Shadows of Nagasaki

World War II: The Global, Human, and Ethical Dimension
G. Kurt Piehler, *series editor*

Shadows of Nagasaki

Trauma, Religion, and Memory after the Atomic Bombing

Chad R. Diehl, Editor

Fordham University Press | New York 2024

Copyright © 2024 Fordham University Press

All rights reserved. No part of this publication may be reproduced, stored in a retrieval system, or transmitted in any form or by any means—electronic, mechanical, photocopy, recording, or any other—except for brief quotations in printed reviews, without the prior permission of the publisher.

Fordham University Press has no responsibility for the persistence or accuracy of URLs for external or third-party Internet websites referred to in this publication and does not guarantee that any content on such websites is, or will remain, accurate or appropriate.

Fordham University Press also publishes its books in a variety of electronic formats. Some content that appears in print may not be available in electronic books.

Visit us online at www.fordhampress.com.

Library of Congress Cataloging-in-Publication Data available online at https://catalog.loc.gov.

Printed in the United States of America

26 25 24   5 4 3 2 1

First edition

For the Lights in My Life

Anri, Yuzu, Beni

Contents

Note on Japanese Names — xi

**Introduction. Imagining Nagasaki:
Religion and History in Postatomic Memoryscapes**
Chad R. Diehl — 1

Part I Catholic Responses

**The "Saint" of Urakami:
Nagai Takashi and Early Representations
of the Atomic Experience**
Chad R. Diehl — 33

**Loving Your Neighbor across the Sea:
The Reception of the Work of Nagai Takashi
in the Republic of Korea**
Haeseong Park and Franklin Rausch — 70

**Faith, Family, Earth, and the Atomic Bomb
in the Art of Nagai Takashi**
Anthony Richard Haynes — 93

**"Love Saves from Isolation":
Ozaki Tōmei and His Journey
from Nagasaki to Auschwitz and Back**
Gwyn McClelland — 112

Part II Literature and Testimony

"Nagasaki" in Akutagawa Ryūnosuke's Taishō-Era Literary Imagination
Anri Yasuda — 131

Lambs of God, Ravens of Death, Rafts of Corpses: Three Visions of Trauma in Nagasaki Survivor Poetry
Chad R. Diehl — 151

Listening to the Dead and Filling the Void: The Prayer and Activism of Akizuki Tatsuichirō
Maika Nakao — 179

Breaking New Ground in Nagasaki: Seirai Yūichi's Ground Zero Literature
Michele M. Mason — 191

Part III Sites of Memory

Fragmented Memory: The Scattering of the Urakami Cathedral Ruins among Nagasaki's Memorial Landscape
Anna Gasha — 215

One Fine Day: The Allied Occupation of Nagasaki and "Madame Butterfly House"
Brian Burke-Gaffney — 243

The Titan and the Arch: Regulating Public Memory through the Peace Statue
Nanase Shirokawa — 264

Part IV Reflections

How I Came to Criticize Nagai Takashi's Urakami Holocaust Theory
Shinji Takahashi — 295

On Rereleasing *The Bells of Nagasaki* to the World
Tokusaburō Nagai   312

Acknowledgments   319
List of Contributors   323
Index   327

Note on Japanese Names

I have followed convention for writing Japanese names in English-language scholarship by listing the surname first, followed by the given name. For example, Nagai Takashi is one of the most discussed people in this book. Nagai is the family name and Takashi the given name. However, I have occasionally switched this order when discussing Japanese authors or scholars whose work appears in English, such as Tokusaburō Nagai, the grandson of Nagai Takashi, and other contributors to this volume, including Maika Nakao and Anri Yasuda. Takahashi Shinji's name appears in both formats in the book; as a contributor to this volume he is listed as Shinji Takahashi, his family name being Takahashi, but when I discuss him in the context of his voluminous Japanese-language scholarship, I refer to him as Takahashi Shinji.

Shadows of Nagasaki

Introduction
Imagining Nagasaki: Religion and History in Postatomic Memoryscapes

By Chad R. Diehl

When the Japanese artists Toshi and Iri Maruki sat down in 1982 to complete their fifteenth and final mural of the *Genbaku no zu*—conventionally translated as *The Hiroshima Panels* but literally meaning the *Atomic Bombing Panels*—they turned their attention, finally, to Nagasaki.[1] The Marukis had taken up the subject of Nagasaki's atomic experience once before in 1952 for a smaller project based on the atomic bombings, but for more than three decades that city's experience did not figure into the *Genbaku no zu*, their most famous and enduring project. It seems that the artists largely understood *genbaku* as meaning Hiroshima, not necessarily the bombings of both cities that occurred on August 6 (Hiroshima) and August 9 (Nagasaki), 1945. They had at least one personal reason for viewing *genbaku* in this way. Immediately after the bombing they traveled to Hiroshima to search for family and provide aid to survivors. During their weeks-long stay they witnessed the human suffering and destruction firsthand, and also lost family members and friends to the bombing.[2] Of course, speculating on their personal reasons alone does not fully explain Nagasaki's long absence in their most famous work, which was, at least nominally, representative of both atomic bombings.

The content of the 1982 Nagasaki panel reflects the layers of history that emerged in the wake of the city's bombing and that have led to a particular treatment of the city's atomic experience in art, literature, and other discursive spaces. At first, the mural looks much like the other panels of the *Genbaku no zu*, especially *Ghosts* (1950), *Fire* (1950), and *Mother and Child* (1959), with dark red and black ink depicting countless suffering bodies, both dead and writhing in pain on the verge of death.[3] But there is one clear difference in *Nagasaki* that sets it apart from the other murals. Amid the suffering of the numerous women (mothers) and babies, who are the main humans within the painting, appear representative images of Catholic postatomic Nagasaki. The central two panels include a depiction of the ruins of the Urakami Cathedral and two crucifixes, including a small one on the cathedral ruins among other statues of saintly figures and another as a large illustration of a bearded Jesus appearing dead on a cross and lying among a group of dying people including babies; both of these depictions reflect the actual crucifix statue that lost a leg in the blast (figure 1).[4] The second panel from the left includes two rosaries among the suffering bodies; under the bodies appear flames and smoke, within which subtle depictions of the ruined cathedral repeat (figure 2). The entire painting is obscured by a thin layer of black ink (*sumi*) to varying degrees throughout, which saturates the profiles of the Catholic relics and the suffering bodies in metaphorical shadows of the atomic bombing. The ink shadows make them seem relegated to the past, far from the viewer's present; and yet the relics and bodies persist in declarations of their existence on the landscape and in the viewer's gaze. In this way, as some scholars have also noted, these ink shadows mimic memory.[5]

Figure 1. Maruki Toshi and Maruki Iri, *Nagasaki, Genbaku no zu*, 1982. Detail of center two panels including cathedral ruins and crucifixes (the entire mural includes eight panels). Courtesy of the Maruki Gallery for the Hiroshima Panels. The mural is housed in the Nagasaki Atomic Bomb Museum.

Figure 2. Maruki Toshi and Maruki Iri, *Nagasaki, Genbaku no zu*, 1982. Detail of second and third panels from left, which depicts rosaries (center-left) and repeated depictions of the cathedral ruins in the fire and smoke (center left to right). Courtesy of the Maruki Gallery for the Hiroshima Panels. The mural is housed in the Nagasaki Atomic Bomb Museum.

The Marukis' mural itself both illuminates and mimics the formation of Nagasaki atomic memory. The painting reveals truths about Nagasaki memoryscapes even while endorsing an image of the city borne out of the memory work of certain groups within and outside of the city. The visual cues of the Catholic imagery—which are the only nonhuman subjects in the painting—link the city's centuries of Catholic history directly to its atomic destruction. This was not simply because the atomic bomb exploded in the valley where most of the city's Catholics lived; rather, the image of Nagasaki's atomic experience as largely a Catholic tragedy emerged out of the inseparable processes of history and memory. Peering into the shadows of Nagasaki's collective memory of the bombing, represented in the mural by the thin but inescapable layer of ink, reveals a complex and dynamic history of memory formation that involved a variety of groups.

In the decades following the atomic bombing of Nagasaki, the residents of the city processed their trauma and formed narratives of the destruction and reconstruction in ways that reflected their regional history and social makeup. In doing so, they created a multilayered urban identity as an atomic-bombed city that differed markedly from Hiroshima's own image. This book pays particular attention to how the city's history of international culture, exemplified best perhaps by the region's Christian (especially Catholic) past, informed responses to the atomic trauma that shaped Nagasaki's postwar urban identity. Key historical actors in the volume's essays include novelists, poets, scholars, Japanese-Catholic leaders, atomic-bombing survivors (known as *hibakusha*), municipal officials, American occupation personnel, peace activists, artists, and architects.[6] The story of how these diverse groups of people processed and participated in discourses surrounding the legacies of Nagasaki's bombing shows how regional history, culture, and politics—rather than national ones—become the most influential factors shaping narratives of destruction and reconstruction after mass trauma. In turn, and especially in the case of urban destruction, new identities emerge, and old ones are rekindled, not to serve national politics or social interests but rather to bolster narratives that reflect local circumstances.

This book traces how Nagasaki's trauma, history, and memory of the bombing manifested through some of the city's many postatomic memoryscapes. The word *memoryscapes* as used in this book, which some peace activist groups in Japan today translate from *kioku fūkei* (lit. memory landscape), means a selection of individual or collective memories that, when taken together, form a larger and more comprehensive view of the past as it is remembered, often in opposition to or complementary of historical narratives. *Memoryscapes* here also delineates the physical and discursive spaces within which these memories and narratives have formed, persisted, and been inherited, such as literature, art, religious discourse, historical landmarks and relics, peace activism, reconstruction plans, and urban architecture.

While Nagasaki has endured in the shadows of Hiroshima in atomic-bombing discourse for nearly eight decades, the city has lived with its own shadows, within which a unique discourse of Nagasaki has emerged. I use the word *shadows* in the title of this volume as a visualization of the contexts out of which the memoryscapes of Nagasaki have taken shape. Drawing on Aleida Assmann's approach to memory studies in her monumental book on German war memory, *Shadows of Trauma*, the present volume focuses on "the dynamics of individual and collective memory in the shadow of a traumatic past." It also takes what Assmann considers the dominant approach to memory studies frameworks, which view "the past as a construction that responds to the needs and possibilities of the present." Finally, as Assmann writes, the notion of shadows illuminates for us "the aspects of involuntariness and inaccessibility in the experience of those who engage with the traumatic past, both those who are directly affected by it as well as those who come after."[7] *Shadows of Nagasaki* presents a study of the dynamics of memory formation in Nagasaki as it manifested in a conversation among public custodians of memory, the Catholic community of Urakami, and members of peace and memory activist groups, including *hibakusha* and other intellectuals. Each of these groups at different times shaped, resisted, and reimagined the memory and narratives of "Nagasaki."

I use the word *shadows* in a few additional ways. First, it points to how the parameters of memory formation within and outside the city have largely been determined by the city's long history as a center of "international" culture. The city's past as a so-called international city shone bright in the dark days of the immediate postwar period, and so officials relied on it in the rebuilding process.[8] Rather than exclusively relying on the needs of the present, people and groups in Nagasaki set out to fit their present into storied versions of the past. The past, not the present, seemed to determine discussions of the significance of the bombing and the city's recovery; or, rather, a dialogue between the "needs and possibilities" of the present *and* the past guided memory formation in and about Nagasaki. In this way, Nagasaki seemed to always be living in the shadow of its history, which, as will be seen, ultimately served as an obstruction to the memory work of *hibakusha* and other activists in the city. In other words, the needs of the present to shine the light of a storied past onto the darkness of the postwar period pushed commemoration of the bombing itself to the backburner during the reconstruction process.

Second, like the idea of ink-as-memory-shadow of the Maruki murals, traumatic memory of the bombing lives on as a persistent shadow in Nagasaki. Indeed, the reality of the human destruction and suffering caused by the bombing washes over the canvas of the history of the city, no matter how brightly prewar history continues to shine in nostalgic imaginations of the past. Traces of the physical destruction of the "international" past, too, such as the cathedral ruins, despite the argument of city officials that the bomb did not destroy history, have cast a long shadow.[9] Part of the intrigue and abundance of the city's memory, I would argue, lies in its juxtaposition of a bright past and the "dark era" (*kurai jiki*) of the postwar recovery years, within which the bright past was reintroduced.[10] Last, the story of the *hibakusha*'s collective experience of human destruction and continued suffering caused by the bombing has contested for space among the memoryscapes of the city while under another shadow of memory, namely the Christian image of ground zero, and especially one prominent Catholic figure, Nagai Takashi. This book will walk with the reader among the shadows of Nagasaki to see what we can learn from that city's atomic memories, and especially what knowledge it imparts to us that Hiroshima cannot.

The Christian Image of Ground Zero

The Marukis' depiction in the 1980s of the Catholic imagery among the shadows of the memory of the atomic bombing of Nagasaki tapped into what I have elsewhere called the Christian image of ground zero.[11] The atomic bomb exploded in the northern valley district of Nagasaki City, called Urakami, which also saw the worst of the destruction. The valley was home to the largest community of Catholics in Japan for centuries, which, from immediately after the bombings, led journalists, city officials, other residents, and groups outside of the city to frame the destruction in terms of a tragedy that befell the Urakami Catholics, and not always in terms of the city as a whole.[12]

From the first newspaper reports about the Nagasaki bombing, and in a variety of media for more than ten years, an image of the cathedral ruins often appeared with the article or essay as a visual mnemonic for that city's destruction. For example, on September 15, 1945, the *Nagasaki Shinbun* newspaper ran an article titled "Hibakusha zokuzokuto shibō: Taenu machi no kasō: Kami no shiren ni tatsu Seikyōto" (*Hibakusha* Continue to Die: Town Cremations without End: Christians Rising up to the Trial of God), which appeared with a photograph of the cathedral ruins (figure 3). The journalists also made a clear distinction between the destruction of Catholic Urakami and the rest of Nagasaki.[13] On the front page of its September 16 edition, the newspaper declared—in contrast to its coverage of Urakami—that "Nagasaki escaped total destruction" because of cloud cover that obscured the central part of the city and led to Urakami's being bombed instead.[14]

The Christian image of ground zero became firmly rooted in discussions of "Nagasaki" over the course of the first decade of the city's reconstruction, leading, in part, to its status as what Takahashi Shinji has called an "inferior atomic-bombed city" compared to Hiroshima.[15] When the antinuclear peace movement needed a symbolic leader in the mid-1950s, eyes turned to Hiroshima, where city officials had enacted a vision of reconstruction that

Figure 3. Clipping of newspaper article "Hibakusha zokuzoku to shibō: Taenu machi no kasō: Kami no shiren ni tatsu Seikyōto" (*Hibakusha* Continue to Die: Town Cremations without End: Christians Rising up to the Trial of God), *Nagasaki shinbun*, September 15, 1945. The original caption to the image of the cathedral ruins, appearing here, reads "Urakami Cathedral reduced to ruins in an instant: the head of a saint's statue (*seizō*) mercilessly torn off."

cultivated an urban identity centered on "peace," which of course grew out of the city's atomic experience. In contrast to Nagasaki, where municipal officials had chosen to revive its historical image instead of making its atomic trauma the center of its identity, Hiroshima had built an industry around its trauma and was thus qualified to lead an antinuclear peace activist movement.[16] Highlighting the contrast between the two cities' approaches to commemorating the atomic bombings during their reconstruction processes, a phrase emerged that disparaged Nagasaki as an atomic-bombed city in comparison to Hiroshima: "Ikari no Hiroshima, Inori no Nagasaki," literally "Hiroshima of rage, Nagasaki of prayer."

Immediately after the war, the word "pray" (*inoru*) was used with great frequency all over Japan as the country began to recover, but by the mid-1950s it came to imply nonaction at a time when action on matters such as speaking out against nuclear weapons seemed mandatory. More than simply pointing out a passivity toward activism (there were indeed antinuclear activist groups in Nagasaki, too), the phrase also bore historical weight in reference to Nagasaki due to the city's Christian history and the image of the city's destruction as centered in the Urakami district.[17] Regardless of the reality that numerous *hibakusha* and other memory activists in Nagasaki labored to convey "rage" against the atomic bombings and represent the atomic trauma through writings and commemorations of the bombing, the image of Nagasaki as lagging behind Hiroshima in this regard persisted for decades, and indeed continues into the present.

Some art and other media like the Marukis' projects both reflected and perpetuated the Christian image of ground zero. The Marukis created a series of twelve mostly smaller paintings from 1952 to 1986, also based on the atomic bombings, titled *Genbaku*, literally "the atomic bombings." The second and third paintings of this series, both completed in 1952 and measuring 180 × 180cm, specifically addressed the Nagasaki bombing and were titled, respectively, "Remains of the Cathedral" and "Remains of the Mitsubishi Steel Works" (*Mitsubishi kōjō ato*). The rest of this series share many of the titles with the *Genbaku no zu* murals, with one exception. The 1973 work, titled *Hiroshima*, stands at a massive 400 × 800cm, larger than any of the other paintings in both the *Genbaku* and the *Genbaku no zu* series.[18] The Nagasaki paintings of the *Genbaku* series, too, illustrate referents familiar to anyone within and outside of the city—the destruction of the Urakami Valley, which had been the home of the Catholics, and Mitsubishi, which was a major component of the city's industrial economy for decades. The latter disappeared in the 1982 Nagasaki mural for the *Genbaku no zu* series, leaving the cathedral ruins and crucifixes to dominate the artistic representation of the city's bombing.

But the 1982 Nagasaki panel also presents a truth about commemoration in the city: just like in the mural, the Urakami Cathedral ruins sit among the shadows of the city's memoryscapes. The ruins were once the city's most salient site of memory (*lieu de mémoire*, in the words of Pierre Nora) related to the bombing, but they were removed in 1958 after a debate among the city's memory-activist groups, the Catholic community, and city council members who supported each group.[19] Despite the removal of the Catholic ruins, which could then no longer serve as a physical site of memory, the Christian image of ground zero grew stronger. For one, the debate that essentially focused on how to appropriately commemorate the bombing, and which had drawn national attention, centered on the Urakami Catholic region. Second, the Catholics got their wish with the removal of the ruins and built a brand new cathedral at the same physical site, making it appear as though the Catholics had significant power over the city's image as an atomic-bombed city.

All of this is not to say that the Christian image of ground zero is an inaccurate portrayal of the city's experience of postatomic memory formation. On the contrary, the story of Catholic imagery and its dominance within representations of "Nagasaki" is as much part of the story of postatomic memory formation as is the trauma, suffering, and memory of the *hibakusha* who contest its accuracy for representing the human experience of the bombing and its aftermath as they lived it. That is, even if such representations of *Nagasaki* as found in the *Genbaku no zu* perpetuate the Christian image of ground zero and fail to capture the complexities of the city's recovery in the years and decades after the bombing, these kinds of representations indeed reflect the reality of what lies within the shadows of the city's memoryscapes. Similarly, discussions of the Christian image of ground zero appears in many of the essays in this volume, which reflects our attempt to acknowledge its dominance in Nagasaki memoryscapes, explore its origins, and confront its limits of representation.

"Inferior Atomic-Bombed City"

Painting the Nagasaki mural in 1982 for the *Genbaku no zu*, the Marukis relied on the persistent imagery about the city's atomic experience that had been decades in the making. The people of Nagasaki, outside observers had long concluded, processed their atomic trauma differently from their Hiroshima counterparts, and since the city was not *the* representative voice of the atomic bombings like Hiroshima had been since at least the 1950s,

Nagasaki seemed to exist as a kind of subset of *Hiroshima* within the Maruki panels. That is, as the fifteenth and final piece to the *Genbaku no zu*, *Nagasaki* had, at least in the realm of art, been completely subsumed as part of Hiroshima—one-fifteenth, to be exact. Indeed, in the realms of art, literature, and other discursive spaces, "Hiroshima" has come to mean the atomic bombings of both cities; *genbaku* has come to mean "Hiroshima."

The timing of when the Marukis finally painted Nagasaki into their most famous work, the *Genbaku no zu*, also indicates that it was an afterthought. Before Nagasaki, they completed two other major works unrelated to the atomic bombings that highlighted the sorrow of war: *The Rape of Nanking* (1975) and *Auschwitz* (1977). Titling the final panel of the *Genbaku no zu* by the name of the city also suggests, or reflects, how Nagasaki's atomic experience is subsumed within *Hiroshima*, because it is the only panel that includes one of the city's names. Most of the panels bear titles with terms denoting characteristics of the human trauma of Hiroshima and commemoration of it, such as *Ghosts, Fire, Water, Rescue*, and *Floating Lanterns*. The Nagasaki panel makes its appearance within the series, then, as a kind of additional characteristic of *Hiroshima*. It does not appear within its own experience, and yet its uniqueness (exemplified by the Catholic imagery) invariably place it *outside* of the experience of Hiroshima and the atomic bombings as the *Genbaku no zu* had come to define it. That is, while Nagasaki has often been subsumed within atomic-bombing discourse as either another Hiroshima or as an afterthought to it, its inclusion in the *Genbaku no zu* does both.

Many scholars have noted the relative omission of Nagasaki in discourse on the atomic bombings beyond art. I have written elsewhere, too, of the historical context surrounding Nagasaki's status as an "inferior atomic-bombed city" (*rettō hibaku toshi*), as Takahashi Shinji has termed it.[20] But that context has many historical roots yet to be explored. In my previous work, I pointed out how the reconstruction of the city as an "international cultural city" (*kokusai bunka toshi*) led municipal officials to rely on and maintain a Christian image of ground zero. It allowed them to separate the bombing as an issue primarily concerning Urakami, which gave them flexibility in sculpting an urban identity in which the atomic bombing was a part of but not the main identity of the city. It also provided a way to link the tragedy of the bombing (in Urakami) to the centuries-long history of the Christian presence, and for the Catholics to their community's centuries-long history of martyrdoms, or "destructions" (*kuzure*), as they call them, thus also providing evidence of the city's "international" culture. The urban identity that both emerged out of and helped maintain the Christian image of ground zero is, of course, only part of the story.

For the *hibakusha* of Nagasaki, framing the tragedy of the atomic bombing with Catholic imagery has been too detached from their lived experience to serve as an accurate representation. As Takahashi writes in the conclusion to his essay here, the religious interpretation of the bombing by one prominent Catholic, Nagai Takashi, was a "useless idea because it was too detached from [the] postwar reality [of the *hibakusha*]." To put it more bluntly, where Nagai Takashi saw "pure sacrificial lambs," *hibakusha* such as Yamaguchi Senji "saw people all around me with extruding eyeballs, men and women showered with penetrating splinters of glass and wood, and weeping young mothers frantically holding on to their lifeless decapitated babies."[21] Nagai Takashi and the Christian image of ground zero more generally have muffled experiences like Yamaguchi's that call out from the shadows of collective memory. And so the *hibakusha* memory-activists' open rejection of Nagai from the late 1960s was the initial step taken by them and other intellectuals to begin deconstructing the inaccurate representations of the city's atomic experience. The dominance of Hiroshima as a representative atomic-bombed city, and Nagasaki's urban identity as an international cultural city, have of course factored into the lack of attention paid to Nagasaki. But shorthand references to Nagasaki as a Christian city give priority to representations of Urakami and its Catholic community in visual, literary, and architectural representations and have caused the persistent obfuscation of Nagasaki *hibakusha*'s collective trauma, suffering, memory, and peace activism. In part because of this, Hiroshima has remained the city to which people look to understand the atomic experience.

Nagai Takashi in This Study

One of the intentions of this volume is to confront the Christian image of ground zero as a precondition for the establishment and development of Nagasaki studies. No one person contributed more to the physical, social, and spiritual reconstruction of the city after the bombing than did Nagai Takashi (1908–1951), a Catholic believer and medical doctor. At the same time, no single person has cast such a long and persistent shadow on memoryscapes both within and outside of the city as he did. The postwar writings and persona of Nagai contributed in large part to the association of atomic memory in Nagasaki with Christianity, and so a prudent confrontation of the Christian image of ground zero must begin with a sustained scholarly discussion of Nagai and his legacy. Many of the essays in this volume, therefore, discuss Nagai at length, not to reinforce the Christian image of ground zero but rather to confront it so that we can, as a field, complicate the image, as well as Nagai, and begin to build new avenues of inquiry in scholarly discussions of the city and its memory. In other words, the large presence of Nagai in the pages that follow is reflective of the memoryscapes of and discourse on Nagasaki, but it is also a manifestation of our attempt to review Nagai Takashi from new scholarly perspectives to be thorough in our understanding of how he and his legacy helped create the Christian image of the city and its atomic memory. This is a necessary first step to opening the door to attending to other perspectives and narratives of the city and its survivors, because Nagai's legacy has for so long acted as a gatekeeper to the city's memory. Moreover, because academic scholarship has explored "Hiroshima" over countless books and for more than seven decades, and because "Nagasaki" has enjoyed no such treatment, *Shadows of Nagasaki* must necessarily delineate the most basic—and yet most important—issues surrounding "Nagasaki."

As a leader within the Catholic community, Nagai sought to give meaning to the bombing by arguing that it was a manifestation of God's Providence and love for the Urakami Catholics because they were the only worthy sacrifice in all of Japan to be placed on His altar and burned in a "holocaust" (*hansai*, "burnt offering") to end the Second World War. It might seem strange to focus so much on a single person, and one who died seven decades ago, but his legacy continues to dominate as a representative voice of the city, including among the Catholics. Moreover, his relevance as an object of scholarly criticism—an academic discussion that began in earnest only in the 1990s—continues into the present. Of special interest to scholars such as Takahashi and myself are the ramifications of Nagai's interpretation of the bombing beyond Urakami. Discussions that include Nagai thus provide insight into Nagasaki's memoryscapes and the social politics of memory formation within and beyond the city. In other words, only by confronting and deeply engaging with Nagai's presence in postatomic memoryscapes can we truly begin to write Nagasaki's place into broader discourses surrounding the atomic bombings, postwar Japan, and the Cold War.

There has been a critical discussion of Nagai taking place in Japan since the 1990s, and it is with that scholarship in mind that our volume's discussions of Nagai also take place. While some *hibakusha*, including poet Yamada Kan, have claimed in their writing that Nagai does not represent the majority of Nagasaki *hibakusha*, few scholars have dedicated themselves to a sustained and carefully articulated criticism of Nagai's interpretation of the bombing. Takahashi Shinji was the first academic scholar to carry out a sustained criticism of Nagai through his books, articles, and public lectures.[22] His criticism, which first appeared in print in his 1994 book, *Nagasaki ni atte tetsugaku suru* (Philosophizing in Nagasaki), and the origins of which he recounts in his essay in the present volume, focuses on Nagai's interpretation of the bombing as a "holocaust" for which the Catholics should be grateful. Takahashi's primary point of criticism highlights the effects of Nagai's interpretation of the bombing beyond the Urakami Catholic community for which he intended it, arguing that Nagai's "Urakami holocaust theory" (*Urakami hansai setsu*) exempted the responsibility of the United States for dropping the atomic bomb, as well as the responsibility of the Japanese wartime government for waging a war of imperialism.[23]

Two Catholic leaders in Nagasaki have published defenses of Nagai, in both cases responding directly to Takahashi. Sister Kataoka Chizuko claims in *Hibakuchi Nagasaki no saiken* (The Reconstruction of the Atomic-Bombed Land of Nagasaki, 1996), which she coauthored with Kataoka Rumiko, that Takahashi missed the point of Nagai's work altogether. She acknowledges in the book that Nagai's words (his interpretation of the bombing) were used for political purposes, but she argues that they were taken out of context and, therefore, criticism of his work ignores his *intent*. Nagai intended his words to offer comfort to his fellow surviving Catholics, who had endured so much loss and suffering in the bombing, and to provide a narrative to which they could relate. Kataoka explains the specific Catholic references in Nagai's interpretation, such as how by "bearing the cross" like Jesus, Urakami Catholics walked in his footsteps to "atone for the sins of humankind," and thus by viewing their suffering as akin to that of Jesus will achieve revival and everlasting life. Furthermore, Kataoka argues, because Nagai never intended his words to be political devices, to criticize him misses the point.[24] The implication in Kataoka's defense of Nagai, it seems, is that one should only engage with Nagai's work from within Catholic theological frameworks, and to identify how he and his perspective on the bombing affected postwar history and atomic memory beyond the Urakami Catholic community is unfair.

Like Kataoka, Father Yamauchi Kiyomi argues that Nagai's *intent* behind formulating a religious understanding of the bombing that viewed the Urakami Catholics as martyrs, as well as his motivation for writing and publishing so much in the final three years of his life, should be the focus of discussion. Yamauchi suggests that criticisms of Nagai's interpretation of the bombing, such as Takahashi's, are invalid because they ignore its Catholic theological meaning as well. Yamauchi agrees with Nagai's critics that his writings failed to include any criticism of the United States or the

Japanese wartime government, but he claims that Nagai's avoidance of seeking responsibility was reasonable (*tōzen*). Quoting from one of Nagai's most popular books, Yamauchi discusses how Nagai based his ideas on Catholic teachings that reject "revenge/vengeance" (*fukushū*) as an appropriate response to conflict. To single out wartime leaders with accusations of war responsibility (*sensō sekinin*), Yamauchi argues, would constitute a kind of *fukushū*, and therefore Nagai, naturally, avoided targeting national leaders for responsibility.[25]

According to Yamauchi, it would have been un-Catholic for Nagai to engage in a discussion of war responsibility. But Yamauchi also sidesteps Takahashi's critical argument of Nagai. It was not simply that Nagai never spoke of the war responsibility of the leaders of Japan or the United States, but, rather, that his interpretation of the bombing as a work of God actively exempted the responsibility of wartime leaders entirely. In this way, Nagai was indeed participating in a kind of discourse on war responsibility because his "Urakami holocaust theory," as Takahashi calls it, made the argument that no human leader held responsibility, because the bombing was the work of God.

Nagai's interpretation of the bombing and Takahashi's criticism of it continue as topics of discussion in atomic-bombing discourse to this day. On October 4, 2021, the *Asahi Shinbun*, one of Japan's largest newspapers, ran an op-ed by Nagasaki-based writer Seirai Yūichi, who is one of the most prominent novelists of what might be called Urakami literature.[26] In 2001, Seirai won Japan's most prestigious literary prize, the Akutagawa Prize, for his novel *Seisui* (Holy Water), and in 2007, he won two literary awards for his novel *Bakushin* (Ground Zero). In his op-ed, titled, "Nagai hakase no chōji: Ito senu kaishaku" (Dr. Nagai's Eulogy: An Unintended Interpretation), Seirai takes up the topic of Nagai Takashi's November 1945 eulogy for those who died in the bombing of August, in which he first expounded the idea that the atomic bombing was an instance of martyrdom in that Urakami was chosen by God as a sacrifice to end the war. Seirai recalls how Nagai's eulogy, as it appeared in his 1949 bestseller *Nagasaki no kane* (later translated as *The Bells of Nagasaki*), moved him as a middle-school student in the 1970s.[27] Around twenty years later, he remembers, he read Takahashi Shinji's 1994 *Nagasaki ni atte tetsugaku suru*, and the criticism of how Nagai's Urakami holocaust theory exempted atomic-bombing and war responsibility opened his eyes. Seirai writes of his surprise at how Takahashi's book made him realize that he had never before considered the ramifications of Nagai's words for political issues like national war responsibility. Seirai acknowledges, too, that Nagai's "Urakami holocaust story" (*monogatari*) traveled well beyond his intent.[28]

The theological correctness, so to speak, of Nagai's interpretation of the bombing would of course require a critique from within Catholic theology, but an objective, balanced discussion of Nagai Takashi's life, literature, and legacy holds value beyond the social context of the Urakami Catholic community. One, it illuminates postwar history, especially the initial democratization process of the occupation years. American occupation leaders were interested in Nagai's books for more than the topic of the atomic bombing, because they promoted Christianity and anticommunist rhetoric, both of which suited the goals of the occupation.[29] Two, the fact that Nagai's idea of the bombing as an instance of martyrdom that ended the war shaped history and memory surrounding Nagasaki speaks to the power of theology in memory formation. It also reminds us of the fact that memory, like history, takes form within a dialogue among disparate groups that are each invested in their own narratives of the past. Three, discourse on Nagai reminds us of how local history and society often become the most fertile ground for a dialectical formation of memory, the results of which are felt far beyond its origins. Nagai Takashi, his books, and his memory have not existed within an Urakami-Catholic vacuum. As the most influential single person to contribute to the reconstruction of Nagasaki city after the atomic bombing, his interpretation directly shaped postwar history and memory, and understanding the ways in which it did so is crucial to advancing discussions of "Nagasaki."[30]

The attention that has been paid to Nagai Takashi since the 1990s and into the present makes it clear that he is perhaps the most prominent single voice echoing from the shadows of Nagasaki. Moreover, because the Christian image of ground zero, of which Nagai is a significant part, persists in discussions of Nagasaki and the atomic bombings, we continue the academic treatment of Nagai with this volume from a variety of standpoints in order to understand how his legacy continues to determine vital components of atomic-bombing discourse. Importantly, however, we also move beyond Nagai and the Christian image of ground zero to listen to other *hibakusha* whose voices are also representative of the city's atomic experience, and to explore the histories of physical sites around the city, which also call out from among the shadowy ink of Nagasaki's memory.

Toward a Field of Nagasaki Studies in English

A study of Nagasaki as separate and distinct from Hiroshima—indeed as something that transcends eight decades of *genbaku* (atomic-bombing) discourse—offers us an opportunity to explore what Nagasaki *hibakusha*, scholars, writers, city-planners, and artists can teach us about *genbaku* that

Hiroshima has not. As such, the reader will notice in the pages that follow the distinct absence of any sustained discussion of the Hiroshima bombing and its aftermath. This is intentional. The "atomic bombings" have long equaled "Hiroshima" in both public and scholarly discussions, and much of those discussions has *relied and been built on* the dismissal of Nagasaki's postatomic experience as a subject for serious study. For too long Hiroshima has been presumed to represent both cities' atomic experiences, when in fact Hiroshima can tell us little to nothing of the afterlife of the bombing in Nagasaki; indeed, discussions of the "atomic bombings" will remain radically incomplete without at least an attempt to see what "Nagasaki" can tell us. Moreover, to rely too much on scholarship on Hiroshima, or on the "atomic bombings," in discussions of Nagasaki discourse in this book, would transfer predetermined conclusions about Hiroshima into a study of Nagasaki in ways that would undermine the rich and individual patterns of history that Nagasaki memoryscapes embody. In short, Nagasaki and Hiroshima have known radically different postatomic stories, and so a comparison of the two cities, while no doubt fruitful in many ways, will remain an empty comparison until we first give primacy to Nagasaki by studying it as thoroughly as we have Hiroshima.

Simply put, this book is about Nagasaki, not the atomic bombings. It also does not rely on previous knowledge gained by looking at Hiroshima. There is, of course, a mountain of scholarly literature on the atomic bombings based on Hiroshima's experience, but as I have indicated, it has been built on an obfuscation of Nagasaki and thus cannot accurately be called atomic-bombing scholarship. Hiroshima scholarship is indeed valuable, and reference to it occasionally appears in the pages that follow. But the limits of comparing the atomic experiences of the two cities must be recognized from the start. Most important, I think, the initial urge to look to Hiroshima for answers to research questions related to Nagasaki must be resisted. Instead, the present volume has sought to draw on bodies of knowledge and methodologies from a wide range of disciplines and topics to give Nagasaki the attention and care it has long deserved.

To that end, the book has two main goals. The first goal is to adequately confront the Christian image of ground zero by recognizing its reality. That is, even though it is not representative of the experience of the majority of the *hibakusha* or the city as a whole, and thus presents a false image of how they have lived through and remembered the bombing, the Christian image of ground zero has its own origins and legacy; it must be sufficiently addressed, understood, and kept in dialogue before it can be dismantled as representative of "Nagasaki." How has this image affected the memoryscapes of Nagasaki, specifically in art, literature, architecture, and commemorative spaces? To what interest groups did the Christian image of ground zero become a locus of memory activism? How did the image determine the discourse on the meaning of the bombing, especially regarding human suffering? How have *hibakusha* engaged with or sought to tear down that image? How have other Catholic believers in the city responded to the bombing? In answering these questions, we seek to disassemble and interrogate Nagasaki's memoryscapes for what they reveal to us about memory formation, especially in the case of the atomic bombings, and especially in ways that the case of Hiroshima cannot.

The second goal of the book is to initiate a field of postatomic Nagasaki studies in English. This book brings to English readers for the first time an edited volume dedicated entirely to Nagasaki.[31] The diverse authors of this book individually and collectively attempt to identify and define the nuances of the discourse of Nagasaki, as materialized in its memoryscapes, bring attention to what lies in the shadows of the city's atomic experience, and show the value of giving Nagasaki our full attention. The human experience of the atomic bombing—traumatic memory, suffering, and recovery—indeed appears in the pages that follow, but our primary subject of study in this volume are the memoryscapes within which intellectual images of "Nagasaki" have taken shape. The origins and components of what we can identify as discourse/memoryscapes emerged out of the literature, testimony, art, architecture, commemorative infrastructure (including ruins and ceremonies), and activism related to the atomic bombing. Moreover, the originators of Nagasaki memoryscapes as we present them to you in this volume are, of course, diverse. The *hibakusha*, artists, novelists, scholars, architects, city planners, and politicians spanning nearly eight decades are some whom you will meet in the pages that follow. Relatedly, one characteristic of the volume that I hope readers will find value in is its overview of current scholarly work on Nagasaki, a major strength of which is its interdisciplinary approach. The essays that follow look at postatomic Nagasaki from a multitude of academic perspectives, including history, literature, religious studies, archaeology, art, and memory studies. In this way, I envision the book as serving as an important introduction to historiographical and other scholarly approaches to discussing Nagasaki.

While so little scholarship and popular writing in English has covered Nagasaki, Japanese scholarship has been much more attentive to the city's atomic experience, yet still less so than the body of scholarly literature in Japanese on Hiroshima. Publications on Nagasaki emerged visibly in the late 1960s and the 1970s and were largely written by *hibakusha* such as Yamada

Kan, Akizuki Tatsuichirō, and Taniguchi Sumiteru, as well as other members of memory activist groups working with the *hibakusha* of the city, such as Kamata Sadao. The focus of these works was largely to draw attention to the traumatic memory of the *hibakusha*, their continued suffering, and the mission of their social and peace activism. For example, the book *Chinmoku no kabe o yabutte* (Breaking Down the Walls of Silence, 1970) was one of the first major collections of analytical essays that opened the floodgates for discussions of the bombing, at least in Japanese.[32]

Shinji Takahashi discusses herein some of the developments in writing on Nagasaki, especially regarding the lived experience of the *hibakusha*. From the 1980s and into the 1990s, writers, which included activists and other intellectuals, took a more academic approach to "Nagasaki," including Takahashi himself. The focus in writing in general shifted here from the *hibakusha* and the "human damage" of the bombing to intellectual discussions of Nagasaki's collective memory, especially its origins and consequences for the city's peace activism and image as an atomic-bombed city. The focus may have shifted, but discussions of the *hibakusha*'s suffering and trauma of course continued in the literature. In what would become a three-volume series, titled, *Nagasaki ni atte tetsugaku suru* (Philosophizing in Nagasaki, 1994, 2004, 2015), Takahashi drew on his decades-long work with *hibakusha*, peace activists, and scholars at institutions around the city, as well as within city archives from the late 1970s, to give the fullest multidisciplinary account to date of Nagasaki's postatomic story, especially as it pertains to the *hibakusha*.[33]

Since the 1990s, books about Nagasaki have been published on a variety of topics in Japanese. An important book about *burakumin hibakusha* appeared in 1995, called *Furusato wa isshun ni kieta: Nagasaki, Urakami chō no hibaku to ima* (My Hometown Disappeared in an Instant: [The Moment of] the Atomic Bombing and the Present in Urakami, Nagasaki). The *burakumin* are a social outcaste group whose ancestors' occupations had been considered unclean, such as butchers, executioners, or tanners, and who continue to endure discrimination today. *Furusato wa isshun ni kieta* was edited by five members of Nagasaki Ken Buraku Shi Kenkyūjo (The Buraku Historical Research Institute of Nagasaki Prefecture) and includes the testimonial accounts of the atomic experience of ten *hibakusha*. In 2016, Nishimura Toyoyuki, who has been writing about the Nagasaki *hibakusha* since the 1960s, published *"Nagasaki" no hibakusha: Shisha no minshū wa kazoekirenai* (The *Hibakusha* of "Nagasaki": The Deceased Are Incalculable).[34] Nishimura's main focus of research for decades has been the atomic experience of social minorities in the city, specifically the *burakumin, zainichi*

Koreans, and *zainichi* Chinese (*zainichi* means, roughly, "resident in Japan," but the term also contains layers of historical significance related to Japan's colonial past). The books mentioned here point to a key aspect of the city's history that has factored into how we understand "Nagasaki" today: that the Urakami Valley was home to both the Catholics and the *burakumin* outcaste community. But they also remind us of the history, including legacies of colonialism and social discrimination, that adds complex layers to the collective and individual memories of the atomic bombing and the war more generally.

There have also been several books by Catholic authors in Japan, many of them clergy, about Nagasaki's atomic experience. Some examples include Takami Mitsuaki, *Kyō mo narihibiku heiwa no kane: Hibaku Maria to hibaku jūjika no messēji* (The Bells of Peace That Also Reverberate Today: The Message of *Hibaku* Maria and the *Hibaku* Cross, 2020). Takami served as archbishop of the Nagasaki Archdiocese from 2003 to 2021. Another book by Yamauchi Kiyomi, a priest also in Nagasaki, explicates the life and legacy of Nagai Takashi from a Catholic perspective, *Nagai Takashi hakase no shisō o kataru* (Discussing the Thoughts of Dr. Nagai Takashi, 2017). An earlier but significant example is Kataoka Chizuko and Kataoka Rumiko, *Hibakuchi Nagasaki no saiken* (1996). Kataoka Chizuko and Rumiko are both Catholic sisters and scholars at Nagasaki Junshin Catholic University.

While the present edited volume appears to be the first of its kind in English to focus on postatomic Nagasaki, there have been several noteworthy multiauthored volumes in Japanese. Most recently, *Genbakugo no 75 nen: Nagasaki no kioku to kiroku o tadoru* (The Seventy-Five Years after the Atomic Bombing: Tracing the Memories and Records of Nagasaki), was edited by six members of the Nagasaki Genbaku no Sengoshi o Nokosu Kai (Association for the Recording of the Postwar History of the Nagasaki Atomic Bombing), including Maika Nakao, who has contributed an essay to the present volume as well.[35] Another important volume in Japanese postatomic Nagasaki studies is *Nagasaki kara heiwa gaku suru!* (Doing Peace Studies from Nagasaki), edited by Takahashi Shinji and Funakoe Kōichi and published in 2009.

It should be noted that what I refer to as the field of Nagasaki studies in Japan does not exist as such, either; rather, scholarly work on subjects related to the atomic bombings today sometimes falls under the term "peace studies," pointing to a more expansive notion of what it means to study the aftermath of Nagasaki and Hiroshima. With *Shadows of Nagasaki*, we hope to complement the work of our counterparts in Japan and extend Nagasaki studies into the realm of English-language scholarship. To achieve this, the present volume provides an interdisciplinary study of a variety of topics to offer a look at the state of the field and to stimulate new research and discussions of "Nagasaki."[36]

Part I, "Catholic Responses," focuses largely on the history of Nagai Takashi, but it also includes discussion of other Catholic perspectives from within and beyond Urakami. In "The 'Saint' of Nagasaki," I trace how Nagai Takashi became the representative voice after the bombing for his community and the city as a whole. I discuss how Nagai's approach to remembering the bombing, supporting his fellow Urakami Catholics, and writing books about the significance of the bombing coincided with the interests of municipal officials and American occupation leaders alike. Early postwar Nagasaki, through the lens of Nagai, reveals a convergence of the interests of various groups of stakeholders, such as the Urakami Catholic community, the municipal government, and the Allied occupation, which led to both Nagai's rise as the representative voice of the atomic experience of the city, as well as the endurance of the Christian image of ground zero. With no exaggeration intended, understanding this early history is key to understanding everything related the memory and memoryscapes of "Nagasaki" since. In other words, the story of Nagai elucidates the concrete ways in which the Catholic past of the city became so easily linked to its atomic present and determined discourse on Nagasaki for decades. A version of this essay first appeared in my book, *Resurrecting Nagasaki* (2018), and it is reproduced here with permission from Cornell University Press.

In "Loving Your Neighbor across the Sea," Haeseong Park and Franklin Rausch take us to Korea for a discussion of the impact Nagai Takashi's life and literature has had on readers there. Through a study of translations and reactions to Nagai's work and by looking at the activities of the Korean Love Your Neighbor Association, Park and Rausch show how Nagai and his works became immortally popular in Korea. While only two of his works, *The Bells of Nagasaki* and *We of Nagasaki*, were translated into English, three times as many of his works have been translated into Korean. For Korean translators and readers, Nagai Takashi's desire to make sense of the suffering caused by the bombing by suffusing his books with both his Catholic worldview and a genuine desire to help his readers overcome tragedy regardless of religion or nationality, became the most appealing aspects of his works. Park and Rausch's essay shows us how a key component of the Christian image of ground zero has reached far beyond Japan, and, importantly, beyond dichotomic comparisons with Hiroshima.

In "Faith, Family, Earth, and the Atomic Bomb in the Art of Nagai Takashi," Anthony Richard Haynes moves us away from a focus on Nagai's life as a medical doctor and writer to provide a fuller picture of his theological and artistic explorations through a lifelong passion for drawing. Haynes identifies themes in Nagai's drawings, including Catholic faith, dedication to and love for family, and themes of what he calls earthiness, which influenced and informed Nagai's artistic depictions of the atomic bombing, such as a mushroom cloud carrying his wife, who died in the bombing to heaven, or as a martyred Jesus with the flame of the sacred heart replaced with the mushroom cloud. Haynes's essay helps us better understand the theological origins and explanations of the atomic bombing as Providence.

In "Love Saves from Isolation," oral historian Gwyn McClelland introduces us to another Nagasaki Catholic *hibakusha*, Father Ozaki Tomei, who took a different path from Nagai. Father Ozaki wrote much about the atomic bombing of Nagasaki and worked as a *kataribe* (a public speaker about the atomic experience), which served as important parts of his identity as both a *hibakusha* and a Catholic. McClelland traces Ozaki's life to show how his physical and spiritual journeys abroad, including to Auschwitz, influenced his understandings of mass trauma and his own communitarian work and peace activism in Nagasaki.

The essays included in Part II, "Literature and Testimony," illuminate for us how both the Christian history of the city and the legacies of the trauma of the atomic bombing have factored into the city's urban identity looking both from within and outside of the city. Anri Yasuda shows in "'Nagasaki' in Akutagawa Ryūnosuke's Taishō-Era Literary Imagination" how Nagasaki's history as an international city, and especially the region's Christian presence, shaped its image in popular cultural discourse as a city that embodied a blend of Western and Japanese influences. One of Japan's most famous writers, Akutagawa Ryūnosuke (1892–1927), in his so-called *Kirishitan* (Christian) works, explored and perpetuated the image of Nagasaki as a Christian city and as a place somehow both simultaneously Japanese and Western. He was always fascinated with Nagasaki's juxtapositions of past and present, tradition and modernity. Yasuda elucidates how Nagasaki fit into the early twentieth-century Japanese literary imagination and how the "Christian" image of the city was ready-made decades before the bombing, as was the idea of the "international" aspect of modernity, both ideals that drove Nagasaki's reconstruction process. The notions of the "international" and the "modern" in Nagasaki that had fascinated Akutagawa in the Taishō era breathed life into the city's revival and its urban image during the decades following the atomic bombing.

In "Lambs of God, Ravens of Death, Rafts of Corpses," I focus on poetry written by *hibakusha*, which was the preferred medium of artistic expression for their atomic trauma. The essay specifically takes up the *tanka* and free-verse poetry written by *hibakusha*, including Nagai Takashi, but with a significant focus on two other survivor-poets, Yamada Kan and Yamaguchi Tsutomu, and with mention of others. I show how these *hibakusha* poets all used their artistic form as a way to process their trauma and grief and how Yamada, Yamaguchi, and another *hibakusha* poet named Fukuda Sumako additionally saw their poetry as a vehicle for social, political, and memory activism. The memory-activism component of their poetry spoke in response to municipal policies that seemed to ignore their plight and in many cases directly confronted the dominance of Nagai Takashi in the memory and memoryscapes of the city. A version of this essay first appeared in *Japanese Studies* 37, no. 1 (2017), and is used here with permission of the publisher, Taylor & Francis.

In "Listening to the Dead and Filling the Void," Maika Nakao focuses on the life and activism of Akizuki Tatsuichirō, who was a doctor, *hibakusha*, and eventually chief physician at St. Francis Hospital in Nagasaki. Akizuki had at one time studied medicine under Nagai Takashi, but he rejected Nagai's interpretation of the bombing as God's Providence, instead embracing the peace and social activism of the Nagasaki-based activist groups in the years and decades following the war. Nakao discusses the way that Akizuki drew on both his work as a doctor and his religious faith in his decades-long work as a peace activist to give voice to *hibakusha*, including the dead who could not speak for themselves, and to reimagine and reshape knowledge and narratives of ground zero. Akizuki's work with other *hibakusha* and memory activists in the city was key to creating the Testimony movement of the city, which began in force in the late 1960s.

In "Breaking New Ground in Nagasaki," Michele M. Mason delves into the relatively recent works of atomic-bombing literature by Seirai Yūichi, who is a second-generation *hibakusha* (*nisei hibakusha*) and a longtime public servant in Nagasaki's municipal government. Seirai has spoken publicly of his "sense of duty" to grapple with and depict the manifold truths of the city. Notably, this award-winning writer proposes a new form of atomic-bombing literature. In his collection of stories, called *Bakushin* (Ground Zero: Nagasaki, 2006), Seirai uses physical space to deftly entangle the reader within fraught emotional terrain, a feature that helps us conceptualize his vision for a so-called ground zero literature.

In Part III, "Sites of Memory," three authors offer a look into decades-long discussions surrounding physical sites and ruins related to the atomic bombing. These essays each explore the way Nagasaki's physical sites of memory have contributed to the creation of environments of memory.

While some sites have worked to bolster the Catholic connection to the city's trauma, other sites have served as sites of alternative memory or narratives about the trauma that contradict the Christian image of ground zero. In "Fragmented Memory," Anna Gasha introduces us to the afterlife of several pieces of the Urakami Cathedral ruins in the years following their removal in 1958. Gasha points out how a visitor to Nagasaki today in search of places of atomic memory finds different pieces of the Urakami Cathedral, and of varying degrees of authenticity, strewn throughout the city. She argues that the physical separation of the cathedral's architectural fabric reveals a dissonance that dismembering and replication create in contemporary visitors' understandings and impressions of the bombing as an historical event.

In "One Fine Day," Brian Burke-Gaffney takes us back to the early years of the Allied occupation of Nagasaki, when some "international" historic sites took on new meaning with a large American military presence. The former house of British merchant Thomas B. Glover and his family, a colonial-style bungalow built in 1863, was nicknamed the "Madame Butterfly House" by American occupation personnel, even though the house had no relation at all to Puccini's famous opera *Madame Butterfly*. Nevertheless, the nickname persisted after the departure of occupation forces, adopted by local authorities as a means to promote tourism and to lift Nagasaki out of postwar stagnation through cultivation of a tourism industry. Burke-Gaffney's essay shares a sliver of postwar history that helps us better understand how sites of the atomic bombing, as I have argued elsewhere, were sometimes overlooked in favor of the city's brighter history to bolster the official identity of the city as an "international" city of culture.

In "The Titan and the Arch," Nanase Shirokawa addresses the topic of regulating public memory in Nagasaki through a sustained discussion of Kitamura Seibō's monumental Peace Statue, commissioned by the city and installed in 1955. Shirokawa puts the most visible memorials of Nagasaki and Hiroshima's peace parks in conversation with one another, showing how Nagasaki's Peace Statue and Hiroshima's concrete-laden Peace Center and memorial cenotaph, designed by Tange Kenzō, sit at opposite ends of an aesthetic spectrum. Tange's design exhibits a modernist sensibility inspired by the likes of Le Corbusier, while Kitamura's appears far less cosmopolitan by comparison and is rarely taken seriously as an artistic object. Shirokawa's essay provides us with a necessary discussion of the disparity in physical sites of memory in the two atomic-bombed cities, and especially how they reveal a tension inherent in attempts to visually memorialize unprecedented forms of violence.

Part IV, "Reflections," offers readers the opportunity to hear from the living history of the shadows of postwar Nagasaki. In "How I Came to Criticize Nagai Takashi's Urakami Holocaust Theory," Shinji Takahashi provides a chronological look at the intellectual origins of the first sustained criticism of Nagai Takashi and his influence over the city's memory. The essay provides a kind of social history of the city from the late 1970s through the 1990s, offering a window onto the driving forces of memory activism there, which has always framed the trauma and suffering of the *hibakusha* as the primary legacy of the city's bombing. Even so, as Takahashi makes clear in his work, Nagai's legacy acted as an obstruction to the memory work of memory activists in Nagasaki who have emphasized the reality of the human destruction and continued suffering caused by the bombing, because his particular Catholic-based interpretation has never reflected the atomic experience as *hibakusha* have lived it. Takahashi's own contribution to the city's memoryscapes, as his narrative reveals, has been to further develop an intellectual engagement with the context surrounding memory formation itself.

In "On Rereleasing *The Bells of Nagasaki* to the World," the final essay of the book, Tokusaburō Nagai reflects on the legacy and status of his grandfather's literature and memory. He discusses the significance of publishing a new English translation of the book *Nagasaki no kane* (conventionally translated as *The Bells of Nagasaki*) as a version that now includes the original Japanese text side-by-side. Tokusaburō is the director of the Nagasaki municipal Nagai Takashi Memorial Museum and serves as the custodian of his grandfather's memory. This essay provides us insight into the ongoing work to keep his grandfather's legacy alive today among Nagasaki memoryscapes.

Notes

1. The official website of the *Genbaku no zu* also gives the English translation as *The Hiroshima Panels*. Art historian Justin Jesty translates it, more accurately, as the *Atomic Bomb Panels*; see Justin Jesty, *Art and Engagement in Early Postwar Japan* (Ithaca, NY: Cornell University Press, 2018). It is not incorrect to translate the word *genbaku* as "atomic bomb," but the term more precisely means the "atomic bombing(s)" when referring to the atomic experiences of Hiroshima and/or Nagasaki, and not just the bomb(s) themselves. The phrases in Japanese, which are both abbreviated *genbaku*, are *genshi bakudan* (atomic bomb) and *gen(shi) baku(dan) tōka* (atomic bombing). Of course, the term "atomic bomb" in English has also come to mean the "atomic bombing(s)," and so this is just me being pedantic. I have decided to refer to the Maruki panels by their original

title, *Genbaku no zu*, to leave intact more of the meaning with which the Marukis painted them. For the official website of the panels, see, https://marukigallery.jp/.

2. Iri and Toshi Maruki, *The Hiroshima Panels* (Saitama: Maruki Gallery for The Hiroshima Panels Foundation, [1972] 2010), 2.

3. See Jesty, *Art and Engagement in Early Postwar Japan*, 1–5, for a discussion of the origins and content of the panels.

4. The entire mural, *Nagasaki*, can be viewed online at https://marukigallery.jp/hiroshimapanels/#gallery-15. See figure 1 in Anna Gasha's essay in this volume for a photograph of the cathedral ruins shortly after the bombing, which shows the actual shape of the ruins that the Marukis depicted in their art.

5. The technique of obscuring the subjects with a thin layer of *sumi* (ink), can be found in many of the *Genbaku no zu*. Justin Jesty, who paraphrases Kozawa Setsuko's analysis of the *Genbaku no zu*, says that Iri "washed the veil of memory over [the suffering bodies] in the watery grey of ink." *Art and Engagement in Early Postwar Japan*, 4.

6. For an explanation of additional nuances of the term *hibakusha*, see note 1 of my essay "Lambs of God, Ravens of Death, Rafts of Corpses" in this volume.

7. Aleida Assmann, *Shadows of Trauma: Memory and the Politics of Postwar Identity*, trans. Sarah Clift (New York: Fordham University Press, 2016), 5–6.

8. My first monograph traces how the municipal vision of reconstruction affected narratives about Nagasaki's atomic bombing in this way: Chad R. Diehl, *Resurrecting Nagasaki: Reconstruction and the Formation of Atomic Narratives* (Ithaca, NY: Cornell University Press, 2018).

9. One economist in the city, Itō Hisa'aki, claimed in an editorial of September 14, 1945, "Nagasaki saiken no kōsō" (Planning the Reconstruction of Nagasaki), in the newspaper *Nagasaki Shinbun*, that the city's "culture," manifested in part by its "exotic cathedral," had survived the bombing: "historical traditions cannot be destroyed by mere violence." See Diehl, *Resurrecting Nagasaki*, 22.

10. The *hibakusha* of Nagasaki referred to roughly the first decade after the bombing as the "dark era": see, e.g., Yamada Hirotami, "Nagasaki no hibakusha" (*Hibakusha* of Nagasaki), *Nagasaki kara heiwa gaku suru!* (Doing Peace Studies from Nagasaki), ed. Takahashi Shinji and Funakoe Kōichi (Kyoto: Hōritsu bunka sha, 2009).

11. For a more complete discussion of the Christian image of ground zero, and especially how it shaped understandings of "Nagasaki" in local, national, and international discourse on the atomic bombings, see Diehl, *Resurrecting Nagasaki*, esp. 8–11, 112–113, and 130–132.

12. See, for example, Funakoe Kōichi, "Jūroku seiki made sakanobotte genbaku o kangaeru" (Thinking of the Atomic Bombing Going back to the Sixteenth Century), in Takahashi and Funakoe, *Nagasaki kara heiwagaku suru*, 29–36.

13. "Hibakusha zokuzokuto shibō: Taenu machi no kasō: Kami no shiren ni tatsu Seikyōto" (*Hibakusha* Continue to Die: Town Cremations without End: Christians Rising up to the Trial of God), *Nagasaki Shinbun*, September 15, 1945,

2 *men*. For a discussion of the origins, content, and significance of the article, see, Diehl, *Resurrecting Nagasaki*, 9, 149, and 203n6. Notice the use of the word *hibakusha* to refer to people who experienced the atomic bombing. The term *hibakusha* gained wide use from 1957, after the passing of the first Medical Relief Law, to generally refer to *survivors* of the bombings and became a legal category of survivor; however, it was also used popularly from immediately after the bombing to refer to people, alive or dead, who experienced the bombing, and without any legal requirement to prove that they did so (this became a requirement later to receive a booklet from the national government to qualify the survivor for financial aid to pay medical costs related to illnesses from the bombing).

14. "Kumo no tame 'tōka' kuru'u: Zenmetsu o manukareta Nagasaki" (The "Bombing" Goes Amiss because of Clouds: Nagasaki Escaped Total Destruction), *Nagasaki Shinbun*, September 16, 1945, 1.

15. See Takahashi Shinji, *Nagasaki ni atte tetsugaku suru: Kakujidai no shi to sei* (Philosophizing in Nagasaki: Death and Life in the Nuclear Age) (Tokyo: Hokuju shuppan, 1994), 193.

16. Many scholars have written about Hiroshima leaders' cultivation of an urban identity surrounding the city's atomic experience and the emergence of the city as the leader of the antinuclear peace movement in the 1950s. See, especially, Ran Zwigenberg, *Hiroshima: The Origins of Global Memory Culture* (Cambridge: Cambridge University Press, 2014); James J. Orr, *The Victim as Hero: Ideologies of Peace and National Identity in Postwar Japan* (Honolulu: University of Hawai'i Press, 2001); and, Lisa Yoneyama, *Hiroshima Traces: Time, Space, and the Dialectics of Memory* (Berkeley: University of California Press, 1999).

17. Diehl, *Resurrecting Nagasaki*, 5. See 132–143 for a discussion of *hibakusha* and activist groups in Nagasaki.

18. Iri and Toshi Maruki, *The Hiroshima Panels*, 187. The English translations of the two 1952 Nagasaki pieces as they appear in the book are *The Remains of the Cathedral* and *Mitsubishi Steel Works*. I have added "Remains" (*ato*) in my translation of the latter to be consistent with the original Japanese title, *Mitsubishi kōjō ato*.

19. For a lengthy history of the events leading to the removal of the cathedral ruins, see Takase Tsuyoshi, *Nagasaki: Kieta mō hitotsu no "Genbaku dōmu"* (Nagasaki: One More "Genbaku Dome" that Disappeared) (Tokyo: Heibonsha, 2009). For a look at how the debates surrounding the ruins played out in the 1950s, especially related to the city's evolving ideas of reconstruction and urban identity, see, Diehl, *Resurrecting Nagasaki*, ch. 6. For *lieu de mémoire*, see, Pierre Nora, "Between Memory and History: Les Lieux de Mémoire," *Representations* 26 (Spring 1989): 7–24.

20. For further discussion of "inferior atomic-bombed city," see Takahashi, *Nagasaki ni atte tetsugaku suru*, 193.

21. Yamaguchi Senji, "No More Hiroshimas, No More Nagasakis," in *Appeals From Nagasaki*, ed. Takahashi Shinji (Nagasaki: Nagasaki Association for Research and Dissemination of Atomic Bomb Survivors' Problems, 1991), 13–14.

22. Two other intellectuals who have published brief criticisms of Nagai in their evaluation of occupation-era literature are newspaper editor Tadokoro Tarō (in 1965) and novelist/playwright Inoue Hisashi (in 1995). Catholic Father Yamauchi Kiyomi, in his *Nagai Takashi hakase no shisō o kataru* (Discussing the Thoughts of Dr. Nagai Takashi) (Tokyo: Bungeisha, 2017), singles out these two men, as well as Takahashi, as the three main scholars who have spoken out against Nagai Takashi, even though Tadokoro and Inoue's criticisms appeared only briefly among other content. Takahashi's treatment of Nagai as a subject of study, however, has been lengthy and consistent since he first began presenting it in the mid-1980s.

23. Takahashi, *Nagasaki ni atte tetsugaku suru*, 201–202.

24. Kataoka Chizuko and Kataoka Rumiko, *Hibakuchi Nagasaki no saiken* (The Reconstruction of the Atomic-Bombed Land of Nagasaki) (Nagasaki: Nagasaki Junshin Daigaku hakubutsukan, 1996), 74.

25. Yamauchi, *Nagai Takashi hakase no shisō o kataru*, 135–143. The critic of Nagai whom Yamauchi is addressing is primarily Takahashi Shinji, but he also includes Tadokoro Tarō and Inoue Hisashi in his "Responding to Criticism of Nagai" (136). It is important to note that Nagai's rejection of *fukushū* as a response to Japan's defeat excited some occupation censors who saw it as useful antiwar sentiment, and one censor pointed to it as an example in support of publishing Nagai's work. See, Diehl, *Resurrecting Nagasaki*, 103–104.

26. Seirai Yūichi is the pen name of Nakamura Akitoshi (b. 1958). By "Urakami literature" I mean that Seirai's novels often take place in Urakami and address themes related to the atomic bombing and Catholic history. Michele M. Mason notes in this volume that Seirai himself refers to his work as "ground zero literature" (*bakushin bungaku*).

27. The eulogy as it appears in *Nagasaki no kane* is different from the eulogy he delivered on November 23, 1945, and in important ways. For a discussion of this, see Diehl, *Resurrecting Nagasaki*, 107. For a full English translation of the original, delivered eulogy, see Chad R. Diehl, "Resurrecting Nagasaki: Reconstruction, the Urakami Catholics, and Atomic Memory, 1945–1970," PhD diss., Columbia University, 2011, 122–125.

28. Seirai Yūichi, "Nagai hakase no chōji: Ito senu kaishaku" (Dr. Nagai's Eulogy: An Unintended Interpretation), *Asahi Shinbun*, October 4, 2021.

29. I have written elsewhere about the relationship between official democratization policy and unofficial Christianization programs during the occupation: Chad R. Diehl, "Praying for Democracy: Christianity as Cultural Diplomacy in American-Occupied Japan, 1945–1952," *The Routledge History of U.S. Foreign Relations*, ed. Tyson Reeder (New York: Routledge, 2022), 90–103.

30. I have never understood the defensiveness of some admirers of Nagai Takashi, because, as I think will become clear in the pages of this volume, scholarly criticism of Nagai, his interpretation, and historical contexts more broadly have never been personal attacks on Nagai himself.

31. There have been a few single-authored books recently about the aftermath of Nagasaki's bombing. In *Dangerous Memory in Nagasaki: Prayers, Protests, and Catholic Survivor Narratives* (New York: Routledge, 2020), by oral historian Gwyn McClelland (who also appears in the present volume), the experiences of some Catholic *hibakusha* of Urakami take center stage in the story, illuminating the complex terrain they have traveled in remembering the bombing as both individuals and as part of a historical religious community. My own book *Resurrecting Nagasaki* looks at how the reconstruction of the city shaped the development of the city's atomic narratives, focusing especially on the people and interest groups who ushered their narratives through the first two postwar decades. Susan Southard's *Nagasaki: Life after Nuclear War* (New York: Viking Press, 2015) traces the postwar lives of five *hibakusha* in a standard format that weaves their stories together with some general history of the time. It is important to mention that Southard's *Nagasaki* is a trade book because, though quite lengthy, it does not serve the same function as an academic monograph that puts forth analysis and original arguments. Rather, her book works better as a collection of materials already available in English than an analytical contribution to the study of postatomic Nagasaki. Others have noted the book's lack of accurate analysis: see, e.g., Ian Buruma, "'Nagasaki: Life After Nuclear War,' by Susan Southard," *New York Times*, July 28, 2015. For my own brief review of the book, see the *Journal of American History* 103, no. 2 (September 2016): 537–538.

32. *Chinmoku no kabe o yabutte* (Breaking Down the Walls of Silence), ed. Nagasaki hibaku kyōshi no kai (Tokyo: Rōdō shunhō sha, 1970).

33. Takahashi Shinji, *Nagasaki ni atte tetsugaku suru: Kakujidai no shi to sei* (Philosophizing in Nagasaki: Death and Life in the Nuclear Age) (Tokyo: Hokuju Shuppan, 1994); Takahashi Shinji, *Nagasaki ni atte tetsugaku suru, II: Genbakushi kara heiwa sekinin e* (Philosophizing in Nagasaki: From Atomic-Bombing Death to Peace Responsibility) (Tokyo: Hokuju Shuppan, 2004); and Takahashi Shinji, *Nagasaki ni atte tetsugaku suru III: 3.11 go no heiwa sekinin* (Philosophizing in Nagasaki: Peace Responsibility after 3.11) (Tokyo: Hokuju shuppan, 2015).

34. Nishimura Toyoyuki, *"Nagasaki" no hibakusha: shisha no minshū wa kazoekirenai* (The *Hibakusha* of "Nagasaki": The Deceased Are Incalculable) (Tokyo: Shakai hyōron sha, 2016). The word *Nagasaki* appears in katakana to point to an implied meaning of the word, i.e., the atomic bombing of the city, and so I have indicated that with quotation marks. Part I, roughly two-thirds of the book, is an updated and expanded version of his 1970 book by the same name, which had the subtitle *Buraku, Korea, China*.

35. *Genbakugo no 75 nen: Nagasaki no kioku to kiroku o tadoru* (Seventy-Five Years after the Atomic Bombing: Tracing the Memories and Records of Nagasaki), ed. Kinaga Katsuya et al. (Nagasaki: Shoshi tsukumo, 2021).

36. There are scholars currently writing on Nagasaki in English who were unable to appear in this volume but whose work I would recommend, among them Tomoe Otsuki, Aleksandr Sklyar, Shi-Lin Loh, and Hirokazu Miyazaki.

Part I
Catholic Responses

The "Saint" of Urakami
Nagai Takashi and Early Representations of the Atomic Experience

By Chad R. Diehl

Nagai Takashi (1908–1951) was perhaps the most unlikely representative voice of Nagasaki to emerge in the early postwar years. He was a Catholic, a historically oppressed minority in Japan for centuries, including within Nagasaki, and he was terminally ill with cancer even before the bombing. But he also seemed a natural choice. As the popular memory of the bombing in local and national narratives became localized as an Urakami tragedy, the Catholic leader who lost his wife in the bombing, lay dying of cancer, and lived in the bombed-out region defined for many, especially those outside Nagasaki, the suffering of the city as a whole. Furthermore, municipal officials found Nagai useful because he promoted an atomic narrative and a vision of reconstruction that complemented, and at times mirrored, their own. Among all of the figures to emerge in the first years of postwar Nagasaki, no single person affected the reconstruction of the city and shaped its atomic narratives on local, national, and international levels as did Nagai.

Nagai's leadership among the Urakami Catholics came in three stages. First, during the Second World War, Nagai represented for his community a paragon Japanese Catholic who served both God and the emperor by dedicating himself to the war effort; on his return from military service in China, he became the parishioner representative. Second, from 1945 to 1947, Nagai led the Catholic survivors into recovery from the atomic bombing, providing for them an explanation for the bombing that drew on their religious beliefs and gave meaning to the loss of their loved ones and their personal suffering. Third, from 1948 to 1951, Nagai acted as the representative voice for Urakami and the city more generally by publishing prolifically; explaining the atomic experience to local, national, and international media; and making large monetary donations to the city to aid in the reconstruction.

During the last phase especially, Nagai's writings and persona supported the municipal vision of reconstruction.

A confluence of circumstances allowed Nagai to rise as the representative of Nagasaki. Nagai benefited from the occupation's being primarily an American venture as Christianity increased in importance, strengthening his position as a Catholic and giving visibility to his religious rhetoric. The focus on reconstruction throughout his books, which encouraged community revival, religious themes such as forgiveness of one's enemies, and the recovery of a historic Nagasaki in which Catholicism played a part, served the purposes of local and national politicians as well as the American occupation, not to mention the Nagasaki Catholic community. Nagai's ruminations on the relationship between God, destruction, and revival also advanced the image of the church in Japan. Nagai exerted efforts in support of recovery through literary and monetary means, drawing national and international attention to the history of Nagasaki, especially its Christians, its plight among the other war-torn cities in Japan, and its desire to fully recover from the tragedy and become a voice of peace. Nagai's point of view as a witness of the bombing, combined with the postwar benefits of his religious position, propelled him to the top of the literary world when the nation thirsted for information regarding the atomic bomb.

Nagai's Catholic interpretation of the atomic bombing became the central motif of his postwar writings. Nagai, drawing inspiration from Mark 8:34 in the Bible, thought that because God loves the Urakami Catholics, they had to walk in the footsteps of Jesus Christ as martyrs for a greater cause, a sacrificial lamb to end the war.[1] Nagai developed this interpretation shortly after the bombing, but his public declaration of it from November 1945 was timely in that it provided comfort to his fellow Catholic survivors, who struggled to make sense of the destruction of their community in the face of anti-Christian sentiments among townspeople. In the weeks and months after the bombing, some in Nagasaki declared that the atomic bomb that decimated the Urakami Valley exemplified divine punishment because the Catholics had not made sufficient pilgrimage to Suwa Jinja, the main Shinto shrine in the southern part of the city. In response to this claim, Nagai declared that it was not divine punishment, but, rather, the love of God that directed the bomb to Urakami.[2] In this way he sought to give meaning to the suffering of the Urakami Catholics. Appearing in his bestselling books from 1948, this interpretation drew the attention of national and international readers, not to mention the American occupiers, and helped shape both the Christian image of ground zero and Nagasaki's place in popular memory more generally.

The "Saint" of Urakami | 35

Within months of publishing his first books in 1948, Nagai, the "saint" of Urakami as some chose to call him, enjoyed overwhelming national and international popularity. Letters of admiration and support poured in to his small hut from actors, community leaders, government officials, and everyday citizens from all over the world, including some American occupation officials and the Vatican. The National Diet took note of Nagai, commending him for his "contributions to reconstruction" and even referring to him and his writings in discussions of postwar issues such as war orphans and the tax code. But not everyone was a Nagai fan. Some argued that Nagai deserved no special attention because everyone in Japan was suffering. The Communist Party criticized members of the National Diet for co-opting Nagai's fame for their own personal gain by attempting to whitewash the memory of the government's militaristic past.

Nagai embodied the Christian image of ground zero. He was a devout Catholic and leader in the Urakami community who suffered the atomic experience and dedicated himself for the revival of the city. Through his writings, he interpreted the bombing as an Urakami sacrifice, not a Nagasaki one. Nagai was always careful to write "Urakami" when discussing ground zero and the atomic destruction, even if decades later translators have replaced the word with "Nagasaki."[3] Urakami figured in all of his bestselling books as a historical center of Christian martyrdom and sacrifice, the atomic bombing having been one more instance on that timeline. His books outsold all others from Nagasaki, creating a popular discourse on the bombing that drew on his voice above others. In the eyes of local, national, and international media and publishers, as well as municipal and national officials, not to mention the American occupiers, Nagai spoke for Nagasaki's atomic experience. Thus, in their treatment of Nagai, these groups enhanced the Christian image of ground zero and, as a result, encouraged the disparity between Nagasaki and Hiroshima in popular memory.

Nagai Takashi as a Community Leader in War and Suffering

Nagai Takashi was not born in Nagasaki. Nor was he originally Catholic. He was born in 1908 in Matsue City, Shimane Prefecture, where his ancestors had lived for generations in the region of Izumo, or as Kataoka Yakichi once wrote, "the land of the foundation myths of Japan."[4] Izumo is home to one of the most historically and spiritually important Shinto shrines in Japan, the Izumo Taisha, and Nagai's father Noboru was a devout worshipper at the shrine.[5] Growing up in Izumo and in a strictly Shinto household gave Nagai a solid patriotic foundation, which later underlay his encouragement of fellow Catholics in Nagasaki to embrace the cause of the nation in the war. Nagai left his hometown at the age of twenty to attend medical school at Nagasaki University, located in Urakami. On a hill near the medical school stood the grand Urakami Cathedral, which mesmerized Nagai with its red bricks and the sound of its Angelus bells. When offered a room for rent, he moved to the second floor of the house of the Moriyama family, which stood directly in front of the cathedral.[6] The Moriyamas were direct descendants of the hidden Christians (*kakure Kirishitan*), Japanese Christians who took their faith underground after enduring persecution from the early 1600s and practiced their faith in secrecy for almost 250 years. The Moriyama family had been the *chōgata* (keeper of the calendar), the most important task of Catholic leaders during the centuries underground.[7] While living with the Moriyama family, Nagai learned the history of the Urakami Catholics and was drawn to Christianity.

When he was drafted into the military as a medic in 1931 after the Manchurian Incident, the young daughter of the Moriyama household, Maria Midori, sent Nagai a book titled *Kōkyō yōri* (Catholic catechism) in a care package. Nagai received Midori's gift under the watchful eye of his commanding sergeant, who was immediately suspicious of the book and sent it to be examined for subversive ideas. Three days later the sergeant returned the catechism to Nagai, saying, "This is a Christian book, so there are many areas in it that make no sense, but because it does not seem particularly socialist, I guess you can hang on to it. However, if you have time to read stuff like this book of a Western God, read the Imperial Rescript to Soldiers (*Gunjin chokuyu*)." Nagai had already memorized the *Gunjin chokuyu*, so he decided to devote his time to studying the Catholic catechism.[8] It was on the battlefield in China studying the principles of Christianity that Nagai began to understand the essence of Catholicism and decided to embrace the Christian God. On his return to Nagasaki, he converted to Catholicism.[9] On June 12, 1934, Nagai was baptized a Roman Catholic and received the name "Paulo."[10] Two months later in August, Paulo Takashi married Maria Midori, thereby becoming a member of one of the most important Catholic families in Nagasaki.[11]

Nagai rose in the community, becoming a role model of an Urakami Catholic who balanced the duties of a devout believer and a patriotic subject. After Nagai was again drafted into the military as a medical officer when Japan entered all-out war with China in July 1937, he sent letters back home addressed to the entire community and meant for publication in the *Katori-kukyō hō* (Catholicism bulletin), a bimonthly publication that kept the parish informed on religious matters and national news, as well as international Catholic affairs. In the letters he stressed the importance of balancing the duties of an imperial subject and a Roman Catholic. On August 29, 1937, when his group was fighting near the Great Wall, he wrote a letter that was published in the September 15 issue of the *Katorikukyō hō*. In it, he encouraged the Catholics to exert all efforts possible for the war. The battles in China were gruesome, he wrote, and "the corpses of Chinese soldiers" lay everywhere. He added, "Tomorrow we are finally going over the Great Wall and advancing the attack. I'm glad." He then put the war in the context of the role of Nagasaki:

> I've mentioned the bombing of Tianjin [in previous letters], but the aerial bombing of that city was actually quite tragic. You had to see it to believe it.[12] I did not take pleasure in Tianjin's condition, but looking back, my heart shivered (*samukunatta*) when I thought what if Nagasaki were bombed....
>
> I want Nagasaki to more seriously build its air defenses. There is nothing more pitiful than a city with no air-defense facilities.
>
> First, you must actively build (*ken'nō*) patriotic airplanes to secure Japan's command of the air. Then comes building air-defense facilities.
>
> Everyday, planes come and the sounds of the Great Wall being bombed ring on. We all raise our hands and shout, "*banzai!*" It feels great. I wish I had a plane.[13]

In retrospect, the letter conveyed an eerie premonition of the city's fate in 1945, but Nagai's point was to encourage his community to mobilize for the war effort, build airplanes, and defend the homeland. Although Nagai was a fervent Catholic, patriotism for his Shinto homeland pervaded his letters from the battlefront. Nagai's patriotism was not atypical of Japanese Christians, his letters from the battlefront echoing the calls of Catholic leaders in Nagasaki to be patriotic.

He spoke of the patriotic duty of the Urakami Catholics again in a New Year's greeting written from Nanjing in December 1937, after the Japanese Imperial Army had occupied and devastated the city beginning the thirteenth of that month. Although Nagai acknowledged years later that he "saw all kinds of crimes being calmly performed on the battlefield" in China, the mood of his letter was cheery.[14] "I respectfully wish you all a Merry Christmas and a Happy New Year from the battlefield," he wrote. "We have greeted this year along with grave current events, but especially this year Japan will soar. This is the perfect opportunity for Japanese Christians to display that essence. As I pray for the activities of everyone on the home front, I, too, will render the duty of a warrior of Japan and repay the kindness of the emperor."[15] Nagai reveals here that the duties of believer and subject are compatible, but separate, as he prays for the Catholics but fights for the emperor. Furthermore, Nagai encouraged his fellow Urakami Catholics to see themselves not simply as subjects, but as "warriors of Japan."

Although Nagai's letters conveyed a proud and cheery sense of unbreakable patriotism, the reality was of course grim. Three years of encountering the violence of war in China shaped his views of death. He witnessed bloody battles and treated countless wounded soldiers, Japanese and Chinese alike; faced with the daily reality of war and death, Nagai turned to the Bible for guidance. He always carried with him a 1910 copy of Emil Raguet's translation of the New Testament (he thought the newer translations had too many errors), and he repeatedly read a particular passage for comfort: "We all face death for the Lord, and through it we are akin to the sacrificial lamb."[16] Nagai wrote years later that during his time in China he realized that "death is never coincidence. It is according to the Providence of God (*Tenshu*)."[17] Nagai later evoked this view of death to give meaning to the atomic bombing.

After he returned from China in 1940, Nagai settled back into a routine at home. He had returned to Nagasaki on March 5 as a decorated soldier, having received the Order of the Rising Sun for his bravery in China, and he continued to wear his military uniform to work at the hospital to show his patriotism and promote military preparedness among his community.[18] He continued his work as a radiologist at Nagasaki University Medical School. Because of wartime scarcity, X-ray film was in short supply, and he could no longer take indirect photographs of patients, but he could also not stop his work. Nagai continued working with X-rays, exposing his body to dangerous amounts of radiation, and in May 1945, he began to feel ill.[19] In June, Nagai was given three years to live. His colleagues estimated that he had contracted leukemia as early as 1940, since he had been living with the pain for five years.[20] Nonetheless, Nagai continued to teach at the university and treat patients.

During the war, Christians all over Japan sought to prove their dedication to the Japanese war effort to allay doubts surrounding their patriotism. Even so, Christians, including decorated war veterans such as Nagai, were under constant suspicion from their fellow citizens and the government of being American sympathizers. In July 1945 the military ordered Catholic leaders to report to army headquarters in Nagasaki for a meeting to address their loyalty to the nation. Military officials had long suspected Japanese Christians of being fifth columnists, but they grew more concerned once American planes began bombing the main islands in late 1944. At the meeting in July 1945, officials berated the Catholics and demanded they report to police headquarters immediately if they discovered any Americans landing.[21] Nagai and the Catholics never had the opportunity to warn of the arrival of the Americans to Urakami on August 9, 1945, when the atomic bomb decimated the only place in Nagasaki that the Japanese military suspected would be sympathetic to the Americans. Even amid the atomic destruction, Nagai's patriotism manifested, when, on the evening of the bombing while he and his medical staff were treating the waves of wounded that flooded their relief station, he took the bandage from his own bleeding forehead and used it to draw a red circle in the middle of a large white cloth. He planted the makeshift flag of the rising sun with a bamboo pole on the hilltop above the university, which overlooked the flattened and burning landscape of Urakami.[22]

When the war ended on August 15 and fewer than two thousand of the ten thousand Urakami Catholics remained alive, the community turned to Nagai to help them understand the loss. In the months following, Nagai established himself as the leading voice for the surviving Urakami Catholics. The atomic bomb had exploded in the northern part of the city, not the main part of the city in the south, which led some southern residents to form explanations of the bombing that revealed a historical tension between the disparate regions of the city. The northern, Christian district of Urakami had long contrasted with the southern part of Nagasaki with its mostly Buddhist and Shinto population.[23] The disparity was such that Nagai referred to Urakami and "Old Nagasaki" as the "City of Maria" and the "City of Eros," respectively. Both Nagasakis were cities of love, Nagai declared, but the "city of the god Eros" was filled with earthly love in contrast to the supernatural love of the "city of Holy Maria."[24] The disdain between the two parts of the city was mutual and did not disappear with the bomb. Instead, the bombing reaffirmed for some residents that the gods disliked the Urakami Catholics because they refused to worship at shrines.

In October, two months after the bombing, Nagai moved back into Urakami from the relief station in Mitsuyama in defiance of the so-called seventy-year sterility theory, building a small ten-foot (3 m)-square shack to live with his two children. In January 1946, Nagai and his children moved to a more stable makeshift hut, and in March 1948, they moved into a better hut built and donated by many in the Catholic community, where he and his children lived until his death in 1951. Nagai named the humble hermitage "Nyokodō," which he derived from the words of Jesus, "Love thy neighbor as thyself."[25] Nyokodō, the "smallest house in the prefecture," as Nagai claimed, represented for him the unrelenting faith of the Urakami believers, including those killed in the bombing. The hut served as the headquarters of Nagai's reconstruction activities, through which he continued to spread his interpretation of the bombing of Nagasaki.[26]

The tragedy of the atomic bombing and especially the death of loved ones challenged the Urakami Catholics' faith in God, and so the first priority for Nagai was to use religious explanations for the destruction to put it into a context that they could understand. A friend of Nagai, Yamada Ichitarō, returned home to Nagasaki to find his wife and five children killed in the bombing. Yamada believed what people were saying, agonizing, "Everyone I meet says so: the atomic bomb was the wrath of God [*tenbatsu*]; those who were killed were sinners [*warumono*]; those who survived received a special grace from God. So, does that mean that my wife and children were sinners!?" Yamada was torn because he could not believe that God, to whom he had dedicated his life, had killed his wife and five children for being sinners, especially considering that it was he who had been a soldier in the Imperial Army. Nagai reassured Yamada that such thinking misunderstood the workings of God. "That the atomic bomb fell on Urakami was great Divine Providence. It was the grace of God," Nagai declared to his troubled friend. And instead of lamenting the destruction and losing faith, Nagai argued, "Urakami must offer thanks unto God" for having been chosen as a sacrifice to end the war. The survivors, he claimed, had failed the entrance exam into heaven and had to remain on earth to continue their studies through suffering. Yamada understood and, feeling reassured of God's love, left Nagai's hut, saying, "I am a sinner [*tsumibito*], so more than anything I look forward to the opportunity to suffer and pay for my sins [*baishō*]."[27]

Shortly after this episode, Nagai shared and expounded his interpretation of the bombing as Providence at a mass funeral among the ruins of the Urakami Cathedral on November 23, 1945, which was attended by survivors as well as some Catholics from around Japan who had returned to help in recovery. As the parishioner representative, Nagai presented the eulogy.[28] On a hill overlooking the devastated landscape of the Urakami Valley in front of thousands of Christians gathered near the cathedral ruins, Nagai spoke words of comfort, reassuring them of the exceptional love of God for Nagasaki Catholics and linking the atomic tragedy with the history of Christian martyrdom in the city. The eulogy was the first instance in which Nagai spoke publicly of the atomic bombing as a providential tragedy.

The eulogy blended religious and historical interpretations of the tragedy to proclaim the exceptional character of Urakami in the eyes of God. For Nagai, the bombing exemplified atonement for the sin of world war. The sin, however, was not the Catholics', or even Japan's, but rather humanity's; that is, responsibility for the war belonged to all of humankind equally, including the victorious Allies. Because Japan had initiated the "fifteen-year war" with the "Manchurian Incident," he said, the war had to end in Japan, but the numerous cities that the Allies firebombed in the last year of the war were "not suitable for the sacrifice." Only Urakami possessed the qualifications to become a sacrificial lamb because the community had endured persecution "for four hundred years, shedding the blood of numerous martyrs." In light of this history of sacrifice, he asked, were not the Catholics of Urakami "chosen from among the world as a flock of pure lambs that should be offered on the altar of the Lord? Alas, the great holocaust [*hansai*] that was made in the presence of this cathedral on August ninth and duly ended the darkness of the great world war and shined the light of peace! Even in the nadir of sadness, we reverently viewed this as something beautiful, something pure, and something sacred." More to the point, he claimed that "the church of Urakami was placed on the altar of sacrifice as atonement for the sin of humankind [*jinrui*] that was the world war. It was chosen as a pure lamb, slaughtered, and burned." Nagai created a theodicy for his community in that he claimed God worked through them in order to expiate the sins of humankind.[29] He hoped that the belief in the exceptional love of God for his community would comfort the few who had not been "summoned to His side" and that they would take comfort in knowing that their loved ones who died were not punished, as some Nagasaki residents had claimed, but rather chosen by God because of their purity and righteousness. The atomic bombing of Nagasaki was not divine punishment. It had ended "darkness," bringing peace and freedom of religion to Japan. Urakami's sacrifice, Nagai declared, "saved billions of people from the calamity of war."[30] Although the rationale and context differed, Nagai's interpretation of the bombing as having ended the war and saved lives echoed the narrative of the United States.

The surviving Catholics took to heart Nagai's message about the bombing as holocaust.[31] Nishida Hideo, who attended the funeral, remembers that when Nagai read the eulogy "in a loud voice," everyone wept. "We were persuaded" (*nattoku*) by Nagai's interpretation of the bomb, Nishida says, "even the people who had thought it was divine punishment." Nagaoka Some, too, remembers Nagai as having inspired the Catholic community. "He was such a good person," she says, "that some people thought God had delivered him to us [*unde kureta*]."[32] To evoke the words of the poet Rainer Maria Rilke, the "eulogy entrusted [him] with a mission" to "gently remove the appearance of injustice about their death—which at times slightly hinders their souls from proceeding onward."[33] In other words, the interpretation of the bombing as an Urakami sacrifice gave meaning to the community's suffering in a way they could comprehend. In the wake of the destruction and misery of the war, the atomic bomb, and defeat, Nagai's voice seemed like a light illuminating a path to recovery. In the months after the November eulogy, many people in and outside of Nagasaki venerated him as a paragon Catholic and Japanese citizen. From early 1946, newspapers in Nagasaki and from around Japan also began to take notice. Reporters came to Nyokodō and turned to Nagai to speak for the residents of the Urakami Valley and about the atomic experience of the city. Nagai used every chance to convey his understanding of the bombing as an act of Providence.

In February, a reporter from the *Nagasaki Shinbun* interviewed Nagai, who took the opportunity to reiterate some of the ideas that he had advanced in his November eulogy. The article began by describing Nagai's leukemia and how he had contracted it, going on to explain how it improved after the atomic bombing, when his white-blood cell temporarily decreased from two hundred thousand to one hundred thousand. Even so, little changed for Nagai, the reporter pointed out, as a healthy person's count is around seven or eight thousand, and "according to common medical knowledge today," Nagai's sickness was still serious, and he had "less than three years to live." Despite his severe leukemia, Nagai performed his duties as a doctor, and, considering that his terminal condition resulted from work as a radiologist, the reporter concluded, Nagai had made an enormous "noble scientific sacrifice." The Ministry of Education's promotion of Nagai to full professor in 1946 was the first of many awards that, the reporter declared, recognized his dedication as a doctor and his ability to inspire strength in his fellow citizens. The reporter went on to extol Nagai: "As an ardent Christian, he makes a point to participate in Church functions no matter how busy he may be with work, and he stands in a position of leadership" in his community, always showing love and affection as he guides them through destitute and painful times. When the atomic bomb exploded, he suffered a severe injury, the reporter explained, but he treated numerous patients with one hand pressing a cloth to his wound to keep the fresh blood out of his face. Nagai "performs acts [*hataraki*] that a normal person could not possibly do, as if he is doing the work of God [*Kamiwaza no gotoku*]."

The reporter's flattering descriptions preceded Nagai's explanation of the significance of the bombing. "The damage of the atomic bomb is the tragedy of the century," began Nagai. "Eight thousand believers died because of it. However, those people are blessed. Bearing the greatest gift of the Temple of Heaven [*jōdo no tenshudō*], they were chosen as atonement for sin to bring about peace for humankind, and they ascended to the foot of God." The reporter concluded, "A man of passion. A man of love. An object of reverence by his colleagues and acquaintances. And just the fact that he is a rising professor of much promise, the thought that [his success] will be short-lived is unbearable, and the Doctor will be missed."[34] The article, appearing just six months after the bombing, depicted the bombing in a way that had become typical in media since September 1945; that is, the bombing was framed as an Urakami tragedy. Furthermore, neither the reporter nor Nagai mentioned the other sixty-five thousand or more Nagasaki residents who died in addition to the "eight thousand believers," illustrating the local narrative of the bombing taking shape around Urakami, not Nagasaki as a whole.

As the article affirmed Nagai's status as a notable figure in Nagasaki, it also echoed the discourse of postatomic Urakami that Nagai had initiated with his eulogy, giving visibility to his interpretation of the bombing beyond his fellow believers. The Ministry of Education's elevation of Nagai to full professor suggests that officials saw the promise of Nagai's strength and fortitude to inspire Nagasaki residents to endure the road of hardship. By February 1946, the image of Nagai and Urakami in postwar popular media was established. Local and national reporters depicted Nagai as pious and undeterred by the atomic bomb, almost superhumanly so, and as someone for all Japanese to emulate as they attempted to overcome defeat and destruction. The fame enjoyed by Nagai from early 1946 led to the next chapter of his life as the voice of Nagasaki that transcended local and national borders.

Nagai's November 1945 eulogy attracted national and international attention after the first part of it was translated and published in 1947 in an American magazine, *The Field Afar*, along with one of his poems. The translated portion of the eulogy included Nagai's declaration that the atomic bombing of Urakami exemplified atonement for the war and that the Catholics were the sacrificial lambs that expiated the sin of humankind. An American named Ruth Giblin wrote to Nagai from Concord, Massachusetts, in March after reading the article to express solidarity and sympathy as a fellow Christian; she offered to help the Urakami community in any way she could. Nagai requested of Giblin only a holy cloth for the church altar, which she enclosed with a letter two months later, along with some soap. The altar cloth and the soap, however, never made it to Nagai, who thought that both had probably been confiscated on entry to Japan, which caused him to "feel sad."[35]

By 1947 Nagai had established himself as the public voice of Urakami's Catholic community and of Nagasaki's atomic bombing. The *Nagasaki nichinichi* newspaper declared in 1947 on the second anniversary of the bombing that Nagai's "religious love that transcends national borders" had allowed the knowledge of the tragedy of the bomb to reach international audiences, as evidenced by the letter from an American admirer. His writings on the medical effects of the atomic bomb, which he began producing and presenting as early as 1946, using himself as a research specimen, would soon be translated into English, the newspaper asserted. Nagai's achievements by 1947 had positioned him to become the "vanguard of international goodwill," not to mention a key to Japan-U.S. relations. The newspaper commented that "Nagai of Nagasaki" had become "Nagai of Japan," and now, at last, he was the "Nagai of the world."[36] From 1948 on, Nagai used his position in the spotlight to publish numerous books and help in the reconstruction of Nagasaki, leaving a lasting imprint on the city and discussions of its bombing.

Writing Nagasaki

If Nagai worked for the spiritual revival of Urakami from 1945 to 1947, then from 1948 until his death in 1951 he worked for the physical reconstruction of Nagasaki through his writings and in his role as representative voice of the city. Nagai wrote and published prolifically on the bombing, Christianity, and the dawn of the nuclear age, donating his royalties to reconstruction projects in Urakami and other parts of Nagasaki. The books brought him considerable domestic and international renown, which he used to advance the image of Nagasaki and improve the position of Catholics in Japan. Despite Nagai's controversial interpretation of the bombing, religious leaders such as Pope Pius XII and others in the international Christian community applauded the "saint of Urakami" for his literary, spiritual, and financial contributions to the postwar revival of the city.

Nagai's fame became a key component of the municipal vision of reconstruction. As the only atomic-bombing author to appear in major circulation and to be read widely, Nagai symbolized the prosperity of Nagasaki as an international cultural city. No representative emerged as equally influential in Hiroshima. In total, Nagai published nine books and numerous medical reports, poems, paintings, and editorials in newspapers and journals. Two additional manuscripts of his were published posthumously as books.[37] Reviewers praised his books for describing the nuclear age and educating the populace on the truths about radiation and the peaceful uses of atomic energy.[38] "Dr. Nagai is quite famous" for his dedication to atomic science (*genshigaku*), wrote Ono Tomoaki, and the way in which he connected the narrative of the atomic destruction of Urakami to the region's history of Christianity and his own faith demonstrated how Nagai "conquered atomic power with faith."[39] Nagai's persona also became a shorthand way to discuss matters related to the bombing in national media, which served the purposes of the municipal government because it located the bombing in Urakami, displayed the Catholic history of the city, and portrayed the special nature of the city that had entitled it to special reconstruction funds above the other bombed-out cities. In many people's eyes, the international nature of Nagasaki's history gave hope to the city's reconstruction efforts, and for them, Nagai exemplified that hope.

The many books that Nagai wrote drew on his experiences after the bombing. A month after collapsing in front of Urakami Station in July 1946 from complications of his leukemia, Nagai produced his first book manuscript. Less than a year had passed since the bombing, and with the experience fresh in his mind, Nagai wrote candidly about the physical destruction, his medical relief team and their futile efforts to treat irradiated patients, the physics of the atomic bomb, and the impact of the bombing on his community. He also included his November 1945 eulogy address as representative of his community's interpretation of the bombing. The manuscript, entitled *Genshi jidai no kaimaku: Igakusha no taiken shita genshi bakudan* (Raising the Curtain on the Atomic Age: The Atomic Bomb as Experienced by a Physician), promised to inform readers outside Nagasaki (and Hiroshima) of the effects of the atomic bomb. Nagai hoped to publish the manuscript as soon as possible, and because he did not criticize the United States for dropping the bomb he did not expect any problems in passing censorship.

He was wrong. The institution of American censorship was not fully understood by authors in mid-1946, even if some knew enough to self-censor. From early in the occupation, Nagasaki newspapers reminded citizens: "Remember without exception to submit publication materials for censorship."[40] Authors did not always know what might be considered unpalatable to the occupiers, and Nagai submitted *Genshi jidai no kaimaku*, in manuscript form, to officials for approval in early 1947. After a lengthy review process that involved several departments of the occupation government, the censorship bureau suspended the decision on Nagai's manuscript for six months.

While waiting for the decision, Nagai continued to write from the perspective of an atomic-bombing survivor, doctor and physicist, Catholic, and father. Those books easily passed censorship and were published in 1948, soon topping the bestseller charts. *Kono ko o nokoshite* (Leaving These Children Behind), *Itoshigo yo* (My Beloved Children), *Rozario no kusari* (Rosary Chain), and his autobiography, *Horobinu mono o* (Grant Me Something Eternal), established Nagai as the first author to emerge prolifically and successfully from the atomic-bombed cities. One bookstore in Tokyo advertised

Nagai's autobiography as the "bible of the modern era" (*gendai no seisho*).[41] His books sold hundreds of thousands of copies. Not bad for "a frail little Japanese doctor who awaits death in a tiny hut on a Nagasaki hill," and who also happened to be "Japan's most popular author-doctor," as Nagai was described in a June 1949 article in the Associated Press.[42]

Kono ko o nokoshite was a huge success, selling 220,000 copies in the first year of publication.[43] Written from the viewpoint of a father contemplating what will become of his two children, Makoto and Kayano, when he dies of leukemia, the book makes several references to the bombing of Nagasaki. At one point Nagai recounts the treatment he applied to the wounds of a little boy with whom he discussed the hundreds of dead schoolgirls whose corpses lined the riverbed. But the way in which Nagai wrote this account, couching the depictions of destruction in lofty religious language, made it acceptable to the occupation authorities. It began with Christian sentiment:

> The Lord giveth and the Lord taketh away. Let us always praise the name of the Lord! . . .
>
> That night, I medically treated Kozasa-*kun* and the others, but according to their story, it appears that in the dead of night on a riverbank two hundred meters east from the [Jōsei] all-girls school, a Latin hymn sung by several people could be heard joining then ceasing, joining then ceasing. When the night expired and we looked, the nuns were clumped into a group and had become cold.—Could it have been these nuns who were singing last night's hymns? Or, couldn't it have been a flock of Angels, come to welcome the souls, who were singing?—Looking at the pure faces of the dead that were lined in a row made you think that way.
>
> Those of us left living who saw the dead thought that the atomic bomb was not divine punishment at all, but that it was no different from the expression of some profound plan of Divine Providence.—That same day I too had become a weak, penniless person and had embraced two small children in the fire ruins. I don't know what it was, but I believed and didn't doubt that this was the expression of Love's Providence.
>
> I have endured three years since that day, but the fact that my faith that day was correct will gradually come to be proven.
>
> Because of the atomic bomb, the obstruction that was blocking my righteous path was removed, and I became able to taste true happiness.
>
> "Death" that will come to me soon is also the greatest gift of love that I confront, I who am God's and who increases in His infinite love.[44]

The chapter in which this excerpt appears, titled "Providence," revealed a transformation in Nagai's views since 1945. No longer was Nagai professing the idea of the providential tragedy as his own, but rather as "ours"; specifically, "Those of us left living," *we*, consider the atomic bombing an "expression of Divine Providence." As parishioner representative since 1945, Nagai spoke for the entire Urakami community, but after the publication of *Kono ko o nokoshite* in 1948, he began to represent the "we" of Nagasaki to the people all over Japan and the world. In addition, the Christian words Nagai used to express the bombing of Nagasaki in the book outweighed the potential of the book to arouse anti-American sentiments. After all, in the eyes of the censors, "they" of Urakami were uncritical of the atomic bombing and even grateful. The book thus posed no threat to the image of the Allies.

Kono ko o nokoshite brought Nagai's Catholic ideas to a wide segment of the population. The book connected with readers both because of his Christian message and because many around Japan related to his experience of hardship in recovering from the ravages of war. The writer Inoue Hisashi wrote that when he lived in an orphanage in Sendai in the north of Japan as a child after the war, he received a piece of chocolate whenever he brought home a book written by Nagai Takashi because of the Catholic message in his books.[45] *Kono ko o nokoshite*, especially, was popular in orphanages, because in it Nagai expresses the unconditional love of a father in the valuable advice he gives to his soon to be orphaned children. An advertisement in the *Nagasaki Shinbun* declared that "the saint of Urakami, Dr. Nagai," had produced in *Kono ko o nokoshite* "a memoir of passionate paternal love, written from his sickbed for his beloved children. It is also a book of love bequeathed on behalf of the mothers and fathers of the world." The ad insisted, "Tears! Tears! [Your] tears will soak this emotional book."[46] Another ad said that *Kono ko o nokoshite* was the representative work of Nagai, which "extracted the sorrowful tears of the nation [*zenkokumin no netsurui*]."[47] Nagai's voice represented the anxiety of his generation, who contemplated the future of their children in a war-ravaged society that had witnessed the violent emergence of the atomic age.

Nagai's books also appealed to people in Japan because he drew attention to social problems facing the reconstructing nation. In a 1949 essay, one scholar admired Nagai's ability to illuminate broader social issues such as the war orphans. Reflecting on the fate of his own children after his death, Nagai drew attention to society for its failure to properly address the problem of orphans in postwar Japan. When Nagai discussed the dire state of orphanages in a story of an orphan who drowned while attempting to escape from an institution, the scholar felt "sharp regret [hansei] boil to the surface, as if I had committed some kind of great crime. Ahh, if only the many bourgeoisie of the world, the directors of social service institutions, and related government authorities—no, the entire nation of Japan—understood orphans even just half as well as Dr. Nagai does, then might we have been able to prevent an extremely large number of tragedies and crimes" against the orphans of Japan?[48] Nagai's discussion of orphanages reached the ears of policymakers in the National Diet. At a meeting of the House of Representatives on March 31, 1949, Fukuda Masako pointed out the destitute conditions of orphanages and argued for the revision of the Juvenile Social Welfare Law (Jidō fukushi hō) and the improvement of facilities throughout the country. The words of Nagai in *Kono ko o nokoshite* emphasized for Representative Fukuda the failure of current facilities to allow for the proper nurturing and psychological cultivation of children.[49]

Japanese actors, artists, and novelists also expressed their admiration for Nagai in personal letters.[50] Actor Chiaki Minoru, who starred in several Kurosawa Akira films, including *Rashōmon* and *Seven Samurai*, and who played Nagai in a 1949 play version of *Nagasaki no kane*, wrote to Nagai on March 14, 1949, after visiting him in Nagasaki.[51] "As a public figure, Nagai-sensei is now everyone's sensei," declared Chiaki. "You are everyone's Nagai-sensei, [including] ordinary people and the many admiring readers from the time [you published] *Rozario no kusari*."[52] Nagai represented the exemplary sensei and a role model for the nation.

At one point, Nagai became the most widely read author in Japan. In early September 1949, the *Mainichi Shinbun* newspaper company conducted a national survey of readers. The Third National Public Opinion Poll of Publications posed the question: "Among the books you read in the past year, are there any that you consider notable books [ryōsho]?" The previous year, Dazai Osamu's *Shayō* (*The Setting Sun*) and *Ningen shikkaku* (*No Longer Human*) had dominated the *Mainichi's* charts, but the 1949 results revealed a change. Three books by Nagai Takashi appeared in the rankings: *Kono ko o nokoshite* stood at number one, surpassing the number-two book by 30 percent of the votes; his *Nagasaki no kane* (The Bell of Nagasaki)[53] won out over Yoshikawa Eiji's popular historical novel *Miyamoto Musashi* for fourth place; and his *Rozario no kusari* was sixteenth. Nagai's books placed far ahead of the Japanese translation of John Hersey's *Hiroshima*, which was nineteenth, and that only in the votes of men. Nagai's books equally dominated sales in bookstores across Japan.[54] Although he was the most read author in the 1948–1949 publishing year, he was not the most popular. Nagai did not even appear in the top ten of the "favorite author" category. Number one in that category was Yoshikawa Eiji.[55] The subject matter of Nagai's books had made them popular.

Some dignitaries took note of Nagai. On May 27, 1949, just two days before the Saint Francis Xavier festival, Emperor Hirohito paid a visit to the sickbed of Nagai, who had moved to an office in the Nagasaki Medical School to allow for more space during the visit. A few months earlier, Nagai had presented the emperor with a copy of *Nagasaki no kane* through his publisher, Shikiba Ryūzaburō.[56] Hirohito asked gently, "How is your illness?" "I am fine" (*Genki de orimasu*), replied Nagai in a respectful tone. "I hope for your quick recovery," added Hirohito. As the emperor spoke, Nagai brought his hands together silently and replied, "My hands still move. I will continue to write as long as my strength allows." Hirohito, smiling, told Nagai, "I saw your novel [*shōsetsu*]."[57] The emperor then turned to Dr. Kageura, the chief physician caring for Nagai and said, "Please take care [of the patient]."[58] The *Nagasaki minyū* newspaper wrote that the kindness of the "human and scientist emperor echoed strongly in the heart of the bedridden Dr. Nagai."[59] Before leaving, Hirohito encouraged Nagai's children, Makoto and Kayano, "Please study hard and become fine people."[60] Nagai was excited to receive a visit from the emperor. Years earlier, he and so many others had fought in China in his name, and as Nagai saw it, the sacrifice of Nagasaki had convinced Hirohito to end the war. Nagai was overwhelmed with gratitude and humility, wishing that the encounter had occurred under better circumstances.[61] Nonetheless, May 27, 1949, was a special day for Nagai, and he composed several poems as mementos of the imperial visit.[62]

The meeting between the emperor and Nagai exemplified the delicate juxtaposition between the wartime empire and the defeated nation. The emperor seemed to understand the significance of Nagai and his books. As one historian writes, the "emperor skillfully tapped" into the "Nagai boom" that swept the nation in the late 1940s and early 1950s.[63] Hirohito, the icon of Japanese imperialism, and Nagai, the "saint of Urakami," came together for a photo opportunity that embodied the hope of a postwar transition. With the issue of the war responsibility of the nation (and of the emperor) left unaddressed, the two men seamlessly combined the wartime and postwar legacies of Japan.

The Nagai boom extended beyond the borders of Japan. By the time *Nagasaki no kane* was published in 1949, Nagai Takashi was already famous. His bestsellers had made him an international figure as a voice of Japanese who repented for the sins of war and struggled to rebuild their nation in the hope of world peace. For Christians, Nagai's ability to find God in the destruction commanded admiration and attracted notable visitors, such as sixty-nine-year-old Helen Keller, who made a pilgrimage to his bedside on October 18, 1948.[64] Eva Peron sent Nagai a statue of Mother Mary from Argentina in winter of 1950.[65] Letters from publishers, editors, and admirers abroad poured in. His fame was such that some letters arrived at his small hut in Urakami without a correct address, as long as the sender had managed to include Nagai's name in some form. One letter was addressed simply to "Dr. Paul Nagai, Nagasaki, Japan," but no matter the language or the address, the letters seemed to arrive safely.[66] The correspondence Nagai received from the United States, Italy, Spain, Mexico, Brazil, and other countries praised him for his books, his courage in the face of leukemia, and his ability to relate the devastation of the atomic bombing in the language of his faith. The success of *Kono ko o nokoshite* caught the attention of foreign publishers, who thought they could sell the Christian aspect to their readers. Indeed, Roman Catholics around the world admired Nagai for his ability to see the love of God where others saw only death and despair; Pope Pius XII sent Nagai a wooden rosary in May 1950. Representatives from the publisher Editorial Marfil in Spain asked Nagai for permission to publish a Spanish version because "we think that publication of this book in Spain would be very interesting for the large mass of the Catholic people of our country."[67]

Other foreign publishers sought to tap into the Nagai boom. In 1949, Duell, Sloan and Pearce of New York approached Kodansha in Tokyo about the possibility of translating *Kono ko o nokoshite*. For the American press, the book had value for readers because of its "Catholic aspects" (*nioi*) and scientific approach to discussing the bomb, both of which the publisher hoped to intensify in the translation.[68] But the deal never came to fruition. Instead, Duell, Sloan and Pearce became interested in an account of eight Nagasaki survivors written by Nagai for an American audience, which Kodansha sent them in November 1949. Charles A. Pearce replied in February the following year that the manuscript, "Genshiun Senjo Shinri (Atomic Battlefield Psychology) [sic] . . . has been carefully examined and read by several reliable advisers. As a result, I am happy to report that we wish to proceed with the translation and publication of this manuscript by Dr. Nagai." The press had already secured the necessary translators, "a professor at Columbia University and one of his colleagues," after having promised to pay them "a substantial royalty on the first 10,000 copies."[69] Ichiro Shirato and Herbert B. L. Silverman translated the book as *We of Nagasaki: The Story of Survivors in an Atomic Wasteland*, which was released in early 1951. Thus, Nagai's voice and that of the Urakami Catholics spoke for all of Nagasaki to the English-speaking world.

Duell, Sloan and Pearce hoped that Nagai's reportorial account of the experience of the Nagasaki survivors—which had been tentatively titled in English *The Fate of Man at Nagasaki*—would outdo the success of John Hersey's *Hiroshima*. In a fall 1950 press release, the publishers declared that thanks to the "acuteness and reportorial detail" with which Nagai told the story of the survivors, the "narratives probably surpass any existing reports, not excluding the Hersey account of Hiroshima." The release pointed out the contribution of the Nagasaki survivor accounts: "Cumulatively, they lead to a moving statement of Nagai's major theme, that the dangerous spiritual degeneration which an atomic war must inevitably beget is being lost sight of in the concern with material loss, physical death, and suffering."[70] Charles Pearce wrote in his letter, "We believe that this book of his is one of the most sincere, impressive and thought-provoking message[s] that could be presented to the world today."[71] Nagai, too, dreamed that his works would garner American sympathy for Nagasaki, just as Hersey's book had done for Hiroshima.

The significance of *We of Nagasaki* as envisioned by Nagai and the American publishers was not lost on its readers. Ruth E. Giblin, who had visited Nagasaki and met Catholic Fathers Nakashima and Nagata, wrote to Nagai after reading *We of Nagasaki*: "I hope all readers cannot fail to see that those of Nagasaki have carried the cross and suffered the crucifixion for all the rest of us weak ones." Giblin agreed that Nagasaki was the sacrificial lamb on God's altar that ended the war. But the greatest impact of Nagai's book for her was that it forced recognition of "our American responsibility for it all," which, she added, "weighs me down. But now we, on our side, are in fear of the bomb being used on us, but most are in great ignorance and have no idea what it could be like." Nagai's book promised to educate Americans on these matters, she thought.[72] Other letters to Nagai noted the importance of the book in teaching the world of the destructive power of the atomic bomb. Mary Rutherford, too, wrote, "I hope many people throughout the world read [your book] and become more aware of the far reaching horror and destruction caused by such a weapon."[73]

The international translations of Nagai's books carried abroad the Christian image of Nagasaki's ground zero. Sister Mary Ambrose, BVM, of Mundelein College in Chicago reviewed *We of Nagasaki* for a journal and expressed her admiration for it in a letter she wrote to Nagai. "I am very sorry that you are ill for your cross of suffering is heavy indeed. When I knew that the bomb had struck Urakami where Christian families, who have so loyally preserved and suffered for their faith since the days of St. Francis Xavier lived, I recognized again the mission of those whom God calls to share the sufferings of Christ, His Only Son. . . . *We of Nagasaki* are doing that—and your reward will be exceedingly great."⁷⁴ That Nagai found God in the atomic destruction did not surprise Ambrose. Rather, as a fellow Christian, it assured her that Nagai understood the workings of God. God requires the faithful to "share the sufferings of Christ, His Only Son," Ambrose wrote, agreeing with Nagai that the residents of Urakami were a natural sacrifice. Like Nagai, she based her views on Catholic theology that sees suffering as the manifestation of God's love for the ardently faithful, "those loyal enough to give everything." For Ambrose and other readers of Nagai's books in translation, the "Christian families" of Urakami who endured numerous historical martyrdoms exemplified the atomic experience of Nagasaki. Other American publishers were interested in books by Nagai, including *Nagasaki no kane*, but *We of Nagasaki* was the only English translation published during his lifetime.⁷⁵

The overwhelming number of printings of Nagai's works brought overwhelming royalties, most of which he donated to fund reconstruction projects in Nagasaki. He began this practice from the time of his first major publication in the postwar period, which had nothing to do with the atomic bombing but everything to do with his religion.⁷⁶ The book, a 1947 translation of the Scottish author Bruce Marshall's Catholic novel and international bestseller, *The World, the Flesh, and Father Smith*, earned Nagai around ¥40,000 in royalties, of which he donated ¥38,000 to the funds to rebuild Nagasaki's famous St. Francis Xavier Hospital, three schools, and the Urakami Cathedral. Among the contributions was a ¥10,000 organ for the cathedral, which was rebuilt in 1959. The ¥2,000 that remained went to feed his family.⁷⁷ Nagai hoped that the book would help propagate "the fact that Christianity forms the foundation of democracy."⁷⁸ The immediate benefit of the book was not ideological, but material. The donation of his royalties for reconstruction efforts set a precedent for Nagai when his own books began selling in the late 1940s.

Nagai's bestsellers produced substantial profits for him and his publishing companies, but rather than keep the wealth for himself, he gave most of it to the city. During the 1948–1949 fiscal year, Nagai Takashi's books earned ¥2,176,333 in royalties.⁷⁹ In mid-1949, when *Kono ko o nokoshite* had sold 220,000 copies and the rest of his books followed closely behind, Nagai experienced a sudden and enormous gain in wealth.⁸⁰ The royalties catapulted Nagai to the eighth-highest income earner in Nagasaki City, yet he remained in his Nyokodō hut and continued his daily life in poverty. Nagai cherished the humble life, but, more important, he never viewed his books and their royalties as his alone—he thought they always belonged in some way to Nagasaki. Indeed, he claimed he wrote "for the sake of Nagasaki," for its culture and history, and so that atomic-bombing "literature by Nagasaki writers will not lose out to Hiroshima."[81]

The majority of Nagai's after-tax income went directly to city reconstruction projects, but taxes presented a challenge to Nagai's charity. Out of the ¥2,176,333 earned in 1948–1949, he paid nearly 90 percent in commercial, national, and city taxes, leaving him with around ¥20,000 to donate to the city.[82] The previous year was not much better: Nagai paid around ¥400,000 in taxes on a royalty income of about ¥800,000.[83] While the city taxes that Nagai paid probably went in some way to reconstruction efforts, the fate of his national and commercial taxes was less clear. But Nagai never had a problem with paying taxes. "I want to pay all taxes," he said, "because the payment of tax is a shared responsibility for the reconstruction of Japan."[84] When Nagasaki residents and journalists expressed their surprise and confusion at the government's exacting exorbitant amounts of tax from Nagai, he told his close friend Kataoka Yakichi, "Taxes are the oil for the reconstruction of Japan. I am working for reconstruction and there is no way I would not pay taxes. I gathered my income documents and filed a tax return without a mistake of even a single *sen*. I will pay my taxes in full."[85] Nagai did, however, sometimes disagree with the way the government used his and other citizens' taxes. "When I hear of [our] hard-earned taxes being misappropriated [*tsumamigui*] or being wasted on banquet expenses, my desire to pay taxes weakens." As he wryly said to Kataoka, at first "I wrote to eat. I then had to pay taxes because I wrote. Now, I must write only to pay taxes."[86] He remarked elsewhere, "It's as if my legs are stuck in a bog."[87] Even so, he took his position as a kind of role model in Nagasaki seriously, encouraging all residents to be sure to pay taxes in support of the International Cultural City Construction Law that was set to make Nagasaki "a beautiful town" and a city of culture.[88]

Nagai dedicated himself to supporting the reconstruction of Nagasaki as envisioned by municipal officials. He declared in May 1949 that he wished to donate all of his royalties to the Nagasaki International Cultural City Construction Fund for projects such as building a medical treatment facility for atomic-bombing survivors, an orphanage, a museum, or a Peace Cultural Hall, as long as it improved the infrastructure of the city. In this way, he believed that donating to the larger city fund would also allow for the revitalization of the Urakami community. But tax law threatened to bleed dry his hopes.[89] Large monetary donations were subject to additional taxation, and Nagai's donations were indeed massive. Newspapers noted that his recently published books, *Horobinu mono o*, *Seimei no kawa*, and *Hana saku oka* (Hill of Blossoming Flowers), promised to bring in around ¥5 million in royalties, but income tax would claim around 80 percent. Of the remaining ¥1 million, Nagai hoped to put away ¥100,000 for his family after he died and donate ¥900,000 to the main city reconstruction fund, but after a hefty donation tax the amount the city received would be reduced to around ¥400,000.[90]

When the tax system compromised Nagai's efforts to donate, he abandoned the large, single donation and continued to donate to smaller projects that were not subject to as much taxation. Whatever money remained after taxes, Nagai gave most of it to the Urakami community or Nagasaki City because he thought that his children, Makoto and Kayano, would benefit from improved infrastructure instead of individual family wealth. Nagai explained to Kataoka Yakichi, who had asked him why he did not save any money for his children, "We must raise the general level of the area. If everyone improves, then my children will also improve. The revitalization [*fukkō*] of Urakami and the reconstruction [*saiken*] of Nagasaki are our serious responsibilities."[91] For Nagai, writing books not only helped the reconstruction of the city, but it also laid the foundation for the future of his children and the other children of Nagasaki.

Nagai's charitable spirit produced tangible results for both the Catholic parish and all of Nagasaki. Nagai intended Our Bookcase (Uchira no honbako), a library aimed at educating the children of Nagasaki, and the Monument for Those Children (meaning those killed in the bombing) to advance social education in the city and improve the commemorative landscape of the atomic bomb–devastated area.[92] His support also made possible the planting of a thousand cherry trees in the Urakami Valley, which were meant to rejuvenate the area in time for the third Christmas after the bombing.[93] Initially called the "Thousand Urakami *sakura* (cherry trees)," the hill of cherry blossoms later came to be known also as the "Nagai *sakura*."[94]

Awards

Nagai's work led to numerous awards. In November 1948, the *Kyūshū taimuzu* (The Kyushu Times) conferred on Nagai the Kyushu Times Culture Award—an award in recognition of contributions to the cultural reconstruction of Japan (*Nihon bunka saiken*)—for his dedicated research on atomic sickness (*genshi byō*) in which he used himself as a subject.[95] On December 3, 1949, the Nagasaki City Council voted unanimously to name Nagai an "Honorary Citizen" (*meiyo shimin*) for his efforts to realize the vision of Nagasaki as an international cultural city through his books and for "spreading the spirit of love to the world."[96] Among other things, the title of *meiyo shimin* entitled Nagai to a municipally sponsored funeral.[97] The list of awards was long, but not everyone in Japan had boarded the Nagai award train. Some saw his national recognition as undue, or they used their criticism of Nagai to point out how some groups appropriated his suffering and status to serve their own political ends. Nagai's loudest critics were members of the Communist Party, but many other citizens around Japan shared their opinions as well. Criticism of Nagai in the late 1940s presents a window onto the relationship between national politics and nascent narratives of the war while also providing us with a more complete picture of Nagai as a person and revealing cracks in the saintliness of his popular image in postwar society. In general, it reveals the way in which various groups in the postwar period, such as the National Diet and SCAP, co-opted Nagai's influence for their own purposes under the guise of promoting a role model for the nation during the recovery period. In reality, they saw Nagai as a medium to help in reshaping Japan's national image from a soldier to a saint, much like Nagai's own life trajectory. At the heart of the criticism of Nagai and his place in burgeoning war narratives was a call for Japan to remember its past and not to whitewash it through false postwar narratives; only by confronting its past could Japan realize true antiwar culture.

Nagai agreed with his critics that the Diet had made a mistake by choosing him for a national award in 1949 because he thought they had overlooked more qualified candidates. Shortly after the nomination, Nagai wrote, "It is a national disgrace that the National Diet would award someone like me, who is a failure at life and a citizen of a defeated nation. There are so many worldly persons [*sekaiteki jinbutsu*] who have truly worked for the reconstruction of the nation, and [the Diet] would do better to award those people." Nagai added, for good measure, "I agree with Representative Kamiyama's dissenting opinion."[98] Nagai's humility had no effect on the special committee, and they moved forward with their vetting process for the award, which consisted of interviewing people close to Nagai, as well as scientists and other academics.

Other critics of the "saint of Urakami" emerged outside the political realm and included normal citizens and scholars, who did not agree that Nagai was the best choice for their country's honor. Konno Setsuzo, a "company employee" in Tokyo, echoed some of the general points of opposition, stating, "I do not think Dr. Nagai is the most eligible for the honor." It must be recognized that "Japan still is in the process of reconstruction; it has not yet been 'reconstructed.' Accordingly, no [single] person can be credited with contribution to its rehabilitation." In addition, "There are many scientists much superior to Dr. Nagai." Nagai's books, Konno concluded, are indeed "replete with his humanitarian sentiments but that is all. He has done no positive service for moral rehabilitation of the Japanese people. What made his books the bestsellers of the year are nothing but the beautiful style, the peculiar circumstances in which he has been placed and the publicity whipped up by publishers."[99] Although the Nagai boom embroiled most of the nation, some people in Japan maintained their skepticism of the circumstances surrounding his sudden fame and recognition.

Opposition to Nagai's nomination was outvoiced by popular opinion that agreed with the Diet that Nagai had made substantial contributions to the reconstruction of the nation. Some artists showed their support of Nagai by satirizing the opposition of the Communist Party. In the September 15, 1949, *Tōkyō taimuzu*, cartoonist Shimokawa Ōten depicted the "achievements of Dr. Nagai" as a giant "stake driven into the heart of the reconstruction of Japan," with a Diet member presenting the award to the stake, which extended up to the clouds. On the other side of the stake stands a blindfolded "Materialist [Diet] Representative" who "can't see" the massive contributions of Nagai in front of him.[100] In December 1949, the Diet voted unanimously to bestow the award on Nagai, and on June 1, 1950, he received the Prime Minister Award and the Imperial Silver Cups.[101] In the end, however, the Diet members decided not to award Nagai on the grounds of academic achievements, which the Communists had contested, but rather for his contributions to social reconstruction.

Other Voices from Nagasaki and Hiroshima

Books on the atomic bombings that did not suit the goals of the occupation did not fare as well as Nagai's writings.[102] *Hibakusha* authors in Nagasaki and Hiroshima attempted to publish narrative and poetic accounts of their atomic-bombing experiences, but their readership remained limited during the occupation, if they were able to avoid censorship at all. The other survivors who did write and manage to publish presented a narrative of the bombings that contrasted with Nagai's Catholic interpretation; they conveyed the horrifying realities of atomic destruction instead of religious interpretations that seemed to undermine the significance of the tragedy. However, regional presses in or around Nagasaki and Hiroshima published much of the early atomic-bombing literature, including the lesser-known works of Nagai such as *Horobinu mono o*. Indeed, for the first eight or so years after the war, the atomic bombings remained a local literary subject.

The *hibakusha* writers who did publish faced challenges that Nagai had seemingly transcended. In addition to basic censorship, dissemination of and interest in Nagasaki/Hiroshima literature remained limited because the genre of atomic-bomb literature (*genbaku bungaku*) was not welcomed into the Japanese literary tradition. Well into the 1950s, as John Treat notes, "atomic-bomb literature was generally regarded as a local literature restricted to the provinces, a minor literature concerned with a minor theme."[103] Many publishers thought that books and other writings by *hibakusha* would not be popular and chose not to publish them. Even the magazine *Hiroshima bungaku* (Hiroshima Literature) ignored *hibakusha* writings. The *hibakusha* claimed that their writings formed a new genre, but literary circles disagreed, including the Hiroshima bungaku kai (Hiroshima Literature Society). Kurihara Sadako and other survivors found it irritating that such pretentious groups determined the fate of writings on the atomic bombings. In 1953, Ōta Yōko spoke out against the *bundan*, which were exclusive, bourgeois groups consisting of writers, critics, and editors, who had historically determined what constituted *bungaku* (literature), and who denied Ōta and other *hibakusha* a position in the literary world as authors of a new genre. Debates on the atomic bombings as a subject of literature waged for several decades.[104] Perhaps what made Nagai's books successful, at least in part, was that he never identified his writings as a new genre or purported them to be so; he intended them to serve as a record of the bombing of Nagasaki to convey the experience of the city and the significance as he saw it, often employing literary conventions to these ends, as did most *hibakusha* authors. However, Nagai had also benefited from the backing of municipal and national leaders, not to mention the occupation government, and so his works found avenues to reach audiences in ways that the works by other Nagasaki/Hiroshima writers did not.

Despite debates over the bombings' place in the Japanese literary tradition, SCAP controlled the publishing industry during the occupation, and thus they controlled which writings on the bombings would be published. Nagai's antiwar message appealed to occupation government officials, who hoped that the message would appeal to a wide audience, and also helped bring his books to print. As he wrote of Nagasaki's place in postatomic Japan, Nagai promoted the phrase "Peace starts from Nagasaki" (*Heiwa wa Nagasaki yori*) in his books, spreading an antiwar message to a nationwide audience at a time when Japan set out to create a so-called peace-loving nation, perhaps best exemplified in Article 9 of the country's constitution (1947), which committed Japan to pacifism. For the occupation government, of course, Nagai's writings offered a steam valve for information on the bombings through prose couched in religious and antiwar sentiment, while his books also helped fashion the American narrative of the war and the bombings as necessary to end the war and punish Japan for its wartime aggression. The Hiroshima writers and the other writers from Nagasaki did not offer the same package.

Some occupation officials were sympathetic to the *hibakusha* and thought that eyewitness accounts of the bomb were important testimonies about the dawn of the atomic age, even if they depicted the human destruction and thus appeared critical of the United States. When Ishida Masako, a teenage survivor in Nagasaki, sought to publish her account, *Masako taorezu* (Masako Shall Not Perish), in March 1947, American officials supported her. Captain Irvin W. Rogers recommended to the Civil Censorship Detachment in Fukuoka that Ishida's book and her father's book-length account be published without censorship. The Nagasaki Military Government Team, he wrote, "feels that the books . . . are worthy of publication. They are true and gripping depictions of a vivid personal experience." Furthermore, he asserted, "The books were examined in manuscript form and were found to contain nothing censorable." Colonel Delnore also attached a note to the letter saying that the two books were valuable in conveying the truth of atomic experience: "They show the reactions of the members of one small family in the holocaust; they show the heartbreak and the pain." Furthermore, Delnore pointed out, "For us to properly realize the significance of the atomic bomb, to experience vicariously the feelings that so many thousands of Japanese people experienced is desirable in these propitious times."[105]

After initial rejection, Captain Rogers sent another letter in June. The district censor in Fukuoka, Major George P. Solovskoy, replied that the book indeed violated the Press Code and could therefore not be approved for publication. "This District believes," Solovskoy wrote in summer 1947, "that the novel, 'MASAKO TAOREZU', would disturb public tranquility in Japan and that it implies the bombing was a crime against humanity." The differing opinions between Rogers and Solovskoy about the content of the book revealed, as in the case of the censors of *Nagasaki no kane*, a disconnect among personnel in the censorship bureaucracy about what was off-limits. Rogers had argued that Nagasaki-based American personnel found nothing censorable, but Solovskoy figured that such descriptions of the bombing as "flesh raw from burns, bodies like peeled peaches" could not be published in a book to be sold "to the Japanese public." Had the book remained "merely for the personal records of the writer's family," Solovskoy implied that it would not have been censored. The book was suppressed, "at least for the time being," or as Solovskoy also explained it, "publication in Japan should be postponed until some future time when it would be less apt to tear open war scars and rekindle animosity."[106]

As a last-ditch effort, however, the local publisher, Fujiki hakuei sha, collected and submitted statements from prominent Nagasaki residents who petitioned for the book's publication, among them Mayor Ōhashi, Governor Sugiyama, and Urakami Catholic bishop Yamaguchi Aijirō. The supporters all testified that the book did not stir in them any anti-American feelings.[107] These efforts were to no avail in 1947, but *Masako taorezu* was finally published by a different company, Fujin taimuzu sha, on February 20, 1949, a few weeks after Nagai Takashi's *Nagasaki no kane*.[108]

Masako's book, however, never attained the popularity of Nagai's book. For one, it did not receive a special allotment of paper for its initial printing separate from its standard allotment of rationed *zara* paper, which was for two thousand copies, far below Nagai's thirty thousand copies of nonrationed *senka* paper. Furthermore, in an updated version of *Masako taorezu*, published by Hyōgen sha in August 1949, the book included a photograph of Masako visiting Nagai, a copy of a letter he had written to her, and a new six-page preface written, of course, by Nagai.[109] Nagai did not appear in the original 1947 version, which was ultimately rejected by Solovskoy, or in the early 1949 version, which included thirty photos of Nagasaki's destruction and recovery. Nagai's *Nagasaki no kane*, by contrast, included only four photos of the destruction.

Other than Ishida Masako, few others published in Nagasaki until the mid-1950s, but in Hiroshima, many *hibakusha* wrote about their trauma, which, if it appeared in smaller publications, generally went unnoticed. Hara Tamiki's famous story "Natsu no hana" (Summer Flowers, 1947) appeared in an obscure journal that escaped the eyes of the censors and, as John Treat notes, "fell, so to speak, between the cracks."[110] American censors based in Tokyo rarely took note of these smaller publications, even if they were well known around Japan. Indeed, Hiroshima writers produced relatively abundantly, and in 1949 several received national recognition in a special issue of the journal *Shūkan asahi* dedicated to "No More Hiroshimas." Among the books mentioned were Hara Tamiki's *Natsu no hana*, Ōta Yōko's 1948 *Shikabane no machi* (City of Corpses), Ogura Toyofumi's *Zetsugo no kiroku* (Letters from the End of the World), Koromogawa Maiko's *Hiroshima*, Tamai Reiko's *Watashi wa Hiroshima ni ita* (I Was in Hiroshima), and Agawa Hiroyuki's 1947 *Hachigatsu muika* (August Sixth).[111] The body of atomic-bombing literature produced by Hiroshima writers was impressive. In Nagasaki, it took decades for the *hibakusha* to strengthen their collective voice and challenge Nagai as the representative of the city's atomic experience by building their own body of atomic-bombing literature.

Nagai Takashi died of leukemia on May 1, 1951, at forty-three years of age, leaving behind his son Makoto, sixteen, and daughter Kayano, nine. Nagai donated his body to science to advance research on radiation-related illness. An autopsy revealed that his organs were badly affected, with his spleen thirty-five times larger than normal and his liver five times larger. Despite the severity of his leukemia, Nagai had lived three years longer than expected. On May 3, the Urakami Catholics held a funeral mass for him, and on May 14, as a privilege of the first Honorary Citizen of Nagasaki City, awarded in 1949, he received a second, city-sponsored funeral, which attracted a crowd of around twenty thousand people.[112] Among the attendees was Prime Minister Yoshida Shigeru, who gave the funeral oration. Nagai's "achievements are truly remarkable with many implications for morality and faith," declared Yoshida. "Today, at the Nagasaki City Public Funeral Service, I extol the virtues of [his] life and reverently present this memorial address." Mayor Tagawa Tsutomu spoke as well, recounting Nagai's many contributions to science on the effects of radiation on the human body and his many books that garnered him and the city so much international attention. A representative from the Vatican attended the funeral and read a message from Pope Pius XII, who had sent Nagai a rosary together with a portrait containing a handwritten note in August 1950 and in December had bestowed on him an "exceptional blessing." "I extend my deepest sympathies to the bereaved family of Dr. Nagai," the pope stated. "Dr. Nagai, who had a deep understanding of Catholic doctrine and who transcended [*yoku shinogareta*] poor health, resides now in heaven as a grand protector of your nation."[113] In the first year and a half after Nagai's death, six books were published: two that he had written, one that he had edited, and three about him by other authors.[114]

Nagai, who originally intended to console his community, based his interpretation of the bombing on specific religious and geographical contexts, but his writings shaped the formation of atomic narratives in at least two ways. First, the dissemination and promotion of Nagai's interpretation of the bombing in the immediate postwar era prevented other narratives of personal trauma and suffering from emerging, including among the Catholics, some of whom did not agree with him. The 1949 book *Masako taorezu* (Masako Shall Not Perish) was no less heartbreaking in conveying the tragedy of the bombing than *Nagasaki no kane* published the same year, but it failed to compete with any of Nagai's books. In other words, the hype surrounding Nagai blinded Japanese readers and politicians, not to mention international audiences, to the other narratives and voices emerging from the atomic experience of Nagasaki. A self-proclaimed martyr replaced the individual experiences of tens of thousands of survivors. Second, in Nagai's formula, the United States did not factor into the bombing—it was all due to the work of God—which impeded discussion of the events surrounding the decision to drop the atomic bombs. Occupation-period censorship also contributed to the lack of discussion, of course, but Nagai's writings supported a view of history in which American responsibility was a nonissue. American censors realized the value of Nagai's writings and sought to use them to promote their own atomic narrative.

The occupation's preferential treatment of Nagai and his books built walls and reinforced others around discussions of the bombing. In subsequent decades, Nagai's works and persona continued to be the voice of Nagasaki's atomic experience, fostering a popular image of the city as having responded to the destruction by praying for peace but performing little real action in the antinuclear and antiwar movements as compared to Hiroshima. This view presented a challenge to survivors who disputed the interpretation of the atomic tragedy as providential and were able only in the 1960s to begin shaking Nagai's hold on the popular memory of the bombing. For more than the first two decades after the bombing, the memory activism of the Nagasaki *hibakusha* worked to break down the walls of silence that had emerged during the occupation.

Notes

1. In Mark 8:34, Jesus encourages believers to bear their cross and follow in his footsteps.

2. Takahashi Shinji, *Nagasaki ni atte tetsugaku suru: Kakujidai no shi to sei* (Philosophizing in Nagasaki: Death and Life in the Nuclear Age) (Tokyo: Hokuju shuppan, 1994), 201.

3. See, e.g., William Johnston's translation: Nagai Takashi, *The Bells of Nagasaki,* trans. William Johnston (Tokyo: Kodansha International, 1984). In his translation of the eulogy of November 1945, Johnston replaced "Urakami" with "Nagasaki" (106–109). The updated English translation in 2022, which is discussed by Nagai's grandson, Tokusaburō, in this volume, has retained Nagai's original use of "Urakami."

4. Kataoka Yakichi, *Nagai Takashi no shōgai* (The Life of Nagai Takashi) (Tokyo: San Paolo, 1961), 12.

5. Takahashi, *Nagasaki ni atte tetsugaku suru*, 195.

6. Kataoka, *Nagai Takashi no shōgai*, 39–44. See also Paul Glynn, *A Song for Nagasaki* (Hunters Hill, Australia: Marist Fathers Books, 1988; repr., Reconciliation Edition, 1995), 31–35.

7. The *chōgata* bore the responsibility of informing the parishioners of religious dates, such as the Assumption of the Virgin Mary on August 15, and passing on the essence of Catholicism from generation to generation.

8. See Nagai Takashi, *Horobinu mono o* (Grant Me Something Eternal) (Nagasaki: Nagasaki nichinichi shinbun sha, 1948), 91–93.

9. Ibid., 93.

10. Takahashi, *Nagasaki ni atte tetsugaku suru*, 231. A different date of June 9 is found in Nagai Tokusaburō, ed., *Nagai Takashi zenshū* (The Complete Works of Nagai Takashi) (Tokyo: San Paolo, 2003), 1:783, but I have relied on Takahashi's date. For a detailed account of Nagai's conversion to Christianity and his Catholic baptism, see Nagai, *Horobinu mono o*, 97–110. Nagai was named after St. Paul.

11. Kataoka, *Nagai Takashi no shōgai*, 360.

12. In Japanese, "Minakerya hanashi ni naranu."

13. *Katorikkukyō hō*, September 15, 1937. The *Katorikkukyō hō*, or *Catholicism Bulletin*, was a bimonthly parish newsletter in Nagasaki.

14. For witnessing "crimes" in China, see Nagai Takashi, "Shi ni chokumen shite" (Facing Death), special issue (Bessatsu), *Shinchō*, January 15, 1951, 20. In the postwar years Nagai did not often discuss his military service in China. The article cited here was written less than four months before he died, when, as the title points out, he was "facing death."

15. Nagai, quoted in *Katorikkukyō hō*, January 15, 1938. In the letter, Nagai makes no mention of the manner in which Nanjing fell to the Japanese military.

16. This passage is from the Bible, Romans 8:36. In Japanese, the verse as it appears in Nagai, *Horobinu mono o*, is "Warera hinemosu shu no tame ni shi no kiken ni ai, hōraru beki hitsuji no gotoku seraruru nari" (189). I have translated the Japanese verse into English instead of relying on conventional English translations of Romans 8:36.

17. Nagai, *Horobinu mono o*, "Providence" on 188; Raguet, "sacrificial lamb" (*hōraru beki kohitsuji*) on 189–190. Father Emil Raguet was once the rector of the Urakami Parish (189).

18. See Kataoka, *Nagai Takashi no shōgai*, 360; Nagai Tokusaburō, *Nagai Takashi zenshū*, 3:772; Glynn, *A Song for Nagasaki*, 82. See also Takahashi, *Nagasaki ni atte tetsugaku suru*, 211. Takahashi argues that Nagai, having seen the destruction wrought by Japanese forces in China, became militaristic (*gunkokushugi*), and his behavior back home in Nagasaki reflected the change. Takahashi discusses an instance where Nagai thought a certain young woman was "slacking" (*tarundeiru*) and threw her into icy water to teach her a lesson. However, Takahashi does not provide a reference.

19. *Nagasaki Shinbun*, February 11, 1946.

20. Kataoka, *Nagai Takashi no shōgai*, 82.

21. Discussed in Glynn, *A Song for Nagasaki*, 92.

22. Josef Schilliger, *The Saint of the Atom Bomb*, trans. David Heimann (Westminster, MD: Newman Press, 1955), 92.

23. Indeed, Christians lived throughout the city, and the Ōura Cathedral, built by French missionaries in the 1860s, is located in the far southern part of the city. The Ōura Cathedral survived the atomic bombing completely unharmed, and the National Commission for the Protection of Cultural Properties declared it a national treasure in 1953.

24. Nagai, *Horobinu mono o*, 97.

25. In Japanese, the phrase is "*Onore no gotoku hito o ai seyo*," or the simplified four-character equivalent, "*Nyoko aijin*." Nyoko is the abbreviated form of *onore no gotoku*, or "as thyself," and *dō* means "temple" or "church."

26. Nagai Takashi, *Hana saku oka* (Hill of Blossoming Flowers), in Nagai Tokusaburō, *Nagai Takashi zenshū*, 1:201.

27. Nagai Takashi, *Nagasaki no kane* (The Bell of Nagasaki) (Tokyo: Hibiya shuppan sha, 1949), 171–179.

28. The English term "parishioner representative" (*shinto daihyō*) is from "Chronology of the Life and Work of Nagai Takashi," in the pamphlet "The Life of Dr. Nagai Takashi" (Nagasaki: Nagasaki City Nagai Takashi Memorial Museum, n.d.). Nagai writes "*shinja daihyō*" at the end of the eulogy manuscript, which has the same meaning.

29. As Max Weber noted, one "can explain suffering and injustice by referring to individual sin committed in a former life (the migration of souls), to the guilt of ancestors . . . or—the most principled—to the wickedness of all creatures *per se*." The pain and suffering of an individual or group, then, represents a martyr complex characterized by the "missionary prophecy" in which "the devout have not experienced themselves as vessels of the divine but rather as instruments of a god"; H. H. Gerth and C. Wright Mills, eds., *From Max Weber: Essays in Sociology* (Oxford University Press, 1946), 275, 285. For an analysis of Nagai's interpretation of the bombing from the perspective of religious studies, see Yuki Miyamoto, "Rebirth in the Pure Land or God's Sacrificial Lambs? Religious Interpretations of the Atomic Bombings in Hiroshima and Nagasaki," *Japanese Journal of Religious Studies* 32, no. 1 (2005): 131–159.

30. Nagai Takashi, *Genshi bakudan shisha gōdō sō chōji* (Eulogy for the Joint Funeral for Those Who Died in the Atomic Bombing), MS, eulogy delivered on November 23, 1945, Nagasaki City Nagai Takashi Memorial Museum, hereafter cited as NTMM.

31. The word *hansai*, which I translate as "holocaust," means "a burnt offering."

32. Nishida Hideo and Nagaoka Some, quoted in *Kami to genbaku: Urakami katorikku hibakusha no 55 nen* (God and the Atomic Bombing: Fifty-Five Years of the Urakami Catholic Hibakusha), television special, produced by NBC Nagasaki hōsō (aired May 31, 2000).

33. Rainer Maria Rilke, "The First Elegy," in *Duino Elegies and The Sonnets to Orpheus—Rainer Maria Rilke*, ed. and trans. Stephen Mitchell (New York: Vintage International, 2009), 7.

34. *NS*, February 11, 1946. The article claimed that Nagai was building a "barracks" hut, but he had just moved out of that makeshift hut into a provisional house weeks earlier.

35. The correspondence between Nagai and Giblin is discussed in a newspaper article, "Kokkyō koeru shūkyō ai" (Religious Love that Transcends National Boundaries), *Nagasaki nichinichi Shinbun*, August 9, 1947. The article identified the magazine as *The Field Affair*, which I then wrote as such in the original version of this essay (2018); I would like to thank Hirokazu Miyazaki for pointing out that the magazine was most likely *The Field Afar*.

36. Ibid.

37. For a list of Nagai's publications, see Nagai Tokusaburō, *Nagai Takashi zenshū*, 1:785–789.

38. Tanaka Shinjirō, review of *Seimei no kawa*, by Nagai Takashi, *Asahi hyōron* 4, no. 1 (1949): 90–93.

39. Ono Tomoaki, review of *Rozario no kusari*, by Nagai Takashi, *Katorikku shisō* 28, no. 4 (1948): 104–5.

40. "Shuppanbutsu wa kanarazu ken'etsu o" (Be Certain to Submit for Censorship Any Works to be Published), *NS*, February 28, 1946.

41. Advertisement poster of Hasumi Shoten in Kanda, Tokyo, for *Horobinu mono o* (1948), Kōkoku folder, NTMM.

42. In *Pasadena Star-News*, "Doomed by Bombing: Leading Japanese Author Calmly Awaiting Death," June 5, 1949. Article written in Tokyo by AP staff, June 4, 1949.

43. *Mainichi Shinbun*, June 10, 1949.

44. Nagai Takashi, *Kono ko o nokoshite* (Leaving These Children Behind) (Tokyo: San Paulo, 2000), 27–30.

45. Inoue Hisashi, *Besuto seraa no sengoshi* (The Postwar History of Best Sellers) (Tokyo: Bungei shunshū, 1995), 55.

46. *Nagasaki Shinbun*, June 25, 1948. From 1948, Nagai was widely known as the "saint of Urakami" (*Urakami no seija*; "*seijin*" was also used). The newspaper cited here is the first public expression of Nagai as the "saint of Urakami," as far as I have seen. Most likely, there is an earlier instance, but I have yet to find it. An ad for the same book in the May 22, 1949, issue of the *Mainichi Shinbun* referred to Nagai as an "apostle of Urakami" (*Urakami no shito*).

47. Advertisement clipping, Kōkoku folder, NTMM.

48. T S, "'Kono ko o nokoshite' dokugo kan (sono ni)" (Impressions after Reading "Leaving These Children Behind," Part 2), *Koe* (Voice) 862 (July 1949): 40–41. This article was part two of two. Part 1 has "T K" listed as the author.

49. Notes of the National Diet of Japan, *Shūgiin, Kōsei i'in kai*, March 31, 1949, no. 3, p. 8.

50. Among them were Anzai Keimei, Hino Ashihei, Suzuki Shintarō, and many others. See Shokan file 1, NTMM.

51. The play was performed by the Bara za (Rose [theater] group) at the Mitsukoshi Theater (*gekijō*) in Tokyo in March 1949; see *Tokyo Times*, March 3 and 19, 1949. The group performed it in Nagasaki as well on March 6 and 7, 1949: see *Nagasaki minyū* (newspaper), May 2, 1949. The play version was arranged by Sasaki Takamaru, Chiaki Minoru's father-in-law. Sasaki and Chiaki starred together in the 1956 Inagaki Hiroshi film, *Kettō Ganryūjima*, about Miyamoto Musashi. Sasaki Takamaru also starred in the 1953 film *Senkan Yamato* (Battleship Yamato). Sasaki's grandson, Chiaki's son, is the actor Sasaki Katsuhiko (b. 1944). The director Ōniwa Hideo made a film version of *Nagasaki no kane* in 1949, and it, too, became a hit. The film was produced by the Shochiku Company. See Eiga "Nagasaki no kane" shashin shū (Movie, "The Bell of Nagasaki" photo album) folder, NTMM.

52. Chiaki Minoru to Nagai Takashi, March 14, 1949, Shokan file 1, NTMM.

53. Although the 1984 English translation of *Nagasaki no kane* translates "*kane*" as "bells" (sound), the title in Japanese refers to a single cathedral bell unearthed by the Catholics in December 1945. This one bell held significant meaning for Nagai and the Catholics after the bombing (discussed in the last part of *Nagasaki no kane*), and so I maintain the nonplural translation of *kane*. For more on the significance of the bell, see, e.g., Hori Noriaki, ed., *Nagasaki yūgaku mappu 1: Genbaku hisaichi ato ni heiwa o manabu* (Nagasaki Travel Study Map 1: Learning Peace among the Ruins of the Atomic Bombing) (Nagasaki: Nagasaki bunken sha, 2004), 23.

54. Results published in *Mainichi Shinbun*, October 26, 1949. The poll also surveyed bookstores: "Name the book that had the best standing at your store in the past year." *Kono ko o nokoshite* secured the number-one spot with a 43 percent margin of votes over the number-two book, *Kyōsan shugi hihan no jōshiki* (Common Knowledge of the Criticism of Communism). Clearly, the publishing year of 1948–49 was defined by Nagai's *Kono ko o nokoshite*. According to a Yomiuri Shinbun Company poll, *Kono ko o nokoshite* was the number-one book in 1948 as well; see T K, "'Kono ko o nokoshite' dokugo kan (sono ichi)," *Koe* 861 (June 1949): 34.

55. *Mainichi Shinbun*, October 26, 1949.

56. Nagai gave a copy each to the emperor and the crown prince. The Imperial Palace acknowledged receipt of the two copies of *Nagasaki no kane* on February 10, 1949, in a document sent to Nagai's publisher, Shikiba Ryūzaburō. See document of receipt in Shokan file 1, NTMM.

57. Emperor Hirohito, quoted in *Nagasaki minyū*, May 28, 1949. Notice that Hirohito did not say he "read" it. He also called the book a *shōsetsu* (novel), which implies fiction.

58. Emperor Hirohito, quoted in Nagai Takashi, *Itoshigo yo* (My Beloved Children) (Tokyo: San Paulo, 1995), 313. Originally published in October 1949 by Kodansha.

59. Notice that the newspaper reporter wrote "human emperor." Hirohito was an amateur biologist, hence "scientist emperor." Nagai felt a deep connection to Hirohito because they were both scientists. For reference to Hirohito's interests in science, see Herbert P. Bix, *Hirohito and the Making of Modern Japan* (New York: Perennial, 2001), esp. 60–62.

60. Emperor Hirohito, quoted in *Nagasaki minyū*, May 28, 1949.

61. Nagai, *Itoshigo yo*, 313, "wished that the visit could have been under better circumstances" (*mottai nai shidai de atta*).

62. *Nagasaki minyū*, May 23, 1949. Nagai Takashi was a prolific poet and painter, in addition to book author, scientist, and theological philosopher.

63. Bix, *Hirohito and the Making of Modern Japan*, 637.

64. Recorded, among other places, in Nagai, *Itoshigo yo*, 279–88.

65. *Nippon Times*, December 1, 1950.

66. One letter had an address in Italian: "Illustre Signor, Prof. TAKASHI NAGAI, Professore della Facoltà di Medicina, Università di, NAGASAKI (Giappone)." For both letters, see Shokan file 2, NTMM. Another letter was addressed to "Dr. Nagi" in "Nagisaki": W. H. Deal to Professor T. Nagi [sic], August 23, 1947, Shohyō folder, NTMM. Incidentally, Nagai's actual mailing address was Nagasaki-shi, Ueno-machi, 373.

67. El Secretario of Editorial Marfil, S. A. to Nagai Takashi, February 9, 1950, Shokan file 2, NTMM.

68. Amino Isao to Nagai Takashi Sensei, September 7, 1949, Shokan file 2, NTMM. Amino Isao wrote on behalf of the Shuppan Kyoku (Publishing Bureau) of DaiNippon Yubenkai Kodansha in Tokyo. The letter to Nagai outlined three issues about which Duell, Sloane and Pearce inquired regarding *Kono ko o nokoshite*: (1) the possibility of obtaining translation rights; (2) the existence of anybody in Japan suitable to translate the book for them; and (3) permission to intensify the Catholic aspects of the book (*Katorikku no nioi o yori koku sakaritai*), as well as the "feelings" of "Nagai the scientist" regarding the atomic bomb. Ray Falk, a reporter for the North American Newspaper Alliance dispatched to Japan, approached Kodansha for Duell, Sloan and Pearce and acted as liaison.

69. Charles A. Pearce to Shinnosuke Owari [sic], February 24, 1950, Shokan file 2, NTMM. *Genshiun senjo shinri* more literally means "battlefield psychology beneath the atomic mushroom cloud."

70. "Fall 1950: Books: Duell Sloan & Pearce," press release, 1950, Shokan file 2, NTMM.

71. Pearce to Owari, February 24, 1950.

72. Ruth Giblin to Dr. Nagai, January 28, 1951, Shohyō folder, NTMM.

73. Mary Rutherford to Dr. Nagai, February 13, 1951, Shohyō folder, NTMM.

74. Sister Mary Ambrose, BVM, to Doctor Takashi Nagai, January 25, 1951, Shohyō folder, NTMM. "BVM" stands for "Blessed Virgin Mary" and means the Sisters of Charity of the Blessed Virgin Mary, a charitable organization established in the United States in the 1800s.

75. *Nagasaki no kane* was not published in English translation as *The Bells of Nagasaki* until 1984. Recently, an organization called the Friends of Takashi and Midori Nagasaki, established in early 2021, has translated and independently published two of Nagai's books that were originally published posthumously: *Otome tōge* (1952) (Pass of the Virgin, trans. Gabriele Di Comite, 2022) and *Nyokodō zuihitsu* (1957) (Thoughts from Nyokodō, trans. Gabriele Di Comite, 2021).

76. From August 1946, Nagai published short writings of his own as series in newspapers and journals. He also gave several lectures and presentations on conditions in postatomic Nagasaki from the latter part of 1946. The early writings were "Kagakusha no shinkō: Gakutō ni okuru" (The Faith of a Scientist: A Gift to Students), *Katorikku Shinbun* (Catholic newspaper), August 18 to September 2, 1946; "Genshino rokuon" (A (Sound) Recording of the Atomic Wasteland), *Seibo no kishi* (Knights of the Blessed Mother Mary), January 1947; "Shi no shinri tankyū" (Investigation into the Truth of Death), *Dokusho tenbō* (Reading Outlook), April 1947; "Kuro yuri" (Black Lily), *Nagasaki bungaku* (Nagasaki Literature), September 1947. However, the 1947 cotranslation of Bruce Marshall's book, discussed later, was the first publication to produce substantial royalties for Nagai.

77. Kataoka, *Nagai Takashi no shōgai*, 233–234; Kataoka Chizuko and Kataoka Rumiko, *Hibakuchi Nagasaki no saiken* (The Reconstruction of the Atomic-Bombed Land of Nagasaki) (Nagasaki: Nagasaki junshin daigaku hakubutsukan, 1996), 83. See also "Inzei o byōin saiken ni: Nagai hakase shōsetsu o kyōdō honyaku," newspaper clipping, n.d., Kiji kirinuki folder, NTMM. The Japanese edition of Marshall's book is *Sekai to nikutai to Sumisu shinpu*, trans. Nagai Takashi and Monfette Proudhon (Tokyo: Shufu no tomo sha, [December 20,] 1947); originally published as Bruce Marshall, *The World, the Flesh, and Father Smith* (Boston: Houghton Mifflin, 1945). Nagai's cotranslator was Father Monfette Proudhon, who was working in the Saint Francis Hospital in Nagasaki. Bruce Marshall lost an arm in the First World War, converted to Catholicism, and became a writer and priest. Nagai's trajectory was similar to that of Marshall's: he converted to Catholicism, suffered leukemia, and became a writer and Catholic leader. Nagai and Proudhon cotranslated another book in 1949, Francis Clement Kelley's 1942 book, *Pack Rat* (*Nonezumi*, lit. "field mouse"): see Nagai Tokusaburō, *Nagai Takashi zenshū*, 1:787. Kelley was the bishop of Oklahoma City and had died in 1948, one year before the Japanese translation of his book; see "Bishop Francis Clement Kelley," http://www.catholic-hierarchy.org/bishop/bkelley.html.

78. See "Inzei o byōin saiken ni: Nagai hakase shōsetsu o kyōdō honyaku," newspaper clipping, n.d., Kiji kirinuki folder, NTMM.

79. *Asahi Shinbun*, June 14, 1949.

80. *Mainichi Shinbun*, June 10, 1949.

81. *Mainichi Shinbun*, March 29, 1949.

82. *Asahi Shinbun*, June 14, 1949. Individual high earners like Nagai paid extremely progressive tax rates from 1947. From September 1946 to March 1947, Japan underwent innovations to its tax system that expanded the nation's tax base as a way to begin relieving the wartime debt, funding reconstruction, and rebuilding the economy. For more on these innovations, see Henry Shavell, "Postwar Taxation in Japan," *Journal of Political Economy* 56, no. 2 (April 1948): 124–137. The progressive tax rates that resulted from the early postwar innovations were also intended as a "key anti-inflation weapon" to subdue the economic chaos of the early postwar period; see Henry Shavell, "Taxation Reform in Occupied Japan," *National Tax Journal* 1, no. 2 (June 1948): 127–143.

83. *Mainichi Shinbun*, June 10, 1949.

84. Kataoka Yakichi, "Nagai hakase to chosaku" (Dr. Nagai and His Books), *Nagasaki Nichinichi Shinbun*, May 15, 1951. The article is reproduced in Kataoka C. and Kataoka R., *Hibakuchi Nagasaki no saiken*, 83–86.

85. A *sen* was the smallest unit of monetary measurement at the time. The saying is akin to "not a single cent."

86. Nagai, quoted in Kataoka, *Nagai Takashi no shōgai*, 218–219.

87. Nagai, quoted in Kataoka, "Nagai hakase to chosaku."

88. Nagai Takashi, *Nagasaki no hana* (Flowers of Nagasaki), in Nagai Tokusaburō, *Nagai Takashi zenshū*, 2:422.

89. *Asahi Shinbun*, May 26, 1949.

90. "Zei de ikinayamu: Nagai hakase no inzei kifu" (Deadlocked over Taxes: The Royalty Donations of Dr. Nagai), newspaper clipping, n.d., Kankei kiji folder 5, NTMM. *Zōyozei* can also be translated as "capital transfer tax." As the head of the Inheritance Tax Department of the National Tax Agency (Kokuzeichō sōzokuzei kachō) pointed out, the donation would not be taxed if it was simply to Nagasaki Prefecture or to the city, but only in the case that the companies (contractors) performing the various projects of the "cultural city construction" were "incorporated foundations" (*zaidan hōjin*), which most likely would be true in many cases. This particular case of taxation, when Nagai paid more than ¥4 million in taxes on ¥5 million in royalties, led to a discussion among policymakers in the National Diet about the need to revise tax law; see Notes of the National Diet of Japan, *Sangi'in, Ōkura i'inkai*, June 9, 1949, 14.

91. Nagai, quoted in Kataoka, *Nagai Takashi no shōgai*, 217.

92. Kataoka, "Nagai hakase to chosaku."

93. *Nishi Nippon Shinbun*, December 26, 1948.

94. See, e.g., *Nagasaki Nichinichi Shinbun*, March 26, 1950.

95. See *Kyūshū taimuzu*, November 15, 1948.

96. *Asahi Shinbun*, December 4, 1949.

97. *Mainichi Shinbun*, December 4, 1949.

98. Nagai Takashi, quoted in *Katorikku Shinbun*, October 9, 1949. Nagai opposed the nomination on similar grounds in other newspapers as well; see, e.g., *Nagasaki Nichinichi Shinbun*, September 14, 1949.

99. Konno Setsuzo, "Letters to the Editor: In the Japanese Press—(To the Mainichi)," n.d., newspaper clipping, unmarked, Kankei kiji folder, NTMM.

100. Shimokawa Ōten, "Ore ni wa mienai" (I Just Can't See It), *Tōkyō taimuzu*, September 15, 1949, newspaper clipping, Kankei kiji folder, NTMM.

101. See various sources, e.g., Takahashi, *Nagasaki ni atte tetsugaku suru*, 225; Mashima Kazuhiro, dir., *Nagasaki no kane: Tsukurareta besuto serā* (NBC Nagasaki Hōseisaku, 2000). The award certificate and silver cups are preserved and on display at NTMM.

102. For a discussion of the American Occupation's treatment of Nagai's books, especially *Nagasaki no kane*, see Chad R. Diehl, *Resurrecting Nagasaki: Reconstruction and the Formation of Atomic Narratives* (Ithaca, NY: Cornell University Press, 2018), ch. 4.

103. John Whittier Treat, *Writing Ground Zero: Japanese Literature and the Atomic Bomb* (Chicago: University of Chicago Press, 1995), 95.

104. See ibid., 92–107.

105. Captain Irvin W. Rogers to Commanding Officer, CCD, Fukuoka, "Censorship of Publication," March 18, 1947, and letter from Delnore to American occupation censors in Fukuoka, March 1947, Victor E. Delnore Papers, Gordon W. Prange Collection, University of Maryland Libraries.

106. Major George P. Solovskoy to Commanding Officer, Kyushu Military Government Region, Hq. & Hq. Det., APO 929, Fukuoka, Kyushu, July 16, 1947, Victor E. Delnore Papers, Gordon W. Prange Collection, University of Maryland Libraries.

107. The comments of those surveyed can be found in the files pertaining to *Masako taorezu*, Gordon W. Prange Collection, University of Maryland Libraries.

108. Copy of Fujin taimuzu sha (1949) version of *Masako taorezu* preserved at the Gordon W. Prange Collection, University of Maryland Libraries. Braw, *Suppressed*, lists the final publication date as April 26, 1949 (92–93, 169n12).

109. Copies of Masako's books used by the censors are preserved at Gordon W. Prange Collection, University of Maryland Libraries.

110. Treat, *Writing Ground Zero*, 90.

111. "Tokushū: Nō moa Hiroshimasu," special issue, *Shūkan asahi*, August 7, 1949, 3.

112. Nagai Tokusaburō, *Nagai Takashi zenshū*, 3:777. Nagai was buried next to his wife, Midori.

113. The orations quoted here can be found in Tomita Kunihiko, ed., *Nagai Takashi hakase: Genshino no seija* (Dr. Nagai Takashi: The Saint of the Atomic Wasteland) (Tokyo: Myōgi shuppansha, 1951), Yoshida on 11; Tagawa on 12–15; Pope Pius XII on 16. See also 311 for details on the pope's gifts to Nagai. For the pope's portrait with note, see also the 1951 film *Nagai hakase no omoide*, produced by Nihon nyūsu and Nagasaki shiyakusho.

114. Nagai Tokusaburō, *Nagai Takashi zenshū*, 3:777.

Loving Your Neighbor across the Sea
The Reception of the Work of Nagai Takashi in the Republic of Korea

By Haeseong Park and Franklin Rausch

Nagai Takashi has attracted significant interest from people in Korea, with responses to his books ranging from admiration to criticism. Certain recurring themes in Nagai's books have resonated among the people of Korea from a variety of backgrounds and perspectives, creating a bridge not only between Japan and Korea, but also, and perhaps more important, across the colonial past, the postwar period, the Cold War, and the present. Nagai's appeal has led authors and translators in Korea to build him up into a popular historical figure and writer, more so than has happened anywhere else in the world outside of Japan. Three main themes that appear in Nagai's works and have driven interest in him in Korea, include issues related to world and regional peace; reconciliation between Korea and Japan, and between Catholic and Protestant Christians; and religious, humanistic, and secular understandings of making sense of human suffering. A focus on these themes implicitly rejects the more nation-focused perspectives that have led to some negative critiques of Nagai in Korea and elsewhere.

Nagai Takashi in Japan, the United States, and Korea

Nagai Takashi was well acquainted with suffering. As a promising young medical student in Nagasaki, Nagai's sudden bout with meningitis caused deafness in one ear. In an age when stethoscopes were key to medical diagnosis, this at first threatened to end his medical career. However, a Japanese doctor who had returned from Germany, where he had been studying the new field of radiology, allowed Nagai to become his assistant. Nagai's work in radiology led him to develop leukemia. Though comforted by the thought that his wife would be with him until his death, she herself was killed in the atomic bombing of Nagasaki, ground zero of which was their Urakami neighborhood. The bombing killed approximately eight thousand of the ten thousand members of the Urakami Catholic community, of which she and her husband were a part. Thus after the war, Nagai was left dying of leukemia, with two young children to care for, in a nation devastated by war. Rather than give in to despair, he began to write, reflecting on what he had witnessed and developing an understanding of war, particularly regarding the use of atomic weapons. His writings helped others make sense of their suffering and gave them the hope to rebuild and live their lives.

Nagai's writings became extremely popular in late 1940s Japan, eclipsing works by many others who had experienced the atomic bombings. While part of this has no doubt to do with the quality of Nagai's work and the power of his writing, key to the comparative success of his works was how they helped advance the agenda of both the Japanese and American occupation governments. As Chad Diehl puts it:

> The focus on reconstruction throughout his books, which encouraged community revival, religious themes such as forgiveness of one's enemies, and the recovery of a historic Nagasaki in which Catholicism played a part, served the purposes of local and national politicians, as well as the American occupation, not to mention the Nagasaki Catholic community. Nagai's ruminations on the relationship between God, destruction, and revival also advanced the image of the church in Japan.[1]

The fact that Nagai's writings complemented the ideas of Japanese and American leadership meant that they would face little to no censorship. Indeed, at a time when paper was still scarce and rationed, his books were printed in large numbers, sometimes on high-quality stock made available by the American occupation government, which approved in particular of his belief in the cause of the bombing as having been general human sinfulness rather than particular choices made by the United States. Thus, key to Nagai's popularity was the unique historical context found in a Japan devastated by war and occupied by the American military. Many Japanese were hungry for hope, for ways of making sense of a war that had led to so much death and ultimately defeat, and so with government support, Nagai provided the Japanese public with some meaning for the tragedy and loss. His books became bestsellers and eventually part of the Japanese canon of literature on the war and the atomic bombings.[2]

Nagai wrote and published nine books before his death in 1951, with two manuscripts published posthumously, as well as a large number of magazine and newspaper articles. One might expect that American public interest in the atomic bombings and Nagai's lack of blame for the United States, as well as the occupation government's support of his writings, would have led his works to become popular in the United States. However, only the edited collection he produced of eyewitness accounts, called, *We of Nagasaki*, appeared in English during his lifetime.³ The English translation of his 1949 book, *Nagasaki no kane*, which describes the atomic bombing and includes his famous eulogy delivered to the devastated Catholic community at the mass funeral for their dead in November 1945, in which he summarized his understanding of the bombing of Urakami as a necessary sacrifice to end the war, was published only posthumously in 1984 as *The Bells of Nagasaki*, translated by William Johnston.

The relative neglect of Nagai in the United States stands in stark contrast to interest in Korea, where at least five of his books have been translated into Korean. In addition to Nagai's own works, at least two biographies on Nagai and a memoir by Nagai's son have also been published. Some books have even been translated and published multiple times by different translators. And while Australian Catholic monk Paul Glynn's biography *Song of Nagasaki* is the only book-length work aimed at a popular audience related to Nagai available in English, numerous works on his life have been translated into Korean, including Glynn's book, or produced by Koreans themselves. Catholics in Korea have been particularly active in these efforts, with many of the publications being undertaken by Catholic institutions. For example, two Korean Catholic clerics, Bishop Yi Munhŭi and Father Sŏ Chunhong have written about Nagai's life and beliefs, the former even establishing an association dedicated to him, discussed below. Moreover, in 2004, the Archdiocese of Daegu, headed by Yi, established the "As Yourself Association" (Yŏgi Aein), the title of which was inspired by the name Nagai chose for his final home, "As Yourself Cottage" (Nyokodō), a reference to Jesus's teaching to "love your neighbor as you love yourself."⁴ Protestant adherents have also shown an interest in Nagai's work. Because both Catholic and Protestant groups continue to keep discussion of Nagai alive, his works are categorized as Christian books rather than as specifically Catholic. However, because not all translators are Christians or are working on behalf of a Christian organization, their translations are frequently included among works on the environment, war, Japan, and social issues. This is particularly surprising inasmuch as there has historically been a significant amount of animosity in Korea toward Japan, not only because the country had engaged in the brutal colonization of the peninsula but also because of the failure by many in Japan to honestly face the legacy caused by Japanese imperialism.

General readers of Nagai's books in Korea, whether Christian or not, have praised him for his self-sacrifice, forgiveness, and love for humanity and peace. Even so, Korean scholars remained relatively silent about Nagai for decades. However, in the 2010s, they began to pay more attention to him and his works, but their treatment has tended to be negative. Scholars and journalists alike have launched scathing criticisms of Nagai, arguing that he exonerated—or was exploited to exonerate—Japanese imperialism and the American use of atomic weapons against Japan. For instance, Pak Sugyŏng, a Japanologist who has conducted extensive research on Nagai, contended that although the death of noncombatant civilians in Nagasaki amounted to "political deaths" caused by "social violence," Nagai distorted the memories of those deaths, consequently altering survivors' reactions.[5] In particular, by describing violent political deaths as a religious sacrifice, Nagai held no one to account and just urged people to move on with reconstruction and rehabilitation.[6] Sugyŏng claimed that advancing forward without critical reflection—honest introspection and apologies—constituted "severance from the dead and the past."[7] Journalist Chŏn Ŭnok agreed with Pak's contentions, saying that just as essential as love and forgiveness are the imperatives to confront the past, clarify who was responsible for the war and the dropping of the atomic bombs, and acknowledge the suffering of the victims (*pihaeja*).[8] In addition, some Korean antinuclear activists denounced Nagai not only for his whitewashing of Japan's war responsibility, but also his support for nuclear energy as well. Kim Hongchung, a sociologist who opposes nuclear power, confessed his uneasiness about Nagai's "holy madness" or "excessive faith and passion for science."[9] Kim pointed out the fact that Nagai lived in the center of the explosion with his own two children to "research the effects of residual radiation on children as well as adults."[10] He contended that Nagai's belief in scientific progress and Catholic salvation made Nagai turn a blind eye to the danger of nuclear energy.[11] Yet, amid mounting criticism of Nagai, his books continue to be reprinted and admired in Korea.

The Catholic Translations of Yi Sŏngwu

Yi Sŏngwu was the first and most prolific individual translator of Nagai's books, completing a total of three. The first, Nagai's 1948 *Horobinu mono o* (Grant Me Something Eternal) was published in 1964 as *Yŏngwŏn han kŏt ŭl* (What Is Eternal). This was a fateful year to publish a book by a Japanese author, since there were massive protests in Korea against the normalization treaty with Japan that would come into effect in 1965. Despite widespread anti-Japanese feelings, Yi continued his work, publishing translations of Nagai's 1948 *Rozario no kusari* (*Rosary Chain*) in 1969 as *Mukchu al* (Rosary Beads) and his 1951 *Nyokodō zuihitsu* (Essays from As Yourself Cottage) in 1971 as *Malli muyŏng* (Bright Moonlight with No Shadows). All of Yi's Korean translations were first published through St. Paul Publishing (Sŏngbaoro Ch'ulp'ansa). Later, Pauline Books & Media, operated by the Daughters of St. Paul (Paoro Ttal Sunyŏhoe) bound *Rosary Chain* and *Malli muyŏng* into one volume and reprinted all three of Yi's translations as part of the series called "masterpieces [that I want] to reread" (Tashi ikko ship'ŭn myŏngjak). Since then, about five hundred copies of *Grant Me Something Eternal* and one thousand copies of *Rosary Beads* (*Mukchu al*, the Korean title of the bound volume of *Rosary Chain* and *Bright Moonlight with No Shadows*) have been printed each year.[12]

In the translation of *Grant Me Something Eternal*, which Nagai wrote as a kind of autobiography, Yi includes a translator's preface. In it, Yi discusses how Nagai's book provides the reader contact with "transcendental truth," which Yi argues gives life a sense of fullness. So moving was this sense of contact with transcendental truth that the translator confessed to weeping several times during his work and was even more deeply moved than during his own baptism. Yi then shifted from the transcendent to the particular, explaining how as an officer in the Japanese army during Japan's invasion of China, Nagai arrived at a parish in the mountain where Catholics had fled seeking the protection of a foreign priest. Seeing Nagai, they were fearful, but after he showed them his rosary, thus identifying himself as a fellow Catholic, all approached him weeping—certainly this was no enemy. Emphasizing this theme of Catholicism as offering reconciliation, Yi explained how Nagai would baptize dying enemy soldiers and pray for their souls.[13]

After expressing his hope that this book, which he thought provided an easy-to-understand explanation of the Catholic faith, would clear up misunderstandings and prejudices about Catholicism and give readers a sense of its beauty and the joy it brought, Yi moved to the devastation caused by the atomic bomb. Rather than present the bombing of Nagasaki as a just punishment for Japan's colonization of Korea, the author quoted his translation of the desolation Nagai felt as he traveled through a city that had "boasted of its modern civilization" and contemplated the destruction he saw, which included his own parish church and congregation, his university and his students, and even his beloved wife. The translator then wrote that, "However, even in this abyss, the light of hope was shining in the heart of the author, that which he was carrying his whole life, that which he could not forget even on the battlefield, the light of faith." The translator then expressed his belief that the faith in God that could be found in Catholicism could be spread by Nagai's book and lead many to convert, and that is why he decided to translate it.[14] Considering that at this time Japan had largely recovered from World War II and was in the middle of its successful plan to double the average income, while South Korea was still at the beginnings of its economic development (and lagging behind North Korea), this hope was likely not only centered on the afterlife but also included a desire for a regeneration in this world as well: just as Japan had recovered from the atomic bombings, so too could Korea recover from the destruction of war. Moreover, during a time of conflict not only between Korea and Japan, but also between the Republic of Korea and the Democratic People's Republic of Korea, Nagai's themes of reconciliation might have been especially attractive to Yi.

Yi's translation of *Rosary Chain* (*Rozario no kusari*) into Korean as *Rosary Beads* (*Mukchu al*, the volume which also includes *Grant Me Something Eternal*) in 1969 continued to focus on the importance of truth and how Nagai's writings carried within them a sense of transcendent truth. This book, too, caused Yi to weep during his translation work as described in his afterword.[15] Part of what made this book so moving to the translator was how its rough and simple Japanese punctuated the message of transcendental truth. The translator then expressed his hope that by translating this book and making it available people who were looking for the way to God would find it. While considerably shorter than his preface in *Grant Me Something Eternal*, Yi ended with a similar emphasis on how truth brought contentment and, transcending national borders and nations, could unify humanity.[16] Perhaps in addition to continuing to find meaning in religious themes, the mild anticommunism of that work, which emphasized victory in the Cold War by loving one's neighbor, would have been appealing to Koreans living in a divided nation.[17]

Yi's third and last choice among Nagai's books was *Bright Moonlight with No Shadows* (*Watashitachi wa Nagasaki ni ita*, lit. We Were in Nagasaki). The book, edited by Nagai, was a collection of thirty-nine essays, as well as correspondence between Nagai and his friends. In the essay from which Yi's translation took its title, Nagai wrote that he wanted to return to his first impression of Nagasaki after it had been struck by the bomb, a field empty save the moonlight that illuminated it. Nagai confessed that the flattened city removed the scales from his eyes and allowed him to realize how meaningless the lust of the flesh and the pride of life were, thus filling his mind with what was eternal—the kingdom of God and His righteousness. Although Yi did not specify why he changed the title of the book, he made it clear in the postscript that he chose which books to translate, including that text, in order to introduce the depth of Nagai's faith to Koreans. Yi believed that the truth that Nagai found in the extreme situation would resonate with everyone everywhere regardless of race, nation, and time, and that anyone who tried to find the "truth"—peace, love, and especially God—should read Nagai. Moreover, themes of rejection of this-worldly desires might have resonated with Yi, too, owing to how such desires had led, in his mind, to the highly visible corruption and social conflict that accompanied South Korea's economic development, as well as the increasingly dictatorial Park Chunghee regime.

Diversification of the Translations of Nagai's Works

It is striking that it would not be until 1994 that a translation would be made of *Leaving These Children Behind* (*Kono ko o nokoshite*), since it was one of Nagai's bestselling works in Japan, more than 200,000 copies being purchased in 1948 alone.[18] However, this text, bound along with *Beloved Children* (*Itoshigo yo*), would be the first translation of Nagai's work by a non-Catholic translator. The fact that these translations were only first published in 1994, more than two decades after Yi's translations, indicates that it took a significant amount of time for interest in Nagai to move outside of Catholic circles. In contrast to the more religiously focused books translated by Yi, these two works express Nagai's fatherly love and advice to his children more than his Catholic outlook. Pak Ilhwa, the translator of the volume that includes these two works and the first dean of the College of Home Economics at Ewha Woman's University, explains in her preface that the books contain words that she strove to express to her own children. As an educator and a Presbyterian senior deaconess, Pak expressed her concern that contemporary Korean homes lacked love and conversation between parents and children and therefore produced many emotional and spiritual orphans. She believed that Nagai's works could help rectify these problems by teaching both parents and children how to love each other, one's neighbors, and God.[19] Pak named the book *Father's Voice* (*Abŏji ŭi moksori*), with father being a rather ambiguous phrase, as it could refer either to God or a human father. This text was first released by a Protestant publisher in 1994 and reprinted multiple times thereafter.

Later, two professional translators published *Leaving These Children Behind* and *Beloved Children* separately under slightly different titles: *Leaving Beloved Children Behind* (*Sarang hanŭn ai tŭl rŭl namgyŏ tugo*) and *My Beloved Children* (*Sarang hanŭn nae aidŭra*). *My Beloved Children* was translated by Chŏng Sŏngho and published through St. Paul Publishing Co. in 1999, whereas the secular company Puksŭk'aen printed *Leaving Beloved*

Children Behind, translated by Hong Sŏngmin in 2003. Both books are out of print now and do not contain translator prefaces. The reason these books were chosen can therefore only be surmised. St. Paul Publishing Co. was explicit in its front matter that publication of was part of St. Paul's mission work.[20] Although it cannot be confirmed whether he is Catholic, Chŏng, the translator, studied philosophy at Catholic University in Taegu and has worked on many Catholic books. Hong Sŏngmin, the translator of *Leaving Beloved Children behind*, does not show any religious affiliation and published his work with Puksŭk'aen, a secular company.[21] That translation was advertised as the inspiring true story of a dying father and his words of encouragement and wisdom.[22] Despite initial interest in these books, they are no longer in print, likely owing to poor sales.

As mentioned earlier, Yi Sŏngwu translated *Rosary Chain* as *Rosary Beads*, and it was published in 1969. Curiously, considering the fact that the title of the book is a reference to the Catholic prayer of the rosary, this work would attract attention from non-Catholics, leading to its retranslation and publication by professional translator, Japan specialist, and non-Catholic Cho Yangwuk as *Rosario ŭi kido* (Prayer of the Rosary) in 1999. Cho's afterword to the text describes how while he was studying Japanese in college, the reader for one of his courses included a selection, without clear attribution, from the *Rosary Chain*. Cho recalled that he was deeply moved by the text, even weeping as he read it. Later, when between projects following the difficulties caused by the 1997 financial crisis, Cho became convinced that it was necessary to "publish a moving book, a beautiful book that would give comfort to wounded hearts," leading him to think back to what he had read while a student.[23]

Cho described in his afterword how he was able to find his course reader from his time in college, but it was only a selection and did not include the name of the author, making it difficult to track down the complete text. He asked around, including his Japanese contacts, but was unable to locate the original text until he met a couple of Japanese journalists who had lived in Hiroshima and knew who Nagai was. Thanks to them, he was able to obtain the book and found within it Nagai's "simplicity and humanity." Out of a sense of courtesy, Cho explained that he had tried but failed to track down Nagai's family. He also sought permission from the publisher St. Paul (San Paolo) in Japan, but they were uncommunicative, and since permission was not legally necessary from a foreign publisher, Cho decided to go ahead and translate it. It is striking just how difficult it was for Cho to find information that would be readily accessible today. Moreover, it must be noted that Cho came into contact with Nagai not through a religious route or through previous Korean translations of his work, but through the study of Japanese.[24]

During his translation work, Cho struggled somewhat because of the difficulty of religious terminology, but through the help of a Korean Catholic priest he was able to complete the translation. While having a drink together to celebrate, the priest received a call from a Catholic nun who informed him that Saint Paul's publishing in Korea had already published a version of the translation, namely, the one by Yi Sŏngwu.[25] Cho wanted to push through with his translation regardless, which he believed was a more easily understood version that would reach a wider audience, since he had removed or simplified the more difficult religious language. Eventually, with the help of his contacts in the Catholic Church and with people in Japan, not only was he able to obtain permission to publish his work, but he was also able to track down Nagai's son Makoto. He concluded his afterword by expressing his hope that readers "would become inebriated with the pure human love of this Japanese person."[26]

Nagai Makoto wrote an afterword that focused on Nagai Takashi's Catholicism.[27] For instance, Makoto wrote of his father's conversion to Catholicism, noting that it must have been "Heaven's will" for him to study medicine in Nagasaki, since that is what led to contact with the Catholic community, particularly with Midori, Makoto's mother. Likewise, Makoto emphasized how he placed a crucifix in his father's hand after he called out "Jesus, Mary, Joseph" as he died. Thus, while Makoto emphasized the importance of Nagai's desire to realize world peace based on the love of neighbor, he contended that in order to end war it was necessary to completely commit to praying for peace. Moreover, Makoto drew explicitly from Christian doctrine, noting that since human beings are the descendants of Cain, they need the help of God in order to overcome the temptation to commit violence (implicitly born out of a failure to love others).[28] And, appropriately enough considering that the title of the book refers to the rosary, a distinctly Catholic prayer, Makoto emphasized his father's own Marian devotion, his frequent praying of the rosary, his meeting with Father Maximillian Kolbe (a Polish priest known for encouraging Marian piety), and Pope Pius XII's gift of a rosary. He also noted how his father taught him the importance of the rosary prayer. Makoto concluded his afterword with a call for peace and reflection on his father's words, "in a world of love there is no enemy, and if there is no enemy, then there will be no war."[29]

While Cho focused on the context of giving hope during difficult economic times (with a subtle message of reconciliation with Japan) and Makoto emphasized the importance of prayer, particularly Catholic prayer, in bringing peace, the preface to Cho's translation, written by Han Su'gan, a professor of literature at Sejong University, focused more on his own reconciliation with Japan within a context that is religious without being distinctly Catholic. For instance, Han usually used the term *sin* (신) to refer to God, which is broad and nonsectarian, rather than the Catholic term *Hanŭnim* (하느님). Han began his introduction noting he had a consciousness, as a Korean, as a victim of Japanese colonialism when he visited Nagasaki. However, he described Nagasaki positively, in his mind, as a place where "twenty-six Catholic saints were martyred" and where he began to think differently about Japan, especially after he visited Nagai's "As Yourself Cottage." There he purchased a book with an old cover that was published by "a religious house" at a time when Korea's "economic situation was not good." That book was *Leaving These Children Behind*. Han, having difficulty sleeping in Tokyo, began to read that book and found that he sniffled and wept through the night as he did so.[30]

Han then noted that *Prayer of the Rosary* (Cho's translation of Nagai's *Rozario no kusari*) was the same, a book suffused with a passion for life by a person who suffered a great deal but did not lose hope. Reflecting on an image of a bearded Nagai in mourning for his wife holding a rosary, Han emphasized Nagai's deep faith and how he had left behind many books that would be translated and go out to foreign lands. In this way Nagai would transform into a dove who informed people of the horrors of atomic weapons and the necessity of peace. In particular, Han praised Nagai's work for overcoming a focus simply on personal tragedy, a kind of victim consciousness he thought had manifested among Japanese people after Japan's defeat in the war, by praying for repentance and accepting responsibility for militarism. Nagai was thus presenting his suffering as emblematic of human suffering in general. Han argued that by reading about Nagai's deep suffering, our own suffering becomes more manageable. Han then concluded his preface by encouraging readers not to think so much about Japan within the historical context of its colonization of Korea or the atomic bomb, but rather to read the work in terms of a "humanity" that elucidates the central issues of "civilization" (*munmyŏng*) and death.[31]

Cho's translation *Prayer of the Rosary* includes secular, generically religious, and Catholic understandings of Nagai Takashi and his work. A distinctly Protestant understanding can be found in Kim Sunghoe's translation of Fr. Paul Glynn's biography of Nagai Takashi, *Song of Nagasaki* (*Nagasaki ŭi norae*), which was published in 2005 (the original English version was published in 1988). Kim's afterword to the translation is rather different from what we have seen so far, beginning not with a focus on truth, peace, or human suffering, but with the uniqueness of individuals.[32] Moreover, a shift in the fortunes of Korea from a country recovering from devastation to one that had weathered the 1997 financial crisis and was enjoying increasing prosperity meant that the translator focused not so much on Nagai's hope when faced with suffering but on the problem of why the bomb detonated over Christians who were the spiritual descendants of people who had endured 250 years of persecution. In other words, the problem Nagai struggled with throughout his books was not so much how to deal with the suffering one was encountering, but with the theological problem of suffering in general.[33]

Thus, after affirming belief that God's grace helped human beings deal with such difficulties, like other translators we have seen thus far, Kim confessed that she had wept, but not so much out of a sense of the impact of truth. Rather, she wept at the realities that science had led to the development of nuclear weapons of war and human hatred, the pitiful circumstances of Nagai and his young children, and the fact that even today many people lived without God. Kim then stated that she was a Protestant and that it was important for Catholics and Protestants to acknowledge and learn from the good points in their faiths, and that the most important thing was their shared love of Jesus. She ended her afterword on a hopeful note, proclaiming that just as Nagai fulfilled his own destiny and so changed the world, the readers, each unique human beings, would also be individuals who could change the world.[34] Thus, while there was a shift across time and among translators—from a focus on truth and the idea of human unity to an emphasis on the fulfillment of the human individual and a plurality that included unity within difference—the idea that Nagai, through his experience as a Japanese and Catholic, could inspire people to hope, faith, and love, illustrates that Nagai Takashi's works were attractive to Koreans living in difficult circumstances.

An additional book by Nagai, called *Nagasaki no kane* (1949, known in English as *The Bells of Nagasaki*), has been popular in the United States since it was translated into English in the 1980s, but it has received the least attention of all his books translated into Korean. This might be due in part to the book being more of a description of what actually happened in the immediate aftermath of the bombing rather than a meditation on the meaning of life and overcoming suffering. Moreover, in this book, Nagai's patriotism and wartime service are most readily apparent, which might make Korean readers uncomfortable. However, this work was eventually translated by a Presbyterian minister named Kim Chaeil, who devoted himself to rural mission work and a cooperative movement.[35] Unfortunately, this book does not include a section written by the translator, likely because it was published in 2011, the year after the translator passed away in 2010.

Kim graduated from Sogang University, a Catholic institution, and perhaps came to learn something about Nagai there. He had been very active in the democratization movement against the military dictatorship during his college days. Even after entering Presbyterian University and Theological Seminary (Changnohoe Shinhak Taehagwŏn), Kim took the lead in democratic activities on and off campus, which led to his suspension and a delay in graduation for a year.[36] He developed a vision of Christian socialism, finding words of support for revolution and resistance in the Bible, and tried to find Jesus's footprints in such figures as Spartacus, Che Guevara, and Ho Chi Minh.[37] Kim also translated two books about Kagawa Toyohiko, a Christian socialist thinker and activist who led a strike in 1921, the largest in Japan until 1945.[38] Kim was thus familiar with both the Japanese language and Japanese history and might also have come to learn about Nagai through those routes. Later, Kim confessed that his failure in the cooperative movement led him to come to his senses, realizing God's revolution was not about hatred or the material world but love and self-sacrifice.[39] In the wake of the first nuclear tests conducted by North Korea in December 2006, Chaeil raised a cry against obtaining peace through strength, including both "Pax Americana" and North Korean nuclear armament.[40] He maintained that Christian peace did not come through force of arms, but through self-sacrifice, so Christians should take up the cross for world peace as Nagai Takashi and the Urakami Christians did.[41] This revolutionary Christian, after a long, winding road, seemed to have found an answer in Nagai Takashi to the problems he thought the world faced. Probably because of the translator's position against nuclear armament, the book included quotes from two antinuclear organizations in Korea, both of which make it appear that Nagai was against all uses of nuclear energy (a position he did not hold).

The Catholic "As Yourself" Association

An attempt to formally organize and maintain interest in Nagai's work can be seen in the "As Yourself Association," which was established by the Catholic Archdiocese of Daegu. According to its website, this organization exists to "encourage lives of peace in this society, advance international peace, and inspire faith through Catholic pilgrimages of Koreans and Japanese to Nagasaki," doing so "in accordance with the spirit of the life of peace of Dr. Nagai Takashi by practicing the commandments of Jesus Christ." In addition to organizing pilgrimages to Japan, the association also hosts an annual contest for middle school and high school students based on the writings of Nagai, the approved works being *What Is Eternal, Rosary Beads*, a biography of Nagai Takashi by Kataoka Yakichi, a translation of a book by Nagai Makoto entitled *The Smiling Bells of Nagasaki* (*Nagasak'i ŭi chong ŭn miso chit nŭnda*), and *A Song of Peace Sung with Love* (*Sarang ŭro purŭnŭn p'yŏnghwa ŭi norae*), the biography compiled by former Archbishop of Taegu Yi Munhŭi, the chief moving force behind the association.[42] Yi was born in 1935, graduated from high school in 1959, and studied political science in college. He decided to become a priest and was sent to study in France. He oversaw the archdiocese of Taegu from 1986 to 2000, served as head of the Korean Catholic Bishop's Conference from 1993 to 1996, retired from active pastoral work in 2007, and passed away in 2021.

Both Nagai Makoto and Yi Munhŭi's works are freely available on the association's website as pdf files. Yi's *A Song of Peace Sung with Love* chiefly consists of a summary of Nagai Takashi's life and thought compiled by Yi interspaced with long quotes from the works of Nagai translated into Korean. Perhaps reflecting on his experience of the Korean War, Yi explains in the beginning of the book that "all people have a heart that desires peace... our nation in particular loves peace." Perhaps with a touch of nostalgia, Yi continued on to note that "people who work the fields and look at the moon do not like to see people bustling around with swords and spears, nor do they like raiding and war." Yi then lamented that "war is always with us and causes a huge amount of damage" but because "only a widow can understand a widow's situation," many people do not know what war is like and thus peace remains elusive.[43]

Yi went on to describe how he discovered Nagasaki and Nagai's "As Yourself Cottage" by accident. He then studied more about Nagai, who charmed him deep within his heart, and who had earned his awe and respect as a person who loved humanity. In fact, Nagai's earnest and sincere desire for peace, in Yi's eyes, made him akin to Jesus when he preached the Sermon on the Mount. This focus on peace was especially necessary, Yi thought, following the creation of atomic bombs in 1945 and even more frightening versions of those weapons since then. No one it seemed knew what to do, including the knowledgeable and intelligent. This led Yi to want to introduce Nagai Takashi to others. The implication is that if more people knew of the life and thought of Nagai Takashi they would know what war is and would therefore abandon it and embrace peace. Moreover, in terms of reconciliation, Yi concluded his preface by noting that as a Korean person who liked a Japanese person, more Japanese people would like Korean people and it was therefore his hope that this book would contribute to harmony and peace among humanity.[44]

In his concluding chapter, Yi sought to provide a theological understanding of Nagai's life and thought. He noted that "people are not just flesh existing in a materialistic world," but instead have souls, leading him to cite biblical references to the spirit of God and how that spirit gives eternal life.[45] After noting that Paul, Nagai Takashi's baptismal name, believed this and lived according to it, Yi emphasized that death did not mean annihilation, recalling a story of Nagai comforting a terminally ill patient by telling him they would meet in heaven. Death is therefore not something to be saddened by, but rather is the greatest gift as an invitation to heaven. Thus, the death of a person who died in the atomic bombing cannot be said to have been in vain. Yi then recalled how in the Nagasaki Atomic Bomb Museum there are televised interviews with people who had suffered from the bombing, including Koreans, illustrating why war should cease. Yi then declared that if we want war to disappear, "hearts for fighting" must disappear. Nagai revealed the path of loving the other as one loves oneself that will end in the cessation of war. Moreover, Yi stated, one can find in Nagai the strength to live in this difficult world by learning his wisdom of living in accordance with the truth.[46]

Bishop Yi included the same themes in his preface to Nagai Makoto's *The Smiling Bells of Nagasaki*. Yi explained that because he thought we should be against war, particularly nuclear war, it was important that Nagai Takashi's life and thought be known and that a book was needed that would make his life and thought approachable for Korean people, leading Yi to have Makoto's book translated and published. Moreover, Yi emphasized reconciliation between Japan and Korea, expressing his concern that it was difficult for Koreans to know Japan without prejudice, and that because of an anti-Japan bias, they frequently failed to recognize the goodness of Nagai. Even so, Yi, perhaps believing his own endorsement and that the "As Yourself" Association would help overcome these obstacles, expressed his hope that by reading Nagai, who believed in world peace and who loved humankind, Koreans would be encouraged to "walk on the path of elevating humanity."[47]

Makoto's own preface to the Korean translation of his book focused chiefly on explaining why he wrote it. After describing the damage caused by the bombing, he recalled that it was fortunate that they had been able to rebuild at all and was grateful that even though times had changed, the church bells could still be heard. Noting the sacrifice of so many Nagasaki residents, including his mother, who "ascended into heaven on an atomic cloud," the living and the dead, including his father Takashi, experienced defeat but still built a new Japan. During the early days of reconstruction, his father studied the emotions of the people, gathered scientific information, and wrote books, articles, and other essays. In 1959 Makoto was encouraged to continue his father's work by writing a book about his own experiences as a child surviving the bombing. In particular, Makoto recalled how his father had made the teaching of Christ the pillar of his life and believed, despite how his family had suffered from the bomb, that it was the will of God. Indeed, Nagai encouraged them to comfort one another. He therefore could not forget the efforts of his father to work for peace while suffering from his illness. Makoto wrote the preface to the Korean translation of his book in 1995, the fiftieth anniversary of the bombing, which led him to reflect on how those who experienced it were still dying. This meant, to him, that the work of writing about the bombing was necessary to help keep those memories alive in order to prevent war. War, unlike the devastating earthquake that struck Japan in January of the same year, could be prevented, and Makoto completed his preface by expressing his hope that there would be fewer wars in the future.[48]

In the 2010s, the "As Yourself" Association continued publishing books about Nagai. In 2014, Catholic priest Sŏ Chunhong, the president of the association at that time, wrote a book about Nagai and the Korean and Japanese efforts to honor and carry on his legacy. Astonishingly, it took less than a month for Sŏ to write a book about Nagai—Bishop Yi had asked Sŏ to write the book in late June 2014, and he completed it on July 11, 2014.[49] What made this fast turnaround possible was Sŏ's nine years of experience as a pilgrimage guide to Nagasaki and the information he had gained from it. The title of the book, *Dr. Nagai Takashi's Love, Peace, and Faith* (*Nagai Tak'asi paksa ŭi sarang kwa p'yŏnghwa, kŭrigo sinang*), manifested what priest Sŏ and the association considered most essential in Takashi's teachings. The book promoted Catholic approaches to peace as being accomplished through selfless love and condemned nuclear energy and Japan's attempt to amend the war-renouncing Article 9 of its constitution, popularly known as the Peace Clause. The book and the As Yourself Association also presented Nagai as a supporter of an antinuclear power campaign, which he never was.[50]

Another book sponsored by the Association was the translation of *The Life of Nagai Takashi* (*Nagai Takashi no shōgai*), a biography written by Nagai's friend, Kataoka Yakichi, and first published in Japan in 1952. In its original Japanese, *The Life of Nagai Takashi* was the first-person observations of Nagai by Kataoka, who specialized in the history of Japanese Christian persecution. The integration of Kataoka's personal and professional views likely appealed to one Peter Sŏ Yun'gyo, which led him to translate and publish Kataoka's book as *Nagai Tak'asi ŭi Saengae* in 2016 through Tosŏ Ch'ulp'an Apsan mit puk k'ap'e, a publisher established and run by the As Yourself Association. Sŏ is a Catholic layman and neither a professional translator nor a writer. He began to work for the Korean government after receiving a master's degree in commercial science from Tokyo International University in 1996. Bishop Yi wrote a foreword to the translation and described how Sŏ, being moved during his visit to the As Yourself Cottage in Nagasaki, began to read voraciously to learn more about Nagai Takashi and spontaneously translated the biography. Sŏ did not include a translator's preface, and only a three-line profile and some remarks by Bishop Yi are included. Perhaps Sŏ sought to imitate Nagai's humility by attempting to shift the focus from him as translator to his subject.[51]

The publication process was a good example of the cooperation that was possible between Korea and Japan based on a shared belief in the power of love that Nagai would have likely found satisfying. The Korean As Yourself Association as well as the translator had no connection with the publisher St. Paul Japan (San Paolo), which owned the copyright of the book. When the association contacted the Japanese publisher through the director of Nagai Takashi Memorial Museum to request permission to print it, they granted it quite readily, revealing a willingness for cooperation between groups in Korea and Japan.[52] The Korean translation was not commercially published and is freely available on the Association's website, showing a lack of interest in earning a profit.

The As Yourself Association has also organized other activities to spread the words and legacy of Nagai Takashi. They have held essay contests, for example, and the essays reveal the impact of Nagai, as well as the Association. The Association published a collection of essays from a contest in 2012, each of which includes reflections on Nagai by Korean students.[53] For instance, third-year middle school student Chŏng Sunghŏn's "Walking together with Nagai Takashi towards love and peace" (Nagai Tak'asi wa hamkkye kŏrŏga nŭn sarang kwa p'yŏnghwa rŭl wihayŏ) began with the author noting that he had not thought about Nagai or the existence of God seriously, but with the encouragement of his mother, read one of the assigned texts for the essay contest.[54] Chŏng recalled that he had approached the book lightly since the book itself was "light" (that is too say, it was not very long). However, upon reading Nagai's work, Chŏng's heart became heavy, as he reflected that the many innocent people who had endured the devastation brought by the bomb would have thought that God was indifferent and unfair to have let them suffer. Yet, God worked an invisible miracle through

Nagai as he was able to give people hope and help them make sense of their suffering. For instance, Chŏng recalled how Nagai had argued that the death of innocents might lead surviving sinners to repent. Moreover, the suffering Nagai endured as he sought to raise his children was like that of Jesus. Chŏng concluded that learning of Nagai's works had strengthened his faith and made him want to be an instrument of God on earth.

Second-year high school student Song Sŏhyŏn grappled with similar issues in her essay "Giving thanks amidst suffering" (Konan edo kamsahage hasosŏ). Song learned about Nagai through a homily given by a parish priest and was struck at the tragedy of how the peaceful and faithful Urakami Catholic community could be "reduced to ashes" in a single day. Song raised the question of how people in such a situation could give hope and then shifted into a retelling of the life of Nagai, focusing on his conversion to Catholicism and his own suffering caused by leukemia and the death of his wife. Song subsequently explained that what made it possible for Nagai to endure such suffering and remain thankful and hopeful was his focus on what is "eternal"—the words of Jesus. This realization gave Nagai the ability to love his enemies and to forgive people even when it was difficult to do so. Song then expressed her hope that having learned about Nagai, she could become "one of the many small seeds" that would bring peace.[55]

Third-year high school student Yi Howŏn's essay "Apostle of True Love, Dr. Nagai Tak'asi" (Ch'am sarang ŭi sado, Nagai Tak'asi paksannim kke) is similar to the preceding entries in that it focused on the suffering of Nagai and how he made sense of and reacted positively to suffering. Yi compared Nagai to Jesus, drawing a parallel between Jesus's walking the Way of the Cross and Nagai's path as a radiologist. Likewise, Yi saw Nagai's decision to move back and live in bombed-out Nagasaki, an act meant to inspire others that the city could be reclaimed, as being in line with Jesus's teaching that the death of a grain of wheat would bring forth an abundant harvest. At the same time, Yi recognized how hard it would be to rely on God amid such cruel circumstances. Yi also explained how he applied what he learned about Nagai to his own life—he had been proud of his volunteer work and role as a prayer leader, but having read Nagai, he realized he had been doing such work only to look good rather than because such acts were good in and of themselves.[56]

While such themes are similar to the first two essays examined, Yi does introduce some ideas that, though different from what we had previously seen, do resonate with the teachings of the As Yourself Association. For instance, Yi praises Nagai for the patience he showed his children and holds him up as an exemplar of paternal love. And the idea of Nagai as encouraging reconciliation between Koreans and Japanese appears as Yi conjectures that Cardinal Kim Suhwan, an important Catholic leader who struggled for human rights during the Park Chunghee dictatorship, and Father Yi T'aesŏk, a popular priest who had been a missionary to Africa, would be good friends in heaven. On a more serious note, Yi tried to understand what the cause of war was and wondered if a lack of faith in heaven and the resurrection led people to fear death and consequently seek wealth and fame, leading to conflict. That being said, Yi expressed his hope that Nagai would pray for people on earth so that his desire for peace would be accomplished. Thus, though there might be some variations, the essay contest winners clearly understood Nagai's life and thought, particularly his Catholic interpretation of suffering and the hope necessary to work to make the world a better place, and they sought to apply it to their own lives. Moreover, the emphasis on the suffering caused by the atomic bombs presented an image of Japanese people as innocent victims rather than as colonizers and the enemies of Korean nationalism. That it was the United States that actually dropped the bombs was not mentioned.[57]

Nagai Takashi's writings were the products of a unique historical context: the devastation of the main islands of Japan in the Second World War, particularly the destruction caused in Nagasaki. Moreover, Nagai's experience as a Japanese convert to Catholicism was particularly unique, leading him to produce works, which, if they had not supported the narratives of war, peace, and reconstruction advocated by the local and national governments of Japan, as well as the U.S. military government, would not have found the audience they had. Moreover, they likely would not have led to the institutional footprint present in Nagasaki today that several of the Korean authors and translators examined in this chapter encountered in person. And yet, despite the particularity of Nagai's experience and work, the Korean scholars featured in this paper found something worthwhile in the writings of a patriotic Japanese person who had served the empire that had colonized their country. And what they found worthwhile could vary dramatically—the advancement of peace, opposition to nuclear weapons, comfort for those suffering, the spreading of Christian faith in general and Catholicism in particular, or reconciliation, with a focus either on harmony between Catholic and Protestant Christians or between Korean and Japanese people. And while we cannot completely discount that the hope of winning a prize shaped the students who submitted their essays to the As Yourself Association contest, it does seem as though their conclusions were at least somewhat influenced by Nagai's life and ideas. Perhaps in the uniqueness of Nagai's thought there was so much depth that different people living in very different times could find something that helped them make sense of their own lives and led them to translate and comment upon his works.

Nagai Takashi, of course, has his critics in Korea. Much of their criticism is similar to that leveled against Nagai in other countries. In particular, one sees the critique that Nagai's approach, by focusing on universal human sinfulness and the idea of redemptive suffering, fails to adequately take into account the crimes of the Japanese empire. In a sense, then, it is a nationalist critique; that is, the focus is on the crimes committed by members of a nation-state, Japan. Reconciliation could then presumably occur when the current leaders of that nation-state accept their country's guilt and make amends to the nation-state of the Republic of Korea. In contrast, one shared characteristic that unites the Korean supporters of Nagai examined in this chapter is a focus on reconciliation as something that is deeply rooted in universal humanity and the idea that it should be affected through relationships and the sharing of Nagai's life and ideas, with prayer being an important means of achieving this goal among his more religious proponents. In that sense, these Korean supporters of Nagai are implicitly challenging the ethnonationalism that dominates discourse not only in their country but also throughout East Asia. In that sense, they are countercultural. And it is in that desire for something eternal and universally humane beyond the nation-state that has driven this group, though small, to continue in their efforts to make better known in Korea a Japanese Catholic Christian and imperial soldier who suffered such terrible losses that he spent the last few painful years of his life trying to make sense of them.

Notes

1. Chad R. Diehl, *Resurrecting Nagasaki: Reconstruction and the Formation of Atomic Narratives* (Ithaca, NY: Cornell University Press, 2018), 66.

2. See, for example, ibid., 130–140; Yuko Shibata, *Producing Hiroshima and Nagasaki: Literature, Film, and Transnational Politics* (Honolulu: University of Hawai'i Press, 2018); Kevin Doak, "Hiroshima Rages, Nagasaki Prays: Nagai Takashi's Catholic Response to the Atomic Bombing," in *When the Tsunami Came to Shore*, ed. Roy Starrs (Leiden: Brill, 2014), 249–271.

3. Takashi Nagai, *We of Nagasaki: The Story of Survivors in an Atomic Wasteland* (New York: Duell, Sloan and Pearce, 1951).

4. As of this writing, the "As Yourself Association" maintains a website that can be found at http://cafe.daum.net/2530666. A municipal museum in Nagasaki, called the Nagai Takashi Memorial Museum, also maintains a website that includes discussion of the Nyokodō: https://nagaitakashi.nagasakipeace.jp/english/stories/4.html.

5. Pak Sugyŏng, "Taejung munhwa ŭi, Chinhon ŭi wŏnp'okto Nagasak'i saengsan: Nagai Tak'asi rŭl chungsim ŭro" (The Production of Popular Culture and the Repose of Souls of Atomic Bomb City Nagasaki: Focusing on Nagai Takashi), *Ilbon munhwa yŏn'gu* 45 (2013): 133.

6. Ibid., 140–141.

7. Ibid., 137; Pak Sugyŏng, "Taejung maech'e e nat'anan rok'al imiji chŏngji: Nagai Tak'asi rŭl t'onghan Nagasak'i parabori rŭl chungsim ŭro" (The Appearance of Local Image Politics in Mass Media: Focusing on an Examination of Nagasaki through Nagai Takasi), *Ilŏ Ilbon Munhak* 57 (February 2013): 431.

8. Chŏn Ŭnok, "Nagasak'i ga sarang han namcha . . . kŭ usanghwa ŭi hamchŏng: Nagai Tak'asi Kinyŏmkwan kwa Yŏgidang" (The Man Nagasaki Loves . . . the Trap of Idolization: The Nagai Takashi Memorial Hall and the As Yourself Cottage), *Oh my News*, April 25, 2013, www.ohmynews.com/NWS_Web/View/at_pg.aspx?CNTN_CD=A0001857267.

9. Kim Hongjung, "Mirae ŭi mirae: Huk'usima wŏnjŏn sat'ae ihu sahoejŏgin kŏt" (The Future of the Future: Social Things after the Fukushima Flood), in *Pip'an sahoe hakhoe haksul taehoe charyojip*, ed. Korean Critical Sociological Association, Conference Proceeding, July 2017, 107.

10. Ibid., 107.

11. Ibid., 108.

12. Email communication with Paul Books & Media.

13. Nagai Tak'asi, *Yŏngwŏn han kŏt ŭl* (What Is Eternal), trans. Yi Sŏngwu (Seoul: Paoro Ttal, 1964), 3. It should be noted that while Nagai's family name is romanized the same in Japanese and Korean, his personal name is "Tak'asi" rather than "Takashi" in Korean romanization.

14. Ibid., 4–5.

15. Nagai Tak'asi, *Mukchu al* (Rosary Beads), trans. Yi Sŏngwu (Seoul: Paoro Ttal, 1964), 218–219.

16. Ibid.

17. In fact, Nagai expressed anticommunist thought in many of his writings. Diehl, *Resurrecting Nagasaki*, 101–102.

18. Ibid., 78.

19. Nagai Tak'asi, *Abŏji ŭi moksori* (Father's Voice), trans. Pak Ilhwa (Seoul: Chul kwa Ch'u, 1999), 5–6.

20. Nagai Tak'asi, *Sarang hanŭn nae aidŭra* (My Beloved Children), trans. Chŏng Sŏngho (Seoul: Sŏngbaoro Ch'ulp'ansa, 1999), 2.

21. Nagai Tak'asi, *Sarang hanŭn aidŭ rŭl namgyŏ tugo* (Leaving Beloved Children Behind), trans. Hong Sŏngmin (Seoul: Pet'elsŭman, 2003). The company that published this book has also been known as Puksuk'aen and Taegyo Puksŭk'aen.

22. This advertisement can be found at http://www.kyobobook.co.kr/product/detailViewKor.laf?ejkGb=KOR&mallGb=KOR&barcode=9788957590225.

23. Nagai Tak'asi, *Rosario ŭi kido* (Prayer of the Rosary), trans. Cho Yangwuk (Seoul: Petŭlpuk, 1999), 246–253. The quote cited here can be found on 246–247.

24. Ibid., 246–253.

25. Because he was largely unfamiliar with Catholicism and the Catholic Church, and Saint Paul's is romanized rather differently in Japanese and Korean, Cho does not seem to have realized that there was a Saint Paul's active in Korea and that it might have already published the book. Moreover, the Korean title of the Saint Paul's version is *Rosary Beads* rather than *Rosary Chain*.

26. Nagai Tak'asi, *Rosario ŭi kido*, 252–253.

27. Ibid., 238–245.

28. Makoto, unlike the other authors cited in this work, talks the most about his father's previous military service. Though seemingly rejecting the idea of a just war in his afterword, Makoto appears to have sought to exonerate his father from any war guilt by emphasizing how he had served in the medical corps faithfully following the principles of the International Red Cross and the Gospel by treating all who were injured.

29. Nagai Tak'asi, *Rosario ŭi kido*, 244.

30. Ibid., 8.

31. Ibid., 16. Curiously, the publisher of Cho's translation focuses on children's books. It is therefore not clear how he ended up publishing with them.

32. Pol Kŭllin (Paul Glynn), *Nagasaki ŭi norae* (The Song of Nagasaki), trans. Kim Sunghŭi (Seoul: Paoro Ttal, 2005).

33 For a study on how Korean Christians have understood suffering, see Franklin Rausch, "Suffering History: Comparative Christian Theodicy in Korea," *Acta Koreana* 19, no. 1 (June 2016): 69–97.

34. Pol Kŭllin, *Nagasaki ŭi norae*, 328–329.

35. Nagai Tak'asi, *Kŭ nal, Nagasak'i e musŭn il issŏtna* (What Happened One Day in Nagasaki), trans. Kim Chaeil (Seoul: Sŏm, 2011); For more on Kim's life, see Kim Tŏgyong, "Yŏlchŏng ŭi saram, ko Kim Chaeil" (Person of Zeal, the Late Kim Chaeil), *Nongch'on kwa mok'oe* (Village and Ministry Association) 46 (Summer 2010): 141.

36. Kim Tŏkyong, "Yŏlchŏngŭi saram, ko Kimjaeil" (A Man of Passion, The Late Kim Jaeil), *Nongch'on'gwa mok'oe* (Rural and Ministry), no. 46 (Summer 2010), 144; Hwang Kyuhak, "Kimjaeil moksanŭn chinjŏnghan ppappiyongiŏtta" (Pastor Kim Chaeil was the Real "Papillon"), July 1, 2010, http://blog.naver.com/PostView.nhn?blogId=cselee59&logNo=100108298326&parentCategoryNo=&categoryNo=6&viewDate=&isShowPopularPosts=false&from=postView.

37 Kim Tŏkyong, "Yŏlchŏngŭi saram, ko Kimjaeil," 141.

38. Kim Chaeil, "Kagawa Toyohik'o rŭl asinayo?" (Do You Know Kagawa Toyohiko?) *News & Joy*, September 23, 2008, https://www.newsnjoy.or.kr/news/articleView.html?idxno=25940

39. Kim Tŏkyong, "Yŏlchŏngŭi saram, ko Kimjaeil," 142.

40. Kim Chaeil, "Haekp'okt'an ŭi sŭlp'ŭn yŏksa wa p'yŏnghwa ŭi kil" (The Sad History of the Atomic Bomb and the Path of Peace), *News & Joy,* October 21, 2006, https://www.newsnjoy.or.kr/news/articleView.html?idxno=18910.

41. Ibid.

42. For information about Yi Munhŭi see his biography: Catholic Bishops' Conference of Korea, http://www.cbck.or.kr/Bishop/10000037. For more on "Nyokodō" (As Yourself Hermitage), please see Nagai Takashi Memorial Museum Nagasaki, "The Life and Work of Takashi Nagai," "Chapter 4: Nyokod [sic]," https://nagaitakashi.nagasakipeace.jp/english/stories/4.html.

43. Yi Munhŭi, ed., *Sarang ŭro purŭnŭn p'yŏnghwa ŭi norae* (A Song of Peace Sung with Love) (Taegu: Kat'ollik sinmunsa, 2000), preface.

44. Ibid.

45. See, for example, John 3:34 and 6:63, as well as 1 John 4:16.

46. Yi Munhŭi, *Sarang ŭro purŭnŭn p'yŏnghwa ŭi norae*, 80–84.

47. Nagai Makoto, *Nagasak'i ŭi chong ŭn miso chit nŭnda* (The Smiling Bells of Nagasaki), trans. Han'guk Yŏgi Dang (Taegu: Taegŏn Inswae Ch'ulp'ansa, 2007), 3–5.

48. Ibid., 6–10.

49. Sŏ Chunhong, *Nagai Tak'asi paksa ŭi sarang kwa p'yŏnghwa, kŭrigo sinang* (*Dr. Nagai Tak'asi's Love, Peace, and Faith*) (Taegu: Taegŏn Inswae Ch'ulpansa, 2014), 11.

50. Ibid., 127.

51. Sŏ Yun'gyo, trans., *Nagai Tak'asi ŭi Saengae* (The Life of Nagai Tak'asi) (Taegu: Apsan mit Pukk'ap'e, 2016), ii and iv.

52. Ibid., v.

53. Han'guk Yŏgihoe Unyŏng Wiwŏnhoe, ed., *Yŏgi Aeinsang Chakp'umjip (2010–2012)* (Collection of Winning Essays of the Love As Yourself Association) (Taegu: Han'guk Yŏgihoe, 2012).

54. Chŏng Sŭnghŏn, "Nagai Tak'asi wa hamkkye kŏrŏga nŭn sarang kwa p'yŏnghwa rŭl wihayŏ" (Walking Together with Nagai Takashi Toward Love and

Peace), in *Yŏgi Aeinsang Chakp'umjip*, ed. Han'guk Yŏgihoe Unyŏng Wiwŏnhoe (Taegu: Han'guk Yŏgihoe, 2012), 296–299.

55. Song Sŏhyŏn, "Konan edo kamsahage hasosŏ" (Giving Thanks Amid Suffering), in *Yŏgi Aeinsang Chakp'umjip*, ed. Han'guk Yŏgihoe Unyŏng Wiwŏnhoe (Taegu: Han'guk Yŏgihoe, 2012), 120–124.

56. Yi Howŏn's, "Ch'am sarang ŭi sado, Nagai Tak'asi paksannim kke" (Apostle of True Love, Dr. Nagai Tak'asi), in *Yŏgi Aeinsang Chakp'umjip,* ed. Han'guk Yŏgihoe Unyŏng Wiwŏnhoe (Taegu: Han'guk Yŏgihoe, 2012), 226–230.

57. Ibid.

Faith, Family, Earth, and the Atomic Bomb in the Art of Nagai Takashi
By Anthony Richard Haynes

The atomic bombing of the Urakami district of Nagasaki both influenced and found expression in the visual art and *tanka* poetry of the radiologist, Catholic convert, essayist, and atomic-bombing survivor Nagai Takashi (1908–1951). In recent years there has been renewed interest in Nagai among both Japanese and Western scholars, although this has mostly centered on his thoughts on the relationship between divine providence and the atomic bombing of Urakami first expressed in a eulogy Nagai gave for the victims of the atomic bombing in November 1945. The manner in which those ideas have been interpreted, as well as Nagai's advocacy of atomic energy, have meant that he now stands as a divisive figure among survivors (*hibakusha*), their descendants, activists, and scholars. Nagai's legacy should not be judged based on these issues alone, for it extends even beyond his scientific contributions, theological ideas, or views on atomic energy, to the arts, a fact that has hitherto been understudied.

Nagai's artistic efforts are an inseparable part of his legacy. The atomic bombing of Urakami led to a new phase in Nagai's artistic life, and it came to constitute one of four underlying themes in Nagai's visual art and *tanka* poetry, along with family, religious faith, and what Anne Primavesi calls our "earthiness." Essential in this task is tracing Nagai's interest in the arts back to his youth, providing a broad overview of the art forms he worked in throughout his life, contrasting the themes of his art before and after the atomic bombing, and presenting a sample of his works that best exhibit the aforementioned thematic changes brought about by the atomic bomb.[1] The artworks Nagai produced after the atomic bombing are indispensable for a fuller understanding of his ideas about the meaning of the bomb for Urakami Catholics, and they furthermore reveal Nagai to be a Japanese Catholic thinker who celebrates the physical senses and the natural world.

Nagai Takashi and Art

The importance of art in Nagai Takashi's life becomes evident on a visit to any one of the locations where his work is exhibited, such as the Nagasaki City Nagai Takashi Memorial Museum, Nagasaki Junshin Catholic University Museum, Unnan City Nagai Takashi Memorial Museum, or Nagasaki Atomic Bomb Museum. Nagai's calligraphic works and paintings—some of which feature *tanka* alongside the image—are displayed alongside his manuscripts, letters, and personal effects. In addition to the artworks on display are lesser-known works that are also useful for understanding Nagai's most pressing concerns and therefore deserve analysis. One indication of the greater recognition that Nagai's artworks are inseparable from his written works is the recent publication of *Heiwa no shito: Nagai Takashi no kotoba* (The Apostle of Peace: Sayings of Nagai Takashi) by the publisher San Paulo in 2020, which features Nagai's artworks along with excerpts and quotations from his written works.

Nagai was born in 1908 in Shimane Prefecture, in western Honshu. While he showed an early love for art, his father forbade him from pursuing art as anything beyond a hobby, and so Nagai followed in his father's footsteps and sought to become a doctor. Nagai received no artistic training. He recounts his childhood love of painting in his 1948 book *Kono ko o nokoshite* (translated here as *Leaving My Beloved Children Behind*):

> Kayano and Makoto both like to draw pictures. I did, too, as a youngster. But being brought up in a small village along Hino River, deep in the mountains of Izumo, there were no mentors for me to emulate, nor did I have any watercolor paints to use. I had an old ink stone and calligraphy brush, but had no ink stick, so I carefully grated charcoal in the ink stone, and used that as ink. ... For color, I used to go to a stream and pick up colored pebbles and grate them on the ink stone to make colored ink.[2]

Nagai goes on to say that despite the fact that there were skilled painters and sculptors among his ancestors, his father forbade him to pursue his interest:

> My father told me that painters tend to be drunk, lazy, and broke. He said I should never become one, and confiscated my paintbrush. ... That was just before I entered elementary school, and I gave up painting as of that day. Instead, I became a physician and eventually took over my father's practice.[3]

Nevertheless, it is clear that his father's prohibition did not stop Nagai from pursuing his interests in the arts in his free time, and this includes both painting and poetry. As a medical student in Nagasaki, Nagai was actively involved in the Araragi school of *tanka*, led by Saitō Mokichi, and the first set of *tanka* which feature in a poetry collection by Nagai, called, *Atarashiki asa* (New Morning), were written between 1926 and 1932, between the ages of eighteen and twenty-four. Nagai also continued to paint, albeit intermittently and with limited materials. Later, when serving as a medic in the Japanese army in China, he made a number of ink paintings and charcoal or pencil drawings depicting his daily experiences of war and of the Chinese people, whom he also provided medical assistance to at that time. One example, probably dating from 1939, depicts a medical examination of a Chinese man, with the doctor using a stethoscope. According to the accompanying text, the Chinese man is from a mountainous area and suffers from a withered or injured leg. The doctor—we do not know if it is Nagai himself or a colleague—gives him some medicine and food.

In 1945, Nagai lost his wife Midori in the atomic bombing and, because of prolonged radiation exposure through X-raying countless patients with inadequate protective equipment, he was diagnosed with leukemia. In the aftermath of the atomic bombing, he built a small wooden hut that he called Nyokodō, where he lived with his two children, and as his conditioned worsened, remained bedridden and unable to move unaided by others for the remainder of his relatively short life. As his leukemia progressed, he came to live, he says, entirely on his back, and he turned his mind to writing and creating a vast number of artworks, including small calligraphic works that he would send to friends and admirers of his writings.

Nagai welcomed visitors to Nyokodō from early in the morning until late at night, by which time his children would be sleeping and he would be ready to use the precious hours he had with his own thoughts for writing. Yet we also know from the abundance of material that Nagai left behind that he spent a considerable amount of time painting, working on calligraphic pieces, and writing *tanka*. There are photos of Nagai with paint pots around his bed. We can conclude from these facts that Nagai was someone who loved the arts and tried his hand at creating genuine artworks with the severe limitations (in terms of physical dexterity and time) imposed upon him. Writing in 1948, he made a remarkable statement about his then current relationship to painting, writing:

> Yet, I still have a lingering love for painting. From time to time, I wonder if it wouldn't have been better if I had taken up painting rather than medicine as my vocation.
>
> The fervor I had when I climbed down the bank of the stream ... was not to be found in my later life as a physician. Throughout my adult life up to now, I've been only a passive admirer of paintings, but recently, bedridden and bored, I have picked up my brush again and begun drawing things I see from my sickbed. Although I'm completely self-taught and have no mentor ... I have revived the love of painting I felt as a child.[4]

Nagai was not a professional artist, but we will see that this fact does not detract from the value of his artworks. At times they burst forth with an unabashed, childlike simplicity, playfulness, and humor. In other instances they encapsulate profound ideas expressed in his written works. An analysis of Nagai's artworks and the themes underlying their composition will tell us much about Nagai's personal preoccupations as a *hibakusha*, father, and widower, as well as much about his approach to Christian spirituality, including his interpretation of the atomic bombing, which has caused some controversy.

The Atomic Bombing of Urakami

The atomic bombing of Urakami forms the major theme underlying Nagai's artistic efforts and constitutes the basis of three other themes: faith, earth, and family. With regard to the first, Nagai's artworks between 1945 and 1948 center on the question of how the Catholic community of Urakami can understand the atomic bombing in terms of God's will or providence (*setsuri*) in order to cope with the loss of their loved ones and homes. With Nagai being one of many Urakami *hibakusha* and having lost his wife Midori in the bombing, the art Nagai produces in this period also centers on the pitiable lives of his surviving children Kayano and Makoto without their mother and living in the atomic wasteland of Urakami with their dying father.

The final chapter of *The Bells of Nagasaki* features an edited version of the funeral address Nagai gave for the victims of the bomb in front of the ruined Urakami Cathedral in November 1945. Nagai famously writes: "It was the providence of God that carried the bomb to that destination.... [The Urakami district of] Nagasaki, the only holy place in all Japan—was it not chosen as a victim, a pure lamb, to be slaughtered and burned on the altar of sacrifice to expiate the sins committed by humanity in the Second World War?"[5]

It is important to note at the outset that Nagai's remarks on divine providence and the atomic bombing of Urakami have been interpreted by some scholars in a literal fashion as amounting to the theory that God himself directed the atomic bomb to the Catholic Urakami district so as to propitiate the divine justice and atone for the sins committed by human beings during the war. While such an interpretation—most commonly referred to as *hansai setsu* ("the *hansai* theory")—has some textual support, it lacks due consideration of context: where Nagai would get this extremely heterodox view of divine providence and morally repugnant view of God, given his very orthodox Catholic formation, the audience of Urakami Catholics to whom he made these remarks and what Nagai was trying to tell them, as well as the other works (prose, poetic, and visual) in which Nagai addresses the atomic bombing. As I have written elsewhere, to believe that God directly willed the atomic bombing of Nagasaki would be to believe that He directly willed the slaughter of tens of thousands. As we have already seen, not only is there no biblical precedent or soteriological basis for such an action by God, as human sacrifice on a mass scale, it would also be morally reprehensible—to the extent that any subsequent faith in God's goodness seems truly baffling.[6]

Yet we know that Nagai *did* believe in God's goodness, to the extent that it served as the very foundation of his Christian worldview and makes declarations such as: "God always loves me, and constantly wishes me to be happy. Just as God gives as an act of love, God takes as an act of love. Everything that takes place around me is an expression of God's providential love."[7] This is why we must distinguish between what God *wills* and what he *permits*, and it is the latter—far more inclusive than the former—that the Urakami Catholic community had in mind when they used the word *setsuri* (divine providence).[8]

When we consider all these factors, we get a rather different picture of how Nagai understood the atomic bombing. When we consider what Nagai writes in later works and what he expresses in artworks pertaining to the atomic bombing, we also achieve a deeper understanding of Nagai's pastoral approach to the suffering caused by the bomb as a lay leader of the Urakami Catholic community. As I have written concerning Nagai's remarks in his earlier work, *Kono ko nokoshite* (*Leaving My Beloved Children Behind*, 1948):

> In writing of the destruction of two Catholic girls' middle schools and the death of the students caused by the atomic bomb, Nagai says: "This was just like in ancient days, when undefiled lambs used to be burned as a sacrifice

on altars in order to please God."⁹ Here we need to pay attention to the phrase "just like," which, in Nagai's original Japanese, is *sanagara*. The resemblance indicated by sanagara is similetic, rather than literalistic. That is, *sanagara* is used to express a poetic resemblance, rather than a visual, logical or theoretical resemblance.¹⁰

In refutation of the *hansai-setsu*, literalistic interpretation of Nagai's remarks in *The Bells of Nagasaki*, this similetic or symbolic resemblance

> precludes the possibility of theologically equating *hansai* in Nagai's work to hansai as featured in the Old Testament—the latter being required by ancient Jews for the establishment of a covenantal relationship between God and Israel, their worship of God and atonement for their sins. Nagai's placing of such practices as having occurred in "ancient days" also highlights the qualitative difference between *hansai* in the Old Testament and the sacrifice of Urakami Catholics, which for him is a kind of *hansai*, but only in a similetic way. Nagai intended to provide a familiar biblical matrix in which the death and suffering of Urakami Catholics could be understood symbolically.¹¹

This symbolic resemblance between the deaths of Urakami Catholics in the atomic bombing and the *hansai* of the Old Testament is a major feature of Nagai's literary and visual artworks in the immediate postwar period. Of particular note in this connection is a poem entitled "Shira bara" (White Roses), which Nagai wrote between 1945 and 1950.¹² In the third and fourth lines of this poem, Nagai writes:

> Singing even in the midst of the flames of the burnt sacrifice,
> may they burn like white lilies, those young girls.¹³

These lines accompany paintings of white lilies and the ruins of Urakami cathedral, as well as letters which Nagai sent to friends from as early as 1948.¹⁴ This symbolic resemblance between the deaths of Urakami Catholics and the biblical notion of *hansai* is further demonstrated in Nagai's use of white lilies in his paintings pertaining to *hansai* and in the lines quoted here. The white lily is a traditional symbol of purity that, over time, also came to be associated with the purity of the Virgin Mary and other saints among Christians. In this connection, in claiming that God took the purest of believers as a sacrifice in the atomic bombing, Nagai intended to give hope and assurance to survivors and the relatives of victims that God had not forgotten their faith, but rather magnified its ennobling and salvific functions and eternally rewarded the faithful in recompense for their sufferings. As I have written elsewhere:

> In providing a similetic rather than literalistic meaning to the sacrifice of Urakami Catholics vis-à-vis the burnt offerings at the Temple in ancient Israel, Nagai's use of the biblical term of *hansai* constituted a unique pastoral device for providing consolation to the victims and families of the victims of the atomic bombing, of which Nagai was a member and which he represented. Nagai's purpose was to remind Urakami Catholics, in a way that would resonate with them, that God had not abandoned those who had departed, would remain with those left behind, and will fulfil His promise that there will be a time for all His human creatures when He "will wipe every tear from their eyes" and "there will be no more death" (Rev 21:4).

For Nagai, it was not that God had sacrificed the community to satisfy any bloodthirsty requirements of his own justice, but rather that Urakami Catholics need not see the deaths of their relatives as meaningless. The deaths of relatives in the bombing, while not intended by God to be a literal sacrifice to or for Himself, should be regarded by survivors as the price paid for peace, and in a Christian manner, so that their relatives can live in the comfort of knowing that the deceased are with God in heaven.

Although we do not know precisely when Nagai produced them, the two paintings of his wife Midori ascending to heaven on the mushroom cloud make sense only if Nagai had been firm in this conviction. The best-known, which is reproduced here (figure 1), does not give one the impression of being produced in a state of despair, fear, or anger at God. Rather, Midori is depicted as meekly accepting what is being asked of her by God, looking up to heaven with her hands together in prayer as in so many depictions of Mary and other female saints.

Another key element of Nagai's theodicy and pastoral approach to the atomic bombing is his insistence that preventing another atomic bombing should be the vocation of survivors. Urakami, Nagai said, should be the last ever instance of an atomic bombing, and Nagasaki residents ought to fight ceaselessly for peace. In this way, the suffering of survivors living in the atomic wasteland and having to rebuild their lives also had a Christian meaning.

In this connection, Nagai referred to the task given to the Urakami Catholics after the bomb as walking the "way of expiation" and, in so doing,

Figure 1. Portrait of Nagai Takashi's wife, Midori. Courtesy of the Nagasaki City Nagai Takashi Memorial Museum.

remembering "how Jesus Christ carried His cross to the hill of Calvary."[15] Such an understanding of the meaning of the atomic bombing for Urakami Catholics belongs firmly in the traditional narrative of the community. The periods of persecution endured by Urakami Catholics were interpreted as tests of faith, or *shiren*, sent by God.[16] In this connection, in both the funeral address and in *Kono ko o nokoshite*, Nagai frames the approach Urakami Catholics ought to take to the suffering inflicted by the atomic bomb in terms of trustful surrender to God in the face of *shiren*: "A great many martyrdoms, constant persecution, and the atomic bomb. These are tests [*shiren*] which have come to reveal the glory of God . . . and for which Urakami has been chosen as holy ground."[17]

Faith

That the atomic bombing, while not planned or intended by God, should nevertheless spur Urakami Catholics on to spiritual betterment and to ensure a peaceful future for Japan and the wider world finds expression in Nagai's incorporation of the atomic cloud in the traditional devotional image of the "sacred heart of Jesus" (figure 2).[18] While Nagai for the most part emulates traditional Western images of the devotion, in the traditional image, flames rise from the top of Jesus's heart, but in Nagai's ink painting of 1948, what rises up from the heart is the mushroom cloud of the atomic bomb. The implication is that Christ is as much in the suffering caused by the atomic bomb as in any other, and that the divine love can embrace and transfigure the suffering caused by the atomic bomb. We may also note that the image is of a post-martyred Jesus (notice the wounds on his hands and the spear

Figure 2. The atomic cloud and the sacred heart of Jesus. Courtesy of the Nagasaki City Nagai Takashi Memorial Museum.

wound under his right chest). This represents the martyrdom of Jesus and his ultimate resurrection. Nagai was clear that Urakami's sacrifice was a similar kind of martyrdom from which the community was resurrecting, represents it in this devotional image.

Together, the painting of Midori ascending to heaven on the mushroom cloud and the atomic sacred heart of Jesus encapsulate Nagai's theodicy of the atomic bombing of Urakami and its pastoral function for Urakami Catholics. Perhaps there is more, however. For if, according to Nagai, Christ's redemption of the suffering the atomic bomb caused is a continual process and not a singular event, and if for Nagai, Christ works through not only Urakami Catholics but also all human beings, including scientists, it may be the case that Nagai's atomic sacred heart mirrors and symbolizes Nagai's controversial beliefs about the peaceful development of atomic energy. In this connection, it is worth quoting Nagai's remarks about "the atomic age," which follow a discussion of the atom and its uses with his son Makoto. Nagai writes:

> Will the human race be happy when it enters the atomic age? Or will it be miserable?
>
> God concealed within the universe a precious sword. First the human race caught the scene of this awful treasure. Then it began to search for it. And finally it grasped it in its hands. What kind of dance will it perform while brandishing this two-edged sword? If we use its power well, it will bring a tremendous leap forward in human civilization; if we use it badly, we will destroy the earth. Either of these alternatives can be taken quite simply. And to turn to the left or to the right is entrusted to the free will of the human family.
>
> The human race, with this discovery of atomic power, has now grasped the key to its future destiny—a key to survival or destruction.... I myself believe that the only way to the proper use of this key is authentic religion.[19]

Based on this, it is clear that Nagai regarded atomic energy as a gift from God, which, just like freedom of the will (also a gift from God), can be used for good or for evil. His enthusiastic support for the use of nuclear power for peaceful purposes has been severely criticized, despite Nagai's being a radiologist by profession and both a *hibakusha* and widower because of the atomic bomb.[20] In any case, Nagai argues that the only way to ensure that atomic power is developed for peaceful purposes is through cultivation of religious faith. It therefore seems reasonable to argue that the atomic heart of Jesus, painted in 1948, expresses this core conviction of the scientist, as part of his theodicy and vision for the "human family" in the "atomic age." Furthermore, based on the preceding quote, it could be also said that for Nagai the development of nuclear energy for peaceful purposes is one of the ways in which Japan could "resurrect" both economically and also religiously, as in the resurrected Christ with the atomic cloud rising from his sacred heart.

The atomic sacred heart marks the beginning of a succession of devotional images Nagai created until around 1950. The majority of these devotional paintings constitute the *Urakami no kodomo* (Children of Urakami) ink painting series and the mostly color "Rosary" series. Both series express the Marian spirituality that Nagai received throughout his Catholic formation, and especially from Maximilian Kolbe and the Conventual Franciscans in Nagasaki.[21] The importance not only of Mary but also of the rosary appears throughout both series, with one ink painting of Mary for the month of October (the month the Catholic Church dedicated to the rosary) exhorting the faithful to "always say the Rosary" and "do everything through the Rosary."[22]

The first artwork to be mentioned in connection to the theme of faith is a devotional work of the Children of Urakami series, which Nagai produced for the month of December. Fittingly, it is a nativity scene, and Nagai attempts to create a focal point of light in what is an extremely dark setting and ensure that the surrounding objects remain distinguishable. The halo around the infant Jesus's head illuminates both his body and the gentle face of Mary, who looks lovingly down at him. Appropriate to his role in the narrative, Joseph serves to frame and foreground Jesus and his mother. He stands slightly off to the side, hands held in prayerful adoration, his body mostly in shadow and his facial features only made slightly visible by the light emanating from the baby.

In contrast to the atomic sacred heart painting, which is one of the most Western in style Nagai produced, the style of the Children of Urakami series is distinctly East Asian in its thick outlines and the clouds on which Mary appears to enjoin the faithful to recite the rosary, in remarkably similar fashion to depictions of the Bodhisattva Avalokiteśvara (in Japanese, Kannon) standing on a lotus in the clouds. These puffy, rolling clouds, delineated by thick outlines, are often in East Asian Buddhist and Chinese Daoist iconography. They feature in the painting of Mary mentioned earlier, and especially prominently in Nagai's representation of the Marian apparitions in Fátima in 1917.[23]

Two other paintings are of particular note in connection to the East Asian influences on Nagai's artistic style and what is something of a fusion of East Asian and Western artistic styles. One is a painting belonging to the Rosary series in which Nagai depicts a lion approaching a martyr in the Colosseum: the lion is depicted in the style of a *komainu*, or guardian lion-dog, as found at the entrances to temples throughout East Asia. The other is a separate ink painting depicting Mary that Nagai produced in 1950. Here, a Mary wearing a kimono and with facial features common in Japanese artistic tradition shoots a beam of light from her hand to reveal a snake waiting in the darkness to bite an unsuspecting victim. This is significant because in most representations of Mary in Japanese churches and devotional art (including by Nagai), Mary is depicted as having Western facial features. In fact, were it not for the halo surrounding Mary's head, one may indeed mistake the woman for Kannon, though it is also possible that the ambiguity is intentional. Nagai could have modeled this particular depiction of Mary on the Maria-Kannon of the "hidden Christians" (*kakure Kirishitan*) of pre-Meiji Japan.

Earth

Given her central role in Christian salvation history, Mary is referred to in the Catholic tradition as the "Mother of God," the "Queen of Heaven," and the "New Eve." Nagai's delicate depictions of Mary capture the theological and emotional meaning of these titles. From a broader perspective, Nagai's depictions of Mary, whether as appearing on the clouds or in the stable of the nativity scene, are also some of the most theologically explicit expressions of the harmony of the celestial or heavenly and the earthly found throughout his artworks.

One less theologically explicit but more visually striking work that expresses this harmony is a separate devotional work of 1949 (figure 3). It is a depiction of the Spanish martyr Antonio González against a background of cherry blossoms. The painting is done in lush pink, purple, green, and yellow, which are allowed to burst forth by virtue of the complete lack of shadows and differences in gradient in the colors. The saint and the halo encircling the saint's head—adorned with hair in the Japanese style—are again delineated by thick, bold lines. His facial features are delineated by means of simple strokes, and the eyes are cast upward in solemn prayer. The impression the work gives is that its unfinished look is intentional, and that embodies the innocent, earthly joy of color that Nagai described earlier in *Kono ko o nokoshite*, as well as a feeling of the belongingness of the human body in the natural world which is so often absent in Western Christian art and spirituality, even as the saint's eyes look to the sky in prayer.

Faith, Family, Earth, and the Atomic Bomb | 105

Figure 3. Spanish martyr Antonio González stands against a background of cherry blossoms. Courtesy of the Nagasaki City Nagai Takashi Memorial Museum.

The beauty of the natural world is a key theme that runs throughout Nagai's artworks, and it may be understood in terms of what Nagai may have viewed as a Japanese love of nature and sense of human belonging in the natural world (as expressed in such well-known terms as *kachō fūgetsu*, or "flowers and birds, wind and moon," some of the most important traditional themes in Japanese aesthetics), or in terms of a Christian appreciation of the beauty and bounty of God's creation. Either way, this celebration of the physical and the recognition of the human body as a product and part of the natural world has often been lacking in Western Christian theology and art. It speaks to what Anne Primavesi calls our "Earthiness" and the need for Christianity to leave behind old dualisms and adopt a more positive view of the physical world not only in theory, but also in practice.[24]

One of Nagai's most well-known calligraphic works, which testifies to the depth and variety of his artistic efforts, states *Donzoko ni daichi ari* ("At the very bottom is the great earth"). The statement is intentionally vague. One of many valid interpretations can be made in light of the historical context of the atomic bombing of Urakami and the religious context of Nagai's call to cultivate self-surrender to divine providence: that it is only at the very bottom, or in grave difficulties, that we finally find the deepest value on which we can build our lives up again. For Nagai, as we have seen, it is Christ's love. Another valid interpretation is more literal in pointing to the physical earth, but still takes Nagai's own experiences into account: that when the earth is stripped bare by the ravages of war and the atomic bomb, it can and does heal itself, and, in time, regains the ability to provide us with nourishment and shelter.

A textual basis of the latter interpretation can be found in Nagai's report of the return of life in Nagasaki shortly after the bombing in *The Bells of Nagasaki*:

> Immediately after the atomic explosion the theory that life could not survive in Nagasaki for seventy-five years was widely spread about It was dangerous, people said, to return to the ruined city. Since we had lost all our measuring instructions, the only way to find a solution to this problem was to observe the plants and animals. This we did. And after three weeks in [the neighboring district of] Matsuyama[machi], the epicenter of the bomb, we found a swarm of ants—and they were vigorous and strong. After a month we found worms in large numbers. Then we found rats running around. Insects that feed on the leaf of the potato multiplied rapidly in one month. And I began to think that if small animals could survive, human life was also possible.
>
> As for plants, the wheat that had been exposed to the atomic blast quickly sprouted everywhere. (A year later this wheat ripened at the same time as wheat elsewhere and the grain was apparently normal.) The corn also began to sprout in winter, but it produced no grain. The morning glory immediately put forth vines and beautiful flowers—though the flowers were small. On the leaves, however, there were deformities. The sweet potato also immediately grew tendrils and leaves but there was almost no crop of potatoes. All types of green vegetables were good.
>
> With this evidence I denied the theory of no-life-in-the-atomic wilderness. I only added the warning that young children should not be brought here since they are particularly sensitive to radioactivity.[25]

The year 1950 marked a change in Nagai's artistic focus, which probably reflected his worsening condition and inability to work for long periods of time. From 1950 to his death in 1951, he produced a number of paintings of fruits in simple ink outline or one or two bold colors, often featuring poignant and amusing epigrams. The fruits range from pomegranates, apples, *nashi* (Japanese pears), peaches, loquats, pomelo (or shaddocks), and dried persimmons. Sometimes the fruit are painted with children, such as the fruit in the baskets of the child working in the fields in the Rosary series, or, more frequently, on their own, though accompanied by an epigram.

While we do not know their date of composition, Nagai's ink paintings of pigs and cows are done in similar fashion and with similarly amusing epigrams. Nagai's happy, cartoonlike pig is the best-known of these and features the epigram *shippo mo hitoyaku* ("Even the tail has a role"), meaning that things and people which are inconspicuous and perhaps even seem useless are often in fact necessary. The epigram accompanying an ink painting of an uncertain-looking calf with rather stumpy legs reads *hoippo* (step by step). This could be referring to the reconstruction of Japan, the psychological and spiritual healing needed by survivors of the atomic bombing and the war more widely, or the slow and halting progress humanity is making toward a civilization based on neighborly love and peace—a key theme of Nagai's books and essays.

Nagai's paintings of flowers range from cherry blossoms, the Chinese or Japanese plum, cineraria, white lilies, cosmos, and cyclamen. In contrast to the bold and amusing paintings of fruit, Nagai's paintings of flowers in the last period of his life are for the most part less impressive, indicating that by this time Nagai did not have the energy to complete them. Some exceptions, however, are two paintings of white lilies accompanied by the *hansai no uta* discussed earlier and a painting of cineraria that he sent to a friend.

Family

As mentioned at the outset of this chapter, a major theme in Nagai's artworks in the immediate aftermath of the atomic bombing was family, reflecting Nagai's attempt to come to terms with his wife Midori's death and the situation faced by his children. In this connection, Nagai writes poignantly in *Kono ko o nokoshite*: "A dying father, two young children soon to be orphans: this is how we live in Nyokodō. I have been searching for the right way to live. I have been tormented by the search, and I have prayed to God for help."[26] As one would expect, the theme of family runs throughout all of Nagai's work, and it is bound up with the devastation and loss of life caused by the atomic bombing of Urakami. Needless to say, then, that the painting of Midori ascending to heaven on the mushroom cloud could be classified under the theme of family.

Nagai's drawings and paintings of his daughter, Kayano, are also important to helping us achieve a deeper understanding of his character and artistic merits. If we include rough drafts in addition to completed works, there are at least six versions of a depiction of Kayano holding a crudely made wooden doll (*kokeshi*) in slightly different positions and from slightly different angles. The earliest draft was produced in 1945, and in this progression we witness Nagai's admirable dedication to his craft. With the exception of the unfinished background, the most technically impressive of these works in terms of anatomical detail and the dynamic presentation of color in the clothing is the following, which is accompanied by a *tanka* (figure 4).

The text of the *tanka* is worth reproducing and transliterating here. It reads:

fuyu gomori
haru sarikuraba
yakehara no

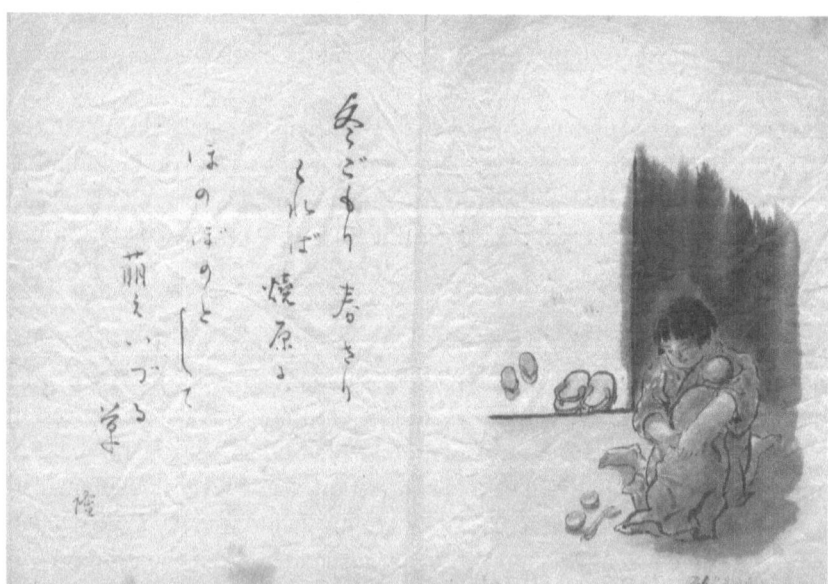

Figure 4. Portrait of Nagai Takashi's daughter, Kayano. Courtesy of the Nagasaki City Nagai Takashi Memorial Museum.

honobono toshite
moeizuru kusa

This can be roughly translated as:

Staying indoors as if hibernating in winter,
and waiting upon Spring's arrival (surely it will come?)—
even in this scorched wasteland there remains
a warm feeling one gets when thinking of
the coming flowering fields and lush grasslands.[27]

The *tanka* operates on many levels. In alluding to the regeneration of the earth and the hope this engenders in survivors of the atomic bombing, the *tanka* echoes the theme of "earthiness" as found in the *donzoko ni daichi ari* calligraphic work discussed earlier.

Given that the subject of the painting with the accompanying *tanka* is Kayano and is one of a series of such paintings of her alone with her doll, it is more likely that Nagai's main motivation in producing it was to highlight the isolation and desolation of his daughter, and at the same time point to the hope that remains for Kayano, symbolized by the cold and dark of winter and the flowering fields and lush grasslands that are sure to come.

Supporting this interpretation is the fact that the draft of the painting is based on, and what is probably the first image of Kayano holding her doll from 1945. It reads *Totan koya no naka ni hitori asobu Kayano* (Kayano playing alone in a tin-roofed hut). Constantly agonizing over the fact that Kayano (and Makoto) has not only lost her mother but has been robbed of the enjoyment of a normal childhood, as well as the fact that he himself is terminally ill, it seems that Nagai sought to portray his daughter in the most delicate, loving way possible so that she could look back on the paintings and still feel close to him in future years.

Nagai was not a professional artist, but just as he was not a theologian and still wrote works of theological importance in relation to theodicy, the artworks he produced—the vast majority after the atomic bombing of Urakami—are an integral part of his legacy, providing an alternative lens through which to analyze his ideas, values, and personal preoccupations in the months and years following the atomic bomb. As we have seen in his *tanka*, *hansai no uta*, and in his paintings of the sacred heart of Jesus and Mary ascending to heaven on the mushroom cloud, Nagai sought to provide consolation to Urakami Catholics (including himself) by reframing the deaths of their relatives in the bomb as meaningful in light of their trust in God's goodness and providential care for his children.

The destruction caused by the atomic bomb and the rapid ecological recovery he witnessed in Urakami led him to celebrate the earth's ability to constantly revitalize itself and sustain human life not only in prose but also in his many paintings of animals, flowers, and fruits. Nagai expresses the unity and complementarity of the physical and the spiritual in his depictions of Mary and the Spanish martyr Antonio González. Indeed, Nagai seems to express his conviction that it is the physical world in which Christians must engage in their spiritual mission, including their prevention of another nuclear bombing and the development of nuclear energy for peaceful purposes.

Finally, Nagai's tender depictions of his daughter Kayano shows his belief in the power of art to capture and preserve emotions for future recollection and consolation. In his many drafts of the Kayano holding her *kokeshi*, one sees what can and should be described as *faith* in the ability of the artifacts made by a dying father to guide and protect his beloved children in the years following his passing.

Notes

1. I would like to express my gratitude to Nagai Tokusaburō for kindly providing high-resolution images of Nagai's artworks and permitting me to reproduce a selection of them here. I would also like to thank Sada Yuka for her assistance in deciphering some difficult passages in Nagai's works and in translating the *tanka* discussed in this chapter.
2. Nagai Takashi, *Leaving My Beloved Children Behind*, trans. M. Tatsuoka and T. Takai (Strathfield, NSW: St. Pauls Publications Australia, 2008), 117.
3. Ibid.
4. Nagai, *Leaving My Beloved Children Behind*, 117–118.
5. Nagai Takashi, *The Bells of Nagasaki*, trans. William Johnston (Tokyo: Kodansha International, 1984), 107.
6. Anthony Haynes, "Nagai Takashi on Divine Providence and Christian Self-Surrender: Towards a New Understanding of *Hansai*," in *Handbook of Japanese Christian Writers*, ed. Yamane Michihiro, Mark Williams, and Van C. Gessel (Tokyo: MHM Ltd. 2022), 127.
7. Nagai, *Leaving My Beloved Children Behind*, 25.
8. See Gwyn McClelland, "Re-Interpreting *hansai*: Burnt Offerings as the Nagasaki Atomic Bomb," in *Colonial Transformation and Asian Religions in Modern History*, ed. David W. Kim (Newcastle upon Tyne: Cambridge Scholars

Publishing, 2018), 247, and Haynes, "Nagai Takashi on Divine Providence and Christian Self-Surrender," 132.

9. Nagai, *Leaving My Beloved Children Behind*, 26.

10. Haynes, "Nagai Takashi on Divine Providence and Christian Self-Surrender," 133.

11. Ibid.

12. Nagai Takashi, *Atarashiki asa* (New Morning) (Nagasaki: Seibo no kishi sha, 1999), 153–154.

13. My translation. Haynes, "Nagai Takashi on Divine Providence and Christian Self-Surrender," 133.

14. *"Heiwa o"—Nagai Takashi: Nagasaki Junshin Daigaku hakubutsukan shozo Nagai Takashi kanren shashinshū* ("Grant Us Peace"—Nagai Takashi: Album of Photographs Related to Nagai Takashi from the Collection of the Nagasaki Junshin Catholic University Museum) (Nagasaki Junshin Daigaku hakubutsukan, 2005), 16, 82.

15. Nagai, *The Bells of Nagasaki*, 109.

16. McClelland, "Re-Interpreting *hansai*," 250–251.

17. Nagai Takashi, *Rozario no kusari* (Rosary Chain, originally 1948) (Tokyo: Nihon bukkuēsu, 2014), 73.

18. "Iezusu no seishin" (Sacred Heart of Jesus), *Katorikkukyō hō*, July 15, 1948, 6.

19. Nagai, *The Bells of Nagasaki*, 116.

20. For example, see Konishi Tetsurō, "Kaku no 'heiwa riyō' to Nagai Takashi" (Nagai Takashi and the "Peaceful Uses" of Nuclear Energy), *Nagasaki gaidai ronsō* 15 (2011): 29–44.

21. See Haynes, "Nagai Takashi on Divine Providence and Christian Self-Surrender,"125, and Nagai, *Leaving My Beloved Children Behind*, 42.

22. *"Heiwa wo"—Nagai Takashi*, 26, 81.

23. Ibid, 38.

24. Anne Primavesi, *Exploring Earthiness: The Reality and Perception of Being Human Today* (Cambridge: Lutterworth Press, 2014), 5.

25. Nagai, *The Bells of Nagasaki*, 111–112.

26. Nagai, *Leaving My Beloved Children Behind*, 176.

27. My translation.

"Love Saves from Isolation"
Ozaki Tōmei and His Journey from Nagasaki to Auschwitz and Back

By Gwyn McClelland

The postatomic Catholic suburb of Urakami, at the hypocenter of the Nagasaki atomic bombing, is frequently epitomized by the work of Nagai Takashi, author and doctor, whose contributions are also highlighted in this collection. Beyond Nagai, though, there are other significant stories and biographies that are continuing to come to light today. Another Catholic contemplative, Ozaki Tōmei, was drawn in the years after the atomic bombing to journey on a pilgrimage to Auschwitz. Ozaki was attracted to the story of the Polish founder, Maximillian Kolbe (1894–1941), of the Seibo no Kishi orphanage in Nagasaki. Here Ozaki had himself found a footing once again after he lost his mother in the atomic bombing at the age of seventeen. Ozaki traveled to Poland a number of times, meeting the man saved by Maximilian Kolbe. Originally Tagawa Kōichi, Ozaki Tōmei took on his new name when he became a Franciscan monk in postatomic Nagasaki. He took on the name of one of the twenty-six martyrs executed by Hideyoshi in 1597. By raising the story of Kolbe in Auschwitz, and re-remembering Ozaki's mother, Ozaki reflected richly upon his own experience, journeying from Nagasaki to Auschwitz and back to his roots in Nagasaki. Drawn to the stories of his ancestors, he reflected deeply on the loss of his mother, an Urakami Catholic, and his father's birth into a Hidden Christian family of Sotome. Ozaki Tōmei proved himself a prolific writer, and in his eighties and nineties he kept an online blog. This chapter reflects on his work as a *kataribe* (a storyteller of the bombing) and on his motto that Life Is Isolation and Encounter (*kodoku to deai*). Ozaki published his autobiography, and his story was told in a manga and an NHK documentary. His journey to Auschwitz and back fed into his own search for identity and his civil and communitarian work in postatomic Nagasaki.

Encountering Ozaki Tōmei

On August 9, 2021, Nagasaki mayor Taue Tomihisa began the annual Nagasaki 2021 Peace Declaration by referring to the life of Ozaki Tōmei (1928–2021):

> This year saw the passing of a Catholic monk. Tōmei Ozaki spent his whole life following in the footsteps of Father Maximilian Kolbe, the man who was called the "Saint of Auschwitz." Brother Ozaki spoke out about his experiences in the atomic bombing up until just before his life came to a close at the age of 93. In his diary he left behind these words: "The countries of the world, all of them, must completely abolish nuclear weapons or there will be no peace on earth. . . . I keep screaming for the abolition of nuclear weapons."[1]

Ozaki, the subject of the mayor's talk, was not a one-dimensional nuclear abolitionist. His life was shaped by multiple forces. These included the demolishing of this city, and his home, 1,640 feet (500 m) from the center of ground zero, the loss of his mother and his consequent orphanhood, and his subsequent rediscovery through a Polish monastery of a religious tradition that had led to his ancestors' traumas. For Ozaki, postatomic Nagasaki and his life were haunted by what is no longer, a pulverized and unrecoverable past. This contributed to a lingering discomfort—which might be termed Catholic guilt, survivor guilt, or a sin-consciousness—he felt about himself and his own motives and desires throughout his life, and even just prior to his death.

Ozaki Tōmei was the final *hibakusha* I met in the course of conducting my oral history project in Nagasaki investigating interpretations of the atomic bombing by the Catholic community. In 2016 I was given an introduction to Ozaki by an author and researcher, and when I phoned him, Ozaki agreed to meet at his hairdresser's studio in the northern suburb of Isahaya. Conducting an interview in a rural hair studio was an unexpected element of my work as an oral historian.

Anamnesis and Embodiment

The philosopher Jean-Francois Lyotard, speaking at the opening of an art exhibition in Jerusalem in 1995, reflected on the Shoah and the platonic concept of anamnesis, saying, "Anamnesis and history keep present what is forgotten. The latter does this by trying to be faithful to the past. . . . Anamnesis is guided by the unknown—because it is engagement with unpredictability and invisibility that allows the event to happen."[2] Lyotard continued,

"The work of anamnesis and its pain, belongs to a talmudic and not a historic order." Theologian Binsar Pakpahan, discussing the process of healing from violent or difficult experiences of the past, describes anamnesis as distinct from simple remembrance, or memorial or commemoration, stating that "the person or event commemorated is actually made present, is brought into the realm of here and now."³ For Pakhapan and for Johann Baptist Metz, anamnesis refers to the sharing of memories with the community. When one shares with their community a personal memory of past hurt, for Pakhapan it is transformed into a liberating experience, and for Metz it enables solidarity.⁴

Others in varied fields raise the concept of anamnesis. Nicole Simek, for example, reflects upon Pierre Bourdieu's sociology of anamnesis as a recalling of the repressed, which, she posits, centralizes embodiment.⁵ Simek writes that "anamnesis represents the process of recovering that forgotten history, of remembering that what is now taken for granted was not always, and need not remain, self-evident."⁶ Rita Nakashima-Brock, a U.S.-based feminist theologian, writes that it is "how we know our lives through acts of recall of our own and others' experiences—the Greek meaning of anamnesis includes recollections of lives that preceded us." She adds that anamnesis captures how we process stories about the past to sustain love and wisdom in the struggle for justice and to enable human flourishing.⁷

Thus, an essential part of coming to terms with the postatomic in Nagasaki is achieved by a communal attention to anamnesis, opening up the forgotten for examination. Ozaki Tōmei journeyed his own postatomic journey by a gradual growth in his own attention to anamnesis, by his enlivening of the forgotten in his own writings and historical research and in his personal encounters with others. He focused in particular on two historic characters, one familial and vanquished by the atomic bomb and the other executed by the Nazis of Auschwitz. The first figure was his mother, and the second is one he knew only through the stories of others, the Polish priest Maximilian Kolbe. Ozaki made his own journeys to Poland, and then developed a community museum in Nagasaki named the Kolbe Museum on his return.

Nagasaki's response to the bombing was popularly called "prayer" (*inori*), as opposed to Hiroshima's perceived "wrath" (*ikari*). Nagai's contributions were considerable, and the Catholic community—albeit a minority, and not the only group impacted extensively by the bombing—is often denoted as a reason for Nagasaki's apparent silence or muted protest in the face of the bomb.⁸ However, the focus on Nagai's representing the Catholic community potentially neglects the contribution of many others, including

Akizuki Tatsuichirō, Kataoka Chizuko, and Ozaki Tōmei. Ozaki forms a part of the consequent generation—post-Nagai if you like—although he remembers Nagai fondly as his own teacher in the aftermath of the bombing, when Nagai was himself accommodated at the Seibo no Kishi (Knights of the Holy Mother) seminary.

Selecting a biographical or life-writing style to "write the postatomic" is only one way in many of representing the myriad experiences of the *hibakusha*. Oral histories, or testimonies of *hibakusha* ever since the bombings of Hiroshima and Nagasaki, have offered important alternatives to allowing the symbolic mushroom clouds to effectively drown out the humanity hidden underneath (Consider the power of the stories published by John Hersey in the *New Yorker* and later published as *Hiroshima*.)[9] One story of a *kataribe* will never represent the whole, and yet understanding Ozaki's story allows us to imagine others who suffered similarly, opening up new worlds. As an oral historian, I have an inevitable influence upon the final written words, the interviewer's presence in the room, especially in this chapter in the form of reflective obituary.[10] Yet as an author I avoid both the stance of a therapist and the danger of hagiographic writing: the subject is not sacred nor infallible.

A cultural hybridity is evident in Ozaki's consideration of self, morality, and identity. As for the *hibakusha*'s treatment of self, Ozaki is sharp in self-examination and assigns to his memory self-problematic motives, avoiding self-aggrandizement. The *Asahi* biographer, Enomoto, begins his obituary with the word for sin or crime in Japanese, *tsumi*, which indicates most often a moral or religious infringement or a divine punishment. "Weighed down by a burden of consciousness of 'sin' and digging into the Catholic history of Nagasaki as a monk, his was a life of encounter with pain." Here, the writer overlaps "sin-consciousness" (*"tsumi" no ishiki*) with pain. There is no doubt that throughout his life Ozaki suffered illness, bookended by his childhood sickness of tuberculosis (before the bombing) and his terminal encounter in 2020–2021 with cancer. On the day he died Ozaki wrote on his blog of his persistent pain: "I can't eat. I sleep day and night. My strength slips away, my stomach hurts. By medicine, at last the pain eases. Please pray for me." Reading this obituary, the audience may well think of various types of guilt, including Catholic guilt and "survivor guilt."[11] Nevertheless, Catholic writer Endō Shūsaku comes to mind, an author who perceived a lack of "sin-consciousness" in Japanese culture, while he also examined evil intent in his writing and the weakness of human beings. In Ozaki's writing, it is difficult to pinpoint a sin-consciousness, although there is no doubt he considers carefully his conscience.[12] Sin-consciousness may be attributable to Catholic guilt and religious piety, or alternatively as what oral historians would call "discomposure," the inability of most people after a traumatic event to hold together a personal narrative or an event that defies interpretation.[13]

When Ozaki neared his own death, he was squeamish and troubled. Ozaki himself was aware all his life of the interruption and irruption of the memory of August 9. His words in his obituary are quoted by Yokoyama Michiko: "Until the last, the 9th of August made me come face to face with my 'weakness.'"[14] On the day he died, April 15, 2021, as was his custom, he wrote a daily blog post. Among his last requests, he asked that a photograph of his body after death be uploaded on the blog.[15] Here, for all to see is (at the time of writing) his embodiment. He lies in the photograph, clasping rosary beads, which represent as well as his prayerfulness and connection to his mother's missing body. The deaths of *hibakusha* including Ozaki so long after the bombings of Hiroshima and Nagasaki inevitably recall "that day" once again.

Ozaki was still tremulous in his later life in facing up to his own death, given his experience as a seventeen-year-old following the atomic bombing. He perceived guilt in his youth experience—perhaps what Enomoto wrote of as sin-consciousness—in his lack of courage; he had an urge to flee, viewing death on all sides, literally piles of human bodies. He ran away when an airplane flew over, betraying an injured young woman, and his sense of guilt about this, stayed with him to the day he died. He spoke publicly via Zoom about this experience in his last public speaking engagement.

The rosary beads he holds on to in his own death are also a significant prop. A Japanese manga-ka (cartoon-author), Shioura Shintarō, produced his manga entitled *Yaketa rozario* (The Burnt Rosary Beads), based on his own interviews with Ozaki in 2009. The story of Ozaki's Hidden Christian ancestry and evidence of redemptive tropes in public narratives are rich in this biographical manga. The illustrator is faithful to the narrative, emphasizing through the visual medium the landmarks, sacred places, and geography that recall the suffering, martyrdom, and death in Nagasaki.[16] Shioura, the author, wrote to me in an email: "I did not want this to be an ordinary religious manga, but rather a story that describes the heart of an ordinary human being." *The Burnt Rosary Beads* adds a unique perspective as an atomic narrative manga, due to the Nagasaki setting and the central protagonist's Catholic faith.[17] For the Catholic community, postatomic Nagasaki and the aftermath of the atomic bombing recall older scenes of devastation, loss, and persecution: traumas of old.

"Love Saves from Isolation" | 117

In the posthumous photograph of Ozaki on his blog, where he clasps in his hands the rosary beads, material memory links him in death to his vanished mother. In an early climax in the manga, Shioura drew the youth Ozaki as he arrives at his burning home, where all that remains for him to claim are burned rosary beads. These beads were reportedly "always on his mother's body" (In the manga: *okaasan ga itsumo hadami hanasazu motte ita rozario*). In 2021, the rosary beads are revisited, grasped by the embodied Ozaki (figure 1).

Figure 1. Page 75 of Shiorua Shintarō, Yaketa rozario: Genbaku o ikinuita shōnen no kiseki na unmei to arata na kokoro no sekai (Nagasaki: Seibo no kishi-sha, 2009).

In my own meetings with him, Ozaki's vivacity and self-deprecating manner conveyed a robust sense of humor. In 2019, prior to the COVID-19 pandemic, I visited Ozaki for the last time at the Franciscan retirement home in Isahaya, with my monograph in hand. My visit on this occasion was simply a courtesy visit, but Ozaki gave me some cards and wrote a quotation for me in calligraphy incorporating three semantic renderings of "life" in the Japanese language. The full writing reads as follows, with the proviso that my Japanese colleagues found it difficult to translate *inochi*. One colleague suggested "Eternal Life," another "Soul." We should note the varied nuances in the word in Japanese of life-force, fate, karma, or destiny.

Living is (*ikiru*)
Solitude and Encounter
Love and Soul (or life) (*inochi*)
Are [human] life. (*jinsei*)

Ozaki signed his personalized calligraphy "Ozaki Tōmei, Nagasaki monk, 91 years old." His obituary in *Asahi* ended with the first words from the motto, "*Ikiru to wa kodoku to deai*": to live is isolation and encounter.[18] These words bring these opposites together. Surely the isolation Ozaki refers to is an attempt to understand the unfathomable loss of his family and community at the age of seventeen.

For Catholic Nagasaki, the obliteration experienced around ground zero incorporated people, buildings, and places, and Ozaki attempted to come to terms with his own resulting isolation. Ozaki, like many *hibakusha* and *kataribe*, remembered what he had lost. He worked out of his own interiority toward an outward anamnesis by an insistence on remembering of those otherwise forgotten.

A Final Lecture

As he entered his final months, Ozaki's distress and emotional trauma was still, or more so, fully evident. His last semi-public lecture as *kataribe* after being diagnosed with pancreatic cancer was held on February 25, 2021, at a Nagasaki Peace Wing Organization (Heiwa Suishin Kyōkai) staff meeting via video link during the pandemic, as reported in the Nagasaki newspaper a couple of days later.[19] On this occasion, Ozaki said, "I think this will be my last day as a *kataribe*. I will speak of my 'mentality' (*shinjō*) for the last time." He explained he wished to talk about something he had not told about or touched upon once since the time: his disturbed mindset. It was to do with an incident that happened before the bombing, when a *senpai* (superior) hit him. He saw the same man, badly injured, in the aftermath, and he remembered a "good feeling" (*ii kimi da*). Ozaki described the feeling as a "superiority complex" (*yūetsukan*) or an elite (*erīto*) consciousness that came to him. As he wept at the lecture in 2021, he said, "This was despite seeing all these people dying. Please study the hearts of *hibakusha*," he implored psychologists, "or war will occur again." The final thoughts Ozaki presented expressed his interiority, guilt, emotion, discomposure, and disrupted psychological state.

Ultimately in life, Ozaki would not transcend the traumatic experience of the bombing—the event reared up again and again, and his memory troubled him to his final days, as shown by his tears. Penny Summerfield writes about such a phenomenon as if sick with grief. In the case of Holocaust survivors, retelling was consistently a painful process, like vomiting, a feeling that makes you feel "humiliated and debased."[20] She writes about the vomiting of narratives because of composure and discomposure, terms that oral historian Graham Dawson used to disclose how people aim for "subjective composure" in our telling of narratives about ourselves.[21] Ozaki's final speaking about his experiences "vomited forth" his utter discomposure, tears streaming down his cheeks. Upon examining Ozaki's experiences through his autobiography and manga, despite his certainty he had not mentioned it, this particular incident is recurrent; replayed time and again, reasserting itself as a recurrent event plaguing the trauma sufferer.[22] In a newspaper article from 2007 or 2008 in the *Nagasaki Shinbun*, the event is discussed, and in 2021 his final discussion of the event reiterated his perception of his own psychological experience at the time.[23] Penny Summerfield writes of the trauma sufferer, "The process of interpretation and reinterpretation never stops. It cannot stop, because the social world is always in flux and we are constantly seeking ways of understanding both it and ourselves within it."[24] Ozaki's reprising of his guilt and pain due to his discomposure erupted forth once again.

Tagawa "Clara" Wasa, Ozaki's mother, was a descendant of the Urakami Hidden Christians, traced back to the early Portuguese mission to Japan. I began to realize the impact of the loss of his mother early in my first interview with Ozaki in 2016. I sat behind Ozaki looking into the mirror to see him as the hairdresser worked. He explained how he had left home on the morning of the bombing and said, "See ya, mum!" At the center of his anamnesis was the vanishing of his mother, with him until she was literally and physically lost. The impact was even more clear in an interview recorded by NHK in 2009. Ozaki related how when he realized his mother was gone at the age of seventeen he felt as though the whole world was at an end. On the day the bomb was deployed, he related that as he left home for work in the Mitsubishi tunnel factory, he prayed with his own rosary beads, the symbol of his mother. In 2016 he explained to me that on the day his mother died, when he left the house he never heard her say goodbye, he faced up to her death and obliteration, noting what had been lost.[25] All his life, Ozaki had no choice but to remember his mother by anamnesis and by the few photographs that remained, in one of which he stood alongside her, a young boy. Ozaki then lived for seventeen days after the bombing in the open, searching for his mother, and crying as he observed the long and excruciating burning of the remains of the Urakami Cathedral and houses outside.

Ozaki's blog assisted him in writing through the difficult days, including the anniversary date of August 9 in multiple years. It was late in his life, at the age of eighty-one, adding to his *kataribe* activities, that he had begun writing his internet blog, entitled, "I want to tell of my life." A tribute to his mother from August 9, 2012, the sixty-seventh anniversary of the atomic bombing, is based on his last memory of his mother, a rendering of his memory of her physical presence.

Ozaki wrote in short sentences: "My sadness is the morning farewell on the day of the atomic bomb. Together we wake, together we breakfast. 'I'll be back soon!' Mum does not reply. A sad bidding bye. That was her last silhouette. Clara Tagawa Wasa, 1945, 67 years ago. I'm now an old man of 84."[26] Trauma theorists explain trauma as an unconcluded event, unintegrated in time, and so his recalling of the parting with his mother represents the rupturing of time. The disappearance of his mother gives the parting from her a special significance. In the same blog entry, he reflected further about his ongoing connection to his mother: "What do I feel when I think of my mum? I'll write it down. *From my mother to me, there was no space between us*—I was a monk with no wife, no children, no descendants, and no relative to occupy this space: [and so] I am directly connected to my mother. I cannot forget her (my heart to think of her is strong). Before the bombing happened, my mother led me to Maria of Lourdes [at the monastery in Nagasaki]. And she must have had a heart which said, 'I leave him to you Mary.' So, that was how it was."[27] No matter who he met, Ozaki's deepest attachment was, he wrote, to his mother—his only relation. He said: "I am directly connected to my mother."[28] So, although his mother disappeared, he sought to bring her love alive to him throughout his life.

Isolation

The beginning of Ozaki's autobiography, *Jū nana sai no natsu* (The Seventeen-Year-Old's Summer, 1996), offers a deeper view of his understanding of "life as isolation." He wrote:

On the day of Nagasaki's atomic bombing,
on a hill in the ruins,
a seventeen-year-old—myself—strangely still alive,
I thought I heard the voice of God within the reality that was destroying this world.

Ozaki then relates God's words as he imagined them: "What is important in this world? Take the rest of your life and come to terms with it." His loss of his mother, the only remaining member of his family, added to the searing impact of the atomic bombing on his life view: "Life is ultimately *kodoku* (solitude)." He continued by describing his motto: it is love that saves us from isolation. Or the Japanese reads in reverse: From isolation we are saved by love (*Kodoku o suku'u no wa ai*).

Ozaki explained how war had broken out at the time when he had made the decision to go to a seminary, presumably at the age of twelve or thirteen. But in order to help out his mother, he was forced in the interim to stay at home to go to work in an aluminum factory. By the age of seventeen he was working as a juvenile at the Mitsubishi ordnance factory in a tunnel known as Akasakō, to the north of Urakami. It was August 1945.

Speaking of his experience following the bombing in his interview in 2016, Ozaki related:

When the bomb was dropped, I was in a tunnel. . . . We were no longer able to stay in there as a navy officer told all the healthy people to leave, so for the first time we left the tunnel and saw that the surroundings had changed. The houses were burning; automobiles had rolled over and drivers had lost their clothes. That was what we confronted [as we emerged]. Then, I turned towards home, worrying about what had happened to my mother and house . . . and I began to walk in that direction.[29]

Emerging from the tunnel, Ozaki had to make sense of a new world. Further visual sources on Ozaki's blog assist in understanding how he makes sense of his memory and story. His detailed sketch map (figure 2) illustrates his journey from the tunnel in the north toward Nagasaki, crossing the railway line and Urakami River, initially 1.4 miles (2.3 km) from the hypocenter and ending 1,640 feet (500 m) away at his ruined house. The sketch map incorporates the concentric circles of the wider public narrative, indicating the hypocenter he was headed toward. Gray marks (red in the original) highlight the significant landmarks, including ground zero, the tunnel, the community's cathedral, and his home. Protected as he was in a tunnel factory

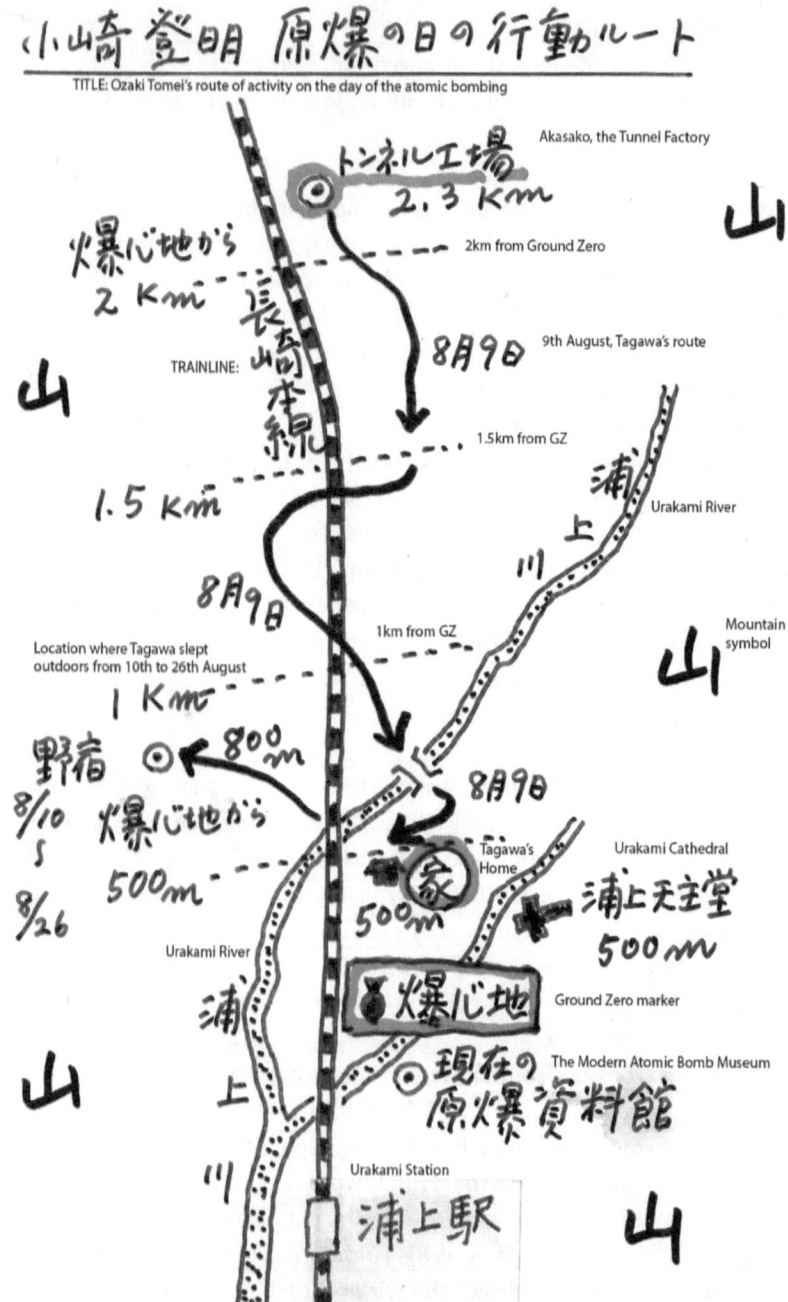

Figure 2. "Ozaki Tōmei's route of activity on the day of the atomic bombing," hand-drawn map. Courtesy of Ozaki Tōmei.

producing torpedoes for Mitsubishi, Ozaki emerged into a world changed forever. Before discussing that new world, however, let us move back in time to Ozaki's early life, up to the age of seventeen.

Reviewing Ozaki's life

First named Tagawa Kōichi, Ozaki was born in occupied Korea, today North Korea, in 1928. His father carried on a trade as a butcher but died when he was only seven years old.[30] Sometime after that, he contracted tuberculosis, and his mother brought him for medical care back to her hometown, Urakami in Nagasaki. This period is colorfully depicted in Shioura's manga. Having returned to Nagasaki, Clara Wasa Tagawa prayed for his restoration from convalescence due to tuberculosis at the sacred places of the Hidden Christians of Sotome, which is where his father had originated. In the manga, her pilgrimage into the countryside to pray for his health is accompanied by a map of the Nagasaki region, allowing readers to understand the memories of Christianity found within the physical landscape. She traverses Mount Iwaya to Kashiyama Akadake in the manga, where she prays facing Kurosaki. Her selection of this location is because Mount Akadake is remembered as *Bastian no kamiyama* (The sacred mountain of Bastian), where seven Christian martyrs reportedly died.[31] Local traditions suggest that a mythical figure, Bastian, was born at Fukabori south of Nagasaki and became the gatekeeper to the local Buddhist temple.[32] He converted to Christianity and ministered to the community at Fukabori with another Christian named Juan during the early 1650s. As a seventeenth-century prophet of the "hidden Christians," Bastian purportedly predicted the priests' eventual return to Japan. "Senpuku," secret Christians, and the Catholic community later believed that a spring in the hills of Sotome where Bastian had drunk, called *maruba no ido*, had healing properties, and many pilgrims traveled there to collect water for healing. Ozaki's mother also prayed for him in Nagasaki at the Polish monastery, Seibo no Kishi, where another spring known as Lourdes, a reference to the sacred spring in Europe, was located. This was the monastery to which Ozaki would return after the bombing. The manga implies that he was healed due to his mother's prayers and pilgrimage.

A path to the postatomic future for Ozaki and others in the Catholic community was in anamnesis of not only the bombing but also of their ancestors who had gone through multiple traumas. (The path to the future winds back in time.) After the war, sometime after wondering the streets, Ozaki approached the Seibo no Kishi (Knights of the Holy Mother) Monastery, which was not destroyed in the bombing, and he became a brother, taking on the name of a martyr of 1597.[33] Even for the Christian community in Urakami, Ozaki's was an abnormal new name. Normally Japanese monks would adopt the name of a Western saint such as Nagai "Paul" Takashi, but Ozaki the young orphaned *hibakusha* took the unexpected path of selecting a Japanese saint. He associated himself with the saints who had come before in sixteenth- and seventeenth-century Nagasaki. The 1597 executions in Nishizaka, which Ozaki commemorated with his new name, were the beginning of many martyrdoms in the Christian (and Hidden Christian) narrative of Japan, including the "1622 Great Martyrdom" and executions in 1635 in Neshiko and Orokunin-sama.[34]

It was here in his early days at the Monastery that young Ozaki learnt about a Polish missionary to Nagasaki, Maximilian Kolbe (1894–1941). Kolbe, ordained in 1918 as a Conventual Franciscan, was a writer and editor-in-chief of a Catholic daily in Poland, that, it should be noted, published anti-Semitic articles. After establishing a monastery west of Warsaw, Kolbe traveled to Japan in 1930 as a missionary, founding a monastery and publishing house, before returning to Poland in 1936. Kolbe was famously executed by lethal injection by the Nazis in Auschwitz.[35] After twenty-six years Kolbe was beatified by Paul VI in 1971 and later canonized by Pope John Paul II in 1982.[36] Kolbe's perceived courage meant he became a figure whom Ozaki would measure his own life and experience by, and his photograph is front and center on the cover of Ozaki's autobiography. Many years later, when he had begun to talk about his own experiences in the bombing, Ozaki showed an acute awareness of a major difference he perceived between himself and Maximilian Kolbe as he understood his story. In a Polish documentary he states his experience of not being able to stay to help those he knew were in pain or in need after the atomic blast, "If it were Father Kolbe, I don't think he would have fled, but would have wanted to help." He went on, "After the atomic bomb experience, I was the complete opposite of Father Kolbe. I ran away and helped no one." Thus, Ozaki wished to emulate Kolbe's story. From his thirties (the late 1950s), writes Enomoto in the obituary in the *Asahi* newspaper, Ozaki researched and wrote about Kolbe in magazines and literature. He visited Poland three times between 1983 and 1994, and there he was able to meet the man, Franciszek Gajowniczek (1901–1995), who had been saved when Kolbe volunteered to take his place in the death camp.[37] Consequently, Ozaki would write two books about Kolbe in Japanese, one of which has been translated into English.[38] The story of Kolbe had a major impact on how he understood himself and his own identity.

Some time on, in the 1980s, from the latter half of his sixties, Ozaki became more and more interested in telling his own story, likely with the additional influence of Pope John Paul II's instruction to the *hibakusha* to talk about their experiences when he visited Japan in 1981. (Ozaki discussed this with me in 2016.)[39] Interpreting and reinterpreting of the story of the atomic bombing of Nagasaki, once begun, never stops for the narrators, the *kataribe*. A *Nagasaki Shinbun* newspaper article notes that from the year 1994 to 2007 Ozaki was attached to the Transmission (Keishō) division of the Peace Wing and spoke during that time to school groups about his experiences of the atomic bombing.[40]

While the sin-consciousness of Ozaki's encounter with the people in the aftermath of the bombing is an aspect of his memory that troubled him until the end, his anamnestic remembering, first of Kolbe and later of his mother, appears to have offered a bridge from his overwhelming emotion of isolation to a new sense of encounter. Rita Nakashima-Brock, a scholar who deals with moral injury, writes that parents in particular are woven into the story of the lives of the next generation as anamnesis in "perspectival and expansive memory."[41] While his memory of his parting from his mother represented for Ozaki a "rupture" in time, and as a result, isolation, his anamnesis of Kolbe and his mother gave him at least some solace.

Ozaki's journey took him from Nagasaki to Auschwitz and back, and his embodying of his mother's love was a key to his coming to terms with the continuing irruption of the events of August 9, 1945, in his life. In contrast to the *Asahi* obituary, while Ozaki did grapple with discomposure in his narrative up to his last days, his interpretation of the atomic bombing does not in fact begin with his sin-consciousness or with Catholic guilt. His own writing and reflecting on the story of Maximilian Kolbe and then his anamnesis focused on his mother initially ushered him in his own words toward courageousness, and to speaking about his own experiences. Life was contradictory for Ozaki, who had experienced both deep isolation and new opportunities for encounter. Ozaki gradually opened up about his own story, especially as he wrote, and he and other Catholic *hibakusha* spoke about their own experiences in Nagasaki from the 1980s. Having written about Kolbe, Ozaki through his autobiography, blog, and interviews opened up about his mother and his loss, driven by his anamnesis of what otherwise might be forgotten. As he remembered his mother, he continued to regret his actions as a seventeen-year-old. Ozaki's own story of the immediate aftermath of the bomb shows that although he believed he ran away, his path actually led him to the center of the destruction, just a third of a mile from ground zero. Faced with and still disturbed by death, Ozaki tightly grasped his mother's burned rosary beads. With this memory, his plaintive words remain with us: "It is love that saves us from isolation."

Notes

1. Tomihisa Taue, "Full Text of Nagasaki Peace Declaration on 76th A-Bomb Anniversary—The Mainichi," *Mainichi Shinbun*, August 9, 2021.
2. Jean-François Lyotard, "Anamnesis: Of the Visible," *Theory, Culture & Society* 21, no. 1 (February 1, 2004): 107–119, at 107.
3. Binsar Jonathan Pakpahan, "To Remember Peacefully: A Christian Perspective of Theology of Remembrance as a Basis of Peaceful Remembrance of Negative Memories," *International Journal of Public Theology* 11, no. 2 (2017): 236–255, at 246.
4. Ibid., 254–255. Metz quoted in Steven Ostovich, "Dangerous Memories and Reason in History," *Kronoscope* 5, no. 1 (2005): 41–58, at 49.
5. Nicole Simek, "Irony in the Dungeon: Anamnesis and Emancipation," in *Bourdieu and Postcolonial Studies*, ed. Graham Huggan and Andrew Thompson (Liverpool University Press: London, 2016), 191.
6. Ibid., 192.
7. Rita Nakashima Brock, "Anamnesis as a Source of Love," in *Asian and Asian American Women in Theology and Religion: Embodying Knowledge*, ed. Kwok Pui-lan (Cham: Springer International, 2020), 31–32.
8. See in particular Shijō's excellent work on this community: Chie Shijō, *Urakami no genbaku no katari: Nagai Takashi kara Rōma Kyōkō e* (The Narration of the Atomic Bomb in Urakami: From Nagai Takashi to the Pope) (Tokyo: Miraisha, 2015).
9. John Hersey, *Hiroshima* (New York: Vintage Books, 1989). See also "Hibakusha Testimony Videos," Ministry of Foreign Affairs, https://www.mofa.go.jp/policy/un/disarmament/arms/testimony_of_hibakusha/index.html.
10. Hans Renders and Binne De Haan, *Theoretical Discussions of Biography: Approaches from History, Microhistory, and Life Writing* (Leiden: Brill, 2014), 174.
11. See for example, Yamagishi, who writes of four types of guilt: Akiko Yamagishi, "Four Types of Guilt and Guilt in the Japanese," *Japanese Journal of Personality* 22, no. 3 (2013): 213–225.
12. Robert Lifton's now classic book based upon interviews with *hibakusha* included some Catholic and Christian respondents, and he reflected at length upon their understanding of guilt. Robert J. Lifton, *Death in Life: Survivors of Hiroshima* (New York: Random House, 1967). In an aside, Ozaki wrote that he assisted Endō when the author sought historical records for the writing of his book that has been recently translated into English as *Sachiko*.
13. Penny Summerfield, "Culture and Composure: Creating Narratives of the Gendered Self in Oral History Interviews," *Cultural and Social History* 1, no. 1 (2004): 65–93; Natalie Thomlinson, "Race and Discomposure in Oral Histories with White Feminist Activists," *Oral History* 42, no. 1 (2014): 84–94.
14. Enomoto Mizuki, "'Kodoku to deai' Saigo made hasshin Hasshin hibakusha Ozaki Tōmei san shikyo" ("'Isolation and Encounter' Transmitted until

the End with the Passing of Ozaki Tōmei"), *Asahi Shinbun Digital*, April 17, 2021, https://www.asahi.com/articles/ASP4J6T82P4JTOLB001.html.

15. See http://tomaozaki.blogspot.com/2021/04/blog-post_16.html.

16. Ozaki's story of victimization by the bomb has not achieved, however, the level of fame of better-known narratives of the atomic bombings captured in cartoon form, such as Keiji Nakazawa, *Barefoot Gen: A Cartoon Story of Hiroshima* (San Francisco: Last Gasp, 2004).

17. Gwyn McClelland, *Dangerous Memory in Nagasaki: Prayers, Protests and Catholic Survivor Narratives* (London: Routledge, 2019), 147.

18. Enomoto, "'Kodoku to Deai' Saigo made Hasshin hibakusha Ozaki Tōmei san shikyo."

19. The Peace Wing organization is linked to the Nagasaki Atomic Bomb Museum, and liaises with *kataribe*, in Urakami. See "Hajimete akashita 17 sai no shinjō Ozaki san 'saigo' no kataribe katsudō o byōin kara" (Final Work in Telling from the Hospital of Ozaki's Seventeen-Year-Old Mentality, for the First Time), *Nagasaki Shinbun*, February 27, 2021.

20. Tess Coslett, Celia Lury, and Penny Summerfield, *Feminism and Autobiography: Texts, Theories, Methods* (London: Taylor and Francis, 2000), 91.

21. Graham Dawson, *Soldier Heroes: British Adventure, Empire and the Imagining of Masculinities* (London: Routledge, 1994), 22–23.

22. Shioura Shintarō, *Yaketa rozario: Genbaku o ikinuita shōnen no sūki na unmei to arata na kokoro no sekai* (The Burnt Rosary Beads: World of the Youth Who Lived through the Atomic Bombing, His Misfortune and Change of Heart) (Nagasaki: Seibo no kishi sha, 2009); Ozaki Tōmei, *Jūnanasai no natsu* (Summer at Seventeen Years Old) (Nagasaki: Seibo no kisha sha, 1996).

23. Okada Gen, "Christmas in the Year of the A-Bomb," *Asahi Shinbun*, December 2008.

24. Coslett, Lury, and Summerfield, *Feminism and Autobiography*, 92.

25. Gwyn McClelland, "Mary, Mothers, Lament and Feminist Theology: The Dead Non-War Heroes of Nagasaki," *Journal of Feminist Studies in Religion* 36, no. 2 (2020): 85–106.

26. Ozaki Tōmei, "Genbaku no hi. 67 nen mae no kanashimi: Haha to no tsunagari. Wasurenai" (The Day of the Atomic Bombing. The Sadness of 67 Years Ago. The Bond with My Mother. I Will Not Forget), August 9, 2012, http://tomaozaki.blogspot.com.au/2012/08/blog-post_3765.html.

27. Ozaki, "Ozaki Tōmei no nikki," ibid. Emphasis mine.

28. Ibid.

29. Tōmei Ozaki, interview with Gwyn McClelland, February 27, 2016.

30. Before 1873, an outcaste community had done the butchering work in Nagasaki, but after the hidden Christians and Catholics returned from exile in the early Meiji period, they took on this work as some had lost farmland. Traditionally, slaughtering animals and working with skins was perceived to make those who

did it "unclean." For more on the interactions between the "outcaste" communities and the hidden Christians and Catholics, see, Gwyn McClelland and David Chapman, "Silences: The Catholics, the Untouchables and the Nagasaki Atomic Bomb," *Asian Studies Review* 44, no. 3 (2020): 382–400.

31. Stephen R. Turnbull, *The Kakure Kirishitan of Japan: A Study of Their Development, Beliefs and Rituals to the Present Day* (Richmond, UK: Japan Library, 1998), 120.

32. Tagita as quoted in ibid., 117.

33. McClelland, *Dangerous Memory in Nagasaki*, 152–153.

34. Turnbull, "Martyrs and Matsuri: The Massacre of the Hidden Christians of Ikitsuki in 1645 and Its Relationship to Local Shintō Tradition," *Japan Forum* 6, no. 2 (1994): 59–74; McClelland, *Dangerous Memory in Nagasaki*, 153.

35. Christian Pletzing, "Legendary Martyr: Maximillian Kolbe," *Kirchliche Zeitgeschichte* 27, no. 2 (2014), 364–373, at 364–365. Kolbe's support of and writing anti-Semitic sentiment is often not described in Catholic publishing companies where his biography is included up to today, writes Pletzing (370). See, for example, "Kolbe, Maximilian," in *The Oxford Dictionary of the Saints*, ed. David Farmer (Oxford: Oxford University Press, 2011).

36. Farmer, "Kolbe, Maximilian."

37. Okada, "Christmas in the Year of the A-Bomb."

38. Tōmei Ozaki, *Nagasaki no Korube Shinpu: Seibo no kishi monogatari* (Father Kolbe of Nagasaki: The Story of the *Knight of the Immaculata*) (Tokyo: Seibo no kishi sha, 1983); Tōmei Ozaki, *Migawari no Ai* (Surrogate Love) (Nagasaki: Seibo no kishi sha, 1994); Tōmei Ozaki, *Father Kolbe in Nagasaki*, trans. Araki Shin'ichirō (New Bedford, CT: Academy of the Immaculate, 2021).

39. Both Shijō and I cite the importance of the visit of the pope for the Catholic community's realization that they needed to speak about their experiences of the atomic bombing. Shijō, *Urakami no genbaku no katari*; McClelland, *Dangerous Memory in Nagasaki*.

40. "Hajimete akashita 17 sai no shinjō Ozaki san 'saigo' no kataribe katsudō wo byōin kara."

41. Brock, "Anamnesis as a Source of Love," 31–46, at 37.

Part II
Literature and Testimony

"Nagasaki" in Akutagawa Ryūnosuke's Taishō-Era Literary Imagination
By Anri Yasuda

Akutagawa Ryūnosuke (1892–1927), the namesake of the Akutagawa Award, the most prestigious literary award in Japan since its inception in 1935, was renowned from during his lifetime as an especially erudite writer whose works reflect a range of literary references. Taking place in a variety of historical periods and cultural settings, many of his stories make oblique as well as overt references to Western, Chinese, and classical Japanese texts, evincing a literary knowledge spanning multiple cultures and eras. Edgar Allen Poe, Pierre Loti, and Matsuo Bashō are among some of the writers that Akutagawa draws on in his essays and fictions. The writer Hori Tatsuo, who had been a close friend to Akutagawa, described his oeuvre as "art made from other artworks."[1] Given this creative cosmopolitanism, it is perhaps not surprising that Akutagawa had harbored a particular affection for Nagasaki and its legacies as a point of cross-cultural contact when Christianity was first introduced to Japan by Jesuit missionaries in the sixteenth century, prior to the Tokugawa shogunate government's ban on foreign religions in the early seventeenth century. Akutagawa's Taishō-period (1912–1926) literary imagination regarded Nagasaki as a unique city that embodied a historical blend of Japanese and imported multicultural influences, as well as a space symbolic of newer possibilities yet to come, ideals that the city would consciously evoke as it rebuilt and represented itself in the postwar era.

The notion of "smooth" versus "striated" spaces, as proposed by Deleuze and Guattari in *A Thousand Plateaus* (1987), their critical purview of modern capitalist societies, helps articulate the fuller implications of how Akutagawa had envisioned Nagasaki. For Akutagawa, Nagasaki had been more than a charming city with a colorful past on the distant island of Kyūshū in Japan's far western region. Instead, Nagasaki represented a "smooth" alternative to the social structures and pressures that defined for him the "striated" urban space of Tokyo, where he was based throughout his life. As Deleuze and Guattari describe it:

> The variability, the polyvocality of directions, is an essential feature of smooth spaces.... The nomad, nomad space, is localized and not delimited. What is both limited and limiting is striated space, the *relative global*: it is limited in its parts, which are assigned constant directions, are oriented in relation to one another, divisible by boundaries, and can interlink; what is limiting ... is this aggregate in relation to the smooth spaces it "contains," whose growth it slows or prevents, and which it restricts or places outside. Even when the nomad sustains its effects, he does not belong to this relative global, where one passes from one point to another, from one region to another. Rather, he is in a *local absolute*, an absolute that is manifested locally.[2]

"Smooth spaces" allow for a "nomadic" way of living in which one is free to move from one absolute position to another, in contrast to "striated spaces" that are gridded and regulated. Striated space is premised on a stable subjectivity that moves along set paths between established points, whereas smooth space envisions the protean malleability of the subjects that traverse its openness. To clarify, "spaces" in Deleuze and Guattari's schema fundamentally refer to epistemic orientations, although they plumb cartographic analogies to further their insights on state power, territoriality, and other related concepts. Akutagawa similarly imagines Nagasaki in spatial *and* conceptual terms, projecting onto the city a complex mode of longing that exceeds a metropole-dweller's idle fascination with a quaint and peripheral locale.

Crucially, Deleuze and Guattari describe striated and smooth spaces as existing in an inseparable relation to each other, with the former seeking to control and contain the latter within an overarching conception of globality, and the latter resisting and undermining such polarity by viewing each local point as a distinctive singularity. This observation that "smooth space is constantly being translated, transversed into a striated space; striated space is constantly being reversed, returned to a smooth space"[3] is important to keep in mind as we assess Akutagawa's comparative views of Nagasaki and Tokyo. Akutagawa experienced firsthand the physical and social continuities between the two cities, traveling between them through a well-developed logistical network of transportation modes and interpersonal relationships. As will be discussed in more detail, he heartily enjoyed his two visits to Nagasaki in May 1919 and May 1922, which impacted his later literary and philosophical trajectories. And in 1925, at around the time that his writing began to take on a more realist and autobiographical flavor as compared to the more dramatic and fantastical settings of his earlier works, Akutagawa had seriously considered moving to Fukuoka for a teaching post at Kyūshū

University but backed out at the last minute, purportedly due to fierce opposition from his family.[4] This indicates that the author had seen Kyūshū as a realistic setting for his life and continued literary production, a viable alternative not entirely disconnected from Tokyo, the city that had for so long been his home.

Yet, Akutagawa's initial interest in the Kyūshū region had been catalyzed by a romanticized attraction to its storied past. From as early as 1916, the year following his literary debut, Akutagawa began writing stories about Kirishitan (Christian) characters in Nagasaki and its environs during and after the era of Japan's first contact with the Namban ("southern barbarian") Spanish and Portuguese traders and missionaries. *Namban shumi*, or a modern, nostalgic enthusiasm for the hybrid culture that was created in this premodern period, had become a popular topic for Taishō period literati thanks to the writings of Kinoshita Mokutaro, Kitahara Hakushū, and their peers in the Tokyo Shinshi-sha (New Poetry) poetry circle. The Shinshi-sha poets were admirers of Namban aesthetics, and they collected a vocabulary of foreign loan words that originated in Kyūshū during this era by perusing historical texts such as the seventeenth-century *Amakusa gunki* jōruri plays about the Shimabara Rebellion of 1637, led by the charismatic Christian youth Amakusa Shirō, and the eighteenth-century *Nagasaki yawasō* that compiled the customs and history of Nagasaki. A trip that the group took to the Kyūshū region over the summer of 1907 inspired them to produce a body of exoticist writings about this long-ago world. The opening lines of Hakushū's poem "Jashūmon hikyoku" (Secret Songs of the Heretic Religion), which became the title poem of his acclaimed debut poetry collection *Jashūmon* (1909), provides an example of the ornate language and dramatic imagery that arose from these efforts:

> I think about that heretic religion, the magic of the Christian Deus.
> The captains of the "Black Ships," the mysterious land of the Europeans.
> The red-colored glass and sharp smell of carnation blossoms.
> The striped "Saint Tomé" fabric [from Southern India], also, araki [likely
>   the Mediterranean *raki* beverage], that strange sunset liquor.[5]

Akutagawa reflects on the *Namban shumi* tendencies of his youth in the opening lines of "Saihō no hito" (The Man from the West, 1927), one of the last texts that he wrote before his suicide at the age of thirty-five. The piece, a free-form rumination on the life of Jesus Christ, was published in the August edition of the *Kaizō* magazine a week after his death. Akutagawa writes:

> About ten or so years ago, I loved Christianity in an artistic sense (*geijutstu-teki ni*); I especially loved Catholicism. I still remember the "Church of the Holy Mother"[6] in Nagasaki [that I visited]. At the time, I was but a crow assiduously gathering the seeds scattered by Kitahara Hakushū and Kinoshita Mokutarō. And then several years later, I developed a special interest in the faithful Christians who martyred themselves for the sake of their beliefs. I was drawn to the psychology of these martyrs in the same way I felt an unhealthy interest (*byō-teki na kyōmi*) in the psychology of all fanatics. It is only recently that I have come to love the figure called Christ as described by his four biographers (*denki saku-sha*).[7]

In his own telling, Akutagawa's earliest attraction to Christianity had been a superficial one spurred on by the fantastical literary trends of his formative years. And in the decades since, his relationship with the religion became more nuanced, but it never developed into one of straightforward faith. Akutagawa stresses that his later fixation with the Japanese Christian martyrs had been purely intellectual, even hinting at the morbid and "unhealthy" nature of his curiosity. Although he admits that in his final period he had come to "love" Christ, the fact that he still took a scholarly, literary-historical approach to the Bible is evinced in his calling the Gospel writers "biographers." Yet, it is undeniable that by his own accounting toward the end of his life, Christianity—and the region of Japan where the religion first took root—had figured significantly in Akutagawa's creative evolution throughout his career.

The "Kirishitan" Writings: The Power to "Remake"

Scholars have dubbed the series of stories that Akutagawa wrote about Christianity-related subjects the "Kirishitan works" (*Kirishitan mono*). In them, he depicts the psychological drama of various characters who attempted to calibrate imported Western Christian thought with traditional Japanese beliefs during and after the Namban period. Rather than explore the religious convictions and virtues of his protagonists, Akutagawa used the context of Japanese encounters with Christianity in the Namban era to probe the question of how to intake Western values while maintaining Japanese perspectives, or on a more general philosophical level, how competing epistemologies and values might be synthesized without contradiction. In the words of Deleuze and Guattari, Akutagawa's inquiries might be recast in terms of the irreconcilability of a "smooth" worldview open to multiplicity, and the rigorous orderliness of "striated" thought. Akutagawa also wrote stories set in the latter-nineteenth century Meiji Enlightenment period, another juncture in Japanese history when individuals had to confront the rapid influx of Western culture and values. But the so-called Kirishitan works enabled Akutagawa to examine his Japanese characters' reactions to their European visitors at a greater remove from the discourses of politics, progress, and profit that more overtly colored cross-cultural contact in the Meiji period and beyond, and this arguably allowed him to engage in freer ruminations on modern Japanese cultural identity.

On both of Akutagawa's two visits to Nagasaki—first for six days in May 1919 and then for almost three weeks in May 1922—he was hosted by Nagami Tokutarō (1890–1950). Nagami was a poet, playwright, and Namban art collector from a family of prosperous merchants whose roots in the city dated back to the Edo period. He often served as a local guide to prominent figures from around Japan when they visited his native city. It was during his second visit to Nagasaki that Akutagawa wrote the story "Nagasaki shōhin" (A Short Nagasaki Story, June 1922). The work was first featured in the *Sunday Mainichi* newspaper in November 1922, and later served as the preface to Nagami's collection of plays entitled *Oranda no Hana* (Blossoms of Holland, 1925). In addition to serving as an homage to Nagami's generous hospitality and his fine tastes as reflected in his collection of antiques, the story reveals Akutagawa's admiration for Nagasaki's historical multiculturalism, which—he seems to imply—might serve as a model for modern Japanese culture's potentials for fostering genuine cosmopolitanism.

"A Short Nagasaki Story" takes place as a present-day dialogue among a display of art objects from Edo-period (1603–1868) Nagasaki, when Japan's contact with foreign countries had been officially restricted to commerce with Dutch and Chinese traders on the artificial island of Dejima off the coast of the port city. The figurines, plates, ceramics, and paintings in the collection are a mix of foreign-made works and Japanese ones made under imported influences during this period. The main character of the story is a Dutch man painted by Shiba Kōkan (1747–1818), an artist who had lived in Nagasaki and became a pioneer of Western style painting in Japan. Kōkan's Dutchman is in love with a woman painted on a plate imported from Holland. The other characters include a Maria-Kannon statue (figure 1), a Western priest painted on a Japanese sword handle, and a Western woman painted on Japanese porcelain ware. The Maria-Kannon tries to relay the Shiba Kōkan Dutchman's feelings to the woman on the plate from Holland. However, the porcelain woman cruelly rejects him, sniffing: "He might pass as Dutch here in this country. But in truth, he's not Dutch and is a weird person who is neither Western nor Eastern."[8] The other objects, also of mixed cultural heritage, are outraged by her snobbery. The Dutchman is reduced to tears.

Figure 1. After the ban on Christianity, some hidden converts continued their worship by using statues of the Buddhist goddess Kannon in place of the Virgin Mary. This image is of a Maria-Kannon statuette that Akutagawa purchased in Nagasaki. Image used courtesy of the Museum of Modern Japanese Literature (Nihon Kindai Bungakukan), where the artifact is held.

The owner of the art collection enters the room at this point with guests who exclaim over his various objects. One immediately compliments Shiba Kōkan's painting of the Dutchman. Another guest admires the image of the Western woman painted on Japanese porcelain and says she is more beautiful than the woman painted on the plate from Holland. The owner picks up the Dutch plate to find that it is wet, to which a guest, perhaps Akutagawa himself, quips that the woman on the plate must be crying in jealousy. The art collector and his guests converse among themselves: "There is a distinct taste to Western-style works made by the Japanese, which are lacking in Western works.... Indeed, for this is where today's civilization was born. In the future, there will be greater works to come."[9]

Akutagawa seems to imply that the "distinct taste" of these art objects, borne from Nagasaki's cross-cultural exchanges, embodied the potential for a multiculturalism in which native perspectives would be maintained alongside imported styles and techniques. Rather than a full imitation of Western aesthetics, the art aficionados in the story seek the charm of works that embody both Japanese and European sensibilities. "A Short Nagasaki Story" is not strictly a Kirishitan work, in that although it features Japanese-Christian iconography, its main focus is on the artistic rather than the spiritual products of the synthesis of Japanese and Western cultural references. But in celebrating the resultant artworks for their hybrid flavors, the story reprises Akutagawa's cogitations on the theme of intercultural exchanges from his earlier Kirishitan stories, even while marking a significant departure from them.

For example, the story "Kamigami no bishō" (The Smiles of the Gods) from January 1922, four months before his second trip to Nagasaki, presents a murkier view of Namban-era Japanese-European interactions, and it implies a less clear assessment about the directions of Japan's cultural identity. The story unfolds in the sixteenth century at the Namban-ji Catholic Church in Kyoto, its main character a Jesuit missionary named Padre Organtino.[10] Despite the growing numbers of converts to his church, including several elite samurai, Organtino has an uneasy suspicion that his new Japanese followers do not truly understand or accept the Christian God whom they call "Deusu" (from the Latin *Deus*, written with the characters 泥烏須). Organtino retires to the chapel to pray and is greeted by a vision of a "Japanese Bacchanalia" wherein a group of Japanese gods dance by firelight. Although he does not recognize it, this is a scene from a Shinto myth featuring the supreme sun goddess Amaterasu-Ohirumemuchi.

The next day, while strolling in the courtyard of the church, Organtino is approached by an old Japanese man who identifies himself as one of the many native deities of Japan. He warns Organtino that the Christian mission in Japan will ultimately fail because of the Japanese tendency to recast all foreign gods and knowledge into their extant frames of reference. He argues that many teachings have come to Japan from overseas—those of Confucius, Mencius, Chuang-tzu, and others from China, as well as of Siddhartha's Buddhism from India—only to be subsumed into the framework of established Japanese worldviews. He explains how the importation of *kanji* characters from China did not lead to the rise of the Chinese language in Japan but instead to the enrichment of the Japanese language, raising the example of the poet Kakinomoto Hitomaro of the eighth-century *Man'yōshū*, Japan's oldest poetry anthology. The old man tells Organtino that the strength of the Japanese spirit lies in "the power not to destroy [other teachings] but to remake them."[11]

On its own, the story can be read as a celebration of Japan's purported power to remake new influences to suit its own needs.[12] Yet, when read against "A Short Nagasaki Story," which praises the vitality of the Namban-style artworks he encountered in Nagasaki, "Smiles of the Gods" seems a critique of the superficial and opportunistic nature of many Japanese people's embrace of Christianity during the Namban era, and by extension, Japan's seemingly uncritical enthusiasm for Western ideas in the modern era. For instance, the Catholic writer Endō Shūsaku observes Akutagawa's ambivalence toward the supposed Japanese "power" to recast all new influences into its existent frames of reference: "If he was affirming this tendency, this would mean that he did not admit the downsides of Japan's methods of absorbing foreign cultures and the power to deform them in the process. If he was criticizing this tendency, it would mean that he was taking on the big task of determining how to resolve this problem. Akutagawa does not remark on this point in 'Smiles of the Gods.'"[13] Karatani Kōjin sees the story as Akutagawa's attempt to address the pressing issue of Japan's cultural identity in the Taishō period as the nation came to view itself as having reached a level of modernity on par with the Western world. Karatani suggests that in the story Akutagawa critically diagnoses Japanese culture as amenable to new ideas not because it recognized similarities between imported influences and extant traditional values, as other thinkers have claimed, but because it tended to "actively take in external things with the clear awareness that these were of foreign origins."[14] That is, the recognition of differences did not lead to a critical engagement with the actual points of divergence between Japanese and imported perspectives. In sum, both Endō and Karatani view "Smiles of the Gods" as Akutagawa's assessment about the insufficiently dialectical status quo of Japanese culture, although it stops short of offering a resolution to this impasse.

In "Jashūmon" (Heretic Religion, 1918–1920), an even earlier Kirishitan work, Akutagawa shows a similar deferral of constructive engagement on the part of his Japanese characters when they are confronted with the alterity of Western perspectives. The story dramatizes a prolonged Heian period power struggle between a Japanese *daimyō* and an itinerant monk of a mysterious foreign religion referred to as "Mari-no-kyō" (the teachings of Mari). This new faith apparently seems to refer to a form of Christianity,[15] with the monk alluding to a "heavenly king" and gaining converts through miraculous acts such as restoring sight to the blind and speech to the mute.[16] The story was serialized in the *Osaka Mainichi* and *Tokyo Nichi-nichi* newspapers, but Akutagawa eventually abandoned writing it before it was completed. Curiously, the story breaks off just as it seems to reach what would have been its climax, when the Japanese domain lord descends into the courtyard of a Buddhist temple to confront the Christian monk. An early draft of the story discovered in 2008 shows that Akutagawa had considered describing the *daimyō* as unusually "decisive and bold (*yūmō kakan*)" at the story's start.[17] From his decision to remove this characterization, we might deduce that Akutagawa was uncertain as to how a direct clash between monotheistic monk and the Japanese lord would unfold and thus had hesitated to raise the stakes of this coming battle by endowing the Japanese lord with a markedly uncompromising personality.

But after witnessing in Nagasaki the artefacts of what he had sensed to be a "smooth" cultural hybridity that he describes in "A Short Nagasaki Story," Akutagawa turns his attention to situations in which a synthesis between different values explicitly fails. The Kirishitan stories written after Akutagawa's second visit to Nagasaki in May 1922 present clearer confrontations between older Japanese worldviews and imported Western ones. "Ogin" (from September 1922) and "Oshino" (from April 1923) trace conflicts between competing native and imported belief systems to their conclusions, not deferring their final outcomes as in his earlier works. Instead of harmonizing competing perspectives, the protagonists of these stories reject the new Western concepts that they find incompatible with their own prior understandings. They display the sort of "striated" logic that Akutagawa seemed to grasp as the organizing tenor of modern life in Tokyo, in stark contrast to the "smooth" openness to aesthetic and conceptual differences that he had glimpsed during his hiatus in Nagasaki.

"Ogin" takes place during the early seventeenth century after Christianity was outlawed in Japan. Ogin was orphaned as a young girl shortly after her family relocated to Nagasaki from Osaka. Her birth parents had been Buddhist, and it is only after she is adopted by "Joan" Magoshichi and "Joana" Osumi, a farmer couple from Urakami, that Ogin is secretly baptized as "Maria." The family quietly practices their religion, but on Christmas Eve, government officials capture them. Ogin, Magoshichi, and Osumi are tied up with ropes and pressured to renounce their heretic beliefs. They refuse and prepare to enter "Haraiso" as martyrs. However, moments before a pyre is lit beneath her bound feet, Ogin announces that she will give up her faith. Her adoptive parents exclaim that she must be possessed by the devil, but Ogin explains: "My dear parents did not know about the teachings of our God and must have fallen into Hell. To enter the gates of Heaven by myself would be inexcusable."[18] Ogin's sudden return to her original Confucian-Buddhist values of filial piety shock Magoshichi and Osumi, who also renounce their Christian faith. The townspeople who had gathered to watch the execution are dismayed by what they perceive as an anticlimactic turn of events. But for Ogin and her adoptive parents, their religious reconversions constitute a momentous psychological reckoning. Faced with the incommensurability of Christian monotheism and Buddhist cosmology, they determined that a compromise was not possible.

"Oshino," written the following year in 1923, also portrays a Japanese heroine who ultimately decides to reject Christian beliefs. Oshino, the title character, approaches a Western priest to ask him to cure her son of his illness. She claims that she is ready to convert to Christianity if her son can be saved. The priest, eager to gain a new convert, relates to her the story of Jesus Christ's self-sacrifice through his crucifixion. But Oshino pales when she hears about how Jesus had cried out on the cross, "My Lord, why have you forsaken me?" Oshino coldly informs the priest that her husband, a samurai, had "never once turned his back" in the face of adversity.[19] As an upholder of Bushido, she rejects what she perceives to be the meekness at the heart of Christianity, and she departs from the church. Like "Ogin" before her, "Oshino" intuits the impossibility of fully accepting Christian values while preserving her original allegiances, even if it costs her access to Western medical advances. A more facile and opportunistic conversion was unthinkable for her.

We can thus perceive a shift in outlook between the Kirishitan stories that came before and after "A Short Nagasaki Piece," which was written during Akutagawa's second visit to the titular city. In the old artworks of Nagasaki, the author seems to have detected a coexistence between Japanese culture and Western influences that was more markedly integrated than what he had known in the supposedly cosmopolitan cultural space of Tokyo. More broadly, perhaps the possibility of a "smooth" synthesis of competing values and imperatives that he had sensed in Nagasaki had underscored for him the rigid "striations" of his usual milieus. After "Ogin" and "Oshino," Akutagawa distanced himself from Kirishitan-themed works until 1927, when he wrote the previously mentioned "Saihō no hito" (Man from the West), which was about the life and mythos of Jesus Christ rather than about the internal struggles of Japanese converts to Christianity. By this point, Akutagawa's personal and creative anxieties had worn down his psyche.

Stories of Modern Life: A Darker Turn

Guilt over a brief affair and the former mistress who harassed him and his family, financial pressures as the sole breadwinner for his extended family, doubts about his position and aesthetic philosophies as a literary writer amid rising socialist movements that questioned apolitical pursuits as frivolous, and his failing physical and mental health, which would eventually lead to a dependency on sleeping pills, compounded in his last years. Akutagawa suffered from dysthymia, if not outright depression. He was torn between his artistic tastes, which remained as cosmopolitan and idealistic as ever, and the growing tensions of his immediate circumstances. As Seiji Lippit puts it, Akutagawa lost "faith in the capacity of literature to organize any coherent narrative of subjectivity."[20] Tellingly, in "Bungei-teki na, amari ni bungei teki-na" (Literary, All Too Literary, 1927), an essay collection about his creative philosophies that ultimately remained unfinished, Akutagawa ruefully called himself a "random and omnivorous (*zappaku na*)" writer, in contrast to someone like Shiga Naoya, often classified as an I-novelist, who remained "pure (*junsui*)" and wrote mainly about autobiographical matters in a poetic but realist manner.[21] When he committed suicide with a drug overdose in 1927 at the age of thirty-five, Akutagawa famously summarized in a letter to his friend and fellow writer Kume Masao his feeling oppressed by a "vague dread about the future."[22]

Akutagawa's depictions of Tokyo, his hometown, reflect the gradual mounting of his despair. Although they evolved over time from unease to outright dread, Akutagawa's writings about the metropolis cumulatively reveal a less than sanguine outlook. For example, the story "Negi" (Spring Onions, 1919) dramatizes the dissonance between the impoverished material realities and the rich inner idealism of city dwellers. The protagonist Okimi is a young and financially struggling café waitress striving for urban sophistication. She admires Beethoven's music and American films. Through her internal monologue, Akutagawa shows the sincerity of her attempts to romanticize downtown Tokyo's sights while her date for the evening, Tanaka, a slick bohemian with artistic pretensions, attempts to lure her into the darker side streets:

> The music of a band advertising the year-end sales, the dizzying lights from a billboard advertising Jintan, evergreen tree decorations celebrating Christmas, flags from multiple nations emblazoned every which way, a Santa Claus in a window display, postcards and calendars in storefronts—to Okimi's eyes, everything appeared to be singing the splendors of love and to continue glittering on infinitely.... Joy, joy, joy ... [23]

Readers worry for Okimi's safety from Tanaka's predations, while she seems distracted by the effort to aestheticize the frenetic, almost schizophrenic, commercial urban landscape around them. But her flowery train of thought is broken when she spots a bargain on spring onions for sale at a vegetable vendor's stall. The gap between her cosmopolitan aspirations and her decidedly plebeian Japanese living conditions creates a sense of humor and pathos. The two sides of Tokyo, one glamorous and seemingly full of possibilities, and the other gritty and harsh, appear to exist poles apart until the intrepid Okimi manages to bridge these spheres with easy grace. Tanaka, Okimi's date, is "struck by the blinding scent of the spring onions, as sharply pungent as real life itself" when she turns to face him with an unfazed smile after her produce purchase.[24]

Tokyo's buzzing cityscape later collapses into an undifferentiated space of generalized anxiety in the story "Haguruma" (Spinning Gears), published in October 1927 after the author's death. The story follows the urban wanderings of Akutagawa's fictional counterpart as he sinks deeper into the neuroses that would soon overcome him. The fashionable shops and crowds of the streets of the modern Ginza neighborhood of Tokyo tax his frayed nerves:

> I could not help but feel depressed by the stores lining both sides of the street and the dizzying whirl of passersby. It was distasteful to me that everyone should be walking so merrily as though they knew nothing of humanity's sins. Amidst the faint glow of the dusk mixed with the street lights, I walked endlessly north....[25]

> I looked up at the high sky and tried to think about how small this earth is amidst the countless number of stars in the sky, that is, how small each of us

are. But the sky, so clear during the day, had at some point become cloudy. I was suddenly overcome with the sense that there was someone out to get me, and I decided to seek refuge in a café on the other side of the train tracks.[26]

At a later interlude, Akutagawa provides some insight into his narrator's desperate mindset: "I suddenly remembered the penname Juryo Yoshi that I had used in the past. There was an anecdote in the *Han Feizi*," a compendium of writings attributed to Han Fei, a Chinese political philosopher from the third century BCE, "about a young man from the city of Juryo, who forgot how to walk in [his native] Juryo style before he mastered walking in the style of [his new city of] Kantan and had to slither home [from Kantan to Juryo] like a snake. To anyone's eyes, I must now appear to be a 'Juryo Yoshi.'"[27] Akutagawa himself was well aware that in addition to the praise he received for the eclectic range of philosophical and literary references he employed in his elegant writings, he was also criticized as an effete dilettante for these very qualities by the growing ranks of politically minded proletarian writers, as well as self-confessional I-novelists, who called for realism in literature. By having his fictional narrator call himself Juryo Yoshi after the cautionary legend of a tragicomic man who had put on airs and lost sight of his own core values and self-awareness, Akutagawa acknowledges his own crisis over his identity as a thinker and writer. Sympathizers saw in his "vague anxiety about the future" a distillation of modern Japan's dilemmas over its core values and future directions.

It was thus as a counterpoint to modern-day "Tokyo," the site of his mounting angst, that "Nagasaki" came to symbolize for Akutagawa a timeless sanctuary space. Despite its later violent history of persecution against the Christian holdouts who refused the Tokugawa shogunate's attempts to suppress foreign religions, Akutagawa was drawn to the brief period when native and imported sensibilities had seemed to merge in a particular blend, and what he perceived—or idealized—as the present-day permeation and continuation of this spirit of tolerance. In addition to "A Short Nagasaki Story," which Akutagawa wrote while visiting the city in May 1922, the poem "Nagasaki," written and published in June 1922 shortly after his return to Tokyo, affirms the special affection he held for Nagasaki. Its lines evoke the gentle, idyllic atmosphere of the sites and scenes of the city:

Diamond-shaped kites. Kites floating in the skies of the Santo Montani mountains.[28] Gently floating kites.

Street vendors selling oranges and bananas. The warmth from the sunlight on the stone pavement. Swallows, flying all throughout the city.

The weeping willows of the Maruyama pleasure district.

The stone "Spectacle Bridge" over the canal. Passing over the bridge, straw hats.—Suddenly, a flock of ducks swimming forth. A flock of ducks, shining whitely.

A lizard on the steps of the Nankin Temple.[29]

The poem guides readers through the mountains of Mount Inasa on the west side of the bay, the Maruyama pleasure quarters, Spectacle Bridge, and Nankin Temple. The kites bobbing lazily in the open sky, the straw hats of the strolling Nagasaki-ites, and even the lizard in the sun add a sense of peaceful activity. Akutagawa creates an active sense of cultural fusion in calling the mountains "Santo Montani," for "sacred mountains," in Portuguese; in juxtaposing the native fruit of *natsu mikan* with bananas, which began to be imported into Japan only in the early 1900s; and in mentioning the famous bridge built in the seventeenth century by the Chinese Zen Buddhist monk known in Japan as Mokusu Nyojō, as well as Kōfukuji Temple (also known as Nankin Temple), where he had served as the head priest. The verses cement Akutagawa's impressions of Nagasaki as a place of beauty, calm, and fertile inclusivity.

Another work that evinces Akutagawa's fondness for the city is the painting that he produced for the Nagasaki geisha Sugimoto Waka, who worked under the professional name of Terugiku. In "Nagasaki nichiroku" (Nagasaki Diary), a partial record of his activities during his second stay in the city, Akutagawa recounts meeting Terugiku on May 18, 1922, with the Nagasaki locals Watanabe Kurasuke and Kamohara Haruo—both of whom became his literary acolytes—at a restaurant in the Maruyama pleasure district. Akutagawa later published the "Nagasaki Diary" in the anthology *Hyakusō* in 1924. In his initial mention of Terugiku, Akutagawa assesses: "She was very different from the geisha in Tokyo."[30] This impression is not explained further, but that he met with her at least once more while in Nagasaki and continued to keep in touch with her after his return to Tokyo shows that he found her "difference" from Tokyo women pleasing. A later entry in "Nagasaki Diary" recounts that he had presented her with the poem "The day-lilies (*hime-kanzō*) have bloomed in Miss Waka's garden, however (*batten*), alas, it is time for us to part," at yet another lively gathering on May

22. The short poem expresses his fondness for Terugiku and the efflorescent beauty he associated with her, as well as bittersweet regret at his impending departure from her city. The playful use of the regional dialect term *batten* shows a lightheartedness that is rare for the erudite and self-conscious Akutagawa.

Before he left Nagasaki approximately a week later, Terugiku asked her new friend to paint a commemorative screen for her. Akutagawa complied, and the result was the ink painting known as *Suiko banki no zu* (Image of a *Suiko* Returning Home in the Evening), now housed in the Nagasaki Museum of History and Culture, where it is displayed each year on the anniversary of his death (figure 2). A *suiko* is a child-sized, bipedal, amphibious creature

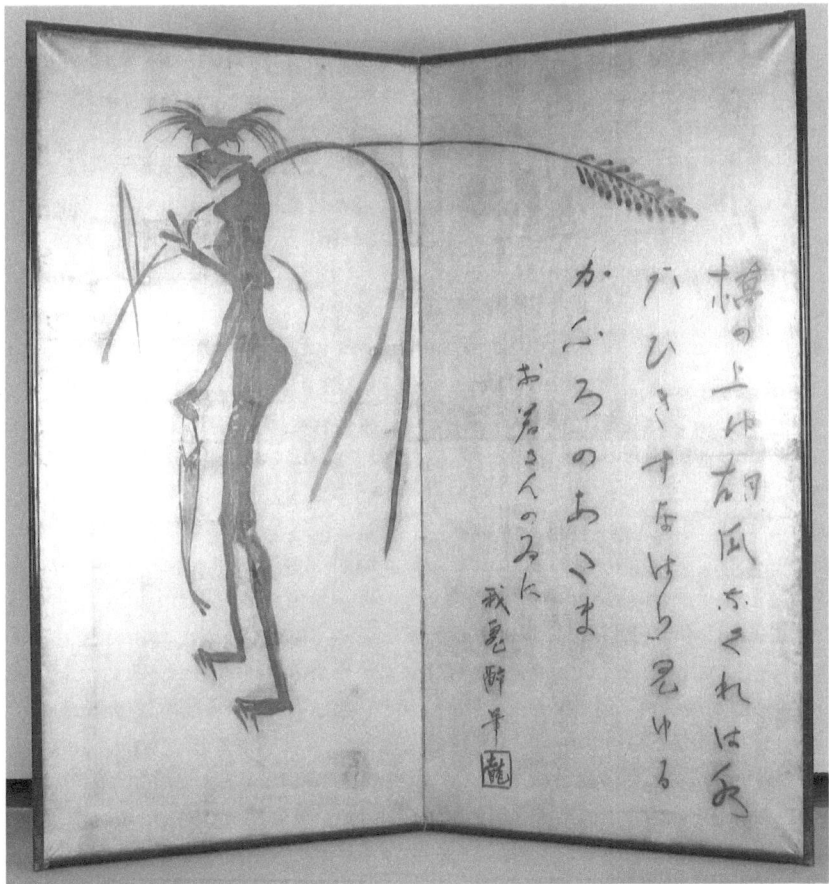

Figure 2. Akutagawa Ryūnosuke, *Suiko banki no zu* (1922). Courtesy of the Nagasaki Museum of History and Culture (Nagasaki Rekishi Bunka Hakubutsukan), where the painting is housed.

of Chinese myth that echoes the *kappa* of Japanese *yōkai* (monster) folklore. Akutagawa seems to have fostered an interest in these mysterious creatures from his youth spent in the *shita-machi* (downtown) area of Tokyo along the banks of the Sumida River, where rumors of *kappa* had circulated.[31] As an adult, he began painting *kappa* in casual correspondences with friends, particularly his confidante Oana Ryūichi, a painter, whom he dubbed the "Kappa of Hongō," while he claimed for himself the epithet of "Kappa of Tabata" after the respective neighborhoods that they resided in. Akutagawa seemed to identify with the liminal status of the *kappa* who resembled human beings and yet remained uncannily other to them; he wrote on a postcard to Oana in September 1920 that he had "begun to find [these] creatures endearing (*kawaiku narimashita*.)"[32] Akutagawa went on to produce ink paintings of *kappa*, often accompanied by poetic inscriptions, on a variety of occasions. Several of these paintings were in the *Suiko banki* composition of a lone *kappa* standing in profile, hoisting a stalk of a grain-bearing plant over one shoulder with a captured fish dangling from the other hand. Yet the *Suiko banki* that Akutagawa gifted to Terugiku has been called "among the best of his kappa paintings"[33] and is unique in its depiction of a clearly female *kappa*.

The *kappa*'s relaxed but supple posture, the gentle curves of her body, and her broad, mischievous grin give this image an air of relaxed ease that is rarely found in Akutagawa's other *kappa* paintings which tend to range between the self-deprecating, the humorous, the slightly grotesque, and the pathetic. For example, the *Shaba o nogareru kappa* (A Kappa Fleeing Worldly Suffering) compositions of his final years express an intense anxiety that reflects the writer's fraught mental state; the *kappa*'s dramatically outstretched arms and crouched running posture, as well as the dead flat whites of the eyes, suggest a terrified desperation to escape a dire threat. Oana states that Akutagawa had begun to paint these ominous images once he decided to kill himself.[34] Curiously, Akutagawa paired the same poem "From atop a bridge/I throw in a cucumber [into the water below]/The water ripples/A bald pate appears" (*Hashi no ue yu/kyūri nagureha/mizu hibiki/sunawachi miyuru/kamuro no atama*) with both Terugiku's 1922 *Suiko banki* and the *Shaba o nogareru kappa* that he painted for his nephew Kazumaki Yoshitoshi a few days before his suicide in 1927 (figure 3). The poem takes on very different connotations against these contrasting images.

To briefly parse the poem, we can understand bridges as symbolic of a transition point between two realms, whether between smooth and striated thought, artistic freedoms and material imperatives, the human and monstrous, or any other competing sets of logics. In tossing into the water a

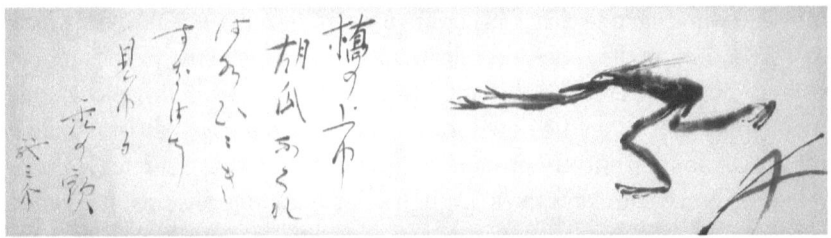

Figure 3. Akutagawa Ryūnosuke, *Shaba o nogareru kappa* (1927). Courtesy of the Museum of Modern Japanese Literature (Nihon Kindai Bungakukan).

cucumber—said to be a favorite food of the *kappa*—from the bridge's midpoint, the poet attempts to temporarily blur the boundaries between these two spaces. The appearance of the *kappa*'s characteristic bald pate as he or she rises to the water's surface to retrieve the offering can be read as either a source of quiet delight for the poet when paired with the calm and smiling *kappa* presented to Terugiku, or of dread when paired with the fleeing *kappa* presented to Kazumaki. In the former instance, the poem seems to celebrate the *kappa*'s liminal status between territories and to affirm Akutagawa's positive identification with such a free and hybrid condition. Under this interpretation, the poem could seem to function as a statement about the expansive breadth of his literary imagination. That the *kappa* is female would seem to indicate more than Akutagawa's thoughtful customization of the image for Terugiku. If we are to read the painting as an act of self-expression that crosses gender lines, it might also imply the writer's conceptual ambitions to question binary limitations at large. But read against the latter image of the fugitive and harried *kappa*, Akutagawa's poem takes on a tone of beleaguered apprehension, implying that he too is perennially unable to find refuge anywhere.

The story "Kappa" that Akutagawa published two months earlier, in May 1927, would support this bleaker interpretation. Through the perspective of a human narrator who wanders into the land of the *kappa* by chance, Akutagawa depicts a society with morals that diverge from those followed by most human beings. The *kappas* are more pragmatic than humankind in certain respects, which leads to shocking customs such as the organized cannibalization of the unemployed in the interest of preventing them from committing suicide or suffering from starvation. The *kappa* also asks unborn infants whether they would like to live, and only those that answer in the affirmative are born. The story's narrator eventually adapts to the ways of his new culture until the death of a *kappa* he had become close with jolts him into wanting to return to his homeplace in the human realm. Once back in Tokyo though, he finds himself unable to fully readjust to society and when he tries to return to the land of the *kappa*, he is forcibly placed in a mental hospital where he now recounts his tale to a psychiatrist. While it refrains from definitively pronouncing which society is preferable, in its relativization of human values through a deadpan tone, "Kappa" has generally been understood as a dark satire of modern life. But for all its gallows humor, the narrator is left in an emotionally and psychically precarious state: he is incapacitated in a limbo between worlds, belonging nowhere. Given his own denouement, it is difficult not to read the story in retrospect as indicative of Akutagawa's painful sense of displacement.

Of course, interpreting an author's oeuvre through the knowledge of his later personal demise can be reductive. Such an approach could lead readers to overlook the aesthetic and imaginative potentials of each individual text. Yet in comparing Akutagawa's consistently positive depictions of Nagasaki and its people against his works set in Tokyo, one cannot help but wonder whether the writer could have met with a different fate had he decided to take up a teaching post in Kyūshū when he had had the chance to do so. It is certainly possible that actually living in, rather than just visiting, the land he had idealized could have destroyed his romanticized visions and plunged him into a new despair. But it is also possible that some distance—both geographically and psychologically—from the metropolitan setting that he had known all his life could have afforded him the respite to critically envisage new directions. For ultimately, Nagasaki came to mean more to Akutagawa than the aesthetic sum of its cumulative valences owing to its multicultural and Kirishitan past or its present-day charms; it embodied for him a bright hope for the future, a new alternative to the increasingly alienating conditions of the present. Akutagawa's vision of the city might thus be said to share the radical optimism of those who dedicated themselves to rebuilding the city in the postwar period following its nuclear devastation.

Notes

1. Hori Tatsuo, "Akutagawa Ryūnosuke ron" (Theory on Akutagawa Ryūnosuke) (1929), *Hori Tatsuo zenshū* (Collected Works of Hori Tatsuo) (Tokyo: Kadokawa shoten, 1964), 1:121.

2. Gilles Deleuze and Felix Guattari, *A Thousand Plateaus: Capitalism and Schizophrenia*, trans. Brian Massumi (Minneapolis: University of Minnesota Press, 1987), 382.

3. Ibid., 475.

4. Niina Noriaki, *Akutagawa Ryūnosuke no Nagasaki* (Akutagawa Ryūnosuke's Nagasaki) (Nagasaki: Nagasaki bunken sha, 2015), 70–72.

5. Kitahara Hakushū, "Jashūmon hikyoku" (Secret Songs of the Heretic Religion), *Hakushū zenshū* (Tokyo: Iwanami shoten, 1984), 1:13. Henceforth, unless otherwise specified, all translations from Japanese are mine.

6. This refers to the Oura Catholic Church. See Asano Yō, "Chūkai" (Annotations), *Akutagawa Ryūnosuke Zenshū* (Complete Works of Akutagawa (Tokyo: Iwanami shoten, 1997), 15:351. Henceforth, the *Akutagawa Ryūnosuke Zenshū* (Tokyo: Iwanami shoten, 1996–1998) collection, numbering twenty-four volumes, will be noted as *ARZ*. Akutagawa visited the Oura Catholic Church on May 20, 1922, according to *Nagasaki nichiroku*, *ARZ* 9:261.

7. Akutagawa Ryūnosuke, "Saihō no hito" (The Man from the West), *ARZ* 15:246.

8. Akutagawa Ryūnosuke, "Nagasaki shōhin" (A Short Nagasaki Story), *ARZ* 9:147.

9. Ibid., 149.

10. Organtino is based on the real historical figure of Gnecchi Soldi Organtino, who had arrived in Japan in 1570. See Kanda Yumiko, "Chūkai" (Annotations), *ARZ* 8:340.

11. Akutagawa Ryūnosuke, "Kamigami no bishō" (The Smiles of the Gods), *ARZ* 8:201.

12. For example, Seiji Lippit notes, "A number of critics have read 'The Smiles of the Gods' as a reference to the process of modernization in Japan and an appreciation of a native culture that is able to assimilate anything from the outside." He continues: "It is important that in this piece, it is specifically literature (in the figure of Hitomaro) that maintains the ability to mediate between outside and inside, between the universal world of monotheistic religion and the multiplicity of indigenous spirits." See Seiji Lippit, *Topographies of Japanese Modernism* (New York: Columbia University Press, 2002), 65.

13. Endō Shūsaku, "*Kamigami no bishō* no imi" (The Meaning of *The Smiles of the Gods*), *Geppō 4*, in *Nihon kindai bungaku taikei*, vol. 38, *Akutagawa Ryūnosuke shū* (Akutagawa Ryūnosuke Collection) (Tokyo: Kadokawa shoten, 1970), 2.

14. Karatani Kōjin, "Nihon seishin bunseki: Akutagawa Ryūnosuke no 'Kamigami no bishō'" (Analysis of the Japanese Spirit: Akutagawa Ryūnosuke's "The Smiles of the Gods"), *Nihon seishin bunseki* (Analysis of the Japanese Spirit) (Tokyo: Kōdansha gakujutsu bunko, 2007), 78.

15. Matsumoto Tsunehiko, "Chūkai" (Annotations), *ARZ* 4:302. Matsumoto suggests that "Mari no kyō" refers to the worship of the Buddhist deity Mārīcī and the Christian saint Maria, and possibly also to Nestorian Christianity which is said to have reached Heian Japan. See also Ozawa Yasuhiro, "Akutagawa Ryūnosuke kenkyū nōto (I. *Jashūmon*, II. *Ryū*, III. *Kōshoku*)" (Akutagawa

Ryūnosuke Research Notes (I. *Jashūmon*, II. *Ryū*, III. *Kōshoku*)), *Ryūkyū daigaku bunka ronsō* (Ryūkyū University Collection of Articles on Culture) 6 (March 2009): 68. Ozawa argues that "Mari no kyō" (the teachings of Mari) refers to Christianity.

16. Akutagawa Ryunosuke, "Jashūmon" (The Heretic Religion), *ARZ* 4:22, 26.

17. Katayama Hiroyuki, "Akutagawa Ryūnosuke shin shiryō shōkai: 'Jashūmon' (bekkō) oyobi shokan ittsū" (Introduction of New Material by Akutagawa Ryūnosuke: "Jashūmon" (Alternate Draft) and One Letter), *Kokubungaku: Kaishaku to kyōzai no kenkyū* (National Literature: Interpretation and the Research of Teaching Materials) 53, no. 3 (February 2008): 179.

18. Akutagawa Ryūnosuke, "Ogin," *ARZ* 9:214–215.

19. Akutagawa Ryūnosuke, "Oshino," *ARZ* 10:44.

20. Lippit, *Topographies*, 69.

21. Akutagawa Ryūnosuke, "Bungei-teki na, amari ni bungei teki-na" (Literary, All Too Literary), *ARZ* 15:154–155.

22. Akutagawa Ryūnosuke, "Aru kyūyū e okuru shuki" (A Letter to An Old Friend), *ARZ* 16:3.

23. Akutagawa Ryūnosuke, "Negi" (Spring Onions), *ARZ* 5:244.

24. Ibid., 246.

25. Akutagawa Ryūnosuke, "Haguruma" (Spinning Gears), *ARZ* 15:56.

26. Ibid., 59.

27. Ibid., 58.

28. See Munakata Kazushige, "Chūkai" (Annotations), *ARZ* 9:322. Munakata explains that Akutagawa refers to the western mountains overlooking the bay of Nagasaki.

29. Akutagawa Ryūnosuke, "Nagasaki," *ARZ* 9:143.

30. Akutagawa Ryūnosuke, "Nagasaki nichiroku" (Nagasaki Daily Log), *ARZ* 9:261.

31. Ikeuchi Teruo, "Akutagawa Ryūnosuke no shoga," *Akutagawa Ryūnosuke no shoga* (The Calligraphic Works and Paintings of Akutagawa Ryūnosuke), ed. Nihon kindai bungaku kan (Tokyo: Nigensha, 2009), 213.

32. Akutagawa Ryūnosuke, Postcard to Oana Ryūichi, September 22, 1920, in *ARZ* 19:98–99.

33. Sagi Tadao, ed., *Nenpyō sakka dokuhon: Akutagawa Ryūnosuke* (A Chronological Reader of the Author: Akutagawa Ryūnosuke) (Tokyo: Kawade shobō shinsa, 2017), 135.

34. Ikeuchi, "Akutagawa Ryūnosuke no shoga," 215. Ikeuchi quotes from Oana Ryūichi, *Akutagawa Ryūnosuke iboku* (The Posthumous Brushworks of Akutagawa Ryūnosuke) (Tokyo: Chūō bijutsu shuppan, 1960).

Lambs of God, Ravens of Death, Rafts of Corpses
Three Visions of Trauma in Nagasaki Survivor Poetry

By Chad R. Diehl

The city of Nagasaki physically reconstructed within years after the atomic bombing of 1945, but the *hibakusha* endured a much slower recovery process.[1] Living with physical and psychological wounds for decades, and in many cases into the present, some *hibakusha* turned to a variety of constructive mediums—art, literature, peace activism—to voice the unvoiceable and give meaning to their trauma. Many among them relied on the city's rich tradition of poetry, which provided catharsis and empowered them with a means of representation. Some survivors were poets before the bombing, while others found poetry only after, but in every case poetry provided them with a tool to articulate their experience. Poetry served as a vehicle of activism for social issues, such as obtaining aid from the national government for medical treatment costs or challenging the popular memory of the bombing both in and outside of Nagasaki. Together with other memory activists, the Nagasaki survivor poets turned to writing and publishing poetry in order to bear witness to the atomic trauma and to challenge the versions of atomic memory that occluded their experience.

It was difficult to confront their personal trauma to be sure, but the collective nature of the atomic trauma impelled the survivor poets to write. As in Hiroshima, many Nagasaki writers, poets among them, saw themselves as writing a literature that held importance beyond themselves. Gotō Minako, a Nagasaki *hibakusha*, declared that writing atomic-bombing literature "means reopening the grave I have tried to cover for good. To reach into what lies at the base of consciousness, to retrieve it and turn it into words, is painfully difficult to endure. Writing becomes distasteful, and I find myself wishing to begin living with these memories of the past interred." Yet Gotō was "urged to go on by another voice; out of my own experiences I still write of Nagasaki and its people since the atomic bombing."[2] Gotō could not bear to put into words the experience because it forced her to recall, and thus relive, the trauma. As for many *hibakusha* writers, Gotō's writing "reopens the grave" in which she had buried her traumatic memories. But the survivors did not always write for themselves. Rather, writing served as a vehicle that also spoke for those who had chosen not to speak about their own experience and suffering, strengthening the peace and antinuclear movements with a collective voice in the process.

In the first decade after the war, Hiroshima surpassed Nagasaki in the popular memory of the atomic bombings and, despite the efforts of activists groups in both cities to work together, emerged as the leader of peace activities in Japan. Already by the late 1940s "Hiroshima" appeared regularly in national publications about the bombings without mention of "Nagasaki."[3] When the antinuclear peace movement burgeoned in Japan in the mid-1950s, Hiroshima became the natural center, not Nagasaki. Some critics considered peace activism in Nagasaki to be lagging behind that in Hiroshima, contrasting the approach of the two cities with the phrase, "Hiroshima rages, Nagasaki prays" (*Ikari no Hiroshima, Inori no Nagasaki*).[4] The dominant narrative coming out of Nagasaki in the first fifteen years painted a Christian image of ground zero, portraying the tragedy as one that primarily befell the Catholics of the devastated Urakami region. People outside of the city viewed Nagasaki through such a lens for decades, explaining the city's "inferiority" as a voice in the peace movement by pointing to its Christian image.[5] Many non-Catholic *hibakusha* in Nagasaki disputed this image and fought for inclusion of their experience in the dominant narrative of the city, or for a rewriting of the narrative altogether. In other words, while survivor-activists in Nagasaki sought equality for their city with "Hiroshima" in popular memory and in the peace movement, they also engaged in a discourse of local memory politics. Poetic expression provided one means to participate in these overlapping activisms for the *hibakusha*.

The poetry of three survivors represents the Nagasaki *hibakusha* experience, illuminating both the city's postwar landscape of contested memory and the nature of trauma poetry more generally. The poetry of Nagai Takashi (1908–1951) echoed his Catholic interpretation of the bombing as Providence that appeared in his popular books and helped shape a Christian image of ground zero that persisted for decades. His verse additionally functioned as catharsis for him and his community as it offered a way to understand the event in terms that reinforced their faith. Yamada Kan (1930–2003), too, wrote poetry as a therapeutic outlet for his psychological trauma, as well, but he often used it as a tool for memory activism. He dedicated a large part of his activism to challenging the "wall of silence" created by the legacy of Nagai. Yamaguchi Tsutomu (1916–2010), who survived *both* Hiroshima and

Nagasaki, wrote poetry that at once represented the experiences of both cities, challenged the lofty verse of Nagai, and functioned as a mechanism for working through trauma.

Walls of Silence

For decades after the bombing, Nagasaki *hibakusha* encountered numerous social and political obstacles, or "walls of silence," which hampered attempts to give voice to their experience. The primary wall of silence, experienced by many trauma survivors, stemmed from the nature of traumatic memory, in that a trauma is often not immediately registered as an experience. Cathy Caruth writes that the experience of a trauma, its memory, is *"not known* in the first instance," but rather "returns to haunt the survivor later on."[6] Dominick LaCapra, too, points out that the "traumatic event is repressed or denied and registers only belatedly (*nachträglich*) after the passage of a period of latency."[7] Indeed, many survivors chose not to acknowledge their trauma, nor to express it in any form, including poetry. More often than not, perhaps, silence was never broken because to remember was too painful, or, as Gotō Minako pointed out, it disturbed the "grave" in which the memory had been buried. In the case of Nagasaki survivors, the period of latency was in part imposed from the outside, by occupation censorship, social discrimination, municipal policies of reconstruction, the Christian image of ground zero, and the persistent Hiroshima-centrism of memory of the atomic bombs.

All survivor accounts, whether prose, verse, or testimony, encountered American occupation censorship in some form from 1945 to 1952, but censorship was not always equally experienced. Nagasaki *hibakusha* Matsuo Atsuyuki (1904–1983) submitted some poetry of his experience in 1946 for publication in the journal *Nagasaki bungaku*, but it was sent back to him because censors had rejected it. Meanwhile in Hiroshima, noted poet Kurihara Sadako managed to publish a poem about the bombing in the Hiroshima's local journal *Chūgoku bunka*.[8] Indeed, censorship of the bombings in media was thorough in the case of both cities for much of the occupation, but in the earliest of attempts at poetic expression of the bombings, Hiroshima found a voice while Nagasaki did not. The end of the occupation in 1952 did not mean the end of silence for all survivors, and the effect of the forced silence during the years of censorship took years to wear off entirely.

Survivors in both cities suffered social discrimination that convinced many of them that silence was better than unwanted attention. The atomic bomb created a stigma that plagued survivors and affected their livelihood for decades. The *hibakusha* had difficulty getting work if they did not conceal the fact, if possible, that they had experienced the bomb, and at work, discrimination continued.⁹ *Hibakusha* also had difficulty in social interactions. Although *hibakusha* frequently married other *hibakusha*, many others had difficulty finding marriage partners for reasons of health or the fear that the effects of radiation would be passed on to their children.¹⁰ Many survivors, including those who moved to other parts of Japan, concealed the fact that they were *hibakusha*, or even related to one, to avoid discrimination.¹¹ The *hibakusha* struggled to live with social discrimination as well as health complications due to the bomb, such as keloid scarring and cancers, including leukemia. The psychological hardships of survival in this context produced among the *hibakusha* what they called "keloid of the heart" and "leukemia of the spirit."¹² Suffering in this way made it undesirable, or at least difficult, to write of their experience, let alone speak publicly about it.

Municipal policies of reconstruction in Nagasaki contributed, in part, to the formation of atomic memory in the city, and in Japan more generally, in which the suffering of the city's *hibakusha* played little part. During the early postwar years, Nagasaki officials implemented a vision of reconstruction that cultivated the city's urban identity in light of its past as an "international cultural city." Commemoration of the atomic bombing was thus not a priority to city reconstruction planners. Meanwhile, in Hiroshima, officials cultivated an urban identity that emphasized the city's role in the postwar world as a "peace commemoration city," meaning that as the site of the world's first atomic bombing, it should serve as a beacon of peace and as a warning to mankind of the effects of atomic weapons. In the immediate postwar context, it was natural for Nagasaki officials to envision a rebuilt Nagasaki in terms of its rich history rather than define it as a city of mass destruction and death.¹³ However, the different approaches to reconstruction in the two cities factored into the rise of Hiroshima as the center of the antinuclear peace movement instead of Nagasaki.

The approach of municipal officials in Nagasaki sometimes appeared as a direct attack on the memory and suffering of the *hibakusha* in that city. When a world conference against nuclear weapons was underway in Hiroshima in summer 1955, officials in Nagasaki installed an enormous "peace statue" in Peace Park, costing the city ¥30 million, more than seven times the amount of money received by the city from the national government for medical treatment of *hibakusha* the same year.¹⁴ The *hibakusha* were livid, failing to see how the statue connected to the bombing at all.¹⁵ Some *hibakusha* saw the statue not only as a confusing symbol of their trauma, but also as a waste of municipal funds. In 1955 *hibakusha* poet Fukuda Sumako wrote an open letter to the city in the form of a poem published in the *Asahi Shinbun* newspaper:

I have become disgusted with it all.
The giant peace statue towers over the atomic wasteland.
That's fine. That's fine, but
with that money, I wonder if something else couldn't have been done.
"We cannot eat a stone statue; it will not alleviate our hunger."
Please don't call us selfish.
These are the honest feelings of the victims
who have barely lived the ten years after the bomb.

Sigh. I have no energy this year.
Peace! Peace! I'm so tired of hearing [that word].
No matter how much one shouts or cries out,
there is a powerlessness, as if it disappears into the deep sky.
I am completely tired
of the unseen anxiety for whatever the reply.

Fukuda expressed the frustration and displeasure of the Nagasaki *hibakusha*, who felt that municipal funds were being wasted on pointless projects in the name of "peace" instead of supporting their medical treatments and improving their living standards. "The more everyone gets excited [over the statue]," she lamented, "the emptier my heart is."[16] The statue reflected the city's approach to commemoration, which rarely took into consideration the voice, and the plight, of the *hibakusha*. Fukuda hoped to draw attention to the state of atomic memory as it excluded the *hibakusha*, by pointing out that the word "peace" had become as meaningless as the "empty symbol" that was installed in 1955 and still stands today. Fukuda's poem, in short, marked one of the first instances of the political voice of a *hibakusha* as expressed through poetry.

The biggest "wall of silence" within Nagasaki grew out of the legacy of Nagai Takashi, a Catholic *hibakusha* who emerged during the American occupation (1945–1952) as the voice of the city's atomic experience. In November 1945, two months after the atomic bombing, Nagai Takashi, who was the parishioner leader of the Catholics and a doctor at Nagasaki Medical School, delivered a eulogy at a mass funeral for the thousands of Catholics who died in the bombing. In the eulogy, Nagai declared that the atomic bombing of Nagasaki was an act of God's Providence: "[the] church of Urakami was placed on the altar of sacrifice as atonement for the sin of humankind that was the world war. It was chosen as a pure lamb, slaughtered, and burned."[17] Nagai believed that God had chosen the Urakami Catholic community as a "sacrificial lamb" to end the Second World War.

During the occupation, when most other mentions of the atomic bombs were suppressed, Nagai was allowed to publish numerous books and poetry in which he expounded the idea of the "Providential" tragedy. Most of his books became national bestsellers, beating out books by popular authors such as Yoshikawa Eiji, perhaps best known for his multivolume work *Miyamoto Musashi*, which, incidentally, two of Nagai's books surpassed in the bestseller rankings of 1949, as well as in the rankings for number of books sold across Japan.[18] Nagai's voice, then, was the loudest coming out of Nagasaki and thus influenced the perception of the city around the country. Because of his strong Christian faith and his donation of royalties from his books to the reconstruction of Nagasaki, Nagai became known as the "saint of Urakami" in local, national, and international media. Some Nagasaki Christians thought that God had delivered Nagai to them.[19] By 1949, he had grown from being the voice of his Catholic community in Urakami to that of Nagasaki City in general, leading to visits from a variety of public, religious, and national figures, including Emperor Hirohito who paid a personal visit to his sickbed in May 1949. Through his position in the Urakami Catholic community and his role as the voice of Nagasaki's atomic experience until his death in 1951, Nagai's uncritical religious views on the bombing contributed to the city's image in popular memory, which contrasted starkly with Hiroshima's "rage."

For many *hibakusha*, poetic composition became a powerful tool for challenging the "walls of silence" because it provided for them a voice for social, political, and memory activism. From the late 1960s on, Nagasaki *hibakusha* peace activists became memory activists, compiling and publishing more than ever before the testimonial accounts and poetry of survivors in order to, as they put it, "break down the walls of silence." The "Nagasaki testimony" movement began in earnest in 1968, but one publication in particular, *Nagasaki no shōgen: 1970* (Testimonies of Nagasaki: 1970), represented the renewed determination of the *hibakusha* as memory activists. Central to their goal of breaking down the walls was encouraging survivors to speak about their trauma, no matter how painful it was to recall.[20] The editors of *Nagasaki no shōgen: 1970* were well aware of the power of poetry to represent the trauma of the bombings. Chapter 3, "The Atomic Bomb Inside Me" (*Watashi no naka no genbaku*), features a collection of personal recollections of the bombing and its meaning. While some of the *hibakusha* in this section chose to recount their story through narrative, the overwhelming choice of medium of expression was poetry, including *waka* and free verse. The *hibakusha* here looked to poetry to capture and represent the trauma "inside" them in order to convey their trauma, keep their memory alive, and break down the "walls of silence" which threatened their personal and collective atomic memories.

Trauma and Poetry

Survivors of trauma have often found it difficult to articulate and convey their experience. The *hibakusha* poet Tanaka Kishirō once wrote:

> However one tries to speak
> However one tries to write
> Of human atrocity
> All tongues and pens are to no avail.

As literary scholar John Treat points out, the "irony here of course is that Tanaka *is* trying."[21] Nonetheless, the poet's point is well taken: "human atrocity" challenges the ability of human language to convey inhumanity and trauma. The magnitude of the atomic experience defies linguistic expression, but to not at least try to speak and write of atrocity presents for the survivors a greater threat to the preservation of humanity in general, and to their own psychological preservation.

Poetry offers a number of appealing means to represent and express trauma. An individual's trauma begins with an experience, but it does not become simply an event in their past. It is also an ongoing experience, manifesting as traumatic memory, or often as psychological, and sometimes physical, suffering. The memory of a trauma mimics the traumatic event in that it ruptures a normal lived experience, and, moreover, traumatic memory is fractured memory. In recounting a trauma, then, one does not recount a "normal" experience. Poetry does not demand adherence to a narrative recounting of events "as they happened," and instead offers a liberating mode of expression that better reflects the multiple aspects of the experience. In other words, among written forms of expression, poetry is well suited to gather the fragments of a traumatic memory and allow the fragments to speak, not in linear fashion as a story of the past, but all at once as a lived and ongoing experience. Furthermore, memory and poetry are also similar, as Mark Freeman has noted, because "just as memory may disclose meanings that might have been unavailable in the immediacy of the moment, poetry may disclose meanings and truths that might otherwise have gone unarticulated.... In autobiographical narrative, memory and poetry meet."[22] When a trauma survivor puts their memory into a poem, then, they exercise a compelling form of autobiographical expression, finding a voice to speak of their experience, empowering themselves to understand it, and, if they choose, to convey it to an audience. When multiple poetic voices come together, the autobiographical expression of each becomes part of a collective voice, which, in the case of the *hibakusha*, facilitates the articulation of their shared experience and a more nuanced historical understanding of the bombings.

The survivors of Hiroshima and Nagasaki turned to poetic composition, in many cases instead of prose, to articulate their experiences, creating a canon of verse about the atomic bombings, which John Treat thinks may have "exceeded [prose accounts] in sheer volume." He conjectures that "no other single specific theme in Japanese poetry accounts for so many examples in such a short span of time."[23] Indeed, after the bombings, poetry emerged before prose as the chosen medium for representing the trauma; publication of poetry began just months after the bombs. Treat attributes the overwhelming preference for poetry in expression of atomic trauma to, among other things, the fact that it is "poetry, by virtue of its consciously ironic relationship with language, that offers the victim-writer his best opportunity for alluding to a truth which apparently resists explicit denotative expression."[24] Poetic composition also empowered the *hibakusha*. Unlike the testimonial voice, unless poetry is published or shared in an oral reading or performance, it remains, simply, words on the page with no audience except for the survivor themself.[25] But, also unlike testimony, survivors do not always undertake poetic composition with an audience in mind. Many *hibakusha* composed poetry in order to manage their personal, psychological suffering; self-reflexive poetry allowed them to identify, isolate, and attempt to work through their trauma.

Though many survivors of the atomic bombings turned to poetry as the primary mode of expression, they did not always choose the same poetic form. Writers of conventional forms of Japanese poetry, such as *tanka* and *haiku*, adhere to guidelines for composition that regulate the total number of syllables, as well as syllables per line. *Tanka*, for example, contains thirty-one syllables spread over five lines, 5-7-5-7-7. Some *hibakusha* favored these forms because they provided a framework and structure within which they could work to capture, translate, and convey the experience. Also, the brevity of traditional Japanese *waka*, such as *tanka* and *haiku*, as Treat notes, appealed to many *hibakusha* because "here was a vehicle capable of speaking about the bombings without entailing the real risk of telling, and thus reducing into some number of words their complex experience." That is, by accessing the aesthetic vocabulary and structure of traditional poetic composition, "one could open imaginative doors to the interior reality of the bombing without baring its entire, and unfathomable, architecture."[26]

Moreover, the power of these short forms of expression also allowed the survivor to speak about his or her experience without the need for what would amount to a prolonged encounter with the traumatic memory itself.

Many other *hibakusha*, including poets trained in *waka*, rejected the conventional poetic forms and instead turned to free verse as the primary medium of expression. These writers felt that the vocabulary of traditional poetry, which did not include sentiments of rage, for example, failed to express the horror of the bombings and the realities of the lived experiences of the survivors.[27] Some *hibakusha*, however, such as double-survivor Yamaguchi Tsutomu, used the language of the destruction in their compositions of *tanka*, thus at once rejecting the traditional vocabulary of conventional forms and using its structure as a vehicle for expression. But the poets who fully rejected the traditional, rigid, forms of Japanese poetry perhaps also recognized the fragmented nature of traumatic memory and the difficulty of herding the fragments into any sort of coherent expression. Free verse poetry gave these *hibakusha* poets a better means for expression than *waka*: they could say whatever they wanted, however they wanted, and present the fragments of their memory in whatever order they wanted. That is, they turned to free verse poetry because it reflected the nature of traumatic memory in that it, too, is often fragmented and defies the limits of conventions of narrative forms of written expression.

The work of the *hibakusha* poets illuminates the human experience of mass trauma, because trauma transcends spatial and temporal boundaries of historical understanding. Cathy Caruth notes that trauma is a historical phenomenon that is at once a product of a particular or unique historical context and one that by its nature shares a common vocabulary of experience with other traumatic events. Indeed, she argues, it is in the "equally widespread and bewildering encounter with trauma" that we can begin to write a history that transcends specific historical contexts.[28] Scholars have also pointed out that cultural forms of expression such as art and poetry have allowed survivors of trauma over space and time to capture, understand, and represent their traumatic memory.[29] Poetry written out of the darkest moments in history incorporates a vocabulary of trauma that conveys a human experience in ways that help us to better understand the historical past than could conventional primary sources alone.

Sacrificial Lambs: The Poetry of Nagai Takashi

Nagai Takashi lost his wife, Midori, in the bombing, and he lived in a small hut near ground zero with his two young children, Makoto and Kayano, until his death in 1951.[30] He was a prolific poet from the time he was a teenager, mainly of *tanka*, but he also wrote *haiku* and free verse. His poems frequently appeared in the local Catholic newspaper, and, after the bombing, were often included in his bestselling books, as well as in the articles about him in local, national, and international newspapers. Nagai's poetry, like his prose, couched descriptions of the death and human destruction of the atomic bomb in Catholic references which conveyed his interpretation of the bombing of Urakami as a holy sacrifice. A bereavement *tanka* for the students of an all-girl Catholic school, who had died in the bombing and who, some Catholics claimed, sang hymns as they burned to death from the bomb, was perhaps Nagai's most famous and most widely read poem.

> White lily maidens, to the Lord singing
> in the flames of holocaust and burning
> even greater with their faith.
> Summoned to heaven as pure lambs that day.[31]

The poem does not access the language of rage and trauma, but instead stays within the conventional lexicons of *waka* and Catholicism. Instead of rage, Nagai is grateful that the death of the schoolgirls had meaning: that is, the schoolgirls were offered up as sacrificial lambs with the rest of the Urakami Catholics, summoned by the hand of God. In his poetry, Nagai never confronted the reality of the destruction of the atomic bombing in the same way that other Nagasaki *hibakusha* did.

Nagai viewed the bombing through the lens of Catholic theology, exemplified best, perhaps, by his reliance on the term "holocaust" (*hansai*). The term, as used by Nagai and the Catholics, meant a burnt offering of sacrifice on the altar of God, which according to the word's Christian etymology is used to identify one's sacrifice with the martyrdom of Christ. As Giorgio Agamben has noted, "Christ's sacrifice on the cross is thus ultimately defined as a holocaust."[32] In the poem, Nagai refers to the destruction of Urakami as a "holocaust" in order to link his community's sacrifice to the martyrdom of Christ dying to expiate the sins of humankind. The fact that so many fellow Catholics burned to death in the bombing only strengthened Nagai's belief that the event was indeed a "holocaust," including in the most literal sense.

Understanding the destruction of Urakami in this way provided a theological explanation to his community for why so many loved ones had been killed in an otherwise incomprehensible tragedy. In other words, Nagai created a theodicy for his community by claiming that God worked through them in order to expiate the sins of humankind. As Max Weber noted of theodicy, one "can explain suffering and injustice by referring to individual sin committed in a former life (the migration of souls), to the guilt of ancestors ... or—the most principled—to the wickedness of all creatures *per se*." The pain and suffering of an individual or group, then, represents a martyr complex characterized by the "missionary prophecy" in which "the devout have not experienced themselves as vessels of the divine but rather as instruments of a god."[33] Nagai had declared that the Urakami Catholics were the instruments of God used to end the Second World War. The theodicy of the "Providential tragedy" provided a way for Nagai and the Catholic community as a whole to understand and cope with their trauma.

Nagai's approach to understanding the destruction of the bombing in the context of his religious beliefs extended to personal loss as well. In a poem he composed after finding his wife's bones among the ashes of his home, he again avoids graphic imagery and instead turns the tragedy into a beautiful scene with Catholic vocabulary. In late November 1945, just months after the bomb, Nagai wrote of what he saw as life's true "treasures."

> Among the ashes of my burned house
> I wonder if there is any treasure remaining.
> Brush away the ash.
> Remove the roof tiles.
> I search, but there is no treasure.
> The medals are melted and shapeless.
> The bones of my wife are all that is white.
>
> Wealth and honor, oh how ephemeral.
> Even the soul of my beloved one.
> Everything has perished and passed.
> But there is only one thing that will not perish.
> Out of the ash, sparkling,
> a silver crucifix appears.
>
> Late autumn rain falls. Mornings are dreary.
> The late autumn windstorm [*nowaki*] blows. Evenings are cold.
> I hang the crucifix on a pillar.
> I roll a staff with my fingers.
> I am with the Holy Father.
> I am with the Holy Mother.
> Oh how lovely
> are thy atomic-field dwellings [*genshino jūkyo*].[34]

The discovery of the bones of his wife among the ashes of their home did not inspire Nagai to compose a poem of anger. Rather, he found peace in a crucifix that had survived among the ashes, the entire scene reminding him of the ephemeral nature of life and the omnipotence of God. Additionally, among the otherwise burned out and destroyed atomic landscape, he finds solace in his faith because he believes in the presence of holy figures.

In his poetry, Nagai never confronted the physical reality of the destruction of the atomic bombing in the same way that other Nagasaki *hibakusha* did, but he did grapple with his personal trauma in his own way. The preceding poem is free verse, which for Nagai was somewhat rare, and so this is perhaps indicative of his own struggle to comprehend his personal rather than the collective trauma of the Urakami Catholics. The turn to free verse poetry to discuss the loss of his wife and discovery of her bones among the ashes gave Nagai the freedom to attempt to understand, express, and work through the trauma. He was not speaking here of the general trauma of the Catholic community as he did in so many of his books, nor was he addressing the specifics of the bombing. Much like other survivors who rejected conventional forms of Japanese poetry, here Nagai is temporarily rejecting the more familiar *tanka* style because, in addition to serving as the representative voice of the Urakami Catholics, he also needed to confront his personal trauma, especially the loss of his wife Midori.

Nagai's poems, and his interpretation of the bombing as sacrifice, martyrdom, and Providence, reached local and national audiences through a variety of media. The "holocaust" poem appeared in one of his bestselling books in 1948, which was widely read all over Japan during the postwar period. During a ceremony held on the third anniversary of the bombing in 1948, which was broadcast over Nagasaki radio, schoolgirls sang the poem in memory of their departed classmates, accompanied by music composed by Kino Fumio.[35] Nagai also incorporated the theme of martyrdom into his paintings, which appeared at times in the Urakami Catholic newspaper, *Katorikkukyō hō* (Catholicism Bulletin), as well as in other media. In one such image from 1948, Nagai added to a traditional portrait of Jesus a mushroom cloud extending from the top of his heart, making a kind of "Atomic Jesus."[36] During the occupation and subsequent decades, while the *hibakusha* in Hiroshima were attempting to convey the horrifying realities of the atomic bomb, Nagai's voice and his Catholic narrative of the bombing were the loudest from Nagasaki.

The dominance of Nagai as representative of the bombing during and after the occupation presented one of the greatest "walls of silence" for the

Nagasaki *hibakusha* to overcome. As survivors and memory activists like Kamata Sadao have pointed out, the "Catholic myth of Urakami" permeated Nagasaki memory for decades because the books and interpretation of Nagai were the only widely available source about the bombs during the occupation. The books developed an image of Nagasaki through Nagai's religious interpretations of the tragedy that expressed gratitude for the bomb instead of horror at its destruction. Nagai's books promoted the "uniquely Catholic, or Nagai-like (*Nagaiteki*), reception of the atomic bomb as aesthetic martyrdom."[37] At the very least, "rage" did not exist in Nagai's writing.[38]

Nagai's views on the bombing erected a "wall of silence." As Kamata has claimed, Nagai's interpretation depicts the atomic bomb almost like a natural disaster, because he writes that the bomb "fell" (*rakka*) on Nagasaki, it was not "dropped" (*tōka*).[39] Nagai had argued that the destruction of Urakami exemplified God's love for the Catholics and since he loved them so much, he forced them to suffer. The "masochistic logic" of this interpretation, Kamata once wrote, was not representative of the *hibakusha*, and it prevented the development of alternatives in logic, sentiment, and literature about the bombing of Nagasaki in the postwar decades.[40] Akizuki Tatsuichirō, a Catholic and an active member in the peace and memory-activism movements, noted that from around 1949, nobody in Nagasaki except the Communist Party said anything negative about the atomic bombing, because to do so implied an anti-American or revolutionary agenda. Because of the hesitation to discuss the bombing, even after the occupation period, he said, "Religious leaders, too, fell silent and offered up nothing but prayers."[41] The general "silence" of Nagasaki residents in the early decades after the bombing, then, left the image of the city in atomic memory firmly in the hands of Nagai.

Ravens of Death: The Poetry of Yamada Kan

When the *hibakusha* began the testimony movement in the late-1960s, many employed poetry as a medium of expression to reclaim the popular memory of the bombing from the legacy of Nagai Takashi. In the face of the long Christian history of the city and interpretation of the bomb, they "could no longer keep silent" and watch their trauma continue to be "concealed" and "forgotten."[42] The most vocal critic of Nagai was the *hibakusha* and poet Yamada Kan. Yamada, one of the most prolific of the Nagasaki *hibakusha* poets, experienced the atomic bombing at 1.7 miles (2.7 km) from ground zero at fifteen years old, along with his younger sister. Yamada began writing poetry in 1948, and he published his first collection of poems in March 1954, two months after his sister committed suicide to escape the psychological hardships of being a *hibakusha*. Yamada published a collection of poetry, *Inochi no hi* (Fire of Life), because he wanted to commemorate her death, but more than that, it was for himself. It was his atonement for not fulfilling his duty as an elder brother to protect her, and it was a way for him to deal with survivor guilt.[43]

Yamada rejected traditional forms of Japanese poetry, because, he thought, the bomb had ruptured the Nagasaki poetic tradition. "The poverty of poetic expression," he noted, "makes one wonder what has happened." He lamented, the "subject of poetry has become greater than tragedy; the immense ruins that repudiate the traditional rhythmic forms of waka and haiku, and the anxiety over death caused by the lingering effects of atomic-bomb disease, mean that the spirit of poetry is extinguished with only powerlessness left to it."[44] If Yamada found the spirit of traditional poetry impoverished and shattered by the bomb, the poetic vocabulary having been replaced with death and destruction, this did not prevent him from picking up his pen. In fact, he may well have composed poetry to prove his own argument wrong, to revive the spirit of poetry despite its new subject matter, and even though he chose free verse as his preferred form.

Before the 1970s, few *hibakusha* publicly criticized Nagai Takashi. Yamada Kan recalled in 1999 that nobody in Nagasaki ever addressed the "Nagai Takashi problem," because "once you touch that, you're on your own." Yamada claimed that even in 1999 Nagai was "untouchable," and peace research institutes and other scholarly institutes avoided the topic altogether, although Yamada never understood the reason for the taboo.[45] In 1972, Yamada wrote a criticism of Nagai in the national journal *Ushio*, in which he called Nagai the "uninvited representative" of Nagasaki *hibakusha* and pointed out that his interpretation of the bomb seethed with "self-righteous Catholic egoism."[46] Shortly after the article was published, Yamada received a phone call from an influential Catholic scholar in Nagasaki, Kataoka Yakichi, who had been Nagai's close friend and was the author of the official biography of Nagai, (*Nagai Takashi no shōgai* (The Life of Nagai Takashi, 1961). Kataoka apparently chastised Yamada for criticizing the "saint of Urakami."[47]

But Yamada was not attacking Nagai as a person but as *the* representative of Nagasaki atomic-bombing literature. As Yamada wrote to author Yasuda Mitsuru, "I am not aware if there is anyone who dislikes [Nagai]. To express my conviction and as part of my literary theory, I published criticism of Nagai Takashi, but there is no one continuing it." Yamada was not interested in the "extraliterary" (*bungakugai*) persona of Nagai, but rather in how his literature affected other *hibakusha* from Nagasaki and muffled the impact of their literary voice in comparison to that of Hiroshima. Yamada claimed that he was not arguing that Nagai himself was bad, only that he wanted to interrogate his work from a literary perspective (*bungakujō no hihan toshite*). He intended to point out how Nagai's books were simply not good literature and were not representative of Nagasaki *hibakusha*-writers. Yet, after the 1972 *Ushio* article, no one in Nagasaki would work with Yamada, not even authors in the broader literary world. Yamada had simply argued that Nagai "was obviously embroiled in the policies of the American occupation," but, he said, "once you point out that fact, everyone hates you."[48]

For years, Yamada had made it a point of his "literary theory" to look at atomic-bomb literature *as* literature, not as something bearing significance simply because it addressed the bomb. Yamada felt especially strong about poetry, as he was a poet himself. Nagasaki *hibakusha*, he argued, needed to transcend the arbitrary genre of "atomic-bomb poetry" (*genbaku shi*) to write poetry that could be called literature. Simply writing a poem about the atomic bombing and calling it literature did not make it so.[49] For Yamada, poetry when composed with sincerity possessed the power of both expression and representation.

Throughout his life as a survivor of the bomb, Yamada made it his mission to battle the domination of Nagai in Nagasaki literature, and his weapon of choice was poetry. Avoiding lofty religious imagery or claims of beauty in death, Yamada depicted the grotesque realities of atomic destruction. He replaced Nagai's sacrificial lamb with ravens perching on the corpses in the atomic-bombed landscape, an image that came from personal experiences. The day after the bomb, Yamada was walking with his younger sister through the Urakami Valley when he noticed some wooden poles on top of a pile of corpses; nearby, a soldier had died with his head in a tub of water and his boots off. All of a sudden, a raven flew down to the corpses and perched calmly on one of the poles. Yamada saw many ravens sitting on the corpses, pecking at the bodies with their beaks, a scene that was burned into his memory.[50]

In March 1972 he evoked the raven he had seen with his sister in "The Dead Raven" (*Shinda karasu*):

... One raven walks along with its head hanging.

Indeed, [the bombing] must have been around here.
It's a wasteland of corpses.
Burned pieces of wood had blown over the browned roof tiles.
Corpses you can see. Corpses you can't see.
Raise their hands. Tear their stomachs.

Raise their scorched heads. Spread their crotches.
Everything lies in the abyss of darkness. Smoke flows.

One raven.
Perches atop the head of a corpse.
It [*soitsu*, the corpse] never moves.
We cried out loud and moved along.[51]
The raven looks from above,
walking along slowly with its head hanging.[52]

Yamada saw no salvation in the destruction. The motionless and charred corpses remained frozen in grotesque poses as ravens perched upon their lifeless bodies that were powerless to shoo away the birds. The scene represented for Yamada the helplessness of human beings in the face of the destruction of the atomic bomb and its aftereffects, where the raven embodied the death that awaited even the so-called survivors. Moreover, the "abyss of darkness" lives on in the present for Yamada. The raven, too, is never in the past for Yamada: it "walks along," it "perches," and it "looks from above" at Yamada and his sister. The corpses, too, though frozen in various horrific poses move through Yamada's memory as they actively pose: they "raise their hands," "tear their stomachs," and "raise their scorched heads." Here Yamada captures the nature of traumatic memory, because even though he moves forward in time and leaves the physical site of trauma in the past tense (he "moved along"), the memory lives on inside him, always in the present tense.

In his 1981 poem "White Blood Raven" (*Shirachi no karasu*), Yamada evokes ravens again to represent the destruction of the bombing as well as the anxiety over impending death that all *hibakusha* experienced. Yamada writes this time from the point of view of the present:

Still in the sky above the plaza
the flesh of the black torso of a raven
in which red blood also flows.
It flies as it caws
and pushes its way through the low rain clouds.
One lonely ominous bird.

Ever since I saw that bird
at ground zero
I have carried it in my heart for more than thirty years, but

the sharpness of the lead-colored beak that pecked
and cut open the eyeballs of the corpses
rests in the deep darkness of the eye sockets.
The raven that is flying now:
no one can say
that it is not a descendant of [the ravens]
that chewed the eyeballs of the corpses with their beaks
and disappeared into the shadows of the massifs burned brown—
they are living thirty years later.

The radiation that was dispersed in the air of the plaza
was inherited by every single body.
Even the flesh-eating birds were violated.
As one takes flight, it weakly drops its white and bloody feces/
    leukemic feces.[53]
One raven flutters gently in the sky above a building.
Vertigo. It flies at me with its beak askew.[54]

    The poem begins and ends in the present, but the raven Yamada sees flying above the plaza brings him momentarily back to the past, to the trauma of seeing ravens feeding on corpses after the bombing. Yamada concludes that the raven of the present is a descendant of the ravens of his memory, and so the "flesh-eating birds" live on, just as the trauma of the bombing lives on through his memory. Indeed, he has "carried it in my heart for more than thirty years." And just like the "sharpness of the lead-colored beak," Yamada's trauma simply "rests in the deep darkness of the eye sockets," waiting for a moment to reemerge.

    The raven that Yamada sees in the square is not only an ever-present physical reminder of the past but also an "ominous" symbol of the persistent trauma of living with the aftereffects of the bomb. In particular, it represents the *hibakusha*'s anxiety about the relationship between radiation and cancer. Yamada commented in 1999 on the presence of ravens in his poetry, saying, "I depicted the anxiety over the occurrence of blood cancer under the pretense of the raven swooping down."[55] In the poem here, Yamada plays on the words "white" (*shiroi/haku*) and "blood" (*chi/ketsu*), which when combined with the character for "illness" (*byō*), means "leukemia" (*hakketsubyō*). "*Shirachi*" in the poem also refers to the white droppings of the raven, which defecates as it takes flight. Nothing was spared the debilitating effects of the bomb's radiation, not even the "flesh-eating birds," which remain flying, ominously, overhead. Even the ravens of decades later seem to behave oddly, causing Yamada to wonder if they are descended from the ravens that fed on corpses in 1945 and have thus been genetically affected by the radiation. The depiction of Yamada's ravens as always in the present represents the overpowering anxiety of dying from the aftereffects of the bomb, even decades later, which has continued to traumatize the *hibakusha*, or rather to keep them from climbing out of and moving on from the traumatic past. Standing in the present, what ultimately connects the traumatic memory of the past to the anxiety of the present for Yamada is the image of the raven, which assaults him "with its beak askew."

For Yamada and many Nagasaki *hibakusha*, the representative image of the atomic bombing was no sacrificial lamb, but death, human destruction, and the persistent anxiety of dying. Yamada's poetry challenged Nagai as the voice of Nagasaki by drawing attention to and contextualizing the issue of Nagasaki *hibakusha* memory and representation. But the resistance he encountered is indicative of the persistence of Nagai in the atomic memory of the city. Today Catholic and non-Catholic residents alike still venerate the memory of Nagai; his city-sponsored museum attracts numbers of tourists, and his books occupy a special shelf in local bookstores. It appears that the Nagai "wall" might still present a challenge to local and national understandings of Nagasaki's atomic experience.

Rafts of Corpses: The Poetry of Yamaguchi Tsutomu

Yamaguchi Tsutomu was another poet who, like Yamada Kan, depicted the grotesque realities of the atomic bombings, and whose work exemplifies the catharsis function of poetry. Yamaguchi was a "double *hibakusha*" (*nijū hibakusha*) who survived the atomic bombings of *both* Hiroshima and Nagasaki. He was a Nagasaki native who began working for the Nagasaki Mitsubishi Shipbuilding Corporation in 1934 at the age of eighteen, and by 1937 he had been promoted to nautical design engineer. In May 1945, the company sent him to the Hiroshima plant to design special submarines. Yamaguchi was scheduled to return to Nagasaki on August 7. On the morning of August 6, the United States dropped the atomic bomb Little Boy on Hiroshima at 8:15 a.m. when Yamaguchi was on his way to the office. He was knocked unconscious by the force of the blast, and when he awoke he noticed that the left side of his face and his left arm were badly burned. He and his colleagues managed to catch a train to Nagasaki the next day, returning home on schedule around noon on August 8. He reported to work the next day, despite being badly burned and against the protests of his wife, who encouraged him to rest. At around 11:00 a.m., when he was explaining to his colleagues what had happened in Hiroshima, the United

States dropped Fat Man on Nagasaki. After his physical wounds had healed, Yamaguchi turned to composing *tanka* to cope with the psychological pain of surviving the double trauma and the scenes that he witnessed. He composed hundreds of poems before his death from cancer in 2010. His wife, Hisako, and son, Katsutoshi, also died of cancer in 2008 and 2005, respectively.[56]

Yamaguchi was a model figure of the Nagasaki tradition of poetry. He studied poetry in school, including the works of western poets (Christina Rosetti was one of his favorites), and after joining the Mitsubishi Tanka Association in 1936, he studied *tanka* composition under renowned poet Kitaoka Nobuo, a disciple of Hashida Tōsei, who was a famous poet, novelist, and literary critic.[57] The trauma of witnessing and living through two atomic bombings, just three days apart, never left Yamaguchi and remained close to the surface until he died sixty-five years later at the age of ninety-three. Poetic composition provided catharsis and allowed him to live with the psychological pain and the aftereffects of being exposed, twice, to the blast and radiation.

Yamaguchi composed in the traditional *tanka* form, but he never shied away from using explicit and graphic imagery to depict the many grotesque scenes he saw in the two cities. Indeed, he relied on a kind of visual realism rather than flowery language or metaphor. After the bombings, the rivers became clogged with corpses to the point that it looked like they clumped together and floated in unison. Yamaguchi called this phenomenon "human rafts" (*ningen ikada*), the term he used as the title for his first full collection of *tanka* poems, *Ningen ikada*.[58] In two of his poems, he writes:

In Great Hiroshima
dawn comes this morning
blazing and roaring.
In the river toward me comes
a human raft a floating.

The "black rain" that falls in my dreams.
The "human raft" that blocks the streams.
The aftereffects of *pika-don* that consume my being.[59]

Like Yamada's ravens, the trauma of the bombs experienced by Yamaguchi—radioactive black rain, "rafts" (*ikada*) made of human corpses, and continuous illness—did not exist in the past, but rather in the present, falling, blocking, and consuming.

Yamaguchi's use of the word *ikada* to describe the scene of the rivers of corpses captured the dehumanizing nature of the bombings. To discuss a raft, something normally made of inanimate objects like wood or other building material, as being made instead of human bodies presents a grotesque and even confusing image, because it disrupts our notion of humanity and the purpose of bodies—the humans whom Yamaguchi saw floating before him in the two cities had been reduced to material akin to logs. Other *hibakusha* poets wrote of the scene of rivers clogged with bodies more literally. Setoguchi Chie, for example, wrote of how "hundreds of corpses dammed up the water of the Urakami River."[60] Setoguchi's poem draws a harrowing scene of the destruction, too, but her poetry stops short of reducing the dead to dehumanized objects such as raft wood. In her *tanka*, the dead maintain their humanity as corpses, even amid the unprecedented destruction. On the other hand, Yamaguchi's choice of words captures the dehumanization lurking within the scene: the dead have lost their humanity and have become *ikada*.

For Yamaguchi, the landscapes and rivers of both cities that were littered and clogged with corpses psychologically traumatized him, but the trauma went beyond his own experience. The trauma of the atomic bombings was both a personal and a collective one.

> Where has it gone,
> the dignity of humans as being humans?
> It lies destroyed and ruined . . .
> corpses in the atomic field . . . [61]

The mass death represented the collective trauma of the loss of humanity.

Various scenes he witnessed in the two cities marked a variety of traumatic moments for Yamaguchi.

> Intending not to step on
> half-burned corpses
> I stepped over them
> and saw boiled thoraxes.
> Their guts
> were yellow tinges.[62]

Scenes such as this stayed vivid and present in Yamaguchi's mind for the rest of his life: he was unable to suppress them no matter how hard he tried. The trauma of seeing guts spilled out from torn torsos, with yellow tinges of fat intermixed, prevented Yamaguchi from watching fish being prepared for a meal because the gutting process reminded him of what he had witnessed in Hiroshima and Nagasaki.[63] In Hiroshima, Yamaguchi walked by a train near ground zero:

> I will never forget
> the charcoaled bodies,
> the corpses sitting I met
> on the train tracks after
> Hiroshima's atomic death.[64]

More revealing of the trauma, perhaps, was that, similar to the scene of torn torsos, the kind of scene captured here helps explain how such traumatic memories prevented him from eating grilled fish. The smell reminded him of burned human flesh.[65] In other poems, Yamaguchi committed to verse the trauma of seeing bodies that were "burned black as coal" (some survivors have used the term "carbonized" to describe such corpses). Yamaguchi writes:

> Burned black as coal
> countless rise, dead souls
> in the dead of night
> from the atomic bombing *mandala*.
>
> They are piled atop one another high.
> And the ground will never dry.
> It is soaked with the fat of all the people
> who burned and died.[66]

Yamaguchi and Yamada both recall the charred corpses that littered the landscapes of Hiroshima and Nagasaki in their poetry, because for them the bodies are not in the past. For Yamaguchi, the ground that was "soaked with the fat" of the corpses would never dry because the traumatic moment never ended in his mind.

Reading his poetry out loud added a layer to Yamaguchi's expression of trauma. He would sometimes read his poems to an audience, or to a filmmaker, especially in his later years, when he became an activist in the antinuclear weapons movement. When he did read his poems out loud, though, he did not simply recite the text. Rather, his reading became an act of working through. When Yamaguchi recited his *tanka* more than six decades after the bombings, emotion still overcame him as the past became palpable once again, choking him with tears.⁶⁷ Often, his words ceased and he only continued once he had regained his composure, usually continuing in a tearful and pained voice. In other words, Yamaguchi's traumatic memory manifested physically. For Yamaguchi and other *hibakusha*, accessing the traumatic memory ruptured the apparent calm of the present, not because it brought the survivor back into the past, but because it brought the past into the present.

Yamaguchi Tsutomu's poems challenge the assertion of Yamada Kan that the atomic bombing had "extinguished" the spirit of poetry in Nagasaki. The atomic bombings had indeed ruptured the poetic tradition, because the subject of traditional forms of Japanese poetry had been replaced with trauma, but it did not extinguish it. Indeed, it was Yamaguchi's place in the poetic tradition that became, perhaps, his salvation from the darkness of so many traumatic memories. The significance of his poetry goes beyond his own salvation, in fact, because it also provides something not found in the works of other *hibakusha* poets: Yamaguchi's work represents a bridge between the experiences of Hiroshima and Nagasaki. For Yamaguchi, there existed no "Hiroshima atomic-bombing literature" versus "Nagasaki atomic-bombing literature." For him there was only the horror that all *hibakusha* witnessed. In other words, there was no point in distinguishing the political and historical differences of the two cities, their reconstruction, and their memory, because in both cities he witnessed rafts made of human corpses and the destruction of humanity.

In 1917, amid the trenches of the First World War and the physical destruction of industrialized warfare, Alan Seeger (1888–1916) wrote a poem that captured the atmosphere of impending doom:

> I have a rendezvous with Death
> At some disputed barricade,
> When Spring comes back with rustling shade
> And apple-blossoms fill the air—
> I have a rendezvous with Death
> When Spring brings back blue days and fair.
>
> It may be he shall take my hand
> And lead me into his dark land
> And close my eyes and quench my breath—
> It may be I shall pass him still.
> I have a rendezvous with Death

On some scarred slope of battered hill,
When Spring comes round again this year
And the first meadow-flowers appear.

God knows 'twere better to be deep
Pillowed in silk and scented down,
Where love throbs out in blissful sleep,
Pulse nigh to pulse, and breath to breath,
Where hushed awakenings are dear . . .
But I've a rendezvous with Death
At midnight in some flaming town,
When Spring trips north again this year,
And I to my pledged word am true,
I shall not fail that rendezvous.

Seeger articulates here one kind of psychological trauma experienced by soldiers: the persistent feeling that death is unavoidable and near. At first Seeger seems to express apprehension, keeping his eye out for Death creeping among the trenches, but it does not frighten him. Rather, he expresses a peaceful resolve to have his fated rendezvous amid the chaos of war, because together with death will come the rebirth and warm days of spring.

Decades later, on the other side of the world and in the context of a different war, Yamaguchi Tsutomu wrote of his experience witnessing both of the atomic bombings in two poems:

I wonder if the radiation
that showered my living frame
that fated second time
will deep throughout my body remain.

When your time's up, you must die.
You've no choice when it is nigh.
Oh how delightful it would be
if death came warm and kind to me.[68]

Yamaguchi speaks of an experience similar to that of Seeger's. After the bombings, Yamaguchi lived the rest of his life worrying that radiation from the bombs remained active in his bones, eating away at his life slowly from the inside. All *hibakusha* shared this anxiety, as seen in the poetry of Yamada Kan as well. Perhaps Yamaguchi was right to worry: he, his wife, and his son all died of cancer. Yet in his poetry he also expresses acquiescence to death, but hoping that when it finally does come, it greets him warmly and kindly, as might the arrival of spring. In short, despite the cultural nuances inherent in their styles of poetry, Yamaguchi and Seeger have both captured the experience of war trauma.

The works of the three *hibakusha* poets discussed here evince overlapping and diverse visions of atomic trauma. Their poetry reveals some of the diversity within the collective of *hibakusha* to be sure, but it also shows how writing of trauma is never easy, because to recall the memory is to relive the traumatic moment. For Yamaguchi Tsutomu, reciting his poetry out loud induced an uncontrollable physical reaction—tears and difficulty speaking—because he accessed the traumatic memory in which rivers were clogged with rafts of corpses. Like Gotō Minako had said of writing her literature of the bomb, Yamaguchi unearthed the "grave" in which he had thought the past had been laid to rest; what he finds becomes too much to bear. His poetry, then, did not simply represent his traumatic memory. Rather, his *tanka* became vessels for the traumatic memories. The radiation-sickened ravens of Yamada Kan's verse haunted him for the rest of his life, but he *chose* to recall them in the hopes of correcting the atomic memory of his city and rescuing the memory of Nagasaki *hibakusha* from oblivion. Nagai spoke in support of a group of *hibakusha*, too, but his interpretations did not translate beyond the Urakami Catholic community for whom he spoke. The sacrificial lambs of Nagai's prose and verse comforted many of the Catholic *hibakusha*, but they also threatened the memory of the larger Nagasaki *hibakusha* community. However, each of the survivor-poets, in the end, composed verse to speak of the atomic experience as they understood it.

The Nagasaki *hibakusha* composed poetry to give meaning to their experience, whether it meant God's Providence or the past and potential destruction of humanity. They laid claim to popular memory, challenging notions of passivity in the face of Hiroshima dominance and criticism. And they have conveyed the terrifying realities of atomic and nuclear weapons. Yet, whether the poet spoke of sacrificial lambs, ravens of death, or rafts of corpses, the cathartic nature of poetic composition allowed him to identify, isolate, and attempt to work through the trauma. Indeed, for each of the authors discussed here, the ability to articulate their trauma through the vocabulary of poetry empowered them to give voice to an experience of trauma and survival that defies conventional linguistic expression. Even if many survivors have given voice to their experience through poetry and have chosen to bear witness in this way, the traumatic memories have never calmed, and they do not exist in the past. The *hibakusha* poets of both Nagasaki and Hiroshima have left us with a body of verse through which we, as readers, scholars, or memory activists, can attempt to better understand the atomic bombings as historical events, as well as the nature of trauma more generally.

Notes

1. The term *hibakusha* literally means "person/people who has/have experienced an explosion," and is sometimes written with a different "*baku*" to mean "a person who has experienced or been exposed to a flash [of radiation]." In the context of the history of the atomic bombings, the term *hibakusha* is generally used to mean "survivors of the atomic bombings" but can also include those who died as a result of the bombings, including from the radiation. In the context of the antinuclear peace movement in Japan beginning from the 1950s, *hibakusha* can also refer specifically to survivors who became peace activists. The term appeared in discussions of the bombings immediately after the war, but it did not become widely used until the late 1950s, so its usage here to refer to survivors in the late 1940s and early 1950s is somewhat anachronistic. Even so, I use the term here to generally mean "survivor/s of the bombings." For perhaps the best book in English on the psychological trauma of the *hibakusha*, see Lifton, *Death in Life: Survivors of Hiroshima* (New York: Random House, 1967). As his subtitle suggests, however, Lifton's study focuses on the survivors of Hiroshima, not Nagasaki.

2. As quoted in John Whittier Treat, *Writing Ground Zero: Japanese Literature and the Atomic Bomb* (Chicago: University of Chicago Press, 1996), 29.

3. One example is the journal *Shūkan asahi*, which published a special on August 7, 1949, entitled, "*Nō moa Hiroshimazu*" (No More Hiroshimas). The publication mentioned Nagasaki only once in passing in a single article. A separate special edition of the journal on "*Nō moa Nagasakizu*" was never published.

4. Literally, "Hiroshima of rage, Nagasaki of prayer." The translation used here, "Hiroshima rages, Nagasaki prays," is borrowed from Treat, *Writing Ground Zero*, 301.

5. For discussion of Nagasaki as an "inferior atomic-bombed city" (*rettō hibaku toshi*), see Takahashi Shinji, *Nagasaki ni atte tetsugaku suru: Kakujidai no shi to sei* (Philosophizing in Nagasaki: Death and Life in the Nuclear Age) (Tokyo: Hokuju shuppan, 1994), 193.

6. Cathy Caruth, *Unclaimed Experience: Trauma, Narrative, and History* (Baltimore: Johns Hopkins University Press, 1996), 4. Emphasis in original.

7. Dominick LaCapra, *History and Memory after Auschwitz* (Ithaca, NY: Cornell University Press, 1998), 9.

8. Tanaka Toshihiro, "Nagasaki no genbaku bungaku: shisōteki shinka e no jikan" (Nagasaki Atomic-Bombing Literature: Time for an Ideological Deepening),

in *Nagasaki kara heiwagaku suru!* (Doing Peace Studies from Nagasaki), ed. Takahashi Shinji and Funakoe Kōichi (Kyoto: Hōritsu bunka sha, 2009), 82.

9. Committee for the Compilation of Materials on Damage Caused by the Atomic Bombs in Hiroshima and Nagasaki, *Hiroshima and Nagasaki: The Physical, Medical, and Social Effects of the Atomic Bombings*, trans. Eisei Ishikawa and David L. Swain (New York: Basic Books, 1981), 420.

10. Ishikawa and Swain, *Hiroshima and Nagasaki*, 420.

11. See "Genten no kokuhatsu: Genbaku kara 25 nen" (Original Accusation: Twenty-Five Years since the Atomic Bombing) *Mainichi Shinbun*, August 1, 1970, 14.

12. Ishikawa and Swain, *Hiroshima and Nagasaki*, 13–14.

13. See Chad R. Diehl, "Envisioning Nagasaki: From 'Atomic Wasteland' to 'International Cultural City,' 1945–1950," *Urban History*, 41, no. 3 (2014): 497–516.

14. Kamata Sadao, "Nagasaki no ikari to inori" (The Rage and Prayer of Nagasaki), in *Nihon no genbaku bungaku* (Atomic-Bombing Literature of Japan) 15 (Tokyo: Horupu shuppan, 1983): 413.

15. Ishikawa and Swain, *Hiroshima and Nagasaki*, 605.

16. *Chinmoku no kabe o yabutte* (Breaking Down the Walls of Silence), ed. Nagasaki Hibaku Kyōshi no Kai (Rōdō Shunhō Sha, 1970), 17–18. All translations are my own, unless otherwise noted.

17. Nagai Takashi, "Genshi bakudan shisha gōdō sō chōji" (Eulogy for the Joint Funeral for Those Who Died in the Atomic Bombing), delivered on November 23, 1945. Manuscript preserved at the Nagasaki City Nagai Takashi Memorial Museum, Nagasaki, Japan.

18. "Dai sankai shuppan yoron chōsa" (Third Public Opinion Poll on Publications), *Mainichi Shinbun*, October 26, 1949, 4.

19. *Kami to genbaku: Urakami katorikku hibakusha no 55 nen* (God and the Atomic Bomb: 55 Years of the Urakami Catholic Hibakusha), prod. NBC Nagasaki hōsō, 2000.

20. Kamata, "Nagasaki no ikari to inori," 409.

21. Treat, *Writing Ground Zero*, 159. Tanaka Kishirō's poem, quoted here, appears on the same page.

22. Mark Freeman, "Telling Stories: Memory and Narrative," *Memory: Histories, Theories, Debates*, ed. Susannah Radstone and Bill Schwarz (New York: Fordham University Press, 2010), 276.

23. Treat, *Writing Ground Zero*, 155–157.

24. John Whittier Treat, "Early Hiroshima Poetry," *Journal of the Association of Teachers of Japanese* 20, no. 2 (1986): 214.

25. Treat, *Writing Ground Zero*, 60.

26. Ibid., 160.

27. Ibid., 163.

28. Caruth, *Unclaimed Experience*, 11.

29. See, for example, LaCapra, *History and Memory after Auschwitz*, 182.

30. For a detailed biography on Nagai, see, for example, Diehl, *Resurrecting Nagasaki*, ch. 3.

31. This is not a literal translation. My translation is based on Nagai's own explanation of the poem: see, Kataoka Chizuko and Kataoka Rumiko, *Hibakuchi Nagasaki no saiken* (The Reconstruction of the Atomic-Bombed Land of Nagasaki) (Nagasaki: Nagasaki Junshin Daigaku hakubutsukan, 1996), 108. The original poem in Japanese is: *Hansai no/hono'o no naka ni/utaitsutsu/shirayuri otome/moenikeru kamo* (In the flames of holocaust, singing, white lily maidens, burned).

32. Giorgio Agamben, *Remnants of Auschwitz: The Witness and the Archive* (New York: Zone Books, 1999), 29.

33. H. H. Gerth and C. Wright Mills, eds., *From Max Weber: Essays in Sociology*, (New York: Oxford University Press, 1946), 275, 285.

34. From *Nagai Takashi zenshū* (The Complete Works of Nagai Takashi), ed. Nagai Tokusaburō (Tokyo: San Paolo, 2003), 3:536–537. The term *genshino* (also *genshiya*) is sometimes translated as "atomic wasteland," but here Nagai means the general condition of the bombed-out area of Urakami, especially considering the context of late 1945.

35. "Genbaku yonshūnen" (The Fourth Anniversary of the Atomic Bombing), *Katorikkukyō hō* (Catholicism Bulletin), August 15, 1948, 1.

36. "Iezusu no seishin" (The Sacred Heart of Jesus), *Katorikkukyō hō*, July 15, 1948, 6.

37. Kamata, "Nagasaki no ikari to inori," 411.

38. This is not to suggest that all Urakami Catholic writers avoided "rage" or graphic mentions of the scenes they witnessed. Takeyama Hiroshi, for example, was a Catholic tanka poet who, starting in the 1950s, published work in journals relating the horror of the bombing; he would begin releasing his own poetry collections from 1981.

39. Kamata, "Nagasaki no ikari to inori," 411–416.

40. Kamata Sadao, "Genbaku taiken no keishō to kokumin kyōiku e no tenbō," in Nagasaki Hibaku Kyōshi no Kai, *Chinmoku no kabe o yabutte*, 192–193.

41. As quoted in Kamata, "Nagasaki no ikari to inori," 415.

42. Kamata, "Nagasaki no ikari to inori," 409.

43. "Kioku no koshitsu: Yamada Kan shi ni kiku" (Persistence of Memory: In Conversation with Yamada Kan), editors' interview with Yamada Kan, *Josetsu XIX* (Fukuoka: Kashoin, August 9, 1999), 58–59.

44. As quoted in Treat, *Writing Ground Zero*, 58. The roman "waka" and "haiku" is in the original.

45. "Kioku no koshitsu," 66–67.

46. Yamada Kan, "Gizensha: Nagai Takashi e no kokuhatsu" (Hypocrite: The Indictment of Nagai Takashi], *Ushio*, July 1972, 231–232.

47. Shinji, *Nagasaki ni atte tetsugaku suru*, 194.

48. "Kioku no koshitsu," 66–67.

49. Ibid., 57.

50. Ibid., 61.

51. The change in tense is in the original: *shita*.

52. This is only half of the poem: see Ienaga Saburō et al., eds., *Nihon no genbaku kiroku* (Record of the Atomic Bombing of Japan) (Tokyo: Nihon tosho sentā, 1991), 20:178.

53. The phrase can be read "*hakketsu no fun*" or "*shirachi no fun*," a play on words through which Yamada was conveying a double meaning. I have put both meanings in the translation.

54. Ienaga, *Nihon no genbaku kiroku*, 20:200–201.

55. "Kioku no koshitsu," 63.

56. See Chad R. Diehl, *And the River Flowed as a Raft of Corpses* (New York: Excogitating Over Coffee Publishing, 2010), 7–11, 128n20.

57. Yamaguchi Tsutomu, *Hiroshima—Nagasaki: Nijū hibaku* (Hiroshima, Nagasaki: Doubly Atomic-Bombed] (Tokyo: Asahi Shimbun Publications, 2009), 112–115.

58. Yamaguchi Tsutomu, *Ningen ikada* (Human Raft] (Nagasaki: Asunaro sha, 2002).

59. Diehl, *And the River Flowed*, 29, 30.

60. See, e.g., Setoguchi Chie, "Keroido no kao" (A Face of Keloid Scars), in *Genbaku kashū Nagasaki* (Nagasaki Collection of Atomic-Bombing Poetry), ed. Nagasaki kajin kai (Nagasaki Association of Tanka Poets) (Nagasaki: Nagasaki kajin kai, 1967), 72.

61. Diehl, *And the River Flowed*, 77.

62. Ibid., 37.

63. Ibid., 126n4.

64. Ibid., 42.

65. Ibid., 126n4.

66. Ibid., 35–36. See 126n3 for discussion of the significance of *mandala*.

67. One particularly powerful moment of Yamaguchi reciting his poetry can be seen in the documentary, *Nijū hibaku II* (Doubly Atomic-Bombed 2), dir. Inazuka Hidetaka (Takiseeds, 2011). This moment from the film currently appears as a clip on my Youtube page, available with permission from the filmmaker at https://youtu.be/wGqJg2TP8LI.

68. Diehl, *And the River Flowed*, 50, 113.

Listening to the Dead and Filling the Void
The Prayer and Activism of Akizuki Tatsuichirō

By Maika Nakao

The phrase "Hiroshima rages, Nagasaki prays" was used to describe the symbolic difference between the two cities that were subjected to the atomic bombings. As defined in this way, Nagasaki has been regarded as a rather silent city in terms of expressing anger about the atomic bombing. This image of Nagasaki comes, in part, from the interpretation of the bombing as an Urakami Christian tragedy, as exemplified by Nagai Takashi's writing. Chad Diehl describes this as a "Christian image of ground zero" that helped create "walls of silence" in Nagasaki that the *hibakusha* began confronting from around 1970.[1] It was not until after a quarter century had passed that Nagasaki's citizens stood up to raise their own voices to represent the atomic experience as they lived it, such as by publishing a collection of accounts of the atomic bombing, the *Nagasaki no shōgen* (Testimonies of Nagasaki). They also worked on a campaign to reimagine the meaning of ground zero, which included a cartography project that sought to revive and preserve atomic-bombing memory by reconstructing the area near ground zero as a so-called hypocenter map. These movements can be seen as a departure from the image of "prayer" to one of more concrete activism. However, prayer and activism were not always separate categories of memory work within the city, and in some cases they proceeded in close relationship.

Akizuki Tatsuichirō (1916–2005) was a physician who experienced the atomic bombing of Nagasaki on August 9, 1945, and became a lifelong peace activist in the city. Akizuki experienced the bombing while working at Urakami First Hospital, a three-story concrete building approximately 1,530 yards (1.4 km) from the hypocenter. In an effort to convey the tragic experience of the atomic bombing, he published several books, including *Nagasaki genbaku ki: Hibaku ishi no shōgen* (An Account of the Nagasaki Atomic Bombing: Testimony of an Atomic-Bombed Doctor, 1966),[2] *Shi no dō shin'en:*

Nagasaki hibaku ishi no kiroku (Concentric Circles of Death: A Record of a Nagasaki Atomic-Bombed Doctor, 1972), and *"Genbaku" to sanjūnen* (The "Atomic Bombing" and the Thirty Years Since, 1975).

Akizuki was also involved in several activist movements in Nagasaki, contributing to the work of the activist groups from the stance of a physician who had experienced the bombing. He was one of the founding members of the testimonial campaign and the project to create the so-called hypocenter map around 1970. He was actively involved in the *hibakusha* activist groups of the city, as well as the worldwide campaign for the abolition of nuclear weapons, contributing to various fields related to atomic-bombing memory and peace activism, including serving as a member of the Nagasaki Council of Atomic Bomb Survivors, the Nagasaki Atomic Bomb Documentation Council, and the Drafting Committee for the Peace Declaration; the chairman of the Nagasaki Testimony Association, the Nyoko Association, and the Nagasaki Peace Promotion Association; and executive board member of the Nagasaki branch of the International Physicians for the Prevention of Nuclear War (IPPNW). For these activities he received the Nagasaki Medical Association Award, the Japan Medical Association's Highest Distinguished Service Award, the Nishi-Nippon Culture Award, the Yoshikawa Eiji Culture Award, the Asahi Prize, the Order of St. Sylvester, and the Order of the Sacred Treasure. He also received the Nagai Takashi Peace Memorial Nagasaki Prize as its first recipient.

In many ways, Akizuki became the successor of Nagai Takashi, who had died in 1951. Akizuki served as a leader of peace activism, and, like Nagai, became a spiritual leader. While Nagai became a spiritual pillar who comforted the Urakami Catholics after the destruction of the bombing, Akizuki became a spiritual pillar who helped survivors confront their trauma and voice their own memory and viewpoints, often in contrast to the religious interpretation of Nagai that had become the best-known narrative within and outside the city. Takahashi Shinji writes, "It can be summed up that since 1966, when *Nagasaki genbaku ki* was published, the thought-work of Akizuki Tatsuichirō, who criticized Nagai Takashi and his 'Urakami Holocaust Theory' [*Urakami hansai setsu*], had been encouraging a new way of thinking in the atomic-bombed city of Nagasaki. The *Testimonies of Nagasaki* movement, which was eventually launched, has undergone several changes and continues to this day, but we can always count on Akizuki Tatsuichirō to lead the way."[3] As Takahashi has written, to understand Nagasaki, we must connect the work of Nagai with the work of Akizuki.[4]

Akizuki's Experience of the Atomic Bombing

Born in Nagasaki City in 1916, Akizuki studied at Nagasaki Junior High School, Saga High School, and the Kyoto Imperial University School of Medicine. After graduating from the last in 1940, Akizuki returned to Nagasaki as a doctor. He sympathized with local tuberculosis doctor Takahara Ken's construction of a tuberculosis sanatorium that linked Buddhism and modern medicine and decided to live as a town doctor. However, the sanatorium was having difficulty securing land, and on Dr. Takahara's recommendation, Akizuki was offered a position as an assistant in the Radiology Department of Nagasaki Medical College, later part of Nagasaki University. Here he became the first understudy of Dr. Nagai Takashi, who had recently returned from serving in China as a field medic during the Second Sino-Japanese War. Akizuki later recalled, "The cheerful Dr. Nagai and my gloomy self didn't really get along, and I looked at his research with a cold stare."[5] Elsewhere he remembered, "Dr. Nagai's extroverted Catholic love for humanity and my introverted Buddhist outlook on life did not match well. I studied radiology only as a tuberculosis physician. In fact, I even tended to look at Dr. Nagai's poetic sentiments and love for humanity and neighbors coldly."[6] Neither Nagai nor the university's medical school suited Akizuki.

After about a year, Akizuki quit the medical school and worked at the Takahara Clinic. Through overexertion, he contracted tuberculosis in 1943, and during his three months in the hospital he read a book called *New Nutrition* by Sakurazawa Nyoichi (George Osawa), which resonated with him.[7] The book criticized the Western medical theory of nutrition that animal protein was good and recommended eating brown rice, sesame salt, miso, hijiki, and burdock. Inspired by Sakurazawa's claim, Akizuki came up with the Akizuki-style nutritional theory of eating mainly wakame seaweed miso soup, root vegetables, carrots, burdock roots, small beans, and soba noodles. He said that he had "no scientific basis, but something like confidence that my illness could be cured by this method."[8] After regaining his health, Akizuki joined the Forty-Eighth Infantry Regiment in Kurume as a reserve army physician in the summer of 1944. When he returned to Nagasaki after a month of training, he was asked by Dr. Takahara to work at Urakami First Hospital as chief physician. He was certain that he would be called up as a military doctor at the time, but the results of his medical examination showed that he had pleurisy, so he was exempted from serving in the war. In March 1945, the Order of Friars Minor (Franciscan) opened Urakami First Hospital at St. Francis Seminary as a tuberculosis sanatorium.

It was August 8, 1945, when Akizuki heard about the devastation of Hiroshima. On that day, Dr. Tsunoo Susumu, president of the Nagasaki Medical College, had witnessed the devastation of Hiroshima on his way back from Tokyo. He informed the university staff and students gathered in the schoolyard about the atomic bomb that had been dropped on Hiroshima. Akizuki and the others were surprised and filled with anxiety when they heard about it from a student at the medical school who was staying at Urakami First Hospital. An atomic bomb was dropped on Nagasaki the next day.

When the atomic bomb detonated, Akizuki was treating a pneumothorax patient in the St. Francis Seminary tuberculosis sanatorium. The moment he inserted the pneumothorax needle into the patient's chest, he heard a loud noise, and with a flash of light and a roar, a violent shockwave hit the hospital. Cupboards collapsed, windowpanes were blown out, and a white cloud of dust filled the room. When Akizuki looked out the window, the sky was covered with black clouds, and the houses were engulfed in flames. Seeing this scene, he remembered what he had heard the day before about Hiroshima: "A new-type bomb!" he shouted and shuddered. The explosion of the atomic bomb set the roof of Urakami First Hospital on fire, which was located approximately 1,530 yards (1,400 m) from the hypocenter, and from there the fire spread throughout the hospital. The hospital staff carried the patients out of the building, and everyone in the hospital managed to survive.

People who had been exposed to the atomic bomb gradually gathered at the hospital to seek help. Akizuki later wrote: "They were all in a state of disarray, moaning, 'Hot . . .' 'Water . . .' 'Help . . .' Half-naked or near-naked people were groaning strangely from the depths of their stomachs, or from the depths of hell. They were white and expressionless, like masks. I had the illusion of seeing the procession of the dead that I had seen as a child, dressed in white and moving slowly in one direction."[9] As the afternoon wore on, the appearance of the people gathering at the hospital changed, and people with darker skin began to gather there. With the hospital facilities burned down, hospital staff were at their wits' end, applying oil to patients' burns. The hospital staff cremated and mourned many of the dead while treating patients. In a simple crematorium built in the hospital yard with three pieces of tin, the doctors and nurses at the hospital continued to burn corpses for two or three months after the bombing with the fear that this might happen to them tomorrow. Despite the loss of all his equipment in the bombing, Akizuki continued to treat patients, seemingly without end, an experience that later shaped his thoughts on activism. His colleagues also worked without a break.

The hospital, destroyed by the atomic bomb, was gradually rebuilt, and St. Francis Clinic opened in November 1945 amid the ruins. The clinic was a source of strength for the recovery efforts and gave hope to the people living around it. In the spring of 1947 a new hospital building was completed in a field next to a damaged hospital, with twenty-five hospital beds, an examination room, and a priest's residence. The new building was called Pruden House and was completed through the efforts of Father Pruden and other atomic-bombing survivors from the Urakami and Motohara churches. Akizuki was amazed at the strength of the Catholic spirit in the construction of the Pruden House, and after seeing its completion, he felt exhausted both physically and emotionally and decided to quit the hospital and live in the surrounding mountains. He explained that first he wanted to abandon the war-disaster mentality, in which a life of hardship was the norm. Second, because of the conflict between modern medicine and the holistic treatments he believed in, he wanted to try mineral therapy again within nature. Third, he felt uncomfortable being in Urakami, which was becoming increasingly colored as a religious center, and he was not a Christian.[10] Last, according to his wife, who had worked with Akizuki at the hospital before getting married, after experiencing the atomic bombing, he no longer desired material things or social prestige and came to think that it would be better if he could live a quiet life with coarse clothes and a modest diet.[11]

In March 1948 Akizuki quit the hospital and began living in a charcoal-burning hut deep in the mountains in Yōkō. There Akizuki began to write a record of his experience of the atomic bombing. The article, "A Week Covered in Blood," which recorded the devastation caused by the atomic bombing and the work of his colleagues in providing relief during the week between August 9 and the end of the war on August 15, was published in the women's monthly magazine *Shufu no tomo* (A Housewife's Friend). Energized by life in the mountains, he also began writing a book on nutritional theory. However, his reputation as a good physician spread, and patients began to flock to his hut every day, which interrupted his writing. The villagers began to build a house for him and recommended that he get married. Akizuki was convinced that the only person who could work with him as a marriage partner was Sugako, a nurse with whom he worked at the hospital, and he asked her to marry him. At the end of 1948, they had their wedding ceremony and began to live together in Yōkō.

In the spring of 1952, after a relapse of asthma and tuberculosis, Akizuki left Yōkō, where he had lived for four years, and returned to St. Francis Hospital (the former Urakami First Hospital) to work and treat himself. Akizuki, who was Buddhist at the time, engaged in lengthy discussions of theology with the Catholics at the hospital, who encouraged him to convert to Catholicism. In October 1953, Akizuki was baptized as a Catholic. He stated that part of the reason for his conversion was that he recognized that "it was just the replacement of prayers to Amitabha Buddha with prayers to our Father in heaven."[12] In other words, through the experience of the atomic bombings and his series of discussions with Christian believers, Akizuki came to believe that Buddhism and Christianity were not so different. Becoming a Christian did not mean that Akizuki abandoned Buddhism. He lived the rest of his life with an eclectic mix of both religions. As seen in his later writings, Akizuki continued to believe in and promote Akizuki Mineral Therapy, which he created from his teacher's Buddhist medical ideas. Such eclecticism became an important element in Akizuki's work to fill in the voids of the history of the atomic bombing.

Testimonies of Nagasaki

The publication of the *Testimonies of Nagasaki* beginning in 1969 was a landmark moment when the *hibakusha* of Nagasaki began to publish their experiences of the atomic bombing. Of course, people had been writing about their experiences before then, but they were few in number, and not the large movement that has continued to this day. Akizuki was one of those deeply involved in this activity, especially in its initiation.

Many citizen groups formed to document both the traumatic memory of the bombing and the postwar daily life of *hibakusha* in Nagasaki. The Nagasaki Life Writing Group (Nagasaki seikatsu o tsuzuru kai) had been active for some time. Kamata Sadao, who was assigned to the College of Naval Architecture of Nagasaki (later the Nagasaki Institute of Applied Science) as an assistant professor in 1962, conceived of the Nagasaki Atomic Bomb Record Society (Nagasaki genbaku kiroku no kai). Along with them, the citizen movement of the Nagasaki Constitutional Council (Nagasaki kenpō kaigi), which began in 1965, the Movement to Protect the Lives and Human Rights of Hibakusha (Hibakusha no seikatsu to jinken o mamoru undō), and the movement of the Citizens Group for the White Paper on the Atomic Bombing (Genbaku hakusho o susumeru shimin no kai), were active in the 1960s. A report on atomic-bomb survivors in Nagasaki, "Twenty-Three Years since That Day: The Actual Conditions and Demands of the Atomic Bombing Survivors," was launched in the spring of 1968 in response to the White Paper on the Atomic Bombing by the Ministry of Health and Welfare, which had stated that "there is no significant disparity between the general population and the atomic bombing survivors in terms of both health and living conditions."[13] *Testimonies of Nagasaki* was published as a comprehensive collection of testimonies by *hibakusha* speaking of their personal trauma of the atomic bombing and their continued suffering as a group, in part in reaction to the national government's erroneous claims about their health and conditions.

The activists began working to improve the lives of the *hibakusha* by bringing attention to their plight with publications beginning in the late 1960s. In August 1968, based on a month-long survey of *hibakusha*, they published "Twenty-Three Years since That Day." In August 1969, they published *Nagasaki no shōgen: Sensō to genbaku no taiken o mitsume shōgen suru Nagasaki no koe* (Testimonies of Nagasaki: Voices of Nagasaki That Look at and Testify to the Experience of War and the Atomic Bombing). In August 1970, they published the *Nagasaki no shōgen* (Testimonies of Nagasaki 1970). In March 1971, in order to further deepen, expand, and maintain the movement, the Nagasaki Testimony Association was established as a volunteer citizens' organization for testimony and essays concerned with the atomic bombing and peace. Over the summer of that year, the group was involved in the publication of *Testimonies of Nagasaki 1971*, Tagawa Seikō's book *Hono'o no naka kara: Hibaku eiseihei no shōgen* (From the Flames: A Medic's Testimony), and Yamada Kan's poetry collection *Nagasaki: Fushoku suru rekijitsu no soko de* (Nagasaki: In the Depths of Decaying Calendar Days), as well as other projects.

As this publication history suggests, documenting the testimonies meant not merely gathering the voices and memories but also participating in the antinuclear peace movement itself. The preface of the *Testimonies of Nagasaki 1970* declares,

> We hope that these "testimonies," in which people of various ideologies and beliefs came together for the repose of the souls of the dead, solidarity, and the rejection of the atomic bombings and nuclear weapons, will be passed on to 1971, and that its depth and breadth will continue to grow. Readers, let us enter together into the blind spot [*anten*] of the history of twenty-five years ago. Let us together ascertain what of the original experience has endured for a quarter of a century, and what is the essence of the anti-atomic-bomb consciousness that has been achieved through the last quarter of a century.[14]

Akizuki explained that what the activists who carried out the testimonial campaign had in mind was to re-create the dark hellscape of the immediate aftermath of the bombing to shed light on the reality of the atomic bomb twenty-five years later. In the first volume of *Testimonies of Nagasaki* of 1969, he wrote, "It is our duty to tell the reality of the atomic bombing. . . .

We, the people of Nagasaki, do not talk about the Nagasaki experience too much. We must talk a lot about it. It is our duty to talk about it. It is our duty to mankind."[15]

For Akizuki, the testimonies were a scientific resource. He wrote, "More than twenty years after the war, people are talking about the 'fading' and 'burial' of [the memory of] the atomic bombings. I believe that the damage caused by the atomic bombing of Nagasaki was a 'void' (*kūhaku*, lit. blank) from the beginning."[16] He also noted elsewhere:

> Seiji Kaya's preface to the photo book *The Atomic Bombing* (published by the Nishina Foundation) states, "In order to make the atomic bombings of Hiroshima and Nagasaki last, it is important to have a scientific record." I agree with him in the sense that "testimony" must be a scientific record. The question is what to do with science. The testimony is material. Listening is also a part of science. What we can do is to "testify" to what we remember, even if it is only a little, and that is important.[17]

In other words, Akizuki thought that only the testimony of the *hibakusha* could fill in the void of knowledge about the human experience of the atomic bombing that seemed beyond the reach of scientific investigation.

The Movement to "Restore the Hypocenter"

There also stood a void that testimony cannot fill. The people in the vicinity of the hypocenter who died immediately could never tell the living of their experience, and there is no other record, testimonial or otherwise, of what happened directly at the hypocenter of the bomb's blast. In that sense, neither scientific investigation nor testimony could fill the void within an 1,100-yard (1,000 m) radius of ground zero. Akizuki called this history's blind spot, writing,

> From now on, I'm going to exclaim that it's not the real bomb, no matter what the records show. In the first week after the bombing, the area 1,000 meters from the hypocenter was beyond the reach of scientific records and research. That is the meaning of the testimony of the atomic-bombing survivors. There are no records, no surveys, and no scientific scalpel has reached the area. Of course, the American military survey team did not arrive until September. After all, there is no other way but for the *hibakusha* to write down what they saw as they searched for a week immediately after the bombing. . . . If we don't fill in the blind spots [*mōten*] of history within a 1,000-meter circumference in the week after August 9, when, and who will

fill them in? If we don't fill it in now, when, and who will? The prosperity and noise of the materials built on top of the blind spot [*mōten*], the scotoma [*anten*] of Nagasaki's history, is irresistibly empty and sad.[18]

The movement to restore the hypocenter map that began in Nagasaki in 1970 was an attempt to fill the blind spot. The movement was enlightened and inspired by a book on the reconstruction of the city, *Genbaku bakushinchi* (The Atomic-Bombing Hypocenter), which had been published in Hiroshima the year before. The work of reconstructing the hypocenter was an attempt to get a complete picture of the damage caused by the atomic bombing using the work of the citizens as a guide. As the book described the project in Hiroshima, "All the *hibakusha* and citizens who are still alive today write down the deaths of their relatives and acquaintances, and each house and alley that is related to them, on a blank map."[19] The project took on a more precise form as a new antinuclear peace movement emerged with the participation of a wide range of citizens, and which emerged in Nagasaki as well.

In Nagasaki, the restoration project began with the Matsuyama and Yamazato districts near the hypocenter and was led by Tsukasa Uchida of Matsuyama and Takatani Shigeharu of Yamazato. With the cooperation of NHK (Japan Broadcasting Corporation), the void, the blank on the map, was unexpectedly filled. The city of Nagasaki had no precise prewar maps and no photographs. Then, through the Atomic Bomb Casualty Commission (ABCC), they were given an aerial photograph of Nagasaki on August 7, 1945. Akizuki was amazed at its precision and accuracy. In addition, they obtained a precise map of the area before it was plotted by the city planning department, and from the memory of those who had survived on the lot number, he wrote down the names of the heads of household.[20]

For those who remained, it was not an objective search but a painful one that involved cutting open, stirring, and healing the wounds in their own hearts. As Akizuki once noted, "Mr. Uchida worked on the restoration with the intention of putting up a gravestone for his family, who were almost completely wiped out, and his only remaining family who were far away."[21] In 1972, he also wrote:

> The Atomic Bomb Relief Law, the Medical Care Act, and the Special Measures Law are gradually becoming more detailed, and medical and pathological research on post-bombing disorders is being carried out. But we feel something empty and sad. In the hearts of those who lost almost all of their family members in the hypocenter area, and only they mysteriously survived, there

is a feeling that, apart from the reconstruction and prosperity of Nagasaki, the lives of these people who were erased and neglected must be written down. Let us restore once again the people who disappeared, the families who disappeared, and the neighbors who were erased. . . . We *hibakusha* have always cried out from the depths of our hearts, from screams of "help" and "water," to demands for "medical treatment" and "fact-finding," to calls to "let's undertake a restoration movement." But our cries only faded into thin air. We searched for the dead and buried them ourselves. Let's look for our dead neighbors ourselves, even now. This was the Nagasaki method of movement to restore that began with the neighbors of Matsuyama and Yamazato towns.[22]

The movement in Nagasaki began by listening to the voices of the survivors and the dead. It was the voices of the dead that moved Akizuki to activism. He explained that the spirits of the dead (*shiryō*) and their grudge compelled him to write. He tried to heal the dead, in a way, by filling in the void of their memory by restoring their place on a map of ground zero. Akizuki's thought and actions to fill in the blanks, so to speak, as well as the memory activism of the numerous other hibakusha and activists with whom he worked, defied the tenet that "Nagasaki prays."

In his life, Akizuki had an experience that drastically changed his view of life and death. He was a doctor, but he was also physically weak, feared tuberculosis and death, questioned modern medicine, and looked to religion for help. Over the course of his life he developed his own way of thought by combining science, experience, and religion. It seems fitting, then, to conclude with his voice through something he wrote in 1972:

It is a peaceful Japan for the time being. It is a world of scientific progress and material prosperity, and it is Japan where associations and temples have been restored in number and grandeur beyond prewar levels. But doesn't religion have the power to stop people from fighting and killing each other, or even to make them stop? Does religion not have the power to bring goodness and peace to the hearts of men, and to make the world of men full of goodness and peace? . . . Religion is not powerless. People do not know God. God is not "silent." God is grieving. I have no other choice but to force myself to think like that.[23]

Notes

1. Chad R. Diehl, *Resurrecting Nagasaki: Reconstruction and the Formation of Atomic Narratives* (Ithaca, NY: Cornell University Press, 2018).

2. *Nagasaki genbaku ki* has been translated into English as *Nagasaki 1945*, trans. Keiichi Nagata, ed. Gordon Honeycombe (London: Quartet Books, 1982).

3. Takahashi Shinji, "Nagasaki genbaku no shisōka o megutte" (On the Ideologization of the Nagasaki Atomic Bombing), *Shakai shisōshi kenkyū* 10 (1986): 33–43, 40–41.

4. Takahashi Shinji, *Nagasaki ni atte tetsugaku suru, 3.11 go no heiwa sekinin* (Philosophizing in Nagasaki: Peace Responsibility after 3.11) (Tokyo: Hokuju shuppan, 2015), 52.

5. Nishino Kenichi, "Ikan henro: Akizuki Tatsuichirō kikigaki" (Medical Observation Pilgrimage: Written Report of Listening to Akizuki Tatsuichirō), *Nishi Nippon Shuppan*, August 6, 1992.

6. Akizuki Tatsuichirō, *Nagasaki genbaku ki* (An Account of the Nagasaki Atomic Bombing) (Kawamata: Nihon Book Ace, 2010), 186.

7. Sakurazawa Nyoichi, *Hakkō ichiu no shokuseikatsu genri: Atarashii eiyōgaku* (Dietary Principle of Universal Brotherhood: New Nutritional Science) (Ōtsu: Musō genri kōkyujo, 1942).

8. Nishino, *Ikan henro*, August 6, 1992.

9. Akizuki, *Nagasaki genbaku ki*, 21–22.

10. Akizuki Tatsuichirō, *Shi no dō shin'en: Nagasaki hibaku ishi no kiroku* (Concentric Circles of Death: A Record of a Nagasaki Atomic-Bombing Physician) (Nagasaki: Nagasaki bunken sha, 2010), 231–232.

11. Yamashita Akiko, *Natsugumo no oka: Hibaku ishi Akizuki Tatsuichirō* (Hill of Summer Clouds: Atomic-Bombing Physician Akizuki Tatsuichirō) (Nagasaki: Nagasaki Shinbun sha, 2006), 35.

12. *Yomiuri Shinbun*, July 30, 1972.

13. "Kenkō chōsa oyobi hibakusha chōsa no gaiyō" (White Paper on the Atomic Bombing), Ministry of Health and Welfare, 1967.

14. "Preface," *Nagasaki no shōgen 1970* (Testimonies of Nagasaki 1970), ed. Akizuki Tatsuichirō and the "Nagasaki no shōgen" kankō i'in kai (Tokyo: Ayumi shuppan sha, 1970), 7.

15. Akizuki Tatsuichirō, "Genbaku hibaku no jittai o kataru koto koso watashitatchi no sekimu" (It Is Our Duty to Speak out about the Reality of the Atomic Bombing), in *Nagasaki no shōgen: Sensō to genbaku no taiken o mitsume shōgen suru Nagasaki no koe* (Testimonies of Nagasaki: Voice of Nagasaki That Looks at and Testifies to the Experience of War and Atomic Bombing) (Nagasaki: Nagasaki shōgen no kai, 1969), 9–10.

16. Akizuki Tatsuichirō, "Thinking about the Atomic Bomb and Science, Education, and Culture (Speech at the 1973 Japanese Scientists Association)," in *"Genbaku" to sanjūnen* (The "Atomic Bombing" and the Thirty Years Since) (Tokyo: Asahi Shinbun sha, 1975), 122.

17. Ibid., 124.

18. Akizuki Tatsuichirō, "Mō ichido ano rekishi no anten no naka e" (Once Again into That Blind Spot of History), *Nagasaki no shōgen 1970*, 13.

19. *Genbaku bakushinchi* (The Atomic-Bombing Hypocenter), ed. Shimizu Kiyoshi (Tokyo: NHK Publishing, 1969), 26.

20. *Asahi Journal*, August 1971.

21. Ibid.

22. *Nagasaki no shōgen 1972* (Testimonies of Nagasaki, 1972) (Nagasaki: Nagasaki shōgen no kai, 1972), 216, 219.

23. *Yomiuri Shinbun*, July 30, 1972.

Breaking New Ground in Nagasaki
Seirai Yūichi's Ground Zero Literature

By Michele M. Mason

For decades, Nagasaki-born Seirai Yūichi (b. 1958) has been offering a vision for and expression of a new form of atomic bomb literature suitable for the turn of the century. Ever cognizant that he is not someone who can speak from direct experience, Seirai makes a case for a genre called "ground zero literature," which stands in contrast to "atomic bomb literature." In his nonfiction writing and literary works, Seirai proposes and manifests this unique perspective, highlighting the many subtle ways the 1945 atomic bombing lives on in the place and people of Nagasaki. His prizewinning novels tie together the city's multifaceted past with contemporary stories of deeply personal pain. These powerful portraits of citizens' lives evoke multiple temporalities on the modern landscape of Nagasaki that reverberate with emotional nuance and a persistent questioning of the meaning of suffering and faith. In doing so, Seirai ensures that uncomfortable truths that otherwise could go unnoticed or relegated to history do not perish with the aging survivors.

A second-generation *hibakusha* (atomic bombing survivor) and a long-time public servant of Nagasaki's municipal government, Seirai has spoken publicly of his "sense of duty" to grapple with and depict the manifold truths of his city. His public service and literature are, in fact, two facets of his life-long activism, each informing the other. In 2010, he took the position of director of the Nagasaki Atomic Bomb Museum. In this post he not only oversaw the preservation of an impressive repository of documents and material artifacts, but he also maintained the invaluable public exhibition space visited by millions each year. Seirai's duties extended to advocacy, outreach, and the support of research through the museum's library that help concretize the many experiences and ramifications of the U.S. bombing of Nagasaki. He is also involved in the Research Center for Nuclear Weapons

Abolition (RECNA), a think tank located within Nagasaki University. Seirai has acknowledged that opportunities through his civil posts—both ordinary and singular—have presented him with "hints" for his writing. These range from meeting with Nagasaki citizens and learning of their lives to preserving the sixteenth-century, distinctly Christian "flower cross" roof tiles found in a dig in the center of Nagasaki.

Despite the many demands on his time, since the 1990s, Seirai has managed to steal precious minutes or hours to devote to his writing. In his early years as a writer, Seirai produced a number of powerful short pieces. "The Cross of Jeronimo" (Jeronimo no jūjika, 1995), which was released in the year of the fiftieth anniversary of the atomic bombings, was his first work to garner attention on the literary scene. It won Bungakukai's New Writer Prize, marking his promise. In 2001, he published *Holy Water* (*Seisui*), for which he earned the coveted Akutagawa Prize. Not long after being appointed the head of Nagasaki City's Peace Promotion Office in 2005, *Ground Zero, Nagasaki* (*Bakushin*, 2006) was published and met with critical acclaim, confirmed by both the Itō Sei and Tanizaki Jun'ichirō awards.[1] *Ground Zero, Nagasaki* received a second consideration in 2013 when a film version, titled *Ground Zero: The Sky of Nagasaki* (*Bakushin: Nagasaki no sora*, dir. Hyūgaji Tarō), came out in theaters. Seirai continues to publish at an impressive pace. Some recent works turn to personal reflection and commentary, for example, *Between Sadness and Nothingness* (*Kanashimi to mu no aida*, 2015) and *Little Finger Burning* (*Koyubi ga moeru*, 2017), the latter paying homage to two formidable literary figures, Endō Shūsaku and Hayashi Kyōko.

Seirai has always been cognizant that he needs to carve out an ethical literary approach that honors the survivors' singular experience while addressing the continued significance of his city's history. Unable to approach the task with firsthand knowledge, he takes another tack. "I am merely portraying the memory of the ground of Nagasaki. In Nagasaki, there are a lot of holes that lead to the past, and from here on I want to continue passing through these holes and writing about them."[2] Wrestling with narrative voice and vantage point, Seirai developed a fresh approach to portray the atomic bombing of Nagasaki in the twenty-first century. In *Ground Zero: Nagasaki*, the focus of this essay, he spotlights ordinary citizens occupied by the details of their daily routines. While their lives seem far removed from the horrors of August 1945, the past suddenly becomes palpable, prompted by the most mundane or happenstance occurrences. A random request, casual conversation, or unexpected reminder illuminates a filament of memory, drawing protagonists into the "holes" of which Seirai speaks. It is such moments of overlapping time-space that interrupt otherwise quotidian lives that are at the center of each of the powerful stories in *Ground Zero, Nagasaki*. These are the stakes and strategies that establish Seirai's reasoning for and conceptualization of his innovative approach to writing about the legacies of Nagasaki's atomic bombing.

A notable feature of this new literary niche is the fusion of the distinct connotations of Nagasaki (長崎) and NAGASAKI (ナガサキ). These two renderings of the name of the city—using different scripts—respectively refer to the city of Nagasaki and the atomic event there in 1945. Much of Seirai's professional vocation and literary output carefully thread the needle between the two. In particular, his concerted efforts toward a thoughtful literary approach asks us to recognize that NAGASAKI is not musty history, but one whose presence—subtle but palpable—deeply informs contemporary lives of Nagasaki citizens.

Seirai's strategic play to accomplish this is to spotlight the power of place. In his works, physical space is palpably entangled with fraught present-day emotional landscapes. The place of Nagasaki is inextricably intertwined both with its atomic past and with other pressing historical realities. Memory of place works simultaneously on two levels: Seirai's conceptualization highlights the memory of a place by its inhabitants and also the tangibility, animacy, and realness of memories of places and experiences. This power exerts itself in the ground, trees, rivers, and monuments, tactile entities that range from the mundane to the reverent. Conversely, trauma manifests in a variety of physical objects. A writer for the *Chūgoku Shinbun* newspaper describes Seirai's fluid linking of the physical and psychic worlds: "A hole in an old tree, the air raid shelters remaining throughout Nagasaki, the hollow spaces that nest in peoples' hearts. In his novels, Seirai Yūichi quietly opens up the dark, melancholic hole-like aspects all around us. This is the entrance to a detour that leads us to the past. By traveling this path, the readers touch 'the ground of memories' that sleeps under the thin flooring of the thing we call present day."[3] Blending the warp and weft of postwar material and emotional realities is the signature of Seirai's singular approach to Nagasaki-based fiction.

Reflecting on his own family members' atomic-bomb history and their differing relationships to sharing experiences has been a key aspect of Seirai's authorial process. Both his mother and father were survivors of the 1945 bombing, and his grandfather was a double survivor of both Hiroshima and Nagasaki. In *Between Sadness and Nothingness*, a touching homage to his father after his death in 2009, Seirai relates how each parent approached their memories. On the one hand, his mother would regularly, even casually, share her recollections in daily conversation. On the other hand, his father, even when pressed, would routinely deflect and equivocate.[4] Not surprisingly, some of Seirai's storylines and characters are inspired by his own family's ordeals, which has instilled in him a keen awareness of the thick history that lingers in and adheres to the city of Nagasaki. He writes:

> My aging mother must have been imprisoned by a sense of powerlessness due to the inability to convey [her experience] in any way, no matter how many words piled up. Above all, when attempting to relate the experiences of suffering caused by humanity's unprecedented bombing, already that feeling of inadequacy shadows you, doesn't it? In the background is the everlasting distress over those victims that did not even have the chance to relate their stories. . . . Really who could possibly make the dead speak?[5]

In imagining the *hibakusha* experience, Seirai has sought to emphasize the pain of impotency and insufficiency that robs them of their voices. In facing the troubled ethical ground that nonsurvivors tread, he has had to navigate a way to write what he cannot "know."

This is the crucible in which Seirai has navigated his career as a writer. From the beginning, Seirai has harbored a deep fear of criticism from *hibakusha* of Hiroshima and Nagasaki, which initially made him unable to discern a path forward. However, Hayashi Kyōko (1930–2017), a prominent Nagasaki author who has written numerous semiautobiographical works based on her experiences of the Nagasaki bombing when she was just fourteen years old, strongly urged him to write. After this gracious encouragement, he felt he could break "free from the constraints": "For me, of course, I can't write like Hayashi Kyōko, whose writing is rooted in her own excruciating experience. I think a novel is not just fiction, but rather another reality that is created from words. I want to ask what was the experience of the bomb from this place. I seek to discover even just a fraction of the memory of the bombing, of being attacked in the middle of ordinary life."[6]

To this end, Seirai's nuanced fictional realities are set squarely in the quotidian unspooling of life in the twenty-first century. Whether a survivor or not, each distinct narrator butts up against the inconceivable weight of the atomic bombing through its effects that are made manifest in bodies, mourning, memories, and the material world.

Ground Zero in History

Ground zero, a military term to denote the point on the earth's surface closest to an atomic bomb's detonation, was most powerfully if paradoxically concretized by the instantaneous carbonization and disintegration of countless civilian women, children, and men on two hot August mornings in 1945. The phrase was coined on the occasion of the world's first nuclear detonation, the Trinity test, which was heralded as a scientific success despite Oppenheimer's immediate response through a prescient quote of the Bhagavad Gita: "Now I have become Death, the destroyer of worlds." These disquieting realities stand in stark contrast to the tactless borrowings that have been bandied about since the beginning of the Cold War era, especially in the United States. That the popular hotdog stand located at the center of the Pentagon was nicknamed "Café Ground Zero" highlights the disturbing dissonance of the term's casual use. Films and video games, whose content ranges from technofix fantasies to zombie horror scenarios, have leveraged the term for sensational effect, confirming the growing, if unsettling, malleability of the phrase.[7]

In the twenty-first century, we witnessed the more somber deployment of "ground zero" for the devastated space left after the attack on New York's World Trade Center. This usage highlights the deadly and devastating implications of the term, but it is divorced from any nuclear explosion component. Certainly, no one can deny the tragic loss and trauma of 9/11. At the same time, one must also note the tension in the ongoing U.S. government's stance vis-à-vis nuclear politics; it appropriates the affective response of the term "ground zero" as it also continues to justify the human destruction in Hiroshima and Nagasaki through the discredited narratives that the atomic bombings ended the war.[8] Moreover, as Joseph Gerson demonstrates, the United States has a long record of using and continues to "use" its nuclear arsenal through both veiled and blatant threats to bomb countries in order to maintain economic and military hegemony across the globe.[9] A tension thus arises from the rhetorical manipulations of "ground zero" that expunge the term from its ghastly historical origins while marshaling its sympathies.

In Japan, the term "ground zero," rendered with two characters whose literal meaning is "heart of the explosion" (*bakushin*), has been at the contentious center of a long-fought battle to secure postwar support for survivors. In the immediate postwar years, the *hibakusha* were left to their own devices to fathom treatments for their unprecedented illnesses, address abject poverty in two cities whose infrastructure was completely destroyed, and struggle with widespread discrimination in regard to work and marriage.

While the Japanese government supported military victims of the war and their families, no material help was extended to the *hibakusha*. However, in the wake of the U.S. Bravo hydrogen bomb test on March 1, 1954, in the Marshall Islands, there was a shift in awareness among the general public and atomic survivors. The first fruit of the *hibakusha*-led activist groups' vigorous advocacy endeavors came in March 1957, nearly twelve years after the atomic bombings, with the enactment of "The Atomic Bomb Survivors' Medical Support Law" (*Genshi bakudan hibakusha no iryō nado ni kan suru hōritsu*).[10] Yet both the legal definition of a *hibakusha* and the few officially recognized "atomic diseases" were grounded in the narrow parameters of "exposure to radiation" via distance from ground zero. Many recognized the limitations of having to prove one's proximity to the epicenter in order to qualify for the assistance and the lack of recognition for injuries from the searing heat of the bomb or the long-term damage of, say, having hundreds of shards of glass embedded into one's body from the blast. The tenacious work of the *hibakusha* over many decades has continued to expand these narrow parameters to ensure that greater numbers of victims receive due care.[11]

Since 1995, Seirai has been "taking a stab at what the structure of post-atomic-bomb literature could possibly be," eventually creating a new term to distinguish his own work from that of *hibakusha*.[12] In 1999, he coined the term "ground zero literature" (*bakushin bungaku*). He explains: "To depict the ordinary life on the bombed-out ground half a century after the bombing, to write about the condition of contemporary people carrying out the mundane business of the present as if nothing happened—if we can possibly name this something like 'ground zero literature,' there might be the possibility of a new way of conveying the bomb."[13] This is the framework for so much of Seirai's work during the last three decades.

Urakami: Catholic Cathedral and Catastrophe

Seirai must also position himself vis-à-vis Nagasaki's long and distinct history connected to Christianity broadly and Catholicism specifically, which is manifest in the city's postwar identity. The prominence of this religious community derives from its rich and fraught record reaching back hundreds of years. Specifically, the case of the Hidden Christians (*kakure kirishitan*)—communities of adherents who were forced to practice in secret when Christianity was banned in the sixteenth century—has loomed large in Nagasaki's collective memory. After the 1614 decree that forbade Christianity in Japan, the ever-increasing campaign to wrest out and eliminate Christians included arrests, separating and relocating family members, exile, and torture.

One revealing form of persecution that prompted believers to go underground was forcing individuals to renounce their faith or face dire consequences by stepping on *fumie*, small iconic images of Jesus or Mary made of metal, wood, or stone. Arguably, the most famous incident of this era is the mass execution by crucifixion of twenty-six Catholics in Nagasaki in 1597. The victims, twenty native Japanese and six priests from abroad, who were publicly tortured and crucified have remained, unsurprisingly, a key facet of Nagasaki history. Their names and stories are memorialized in museums, monuments, and the Basilica of the Twenty-Six Holy Martyrs, which form the trinity of prominent Christian-themed tourist destinations in the city.

The Christian community was again placed in the murderous crux of history when in August 1945 U.S. bomber pilots flying high above the clouded-over city of Nagasaki unknowingly dropped an atomic weapon on the Immaculate Conception Cathedral in the Urakami district. In the aftermath, U.S. officials discovered that what was once the largest Catholic cathedral in East Asia stood on its hill in ruin, stone statues of Mary in pieces, once-soaring steeples reduced to red-brick rubble, rosaries burned into indistinguishable clumps. As leaders bemoaned this strategic misstep, in the following years and decades they made concerted efforts to control images of the cathedral's destruction in order to prevent Christian-minded Americans from forming sympathies that could override the U.S. doctrine that the atomic bombings in Japan were necessary to end the war and save lives.

While the suppression of damage to Urakami Cathedral is the story in the United States, in Japan, Nagasaki's efforts to define "ground zero" has had its own particularly contentious history. Once the emperor declared the war over and the citizens of Nagasaki attempted to build new lives, two groups emerged with very different aims and narratives regarding the church and its role as a place of postwar memory making.[14] On the one hand, the powerful Catholic community emphasized the need to move on from the tragedy. Informed by writings and speeches of Nagai Takashi (1908–1951), generally, and his pronouncement that the bombing was "an act of God's providence" (*Kami no setsuri*), specifically, Catholic leaders called for the complete removal of their destroyed church, stating that rebuilding their house of worship and lives was the priority. On the other hand, other survivors viewed the former cathedral as a powerful symbol of the devastating effects of the atomic bomb and hoped to preserve it for memorial and educational purposes along the same lines as Hiroshima has done with the Prefectural Industrial Promotion Hall, now known as the Atomic Bomb Dome (*Genbaku dōmu*). In their view, the ruins of the Urakami Cathedral would serve as a tangible memory marker, a place that could hold space for not only mourning but also the remembering of and learning about the damage and destruction to the civilians going about their day and their city on that fateful day. As is adroitly laid out by historian Chad Diehl, ultimately, "the municipal government removed symbolic relics of the bombs, supplanting them with what the hibakusha considered *kyozō* (empty symbols) that failed to convey the reality of the bombing."[15] Today, a newly constructed church stands on the hill in the Urakami District, and the Nagasaki Atomic Bomb Museum and Peace Park serve the predominant memorial functions.

Just as Diehl highlights *hibakusha* as "memory activists," I suggest that Seirai is yet another contemporary example. Seirai is, by his own admission, captivated by the stories of Christian martyrs, although not himself a Christian. Historically there has been a palpable resonance between the sacrifice of these religious figures and the victims of the atomic bombing. Seirai explains the connections between his family stories, his work as a civil servant tasked with preserving physical artifacts from the atomic landscape, and his first publication, "The Cross of Jeronimo," as follows:

> The hardships of Catholics as well are piled up in various places in the city of Nagasaki. When city employees were tasked with the job of protecting cultural artifacts, we conducted excavations in the area between the current prefectural office and the municipal building, we uncovered many of what we call "*hana-jūji-mon-kawara*" [flower-crucifix-crest-tiles] or clay tiles that have a crucifix etched into the decorative eave-ends. In my debut work, "The Cross of Jeronimo," I use the anecdote of my grandmother's dream wherein she dug up a golden crucifix from her garden, which I heard when I was in high school, as a motif.[16]

In this way, Seirai stresses that the material history is part and parcel of the landscapes and memoryscapes of post-1945 Nagasaki.

In each of the six stories in *Ground Zero, Nagasaki*, Seirai focuses on how 1945 is always already here and now. He establishes the ground for his own writing by shifting from the events of August 1945 to individuals who live in the physical place of Nagasaki, highlighting the ways in which the past erupts in unexpected moments as they go about their very twenty-first-century lives. In an interview, Seirai explained, "I think that there are moments in which suddenly the place's memory surfaces in the recesses of the consciousness of people who are [otherwise] unconnected to the place. If there is something like '*post*-atomic-bomb literature,' it likely is nothing more than capturing those moments in writing" (203). Below, I examine the strategies that scaffold Seirai's unique vision of "ground zero literature." I offer close readings of three of the six stand-alone stories in *Ground Zero, Nagasaki*, each with punchy one-word titles: "Nails," "Insects," and "Honey." Sixty years hence, each narrator amid his or her very ordinary twenty-first-century lives are in some way bound to NAGASAKI and their efforts to wrestle with questions regarding God, suffering, faith, identity, and desire define the stories. These short works highlight Seirai's exposition of the contemporary tensions and humanity of everyday struggles that occasionally open up explicitly on August 1945 and its aftermath.

"Nails": The History of Persecution and Secrets

The first chapter in *Ground Zero, Nagasaki* is suffused with a heaviness that gives weight to an incisive interrogation of the themes of secrets, faith, and delusion. "Nails" starts with dark gray skies hanging over an elderly couple attempting to discover any telling secret that would explain the horrible act their son has committed. As they pry open the door to the two-room cottage storehouse—occupied for a time by their son after his wife asked for a divorce—they pray for a revelation. Threads of the past and present are unspooled through the husband's streams of thought. A retired man who deeply connects with his heritage as a descendent of the Christian martyrs, the unnamed husband ferries readers through memories of earlier times when his aunt recuperated in the cottage in the aftermath of the atomic bombing, when the couple's sole heir finally fell in love and married, when Pope John Paul visited Nagasaki, and when the man visited his son, diagnosed with delusional schizophrenia, in a mental hospital. The fictional timespan of the story might be less than an hour, but "Nails" wrestles with the legacy and legitimacy of faith through a narrative that travels across great expanses of time and the terrain of trauma, all grounded in the couples' ramshackle cottage, where the two discover a confounding scene for which they are unprepared.

In "Nails," faith and secrets play out in multiple temporal frames, invoking both pride and shame. The couple have resided for decades on a plot of land with views of the stately Urakami Cathedral. Counted among the devout, the two have, until late, attended Mass without fail. We are told the wife believes their land to be a "sacred place," which might be due to its vicinity to Japan's most storied Roman Catholic church or its direct connection to the history of Hidden Christians (1). It is a source of reassurance that the man's family are descendants of these believers who kept their faith despite dreadful persecution—some paying for it with their lives. As a youth, he had been told the "stories of distant ancestors who had gone, praying, to their deaths, burned alive at the stake; or of the narrow cages in which the faithful were imprisoned when whole families were removed to Yamaguchi in the final days of prohibition" (6). Moreover, the narrator learned from his elders how the disciples "had hidden an image of the Virgin and Child in this cottage and how they had prayed here in secret during the years when our religion was outlawed" (6–7). If secrets are frequently valanced with tinges of the illicit and improper, the actions of staggering fidelity in the face of persecution of the Hidden Christians are understandably lauded and respected. Now, in the present, as the couple are shunned by neighbors and alienated from their religious community, the model of faithfulness in the distant past lives on in a palpable present as the elderly couple prepare for a modern-day exile from their hallowed grounds.

The humble cottage on the family's plot of land also provided sanctuary in a more proximate time in Japanese history for another family member, whose story likewise reaffirms it as an architectural talisman and time capsule of believers' enduring faith. In August 1945, the narrator's paternal aunt, O-Ryo, returns to her natal home, having lost not only her house but also her four children in the devastating atomic-bomb attack. It is there that this woman, injured and desolate amidst unfathomable circumstances, recuperates. The narrator recalls fond memories of times when O-Ryo doted on her young nephew and niece, the three eating sweet persimmons together as she proudly recounted stories of their ancestors. He notes the faded scar on his aunt's face, but as a child he does not fully comprehend her pain. Only later, amid his own period of suffering and doubt, does he ponder how she may have questioned her own. He ruminates, "People have probably always asked the same questions when some disaster has occurred. Our martyred ancestors, our dead parents, O-Ryo-san—all of us at some time in our lives have turned our eyes to Heaven and asked: Why?" (9) Within the logic of faith, however, the storehouse ultimately serves as a reassuring confirmation of a familial legacy of fortitude and honor in the face of physical and moral tribulation shared over generations.

Even the smallest of anecdotes in "Nails" underscores the way time is layered upon itself in Nagasaki, shepherding believers through centuries of difficulty. The husband recalls that when Pope John Paul II visited Nagasaki, he and his wife had taken their son and daughter to attend the outdoor Mass on a snowy day. He remembers, "I was overcome by a feeling that the people standing in line to receive the pope's blessing weren't people from this day and age, but our ancestors" (17). He is reassured in his faith because he can "feel their shadowing presence by my side. Prayer is never a solitary occupation" (17). Such ethereal companionship is what helps him and fellow adherents to endure the trials of life.

However, a third calamity, still unfolding in the narrator's present, harbors unfathomable secrets that force him to confront troubling questions regarding the nature of his faith. Just a short time after the "miracle" of his thirty-year-old son's marriage to a woman named Kiyomi, the otherwise tenderhearted man who when a youth would pick up a ladybug to take it to safety, exhibits symptoms of an irrational obsession over "secrets" she was keeping from him. The son inexplicably displays unfounded rage over imaginary affairs and spends unthinkable sums to hire detective agencies to spy on Kiyomi, only to receive reports categorically absolving her. His ever-increasing delusional speech and behavior forces her to move back to her parents' home. The son moves into the cottage, and once the parents witness his irrational rants and behavior, they warn Kiyomi and confer with the police about what to do, to no avail. Eventually the son confronts his wife in public with a knife, and when bystanders pin him to the ground, Kiyomi falls, and her neck is cut by the knife that is still in the son's hand. She is pronounced dead at the hospital. Subsequently, the son is diagnosed with delusional schizophrenia and housed in a modern mental institution, uncomprehending of Kiyomi's death and still tormented by his delusions. The burden of this "living nightmare" has tested the couple and their faith (12). They rejected the fleeting thought of committing suicide together but decide to sell their home and plot of land to pay compensation to Kiyomi's parents for their son's actions. Still, the pain remains unabated: "To be driven out, as we had been, from a place where our ancestors had quietly yet firmly kept their faith for three hundred years brought regrets that seemed unlikely to heal" (2).

The sharpest pain, however, is delivered to the narrator by his son after the tragedy in a fashion that brings to the fore the shared territory of faith and fabulation. The father is torn that the last of the family line is an unbeliever, bringing a wretched end to a legacy of the devoted. His memory strays to a recent visit with his son, when in hopes to orchestrate some sort of redemption, the narrator pleads with his son to write a letter of apology to console Kiyomi's family. But the son, believing Kiyomi to still be alive repeats his disturbing diatribes. When the father makes one more plea for reason—"Kiyomi never did anything wrong. It's a delusion"—his son's resistance puts him on his back foot (15):

"Tell me, Daddy: Do you believe in God?"
My body stiffened, and I sat bolt upright. What kind of thing is that to say? I began to shout.

> "Of course, I do! This family has always believed. Our ancestors gave their lives for the faith!"
> With his long fingernails, he wiped away a spot of yellow cream from the corner of his mouth and licked it as he spoke.
> "And you call me deluded?" (16)

The conversation tips the notion of faith on its head with delusion as the punch line. As such, the readers are meant to see the father as the latest in a familial line to wrestle with the question of faith.

As the story nears the end, the narrator returns readers to the cottage as they attempt to fathom the "horror" they encounter upon entering the second room of the storeroom cottage. In the darkness all they can discern is an empty space except for one hammer and a stepladder. The narrator senses the smell of iron. But when he turns on the light, the couple are unprepared for the mystifying sight: the walls pierced with thousands and thousands—maybe hundreds of thousands—of nails. In shock, the two try to fathom the meaning. The narrator muses, "Is it too much to ask and expect an answer? All these nails.... Will we ever get an explanation?" (17). As the nails conjure up images of the crucified Christ, the senselessness of the son's preoccupation shocks the senses. In this way, "Nails" brings together the crimes against his faithful ancestors, the innocent civilians in Nagasaki in the summer of 1945, and Kiyomi, challenging readers to question the nature of faith and delusion.

"Insects": The Tangle of Time and Bodies

Several works in *Ground Zero, Nagasaki* rely on exquisite if often painful "time slips" that convey a survivor's body and mind back and forth between crystallized memories of the nuclear tragedy and resonant aspects of their current life. This crystallization is especially evoked in "Insects," the third chapter, whose narrative deploys a seemingly innocuous request that elicits an interweaving web of emotions and recollections. The main character, Mitsuko, is a survivor who lost her entire immediate family in the flash of the bomb and only barely survived herself. Sixty years later, now seventy-five years old, she receives a letter asking her to share a memory with a woman, Reiko, who knows that Mitsuko was a coworker and friend of her late husband, Mr. Sasaki. This request incites both anger and anguish in Mitsuko, who had a brief but intense sexual experience with Reiko's husband. The solicitation—"maybe you could tell me about a side of him I never knew" (53)—brings to the fore a whole range of powerful emotions that Mitsuko, a self-proclaimed "warm-blooded woman," has harbored for six decades (52).

She wrestles with the many possible futures that were extinguished by the bomb. Mitsuko did not finish nursing school, marry—because "the bomb made her ugly" (59)—or have children. She did not have support or comfort from her parents as she carved out a lonely and limited existence. Envy and desire flood her being as she questions the value of life.

Mitsuko's psychosexual musings and Nagasaki's postatomic landscape are fused in her powerful memories prompted by the letter, evoked through fusing of fire and desire. Though it was a fleeting interlude, Mitsuko has had never-ending ardor for her longtime friend and brief lover. She recalls feeling most alive when she had sex with Sasaki and has cherished this singular sensual encounter. It is suffused with the power of desire and equated with aliveness and connection. Her imagination conjures up this vision: "The candlelight must have cast our shadows on the walls, our long thin arms entwined, like a pair of huge insects locked together" (67). Prompted by the letter, Mitsuko acknowledges "the longing for him still burns inside of me. Most the time it's a small flickering of light, like the dying embers in the ruins of a burned-out city. But sometimes, late at night, it still bursts into flame and scorches my heart" (53). The smoldering flames in the postapocalyptic aftermath and her powerful yearning for Sasaki are described in the same terms, evoking both the persistence and volatility of the bombing and her craving. Despite being denied the comforting normality of socially sanctioned expectations due to her disabilities, Mitsuko acknowledges that "a warm-blooded woman still lurks inside this decrepit body, threatening to come crawling to the surface" (52).

The narrator's fascination with insects and their symbolic significance across a wide range of contexts is grounded in several immediate postbombing memories. Although she is knocked unconscious, Mitsuko recalls being asked by a disembodied voice, "Are you still alive?" (77). In the confusion, she cannot discern from whom or where the voice originates, but her mind conceives that it is a "bright green insect" that inquired about her condition. The insect climbs up her injured leg, and Mitsuko is immediately comforted. She is encouraged by the "dopey and amiable" quality of the inquiry (51). Later, a family member comments that her disfigured leg makes her look like a cricket, and a conscious fascination with insects is solidified (69). Thereafter, crickets take on the role of Mitsuko's "guardian angel," and she is unable to callously kill mosquitos and other insects (61).

Seirai's "Insects" suggests that when an unfathomable new technology turned everything on its head in a split second in Nagasaki, God's ostensible hierarchy of beings collapsed. The narrator's conceptualization of insects, which appearing repeatedly both in name and metaphorically, assigns them agency and importance and confers on the lowly creatures the status of precious talismans. Regaining consciousness after the blast, Mitsuko takes in her surroundings. In particular, she perceives a tapeworm in the exposed abdomen of another victim and imagines that a force of ants carries her to safety. With unexpected clarity she thinks, "the human world is over . . . and the world of insects was about to take over" (52). As her experiences converge, Mitsuko ascribes great power to these small creatures, wondering "if only a cricket, ant, or tapeworm had been on hand to speak to [the other victims], maybe they, too, would have made it out of the debris" (53). In this way, Mitsuko attempts to shape some sense of the incomprehensible by assigning protective powers to these creatures that often induce revulsion or fear.

Moreover, the topic of insects underscores both Mitsuko's particular and powerful connection to Sasaki and the distance between them. Mitsuko, who is ever careful to keep her relationship with and reverence for insects a secret, reveals her thoughts about them only to Sasaki, a signal of her implicit trust. One night, when he escorts her home after she becomes tipsy at a dinner, Mitsuko initially resists his advances, feeling the eyes of the Virgin Mary statue upon her. When she voices her hesitancy—"God is watching"—Sasaki rebukes her for still believing in a higher power after experiencing the atomic bombing (67). He rejects any notion of "God's plan": "We're like your insects. Eat, mate, reproduce. Who lives, who dies? It's just luck, and that is all there is to it" (67). She attempts to reject this despairing and disparaging retort, but soon she relinquishes to the building passion.

To the degree that the categories of human and insect gain proximity, the notions of faith and God's grace become ever more tenuous. Mitsuko assumes Sasaki to be a believer because he works at a Christian school and is a descendent of the "Hidden Christians." She is, therefore, taken aback by his rebuke of "God's plan." Later, however, she reasons that his experiences during the war, including his narrow escape from death when his plane was grounded just as he was ordered to carry out a suicide mission, "had trimmed the flab from his faith" (57). Sasaki does not reject the existence of God, but he concludes that the deity pays no more attention to individual humans than he does individual insects. Thus, humans are no better than insects—both part of a swarm that God does not see as distinct beings. Later, when he uses the phrase "by the grace of pure luck" to counter Mitsuko's "by the grace of God," the religious language of grace is incongruously paired with random chance rather than divine intervention. Finally, Mitsuko muses, "Perhaps [Sasaki] wasn't quite human, but a beautiful, faithless insect, spreading its wings in a clear blue sky. When the bomb was dropped and people rejected God, they all became insects of a sort." (68) Under the weight of the physical and psychic trauma of the atomic bomb, indifference to an all-powerful being and its ostensible mercy on humans provides a protective exoskeleton that protects them from the incomprehensible dissonance of the "advancements" of the atomic era.

This persistent equating and questioning of the relationship between human and insect in the work brings past and present into a larger picture of meaning-making. Throughout *Ground Zero, Nagasaki*, Seirai focuses on characters' struggles with the intangibility of themselves and their lives shaped so deeply by the tricks of fate. The "Insects" chapter in particular depicts the challenge of forming coherence out of a life that contains so many lacunae arising from lost loved-ones, diminished health, and stolen futures. Since fate has decided her life so quickly and cruelly, Mitsuko questions the meaning of existence: "Am I glad I survived, or would it have been better to have perished along with everyone else? I honestly can't say" (55). A random lot, mere chance of location, and an unprecedented, destructive catastrophe kills thousands of people in an instant and still leaves "a spider with vivid yellow and black stripes wait[ing] patiently in an unbroken web" (55). Mitsuko, ultimately, aligns the human and insect experience, with her understanding that "everything on this earth—however insignificant—has had to struggle to survive" (54). In this way, Seirai keenly underscores the fractured nature of memory, faith, and identity in Nagasaki's postatomic landscape.

"Honey": Faith and Desire in the Garden of Eden

Of the six independent stories in *Ground Zero, Nagasaki*, only the central characters of "Insects" and "Honey" are female. In very distinctive ways, each woman fails to meet conventional expectations of womanhood and domesticity: one is a pious seventy-five-year-old, unwed *hibakusha* with no children and a notable disability; the other is an attractive thirty-year-old in a lusterless, childless marriage who is neither skilled at nor interested in domestic chores. Both narratives spotlight the women's relationship to sexual vitality, but while "Insects" features a woman whose life is shaped by a singular, especially meaningful sexual encounter, "Honey," the fourth chapter, focuses on a sexually experienced woman who is drawn to seduce a young man. By giving voice to the main character in "Honey," Seirai opens up space for a nuanced rendering of her doctrinal grievance with God through varied allusions to the Garden of Eden. In so doing, the work explicitly questions Christian theology, especially that of "original sin," in the terrain of contemporary life.

The narrator is Mihoko, a thirty-year-old, born and raised in Nagasaki, who relocated to work in Tokyo and then returned to settle into a conventional life. Married to an affluent cardiologist fifteen years her senior and living in a dual household with her in-laws, she is generally satisfied with her decision to move back to the city. She gets along with her in-laws, devout believers and *hibakusha*, who graciously welcome her into their lives. When Mihoko meets up with former high-school classmates, she is surprised that almost all confess to flings and affairs. She too had an earlier relationship with a married man in Tokyo, and remembers, "Other men used to ask me out from time to time, but I stayed faithful to him. I liked the way he was—aloof and mean. He used to treat me roughly, like a plaything" (95). In fact, the title of this story comes from an anecdote when this former lover, her superior at work, called her his "Honey Girl," claiming that her sweat smelled like honey (82). Mihoko realizes afterward that one woman's "story that night awoke something inside me" (93). She becomes held in the grip of a sexual fascination with a young man who repairs bikes at a shop just down the road from her home and offers a seductive invitation to come to her house on the morning of August 9, knowing her family will be attending the annual anniversary ceremony for the atomic bombing. The casual and even flippant inner musings about her carnal appetites seem to be at odds with the seriousness of the city's history, but it is the juxtaposition of Mihoko's desire to confirm her vitality and the backdrop of atomic devastation that produces a work that resonates with palpable and believable tension.

In "Honey," notions of faithlessness and faithfulness play central roles in both the characters' relationships with each other and with God. While the apple is conventionally imagined to symbolize the "forbidden fruit" in the parable of the Garden of Eden in the Western world, in Seirai's hands the kiwi takes on varied associations with "desire," both carnal and existential. We are first introduced to the fruit in the family's garden with its trellis loaded with impressive kiwi trees. Mihoko has a clear-eyed understanding that her motive for accepting the marriage proposal was the family's garden. "When I saw the garden and the kiwi vines in fruit, I remember thinking: I've had enough of Tokyo, this is where I want to live" (96–97). Yet the garden is not all paradise. The spot where the trellis stands is, in fact, fraught with historical resonance: it was the spot in 1945—then featuring wisteria vines—where all of the bones of the father-in-law's family members where found. It is the place where he has fostered a desire for and commitment to peace by planting kiwi, inspired by a bold proclamation of a New Zealand statesman. And it is also the location where Mihoko arranges for the tryst. In this way, history piles on itself evoking the incontrovertible march of time.

Mihoko is nominally a Christian, but she has a grievance with God, which causes her to struggle with both theological doctrine and her own relationship to it. She is not prepared for the devout family she has married into and rarely goes beyond merely saying grace at each meal. Still, she has become accustomed to the prominent shrine with a statue of Our Lady in the middle of the home. While gardening one day, Mihoko reaches into the hollow of a tree trunk after which a large, black snake slithers out. She is reminded of the biblical story of the Garden of Eden and equates her flirtatious adventure with the youth as an equivalent of eating the "forbidden fruit" (98). Tied as it is to women's submission, the expulsion of Adam and Eve from paradise, and laying blame on the woman for the "fall" of humankind, this heavily weighted parable lies at the crux of Mihoko's inner dilemma. At one point, she muses, "Where did the snake go after that? Sometimes I wonder if somehow it might be hiding in a hollow inside of me" (87). Rather than feeling shame, however, Mihoko instead airs her grievance with God: "Personally, I think it is unfair of God. He must have known that his two newly created people would sin—and still he let the snake wander around the Garden. HE could have dealt with the thing before the trouble started" (100). Still again, she finds herself questioning her "twisted heart": "Why is this descendant of your Eve about to commit a moral sin without so much as a twinge of guilt?" (100). With the prospect—both tantalizing and bewildering—Mihoko muses, "Like the snake that was sleeping peacefully under the dead leaves until I prodded it and drove it out of its refuge, it seems only a matter of time before I get chased out of Paradise, too" (87).

Despite the skewed gendered overtones in the original religious story, the narrative resists rather than reinforces any condemnation of Mihoko, forgoing typical double standards regarding sexual liberties. Although her husband treats her "more like a daughter than a wife," Mihoko understands that hers is a marriage of convenience for both parties and is satisfied to have independence, economic stability, and in-laws who are kind and caring (99). Thus, when she discovers that her husband is having an affair, Mihoko is impressed rather than jealous. She pretends that she did not see the revealing text and has no inclination to probe him for a confession lest she "risk waking up some big black snake that might be inside him" (99). In this way, the work, suffused with biblical references, gives Mihoko an unapologetic voice and unexpected independence to a woman who finds no comfort in patriarchal restrictions or idealized forms of femininity.

Alongside the association of the "garden" with sexual desire is also an unexpected link to a deep commitment to peace in a world free of nuclear weapons. Mihoko learns that it was the father-in-law who began growing the kiwis, starting with saplings that have since grown into robust bushes covering a trellis that dominates the garden and produces an abundance of fruit from May to June. He was inspired by the outspoken antinuclear position taken by a New Zealand prime minister. David Lange's 1984 declaration that nuclear weapons were "morally indefensible," and New Zealand's successful passing of the 1987 legislation, which made the country a nuclear-free zone, spurred the father-in-law to rebuild the trellis where is kin were killed in 1945.[17] The father-in-law explains, Lange was a "wonderful man. Refused to allow nuclear weapons into his country. And he took a leading role during the talks to ban them all together" (85). In a conversation with Mihoko, the mother-in-law casually quips that her husband believes "New Zealand is like a modern Garden of Eden" (85). Thus, the Garden of Eden takes on two radically different roles in the short work. The in-laws have tended peace not only through their participation in the yearly rituals to memorialize the loss of life in August 1945, but also in their dedication to tend the symbolic growth of peace.

"Honey" does not smooth over the tensions of contemporary life sixty years on. Rather, the work carefully threads together both the palpable presence of and unmistakable distance from Nagasaki's traumatic history. At the end of the story the family attends the yearly memorial of the atomic bombing on August 9 to pay respect to those whose lives were taken by the bomb, while Mihoko stays behind, tingling with anticipation for more than just the return of her bike from the shop. When the youth arrives with her bicycle, the two crouch down in the garden so he can demonstrate that all has been properly repaired. Mihoko, with her skirt purposely hitched up, catches a glance of the "silhouette of Our Lady," her arms reaching out. The last line reads, "I feel misgiving for a moment. But the brakes are long past working now, and when the boy's oil-stained fingers reach out to touch me, there is not so much as a screech" (113). Thus, in the closing passage, Mihoko's deep-seated craving for a confirmation of her aliveness is contrasted to the somber remembrance of the dead. Seirai's play on Christian visual and linguistic vocabulary highlights both the ever-present reminders of the presence and the distance of the atomic bomb. "Honey," like all of the stories in *Ground Zero, Nagasaki*, is a nuanced meditation on the physical and psychic landscapes of life and death.

Seirai's provocative and impactful body of literature represents his quest for the appropriate mode for a non-*hibakusha* to address the ongoing significance of the atomic bombings. He mixes memoir and commentary, illuminating what he has inherited from both the stories and the silences. Embodied in the three stories discussed above, his manifestation of the concept of ground zero literature intricately braids the lingering questions and pain of those who survived the atomic catastrophe with the emergent questions and pain that arise in contemporary life. In so doing, Seirai has been able to evoke the subtle and palpable ways that this city cannot but inhabit multiple temporalities.

More recently, Seirai contributed a short opinion piece for *Asahi Shinbun* newspaper's regular column, titled "Between Belief and Doubt" (*Shin to gi no aida*), which returns to the ethical imperative of engaging with Nagasaki's "stories" of the atomic bomb. In it, the author revisits the language of the famous eulogy given by Nagai Takashi at a memorial Mass on November 23, 1945, just a little over three months after the atomic bombing. Visibly injured and wearing tattered clothing, Nagai spoke to a crowd of a reported six hundred Catholics who held about eight thousand small white crosses to represent their lost loved ones.[18] A well-known member of the Catholic community of Nagasaki and a prominent medical doctor who dedicated himself to rescue and support efforts even as he dealt with the death of his wife and own injuries in the immediate aftermath, Nagai was an obvious person to invite to speak at this solemn occasion. One phrase in his speech, however, precipitated considerable debate, which continues to this day, namely, Nagai's "theory" that the U.S. atomic bombing of Nagasaki was "divine providence" (*setsuri*), repeated with some edits in his 1949 autobiographical work *The Bells of Nagasaki*. In the ensuing decades this has also been referred to as the "burnt offering theory" (*hansaisetsu*).[19] The prominence of the Catholic community broadly and Nagai's interpretation of the event specifically have contributed to the creation of the oft-repeated but misguided phrase "Hiroshima Rages, Nagasaki Prays," which continues to invite reflection and commentary.

Seirai, who admits to having a complicated relationship with the figure of Nagai, titles his short essay "Dr. Nagai's Eulogy: An Unintended Interpretation/Somehow the 'Consoling of Believers' became a 'Story of Peace'" (Nagai hakase no chōji: ito senu kaishaku/'Shinto e no nagusame' ga itsushika 'heiwa no monogatari' ni). He once again brings us back to 1945, explaining that amid the unfathomable atomic destruction, a rumor (*kageguchi*) spread that the bombing was "divine punishment" (*tenbatsu*).[20] Naturally, voices were raised to counter this interpretation of the horror, emphasizing, for instance, the blamelessness of the children who were cruelly killed or injured. In Nagai's funeral address, the notion of divine providence is first mentioned. In the piece, Seirai refers to Takahashi Shinji's *Philosophizing* in *Nagasaki: Death and Life in the Nuclear Age*,[21] which takes issue with Nagai's framing. Takahashi seeks to ground the atomic tragedy in a more worldly realm, stating, "a two-fold dereliction of [wartime] responsibility falls on the Japanese government, which sacrificed the lives of Japanese subjects in a senseless war, and the U.S. government, which indiscriminately slaughtered a civilian population with a bombing that had no military purpose."[22] Serai, who had been deeply moved by Nagai's *Bells of Nagasaki* as a youth, admits that he found Takahashi's critique to be revelatory and thought-provoking.

In parsing and interpreting the language of Nagai's writings, which suggest that the atomic bombings were Japan's burnt offerings (*hansai*) or atonement (*tsugunai*) for waging war, Seirai comes to a further realization. "Recently, it suddenly occurred to me that the 'theory' in the 'Burnt Offering Theory' is really a 'story' (*monogatari*). That the pilots dropped a bomb through an opening in the clouds onto Urakami was merely a coincidence and there is no basis for such an argument. Attaching meaning to randomness is to make a story."[23] He notes that historically Japan's national "stories" have changed with the winds of time. In the immediate postwar era, for instance, the wartime stories that heralded the legitimacy and righteousness of Japan's imperial and wartime projects broke down while new narratives were, with surprising swiftness, drafted and adopted. Thus, while sympathetic to Takahashi's critique, Serai proposes to read the implications of Nagai's motivation through another lens. He writes, "didn't Dr. Nagai change the rumored 'Urakami Divine Punishment Story' to the 'Urakami Burnt Offering Story' in order to give meaning to the deaths of the believers? A story is something that soothes the soul, but unlike theories they circulate within society without the process of supplying proof or undergoing critical discussions."[24] Therefore, just as the Ptolemaic theory, which posited that earth was at the center of the universe, was eventually found to be mistaken, any number of our current "theories" could be equally erroneous. Stories are, he laments, "outrageous" (*keshikaran*). Seirai's musings draw him to a critical conundrum. If the notions of even the "self" and "reality" are stories, we humans are left on shaky ground. Still, he encourages us to carry on, taking short breaks (*hitoikitsuku*) in order to avoid "drowning" in the stories of our own era.

Ground Zero, Nagasaki features characters that could be taken off the streets of Nagasaki today. It evinces a persistent doubling or layering of time that is anchored in both tangible and ephemeral realms. Seirai's entanglement and layering of past and present not only underscore the recurring eruption of the past in the present but also the kinds of pain and longing that take hold of people in our contemporary moment. In this work and his many others, Seirai has followed through on his duty to write the multiple layers of history and personal pain and desires that inhabit the space of Nagasaki. His works underscore the ways residents bridge key junctures of history that continue to make thinking through NAGASAKI/Nagasaki productive. And in doing so, Seirai asks us to see this as our responsibility as well.

Notes

1. Translated into English as *Ground Zero, Nagasaki*, trans. Paul Warham (New York: Columbia University Press, 2015).
2. *Nishi Nihon Shinbun*, October 23, 2008.
3. *Chūgoku Shinbun*, February 11, 2008.
4. Seirai Yūichi, *Kanashimi to mu no aida* (Between Sadness and Nothingness) (Tokyo: Bungei shunjū, 2015), 43.
5. *Nishi Nihon Shinbun*, August 6, 1999.
6. Jinno Toshifumi, *Sensō e, bungaku e "sono go no" Sensō shōsetsuron* (Towards War/Towards Literature: Theories of Wartime Novels in the Aftermath [i.e., Post-9/11]) (Tokyo: Shueisha, 2011), 206–7; *Nagasaki Shinbun*, January 3, 2005.
7. *Ground Zero: The Deadly Shift*, dir. Fred Olen Ray, 2008; *Ground Zero*, dir. Channing Lowe, 2010; *Ground Zero* (game) SEGA CD, 1993.
8. See, e.g., Gar Alperovitz, *The Decision to Use the Atomic Bomb and the Architecture of an American Myth* (New York: Vintage Books, 1996).
9. Joseph Gerson, *Empire and the Bomb: How the U.S. Uses Nuclear Weapons to Dominate the World* (London: Pluto Press, 2007).
10. Literally, the "Law Related to the Medical Treatment and Other Needs of the Atomic-Bombing Survivors," also known as the "Hibakusha Relief Law."
11. The practice of public testimony used in abolition activism is profoundly shaped by this law's definition of a survivor, many starting their deeply painful stories by introducing themselves, the city, what they were doing where at the time of the blast, indicating the distance from the later-determined epicenter as the crow flies to their location.
12. Jinno, *Sensō e*, 195.
13. *Nishi Nihon Shinbun*, August 6, 1999.
14. Chad R. Diehl, *Resurrecting Nagasaki: Reconstruction and the Formation of Atomic Narratives* (Ithaca, NY: Cornell University Press, 2018), 2–4.
15. Diehl, *Resurrecting Nagasaki*, 5–6.
16. Yoshimi Michio, *Hidankyō Newsletter*, December 6, 2014.
17. David Lange, "Nuclear Weapons Are Morally Indefensible," Public Address: Great New Zealand Argument, https://publicaddress.net/1578#post.
18. Konishi Tetsurō, "The Original Manuscript of Takashi Nagai's Funeral Address at a Mass for the Victims of the Nagasaki Bomb," *Journal of Nagasaki University of Foreign Studies* 18 (2014): 55–68.

19. I understand that there are other possible translations of *hansai*. I chose "burnt offering" since the first Japanese character includes "fire," and this is a common phrase used in Christian theology to describe what Nagai is suggesting.

20. *Asahi Shinbun*, October 4, 2021.

21. Takahashi Shinji, *Nagasaki ni atte tetsugaku suru: Kakujidai no shi to sei* (Philosophizing in Nagasaki: Death and Life in the Nuclear Age) (Tokyo: Hokuju shuppan, 1994).

22. *Asahi Shinbun*, October 4, 2021.

23. Ibid.

24. Ibid.

Part III
Sites of Memory

Fragmented Memory
The Scattering of the Urakami Cathedral Ruins among Nagasaki's Memorial Landscape

By Anna Gasha

In her monumental study of postatomic memory in Hiroshima, Lisa Yoneyama speaks of the potential of the city's ruins to serve as memorial guides. She writes that many preservationists in the city "understood that the loss of the ruins meant the ultimate erasure of clues through which one might be invited to think everything from the beginning, to reflect critically on how the present is situated vis-à-vis its history." Ruins in general prompt visitors to consider the origins of preserved relics and recognize that the events of the past were never predetermined, but rather were the results of human actions and decisions. Yoneyama encourages viewing Hiroshima's ruins beyond the destructive moment of the atomic bombing to see also the history of production and preservation of atomic ruins that followed. Indeed, emphasizing the instance when the ruins were created (that is, the atomic bombing) draws attention away from related issues of importance within the nexus of destruction, reconstruction, and memory formation. As Yoneyama puts it, "At these resurrected sites of storytelling, one could begin to ask how the original loss was produced, if in fact the loss was inevitable, and what is at stake in remembering and forgetting the past. As a space of criticism, the ruins, together with other narrative spaces for the dead, question the automatism of historical progress."[1]

The object of my study here is the historical trajectory of the creation of Nagasaki's atomic monuments and the decisions surrounding their preservation that have led to the geographic, curatorial, and aesthetic contexts in which they are located today. In particular, I focus on the components of the memorial landscape pertaining to the Urakami Cathedral, which was heavily damaged from the atomic bombing due to its proximity to the hypocenter. In 1958, the ruins of the cathedral were demolished, and a new cathedral was built in its place, but only after an extended debate among residents in the city over whether the ruins should be preserved unchanged as a memorial site. Ultimately, some pieces of the prewar cathedral were preserved or relocated to other parts of Nagasaki, and replicas of the bombed ruins were created for the city's Atomic Bomb Museum. The proliferation of material and sites linked to the Urakami Cathedral scattered across Nagasaki, however, has made for a complicated memorial landscape. The underlying thread of the Urakami Cathedral and its history of atomic bombing ontologically if not geographically bind these various sites together. This connection means that the reconstructed Urakami Cathedral serves as a central referent for each of these sites. Yet, the reconstructed building's status as a unifying locus poses a paradox: the history of the cathedral's destruction itself is challenged or negated through the material presence of an architectural double at the very same site.

Meanwhile, the tragic nature of the atomic bombing has understandably given way to a discursive focus on loss. The narrative that best suits this perspective is that of the irrevocable demolition of the Urakami Cathedral ruins and how their removal from Nagasaki's urban landscape has deprived survivors and future generations of powerful evidence of the atomic bombing. This lament is often accompanied by an invocation of Hiroshima's Atomic Bomb Dome, with its UNESCO World Heritage designation, a recognition that many feel has been denied to Nagasaki because of the absence of the cathedral's ruins. While understandable, this view of the loss of the Urakami Cathedral ruins as a form of memorial dispossession has also led to the discursive overshadowing of the other fragments from the same ruins that do survive in Nagasaki today. In emphasizing this sense of loss, what does remain from the cathedral ruins has been, in effect, devalued and thus overlooked.

The Destruction of and Preservation Campaign for Urakami Cathedral

The construction of the original cathedral structure began in 1895 and was completed in 1925. By this point, Urakami, an enclave north of the city center of Nagasaki, had been home to a population of Japanese Catholics who had faced religious persecution and discrimination from the state and non-Catholics, including exile from their communities starting in 1867. Only after the repeal of the national ban on Christianity in 1873 did the exiled Catholics return to Urakami. During this resettlement, the Urakami Catholics decided to erect a cathedral to mark their presence and demonstrate their resilience through experiences of marginalization. The resulting structure, built with donations in material, labor, and funds from members of the congregation, was the largest cathedral in East Asia.[2] Correspondingly, the cathedral and its location had become a central place of history, community, and faith for the Urakami Catholics.

On August 9, 1945, American forces dropped an atomic bomb on Nagasaki, which detonated above the Urakami neighborhood. As a result, in addition to the lives lost, the Urakami Cathedral was mostly destroyed; only two portions of the exterior wall remained standing (figure 1). Given the dilapidated condition of the remains, the structure could no longer functionally serve as a cathedral. Survivors within the congregation, still attached to the site of the ruins as a significant location within their religious history, established a temporary place of worship adjacent to the ruins. Meanwhile, non-Catholic survivors also came to valorize the ruins of the Cathedral not as a religious center but as a symbol for the destructive power of nuclear

Figure 1. Photograph of the remaining walls of the Urakami Cathedral following the atomic bombing. Source: United States Department of Defense, Department of the Air Force. Original caption (on the back) reads, "Panorama Of The Urakami Roman Catholic Cathedral After Atomic Bombing of Nagasaki, Japan. 16 October 1945." Identifier within the National Archives Catalog reads, "U.S. Air Force Number A60652AC." Public domain. Full image viewable online at: https://catalog.archives.gov/id/204836855.

weapons and the suffering of the victims of the bombing—and thus, a call for future peace without such flagrant displays of devastation.

Given the various constituencies that found meaning in them, the future of the cathedral's ruins became a widely discussed and debated subject as reconstruction efforts proceeded in Nagasaki. The two segments of the wall that had survived the atomic blast were included among the purview of the Nagasaki City Council's Committee for the Preservation of Atomic Bombing Materials (Genbaku shiryō hozon i'in kai), established in 1949 to designate and conserve materials that could serve as physical evidence of the bombing.³ This Committee comprised largely non-Catholic Nagasaki leaders, who were inclined to preserve the cathedral ruins as a monument to the atomic bombing that could communicate its horrors to subsequent generations. Indeed, the committee had voted in support of the preservation of the ruins nine separate times, with the mayor, Tagawa Tsutomu, also in favor of this plan. Mayor Tagawa had also commissioned Niwa Kankichi, a technician retained by Nagasaki Prefecture, to devise a method to structurally stabilize the ruins; Niwa had in turn submitted construction documents to reinforce the compromised structure from behind with reinforced concrete additions.⁴

In the face of this movement toward preservation of the cathedral walls, the Urakami Catholics advocated for demolition of the ruins in order to make way for a new, usable building for the congregation. Practically speaking, the temporary wooden church structure had become too overcrowded to accommodate services comfortably. Further, the city had capitalized on the new significance of the cathedral ruins as a memento of the atomic bombing by promoting it as a tourist destination, which imposed constant distractions on worshippers.⁵ Gwyn McClelland has argued that the presence of the cathedral ruins also proved an impediment to the Urakami Catholics' self-image and narrative, wherein the persistence of the ruins betrayed the parallelism they hoped to draw between the historical repression and persistence of the Catholics of the region on the one hand and the survival through the tragedy of an atomic bombing on the other. Thus, the ruins not only "represented a dark presence of death, or even the absence of God" for the Urakami Catholics, but they also stifled the "Urakami Catholic faith meta-narrative" and its "hope of resurrection: this hope was discarded whilst the church remained in ruins."⁶

Ultimately, Mayor Tagawa sided with the Catholic leadership of the Urakami congregation, approving the request to demolish the ruins and erect a new church structure on the site. At a city council meeting on March 5, 1958, Tagawa made an announcement on behalf of Bishop Yamaguchi Paul

Aijirō and himself, expressing their conclusion that preserving the structure as it was, where it stood, would be "impossible" (*fukanō*).⁷ This statement marked an about-face for Mayor Tagawa, who had voted in support for preserving the ruins up until this point.⁸ Tagawa still attempted to humor advocates of preserving the ruin by urging the evaluation of the possibility of relocating the ruins elsewhere for their conservation at this meeting.⁹ However, only part of the ruins were in fact transplanted, as we will see. The remaining walls were demolished beginning March 14, just over a week after the mayor's announcement.

A central question that both proponents and detractors of the cathedral ruins' preservation grappled with was whether the remnants on that site possessed a particular potency that would enable future generations to learn about the atomic bombing and its aftermath. Those in favor of preserving the ruins resoundingly insisted that they were indeed the best material articulation of the tragedy. Such an opinion had been presented since some of the earliest debates in the public arena about the fate of the ruins. For example, a city councilman who was also a *hibakusha* had argued at a city council meeting on October 6, 1945, that the preservation of the ruins, along with all other potential "research material," posed "a human obligation" toward the entire "world."¹⁰ The discussion persisted for years as commissions were established and numerous petitions submitted for the preservation of the Urakami Cathedral ruins. At the 1958 meeting where Mayor Tagawa announced his intent to permit the Urakami congregation to demolish the cathedral remains and rebuild on the site, councilmember Iwaguchi Natsuo fervently pushed back on the mayor's decision, drawing from the same line of argument that the ruins were an irreplaceable historical resource that must be passed on to future generations. Iwaguchi argued in the council meeting that beyond touristic (in other words, economic) value, the Urakami Cathedral ruins must be seen through the lens of historical value (*rekishiteki kachi*).¹¹ He further specified that the ruins merit respect not simply by virtue of their age, but, as with all other ruins (*iseki*), their ability to "speak" (*katari*) of the past, "teach" (*oshie*) history, and provide lessons and warnings for a new era.¹² Seen in this light, the elimination of the cathedral ruins from Nagasaki's landscape posed an irreversible erasure and a failure to transmit the heritage and legacy of the atomic bombing, an understanding fundamentally built on the assumption that the ruins were indeed the most effective material expression of this history.

Mayor Tagawa responded to Iwaguchi that the only way for a non-*hibakusha* to understand the full devastation and tragedy of the atomic bombing would be to maintain the *entirety* of Nagasaki or Hiroshima in its exact state immediately after the attack. The selective preservation of just "one part," he continued, would be offensive to or betray the memories of the survivors—they would feel that the remaining representation, confined to a single location, was smaller and more limited in its wreckage than what they had actually witnessed.[13] Putting aside the extreme and impractical nature of Tagawa's sole alternative of freezing an entire city in time, his reply raises some important questions. Is it possible to distill the memory of a traumatic event, which has further mutated into thousands of subjective experiences, into one physical remnant? Does the quantity of historic material affect the way that event is remembered? The scattering of material from the Urakami Cathedral ruins across various locations has led to a particular site of memory ultimately being broken up into smaller fragments that visitors experience separately. If we are to follow Tagawa's dismissal that one site would be too narrow and inadequate to remember the atomic bombing, would it not be the case that the eventual solution, to separately display smaller parts of the ruins, was *more* deficient and insulting to the lived experiences of the *hibakusha*? With such questions in mind, let us turn our examination to the decentralized network of sites related to the Urakami Cathedral ruins that still exist in Nagasaki today to understand the consequences of the fragmentation of a previously singular site of memory.

Overview and Description of the Fragments of Urakami Cathedral

The various fragments of the Urakami Cathedral that have been relocated fall into three general categories: "authentic" (that is, comprising original material from the building completed in 1925), reconstructed, and replicated. (For reference, figure 2 provides a map of the locations and relative distances between each of these sites.) The pieces that make up this architectural fabric, though originating from the same source, vary by location, degree of authenticity, and supplementary interpretive material across this scattered geography, revealing how the resulting memorial landscape is by no means a coincidental creation. Rather, it is the result of human decision making and negotiation among various parties about how the atomic bombing might figure into the urban experience of Nagasaki residents and visitors.

The Reconstructed Urakami Cathedral

The reconstruction of the cathedral began shortly after the rubble had been fully removed from the site. Upon completion in October 1959, the reconstruction project had totaled the cost of ¥50,000,000, according to the *Mainichi Shinbun* newspaper.[14] The church was rebuilt based on the original

Figure 2. Map of sites with fragments or replicas of the Urakami Cathedral ruins. Source: Created by author with ArcGIS Online, Esri.

design of the structure completed in 1925, although there are some discrepancies in dimensions, detailing, and the use of reinforced concrete.[15]

In addition to the reconstructed cathedral building, there are statues and memorials outside on the grounds of the Urakami Cathedral. Of those, there are groupings of statuary and other decorative elements, damaged from the atomic bombing. These "sculpture gardens" serve as sites of remembrance for the atomic bombing, as is evident from the practice of leaving strings of folded paper cranes by these statues. However, there is no signage accompanying these sculptures to explain their historical significance or origins.

The Original Belfry

The atomic bombing rendered the structure of the Urakami Cathedral into countless pieces of rubble, most of which was cleared away from the site after the war. However, despite the rhetoric of complete loss surrounding the demolition of the cathedral, one sizable part of the original cathedral has in fact remained where it was found following August 9, 1945. A belfry, weighing approximately fifty tons and a diameter measuring about eighteen feet (5.5 m), can be found at the foot of the hill below the reconstructed Urakami Cathedral. There are also two explanatory signs with images of and text about the belfry, the cathedral, and the atomic bombing: one was placed in 1987 across a small stream from the cathedral, where a visitor can take in the belfry from a better vantage point, while the other, installed after the belfry was included in a national scenic monument designation in 2016, is atop the hill closer to the reconstructed cathedral.

The twin belfries topping the cathedral were the last parts of the cathedral to be erected in 1925, marking the completion of the construction project: its height and decorative splendor were signs of Catholic triumph.[16] The southern belfry did not survive the atomic blast, collapsing into the main structure itself. The northern belfry, however, remained relatively intact atop the building immediately after the bombing. But on the night of August 9, the damaged belfry gave way to gravity and wind and fell into the stream running along the north edge of the cathedral building.[17] Given its considerable weight, the belfry could not be moved with manual labor, and even explosives were not thought sufficient to demolish it. This conundrum led Father Nakajima Banri to suggest that by redirecting the flow of the stream, the belfry would no longer be covered by water and could be buried instead along the stone wall surrounding the cathedral grounds.[18]

In 1950, Nakajima's proposal was taken up to divert the course of the water away from the belfry. Those examining the scene observed the rubble from other parts of the cathedral building buried below with the belfry, evidence that the belfry's position had not changed since the night of August 9, 1945 when it collapsed and settled into the riverbed.[19] Thus, if we are to judge the degree of authenticity of the various fragments of Urakami Cathedral extant in Nagasaki, this belfry may qualify as retaining the highest level of truth in terms of its siting. Indeed, Takase has commented in his book that as one can still see the belfry as it was found and "up close" (*majika ni*), it "may be the most powerful remains [of the cathedral]" where one can "imagine the vivid scene [around the cathedral] just after the atomic bombing."[20] This potency that Takase refers to derives from the magnitude of the belfry ruin that has remained intact, as well as the knowledge that there is some sense of "truth" to the fact that this artifact has not moved since the moment of the atomic bombing that it seeks to narrate to those who encounter it. However, this judgment of authenticity hinges upon the assumption that the atomic bombing is the defining moment over the course of the "life" of the belfry. Its location is "original" only when considering the particular instant of August 9, 1945, thereby minimizing its prior significance as a component of the cathedral when it was intact.

One of the plaques explaining the history of the cathedral belfry is somewhat removed from the belfry itself, requiring the visitor to traverse a crosswalk spanning the stream. Due to its location away from the cathedral grounds, visitors may see the belfry itself, but miss this sign altogether. Those who do seek out the sign, however, will also find below it extracted courses of original brickwork from the cathedral, discolored both from the bombing and organic growth from its exposure to the elements in its current arrangement. A small label above them identifies them as "bricks from the Urakami Cathedral that survived the atomic bombing [*hibaku shita*]."[21] While these have ostensibly been relocated from their original location, from just above the hill to the foot of the hill, this set of bricks is arguably even more, to borrow Takase's words, "up close"—even offering a tactile immediacy—to a visitor seeking to identify what remains of the atomic bombing in Nagasaki's landscape.

The Stone Wall

The original stone retaining wall surrounding the Urakami Cathedral grounds predated the cathedral structure completed in 1925, and therefore it was also present at the site during the atomic bombing in 1945. This history is explained by a single, understated plaque at the foot of the hill below the cathedral. According to this plaque, issued in March 2000 by the city's Atomic Bomb Museum, the stone wall had been part of the property on the site that the Catholic Church eventually purchased in 1880 for the construction of the cathedral. The plaque's text further describes its survival through the atomic bombing, the restoration that was necessary by consolidating the soil retained by the wall and replacing some of the most damaged bricks. It concludes by commenting that the wall, having experienced all of these events across time, has "continuously convey[ed] its message of peace"; the plaque has been placed with the wish that such "tragedy is never repeated."

The Relocated Wall Fragment

The three sites discussed so far are on or near the site of the original Urakami Cathedral. Farther afield, there is yet another piece of the original cathedral. About 1,640 feet (500 m) southwest of the cathedral site is Hypocenter Park, home to a cenotaph mourning the lives lost in the atomic bombing, located directly beneath where the atomic bomb detonated. Radiating outward from the cenotaph are shallow steps leading to the rest of the park, where there are several additional monuments and memorials honoring the victims of the bombing. Ascending the concentric steps eastward leads to one such marker: the segment of the Urakami Cathedral ruins that was spared demolition and moved from its initial site to Hypocenter Park on July 11,

1958, months after the rest of the structure had been razed to the ground. While Mayor Tagawa had promised to investigate the feasibility of relocating the cathedral ruins elsewhere, this plan was only acted upon partially. What stands in Hypocenter Park today comprises one pier, excised from the multiple arches of the cathedral that had remained standing. The steps leading up to the arch can be found on the ground by the pier, and sculptures of saints and gargoyles accompany the remnants. City council records indicate that the transportation to and installation in Hypocenter Park of this material cost ¥1 million.[22]

As an isolated segment of a building's remains, the wall fragment takes on a more sculptural presence. While certainly monumental in its height, there is no longer an "interior" as such, let alone a distinction between interior and exterior, and the resulting encounter with the cathedral wall may be disorienting or confusing. In one of the beginning sections of his book, *Nagasaki: Kieta mō hitotsu no "genbaku dōmu"* (Nagasaki: The Other "Atomic Dome" That Disappeared), Takase Tsuyoshi describes his experience with the cathedral wall monument as something he first registered only as "strange" (*kimyō*). He also reveals a degree of uncertainty or hesitance about the monument's identity: "It is a wall, but slender like a column, and it may be that someone who first sees it does not immediately understand what it is. It is hard to understand with a glance what something like this has been left there, and for what purpose. It would not be strange to pass by it without giving it serious thought.... Even having been born and raised in Nagasaki, I had never deeply considered... the cathedral wall until the year I graduated high school."[23]

If Takase's reaction can be extrapolated as a typical response to the wall fragment, perhaps the most straightforward way to determine what it is and where it came from is through the signage provided nearby. A plaque, placed March 2001, explains the history of the original Urakami Cathedral's construction, its destruction due to the atomic bomb, the relocation and stabilization of the fragment of its ruins, and a call for peace similar to that mentioned in the plaque near the stone retaining wall. The signage also features a photograph of the cathedral ruins, visually annotated to demonstrate which portion of the cathedral ruins had been moved.

Replicas and Fragments in the Atomic Bomb Museum

Closer to the Hypocenter Park is the Nagasaki Atomic Bomb Museum. The museum, technically called an "archive" (*shiryōkan*) in Japanese, is a common destination for those visiting Nagasaki who seek more information about the atomic bombing. The visitor's experience of the permanent exhibition begins with a panoramic photograph of the urban landscape of Nagasaki prior to the atomic bombing, and a clock whose hands were—and have remained—stopped at the time the bomb exploded at 11:02 a.m. This first room is labeled on the museum map as its own section, focusing on "August 9, 1945." The gallery then transitions into the next thematic section, "Damage Caused by the Atomic Bombing," which attempts to re-create "the tragic state of Nagasaki immediately after the bombing, giving visitors a sense of the destructive power and fear of the atomic bomb."[24] While this section of the exhibition takes up several large halls, its first room is dimly lit, evoking a sense of darkness and dread in the visitor. Opposite the entrance to this gallery there is a large replica of part of the Urakami Cathedral ruins—indeed, this is the image on the cover of the museum pamphlet from 2019, indicating that the museum considers and advertises this scene as one of its most iconic or impactful moments. Signage in the gallery explains that what the visitor sees is "a reproduction of part of the wall that remained standing on the southern side of the ruins" of the cathedral following the bombing. The size of the replica ensures that the visitor would take note of it, especially as one faces it upon entering the room, then passes by it upon exiting onto the next gallery.

The gallery with the replica of the ruins also contains several original artifacts, including a sculpture that was blasted off of the exterior of the cathedral in the bombing and molten fragments of the stained-glass window. Also in this gallery are numerous rosaries, signifying the spirituality of the many Catholic victims of the atomic bombing. These objects, unlike the replica, are held in vitrines typical for museum display.

The Missteps of a Preserved vs. Lost Dichotomy

Despite the continued presence of the fragments, a discourse focusing primarily on the loss of the original Urakami Cathedral has persisted. Nagasaki residents and scholars alike have tended to position the cathedral as an emblem of what has been forsaken in the remembrance of the atomic bombing. In turn, the story of the original cathedral is presented almost exclusively as a narrative of loss, crystallized in the moment of its demolition. Although the Catholic *hibakusha* from Urakami had, as a group, generally pushed for the demolition of the ruins to construct a new structure for worship in the decades following the war, some members of that community have indicated in more recent oral histories that they regretted the loss of the ruins as a potent landmark and conceded that the city might have done well to preserve the ruins to memorialize the atomic bombing.[25] Meanwhile, memory studies scholar Tomoe Otsuki, for example, has described that in removing the cathedral ruins, "Nagasaki perpetually lost its most powerful symbol of the dawn and suffering of the nuclear age."[26] Similar characterizations of Urakami Cathedral as an irrevocable loss of memory abound.

In particular, atomic-bombing survivors, local preservationists, and historians of Nagasaki alike have tended to frame this absence of the Urakami Cathedral through its comparison with the continued presence and worldwide recognition of the Atomic Bomb Dome (Genbaku dōmu) in Hiroshima. The origins of such a contrast were formed shortly after the conclusion of the war. As Chad R. Diehl writes, having become Nagasaki's primary "symbol of the tragedy of the atomic bombing ... [and] the center of its commemoration," the Urakami Cathedral ruins in Nagasaki "usually appeared alongside the Hiroshima Atomic Dome in media discussions of the bombings" from the late 1940s onward.[27] Such visual juxtapositions gave way to and transformed into a conceptual equivalency of the two sites of remembrance across the two cities that had experienced the atomic bomb.

This sentiment has evolved today into a sense of deprivation among those in Nagasaki who frame the demolition and subsequent reconstruction of Urakami Cathedral as a memorial injustice, particularly considering the recognition given to the Atomic Dome in Hiroshima. On a visit to Nagasaki's Atomic Bomb Museum in January 2020, the local *hibakusha* volunteering as a tour guide during my visit pointed to the replica of the bombed Urakami Cathedral, explaining its ultimate demise and how the ruins, if not demolished, would have served a role similar to the Atomic Dome.[28] Similarly, Japanese authors who have published recent works on the Urakami Cathedral emphasize this feeling of dispossession in their titles: Takase's book *Nagasaki: Kieta mō hitotsu no "genbaku dōmu"* directly draws a parallel between the two structures in Hiroshima and Nagasaki while emphasizing the absence in Nagasaki through the word "disappeared" (*kieta*). Within his first chapter, Takase frames the significance of his study of the fate of the Urakami Cathedral as one of addressing why, if the Atomic Dome remains in Hiroshima, the Urakami Cathedral no longer stands in Nagasaki. In other words, although both are cities that experienced atomic destruction, "why are the remains symbolizing the experience of the atomic bombing left in one city, while the other has nothing of the sort to speak of?"[29] Takase's book later recounts an interview with Iwaguchi Natsuo, a fervent champion of the preservation of the Urakami Cathedral ruins who had spoken forcefully against Mayor Tagawa's sudden abandonment of plans to protect the ruins in the 1950s. Takase quotes Iwaguchi, reminiscing on this debate: "Truly, if [the ruins] still remained, it would have been World Heritage. Everyone should regret [its loss].... A Christian country dropped a bomb right above

Catholics in Urakami—above believers of their own religion. It would have been a World Heritage site with a narrative that almost seems made up."[30] Thus, through his own commentary and testimony from preservation advocates, including *hibakusha*, Takase has portrayed Nagasaki as having been denied a rightful World Heritage site.

A similar focus on loss is also evident in the book *Nagasaki kyū-Urakami tenshudō 1945–58: Ushinawareta hibaku isan* (Nagasaki's Former Urakami Cathedral, 1945–58: An Atomic-Bombing Relic Lost), which features photographs by Takahara Itaru with text in Japanese by Yokote Kazuhiko and in English by Brian Burke-Gaffney.[31] Yokote and Burke-Gaffney likewise make reference to the UNESCO World Heritage status that the Atomic Dome acquired in 1996. Burke-Gaffney's text argues that had the Urakami Cathedral ruins been preserved, its "significance for humanity would have undoubtedly been acknowledged in the same way," that is, with a World Heritage label.[32] The corresponding Japanese essay by Yokote includes a phrase that is not included in the English translation, but augments the sense of remorse and longing: "But now, it is the phantom [*maboroshi*] of a World Heritage site."[33] Permeating through these accounts of Urakami Cathedral and its eventual demolition is one that focuses on loss and absence and, by virtue of an assumed equivalency between the Atomic Dome and Urakami Cathedral, how that loss has deprived Nagasaki—and, perhaps by extension, Japan—of worldwide recognition in the form of World Heritage status.

That this lack of recognition has espoused some envy or resentment is entirely understandable. As Diehl has argued, compared to Hiroshima, Nagasaki has historically gotten the short end of the stick in terms of its status as a site of nuclear remembrance. This resulted, in part, from postwar legislation and urban planning schemes that concentrated the construction of Hiroshima as a "peace city" rising out of an atomic bombing and the reconstruction of Nagasaki as a city of "international culture."[34] Meanwhile, several studies have provided data indicating that World Heritage status, perhaps expectedly, does increase the number of visitors to the site and, correspondingly, revenue streams into the local community.[35] However, that the particular vehicle of World Heritage has become such a common theme in lamenting the perceived loss of Urakami Cathedral, procedurally speaking, appears somewhat misguided. The UNESCO World Heritage Convention is upheld through the ratification and participation of States Parties—that is, on the national level. Consequently, national representatives are in charge of selecting sites within their political borders, for which extensive nomination dossiers are compiled for review by the international World Heritage Commission. Considering that in Japan and elsewhere the image of Hiroshima as the "peace city" associated closely with the atomic bombing has long overshadowed Nagasaki, it would have been unlikely that Japan's World Heritage representatives would have put the two sites on equal standing for consideration on the international arena. In fact, the nomination of two sites illustrating similar histories or significance would also not have been strategic for Japan as a state party, considering the World Heritage Commission's mandate and efforts to minimize redundancy among World Heritage sites in terms of building type or historical associations. Arguably, this directive was launched in the 1990s with an eye toward correcting the overrepresentation of European sites on the World Heritage List and so may not have been fully applicable toward Japan, especially for a historical circumstance as exceptional as an atomic bombing.

Nevertheless, the nomination and inscription process for the Atomic Dome in Hiroshima on the World Heritage List was rife with political tensions that sought to undermine the conferral of World Heritage status to the Atomic Dome. In particular, the United States, as a state party, objected to the inclusion of the Atomic Dome as a World Heritage Site on the grounds that the site would offer only a one-sided interpretation of the historical circumstances behind the atomic bombing of Hiroshima.[36] It is not a stretch to imagine that a proposal to inscribe a similar site that represented the nuclear actions of the United States would have met similar opposition—all the more so if it were to follow the Atomic Dome as a second World Heritage site. While these are all counterfactual assertions, the point is that the insistence on a hypothetically guaranteed World Heritage inscription for the Urakami Cathedral ruins is not necessarily a realistic aspiration. In fact, this rhetoric serves only to deepen the emphasis on the sense of loss and an accompanying indignation that distracts from or neglects what does still remain of atomic memory in Nagasaki.

Underlying this insistence on the premise of loss and the constant mention of the counterexample of Hiroshima's Atomic Dome is a firmly embedded dichotomy that pits continued presence and survival against absence and permanent destruction. Indeed, this polarity is revealed in the language that Diehl has indicated as characteristic of the debates among Nagasaki's government and citizens on the future of the Urakami Cathedral ruins after the war: "Discussion over the fate of the ruins, including in newspapers and journals, was often phrased as 'preserve or remove?' [*hozon ka tekkyo ka*]."[37] In such a conception, preservation is considered diametrically opposite to removal or demolition. There is no intermediary option, and the two are seen as mutually exclusive.

And yet, the survey of remaining parts of the Urakami Cathedral extant throughout Nagasaki—indeed, most of the pieces deriving from the original structure, albeit relocated—necessarily complicates such dualistic thinking. There are multiple axes on which to evaluate authenticity, and the fragmentation of a previously singular building into multiple, physically separate sites of memory requires a more nuanced conception of how one engages with the memory that still essentially forms the common thread across these various sites. In the meantime, the persistence of the preserve vs. remove mindset, commonly manifested through discourse on the utter absence of the Urakami Cathedral in today's Nagasaki and the corollary claims that Nagasaki deserves what Hiroshima has in its presence of an atomic ruin, works to devalue what *does* remain of the Urakami Cathedral. Further, averting the possibility of more complex options beyond the two poles of saving and destroying precludes serious consideration of the consequences of this fragmentation, and thinking through if and how such a network of sites of memory pertaining to the Urakami Cathedral poses unique characteristics, experiences, or challenges in transmitting the legacy and heritage of Nagasaki's atomic bombing. In other words, even if the sites are physically separated, does that inevitably entail an analogous disintegration of the memory associated with these artifacts?

What Does Fragmentation Do to Nagasaki's Atomic Memory?

Conflicts and Omissions in Signage

Examining the intertextuality (or lack thereof) among the content of the signage at the various sites pertaining to the Urakami Cathedral indicates the complexity of maintaining a consistent and cohesive historical narrative across these fragments. Geographers Ken Foote and Maoz Azaryahu write of the importance of paying attention to such supplementary interpretive material at historic sites: inscriptions and signage are "crucial for the production of meaning" due to their function as "complementary modes of representation" along with the historical material and artifacts they explicate. They continue: "The different modes of cultural production employed at a site are intended to complement each other in propagating its official story."[38] In this conception, it is only through the explicit verbalization of the history associated with the site through media beyond the historical material itself that solidifies and conveys an understanding of the site's significance. Foote and Azaryahu's implication that the transfer of knowledge is unforgivingly one-directional—an authoritative history is successfully communicated to and unequivocally understood by any and all visitors to a given site—has been contested. Nevertheless, there is value in examining textual materials as evidence of how those in charge of curating these sites *intended* for them to be understood. The Urakami Cathedral fragments in Nagasaki presents a case in which there are multiple sites pertaining to the same history or origin, an arrangement that Foote and Azaryahu's discussion of how an imagined visitor engages with a singular site did not treat. What is shown on the various signs at these sites, then, helps to demonstrate the practical and intellectual challenges that come with the physical separation and multiplication of the sites that theoretically have the same referent of the Urakami Cathedral ruins.

When considered altogether, the signs contain omissions and contradictions that impede a straightforward understanding of how this network of Urakami Cathedral's fragments came to be and fail to paint a complete picture of the extent to which the Urakami Cathedral still persists, albeit in pieces, in Nagasaki. For instance, the signage at the belfry, placed in August 1987, mentions how the "belfries and walls that remained upright collapsed soon after, leaving only a remnant of the church wall." Ostensibly, both the ruins of the two belfries and cathedral walls are offered as material evidence of atomic ruins, but the next sentence narrows the focus to the north belfry: "One of the belfries . . . rests today on the spot where it fell that day." The narrative thread about the ruined walls is stopped short, with no further mention of its demolition and partial relocation to the Hypocenter Park. Meanwhile, at the Hypocenter Park, the wall section is accompanied by a sign that insists that "Only the broken church wall remained," denying the presence of the belfry, the stone wall, or the fragments housed at the Atomic Bomb Museum. Meanwhile, the supplemental material for the replica of the Urakami Cathedral ruins in the Atomic Bomb Museum shows a photograph with arrows to indicate the portion of the wall that has been reproduced in the gallery, and the portion that has been "relocated to Peace Park (near the Hypocenter Monolith) and still stands today." This gallery makes no mention of the subsequent reconstruction of the cathedral. Perhaps because this area of the museum, still early on in the visitor's itinerary, seeks to highlight the devastation and destruction wrought by the atomic bomb, the reconstruction is omitted from the narrative to undercut signals of hope or recovery at this point. Regardless of the reason, none of the Urakami Cathedral ruin fragments fully explicates the presence of the other sites throughout Nagasaki in order to form a textual network that weaves together the various pieces remaining of the cathedral.

It is worth noting that all of the explanatory texts across the various sites are under the purview of the Atomic Bomb Museum. The signs were issued at different points in time over many years, which may have forced gaps in staff and created inconsistencies in the narratives presented at each site. Nevertheless, if a single institution still has sway over these signs, an effort may be made to compare and revise these signs to present more explicitly the interconnectivity between these sites, if such a strategy is thought beneficial for the effective communication of Nagasaki's atomic history.

Administrative and Preservation Policy Issues

The official designation of a site as a historic landmark is often contingent upon the recognition that it integrally fulfills specific criteria of historical significance and value. This prerequisite condition makes designation status and any official historical narratives for those sites a useful source to determine the assumptions underlying a judgment that a site meets baseline criteria and expectations for historical value and authenticity.

Of the sites pertaining to the original Urakami Cathedral, only the belfry has been designated as a historic landmark. The belfry is part of a group of sites inscribed in 2016 as a national historic monument (*shiseki kinenbutsu*) that attests to the aftermath of the atomic bombing, referred to as the "Nagasaki Atomic Bombing Remains" (*genbaku iseki*). In addition to the belfry, the monument designation also includes the hypocenter, ruins of Shiroyama School, the Nagasaki Medical College Gate, and the one-legged *tori'i* gate at San'nō Temple. These five sites are isolated from each other in geographic location, albeit all are within an approximately 2,625-foot (800 m) radius from the hypocenter.[39]

In Japan, there are three levels of governmental landmarks designation: municipal, prefectural, and national. While the city of Nagasaki or Nagasaki Prefecture can designate sites to its own lists of cultural properties, designation as a *national* historic monument means that the entity managing its maintenance and preservation may request federal funds to help finance those efforts, as well as technical advice and recommendations from a central body of experts.[40] Meanwhile, the national designation status does not preclude municipal or prefectural aid—in fact, it is anticipated and encouraged that local bodies participate in affairs around the heritage that surrounds them. To that end, municipal and prefectural governments can promote preservation and interpretation of sites and facilitate administrative processes for nationally designated cultural properties within their boundaries.[41] In this sense, the designation of the cathedral belfry ruin affords it benefits and increased oversight that has not been extended toward the other sites.

Following the 2016 designation, new directional and explanatory signage has been installed on the grounds of the Urakami Cathedral to refer to the belfry at the foot of the hill on which the cathedral stands. Even the directional markers point out that the belfry is a component of the national monument group, stressing the prestige that accompanies such designation. The text on the explanatory plaque abides by the statement of significance of the designations, which explains that the belfry's significance and uniqueness is based on its ability to "authentically" (*nyojitsu ni*) convey the "historical truth" of the atomic bombing, the damage caused by nuclear weapons, and the miseries of war.[42] The plaque supplements this historical understanding by claiming that "the North Bell Tower, still in the same place as when the cathedral was destroyed by the bomb, is all that remains of the original structure to tell the story of the damage done to the Urakami Cathedral." Such a statement hinges upon the necessity of an artifact to be *in situ* in order to be effective in communicating its history, thereby demoting the value of other pieces of the cathedral that have been relocated since the atomic bombing. This particular site and the regulatory mechanism of designation creates a sense of hierarchy and asserts a specific definition of authenticity that may rhetorically undermine the impact of other sites.

Redundancy and Confused Conceptions of "Authenticity"

Not only does the single designated site containing material from the Urakami Cathedral ruins assert its own authenticity at the expense of the building's other remaining fragments, but conversely, the presence of these other sites has come to be typically understood as a sort of abundance that is self-effacing in its redundancy. For example, Kaori Yoshida, Huong T. Bui, and Timothy J. Lee, in their analysis of materials promoting tourism in both Nagasaki and Hiroshima, assert that "owing to the absence of any authentic structure around the Nagasaki hypocenter, monuments in the complex are mainly reconstructed or were brought over from other affected sites. Therefore, A-bomb sites in Nagasaki display *less authenticity* than the actual sites of events such as the Genbaku Dome in Hiroshima" (emphasis added).[43] Note again the use of language about loss and the pitting of Nagasaki's atomic relics against Hiroshima's Atomic Dome. Their conception of authenticity is, as before, one based on the object having remained in its original place, in addition to an assumption that the constituent materials must be historically original rather than replacements or reconstructions. As discussed previously with respect to the designations, these authors resort to ranking these sites, including those in Hiroshima, based on a set standard.

The idea that multiple sites attesting to the same history compete for historical authority and primacy is not new, nor is it unique to Nagasaki. K. E. Foote and M. Azaryahu have insisted that, in general, "*The location itself*, as the scene of past events, together with any available physical remains, can be used to create a sense of authenticity" (emphasis added).[44] That is, according to Foote and Azaryahu, the site is understood to have become imbued with the historical events that it has "witnessed." Following this logic, the location and the "physical remains" should ideally be considered inseparable if they are to communicate its past to the viewer harmoniously and most effectively. Additionally, to offer a concrete example, Jing Xu has discussed the differences in visiting experience before and after the material contents of the Unit 731 Museum in Harbin, China—a historically loaded site that housed a former chemical warfare research facility under the Imperial Japanese Army—were removed to a newly constructed exhibition hall near the original site. Xu argued that the new exhibition hall is "contested," competing with the original site in attracting visitors and conveying a sense of authenticity, even as "it both connects to and disconnects from the old exhibition hall in terms of temporality and spatial functionality." In other words, the new structure is "paradoxically and simultaneously communicating both a historical continuity and a loss of place-based memory."[45] A similar tension—that of concurrent competition, contradiction, and survival—can be applied to the fragmented sites of the Urakami Cathedral.

The standard upon which authenticity is judged has been contested as of late, however, and such interrogations could be usefully transposed onto a revised understanding of the merits of the various Urakami Cathedral ruins. Both the removal of sites from their original locations and reconstruction of lost or damaged sites have been traditionally considered taboo in its affront to orthodox conceptions of historic authenticity.[46] Nevertheless, encroaching forces of urbanization and speculative development, along with the accelerating threats due to climate change, have lately rendered relocation a more commonly practiced option in saving built heritage. Indeed, Cornelius Holtorf has argued that tolerance for loss of and changes to built heritage will become increasingly necessary as humanity faces unprecedented scenarios requiring adaptation and resilience, which in turn implies the urgency to embrace more nuanced understandings of authenticity.[47] What was once a last resort may become more standard and thereby more accepted, which retroactively challenges the more limiting notions of authenticity that have been upheld within the cultural heritage sector. On the other hand, reconstructions such as that of Urakami Cathedral have come to be increasingly suggested as a viable method for heritage preservation. For instance, Francesca Piazzoni has argued that the categorical rejection of reconstructions for their fakeness is reductive and misguided.[48] Specifically, Piazzoni has contended that rebuilt sites in fact enable communities to construct a reworked sense of the authentic that is still continuous to what previously existed. In the materiality that they offer, reconstructions empower people through spatial experiences and enabling them to negotiate historical meaning, which can help establish a new sense of understanding and belonging. Understood through these lenses that challenge traditional tenets of historic preservation, it is possible to reassess and take more seriously what the various fragments of the Urakami Cathedral are able to offer today without dismissing them outright as "lesser" artifacts.

Room for Subjectivity: Experiential and Cognitive Variability

At the simplest level, the dispersion of Urakami Cathedral ruin sites creates spatial and therefore chronological gaps in visitors' experiences. There is no prescribed path to navigate from site to site; some visitors may choose not to see particular sites over others, and the physical distance between the sites may create opportunities for experiences that occur between leaving one site to arriving at another to influence how the visitor understands or reacts to the latter. Arguably, for any given site, there are degrees of freedom introduced based on the visitor's agency—some even contradict given instructions or itineraries at heritage sites outright. A recent turn toward understanding the role of affect in encounters with heritage sites has exposed the fluidity and unpredictability of visitors' reactions, which may even subvert the intent of the official narrative that authorities sought to impart at the site. As Margaret Wetherell, Laurajane Smith, and Gary Campbell have put it, "Affect and emotion are flowing, dynamic, recursive and profoundly contextual, challenging static and neat formulations." Affective responses depend not on "the expression of an underlying basic emotion program but a flexible, contextual, contingent and ongoing construction and assembling of bodily sensations, events, meanings and consequences," which in turn renders visitors' responses, guided by these ever-changing forces, similarly variable.[49] Further, as Hamzah Muzaini has explained, "what actually happens when one implicitly and explicitly engages with these memoryscapes may differ not only between individuals but also with the same individual experiencing the same memoryscapes at different times."[50] Even for a singular site, a particular visitor carries preconceived notions and biases that color their encounter, and the experience at the same site is dynamic over multiple encounters. Extending this reasoning, the multiplicity and separation amongst the Urakami Cathedral ruin sites in Nagasaki augment the discrepancies in visitor experience and understanding that may arise based on the experiential discontinuity and breaks from site to site.

To gain an understanding of how these affective processes come into play at the Urakami Cathedral ruin sites, web-based platforms where tourists can write reviews of their experiences at particular sites are useful. Reviews on sites like TripAdvisor are insightful in that they often include information on the most memorable components of the visit, framed for an audience of other potential visitors.[51] This imagined but clear, intended reader motivates reviewers to share what other visitors need to experience or learn. Scholars such as Laurajane Smith have shown that although heritage sites are commonly considered "educational" resources—that is, people visit them in order to learn something—a critical discourse analysis of interviews with visitors upon exiting the site revealed that instead of learning anything new or considering viewpoints contrary to their own preexisting conceptions, visitors tend to selectively pay attention to and construe meanings from the material at the site in a process of "embodied commitment, reminder and legitimation of political positions held by the visitor."[52] Thus, Smith argues, the "learning" that visitors imagined to occur at heritage sites was for "children and/or communities or groups *other than* the one to which the visitor belonged."[53] Thus, recommendations or opinions made in TripAdvisor reviews about how to visit and understand sites could provide clues for both the visitor's positionality and previously held beliefs, as well as what they believe is the "right" way for others to "learn" from these sites.

The various sites with components or replicas of the Urakami Cathedral ruins outlined herein each have separate pages on TripAdvisor, mirroring their geographic independence from each other.[54] However, all of these pages—along with other sites in Nagasaki pertaining to the atomic bombing—predominantly feature reviews that contain or consist entirely of generic messages about the horrors of war and the need for world peace. This corresponds with what Lisa Yoneyama wrote in her influential book on atomic memory in Hiroshima about the overdetermined nature of remembrance about the atomic bombing: "most visitors to Hiroshima have been preexposed to many versions of stereotypical stories that the mass media provide year after year. . . . Saturated with such simulations and a deluge of objectified information, many of us feel that we have enough knowledge about the atomic bomb, even prior to our visit to the site. As a result, we . . .

often conclude our visit to Hiroshima by reaffirming what we already know."[55] Combined with the universalist rhetoric surrounding contemporary understanding of the atomic bombings—that all of humanity is figuratively in the same boat, threatened by nuclear weapons, and so must all strive for the common goal of peace—virtually all visitors who take the time to reflect on their visits to these sites in Nagasaki were inclined to repeat, presumably with sincerity but perhaps mindlessly, the most common clichés. It is also interesting to note the parallelism between Yoneyama's claim that visits to nuclear sites only reaffirm "what we already know" and Smith's data-based conclusion to the same effect. In this case, the proliferation of official (top-down), standard understandings of the atomic bombing render much of the reviews into rote platitudes.

Looking beyond these repeated wishes for peace, however, reveals more relevant information about how visitors have made sense of the fragmentation of these various sites. The multiplicity of sites that all derive from the narrative of the Urakami Cathedral's destruction appears to have led to factual confusion and conflation in many visitors' minds of the various sites. This disorientation is evident through the pattern of photos of one site being uploaded and therefore associated with a geographically different site. For instance, twenty-four images of the wall fragment from Hypocenter Park have been uploaded for the Atomic Bomb Museum and approximately 20 percent of the forty-six images uploaded for the Urakami Cathedral Wall page. The confusion also carries over to the verbal content of the reviews. Some visitors wrote reviews entirely about their experiences at other Urakami Cathedral–related sites on a page for a different site altogether. The page for the Urakami Cathedral wall ruins at Hypocenter Park contains reviews that commented on the reconstructed cathedral or the nearby belfry ruins, with no mention of the wall ruins at Hypocenter Park. Thus, in general, the various fragments became entangled and even interchangeable in the visitors' recollections. Interestingly, however, reviewers generally seemed to understand that the Urakami Cathedral was a rebuilt structure and not the "original." Nearly 20 percent of the studied reviews for the cathedral explicitly mention the reconstructed nature of the structure they visited. While photographs from different sites (the wall fragment, the replica from the Atomic Bomb Museum) were posted onto the reconstructed Urakami Cathedral page, perhaps the visitors found it necessary to reconcile the contradiction of the images showing duplicate materials (e.g., a new cathedral that has replaced the portion of the wall moved to Hypocenter Park) and attempt to articulate an explanation for this contradiction to others in the text of their reviews.

A number of reviews also contained recommended routes to visit the various Urakami Cathedral sites throughout Nagasaki, both demonstrating the visitors' understanding of the interrelationships between and value judgments about these fragments. Some visitors recall and endorse the way that they ordered their itinerary, and thus in effect attempt to convince others by way of a suggestion that the way that they had experienced and made sense of these multiple sites was "correct." Such instructions to others comprise not only different sequences of visiting the various sites but also advice on which sites feel redundant or not worth visiting. In fact, the rebuilt Urakami Cathedral was the site with the most reviews that discouraged others from visiting or described an experience that was not rewarding or did not meet expectations.[56] Further, this negative reception was often rooted in a sense that the site did not convey a sufficiently "authentic" sense of the atomic bombing; its reconstructed status detracted from a deep or meaningful affective response or opportunity to reflect on the site's history of destruction. Interestingly, many reviewers on the Urakami Cathedral page instead recommend that readers see the belfry as a more effective remnant of the atomic bombing owing to its perceived "authenticity" in its preservation on site and in its ruinous state.

Thus, the reviews provide windows into visitors' retrospective understandings of and projected expectations for other visitors' experiences of the Urakami Cathedral sites in Nagasaki. The itineraries that visitors record and suggest to others are immense in variability. Taken together, they point to the numerous potential permutations for a visitor's experience while also conveying the sense that visitors tend to feel that they had pieced together the correct "route." They also indicate different levels of confusion and a loss of specificity due to the sites all relating to an interconnected and inseparable narrative.

Memorials and monuments tend to be taken for granted. The very human processes that led to their creation and preservation often become overlooked as they become embedded into the imaginary of a particular place or their narratives are solidified and standardized. The atomic ruins of Nagasaki are no different. Nonetheless, the sites of the Urakami Cathedral and its various fragments pose a worthwhile and unique case study because of the historical circumstances that have led to the dispersion and reproduction of the memory associated with a particular place. The continued presence of these fragments defies the potent but simplistic narrative that Nagasaki was deprived of its own version of an "Atomic Bomb Dome" with the reconstruction of the Urakami Cathedral, a limiting view that pits preservation squarely and irreconcilably against demolition without considering any intermediary options, including the persistence of pieces of the ruin within the city. This perspective has prevented a holistic analysis of these fragments acting in conjunction with each other, as the destruction/reconstruction of the Urakami Cathedral itself drew attention away from the other relevant sites. This essay has attempted to take these relationships seriously in identifying and describing these other components of the Urakami Cathedral in Nagasaki's memorial landscape and providing some preliminary ways to consider what this physical and cognitive fragmentation of the cathedral's history might mean in terms of how visitors value (and even rank) the various sites, and what they perceive to be most "authentic," impactful, or effective in engaging the history of the atomic bombing. While it is perhaps overly ambitious to predict or cleanly analyze subjective reactions across all potential visitors, the different sites connected to the Urakami Cathedral ruins offer a way to think not only about the atomic bombing as an event constrained in time but also about the human values and priorities reflected in its dispersal through preservation, relocation, and replication since 1945.

Notes

1. Lisa Yoneyama, *Hiroshima Traces: Time, Space, and the Dialectics of Memory* (Berkeley: University of California Press, 1999), 81.

2. Gwyn McClelland, *Dangerous Memory in Nagasaki: Prayers, Protests and Catholic Survivor Narratives* (New York: Routledge, 2020), 113.

3. Chad R. Diehl, *Resurrecting Nagasaki: Reconstruction and the Formation of Atomic Narratives* (Ithaca, NY: Cornell University Press, 2018), 149.

4. Takase Tsuyoshi, *Nagasaki: Kieta mō hitotsu no "genbaku dōmu"* (Nagasaki: The Other "Atomic Dome" That Disappeared) (Tokyo: Heibonsha, 2009), 115–116.

5. Diehl, *Resurrecting Nagasaki*, 156.

6. McClelland, *Dangerous Memory in Nagasaki*, 56.

7. Takase, *Nagasaki*, 149. All translations cited from Japanese sources are mine, unless otherwise noted.

8. This course of action has continued to raised suspicion among survivors who had lived through these debates, as well as historians attempting to recover more information about the circumstances of the cathedral's demolition. Takase Tsuyoshi, for example, posits that Tagawa was likely to have been influenced by U.S. postwar public diplomacy efforts toward the elimination of damning evidence of the country's nuclear aggression, such as the cathedral ruins. See Takase, *Nagasaki*, 223–225.

9. Ibid., 149.

10. Chad R. Diehl, "Resurrecting Nagasaki: Reconstruction, the Urakami Catholics, and Atomic Memory, 1945–1970," PhD diss., Columbia University, 2011, 83.

11. Takase, *Nagasaki*, 136–137.

12. Ibid., 138.

13. Ibid., 144.

14. "Urakami tenshudō saiken" (Reconstruction of Urakami Cathedral), *Mainichi Shinbun*, November 1, 1959.

15. The reconstructed building had a total area of about 18,000 square feet (1,700 sq m) and reached a height of 108 feet (33 m); both of these dimensions were larger than the original. However, allegedly due to budget shortages and rushed construction, some parts were considered "somewhat incomplete" and "architecturally regrettable" (*oshimarete iru*). "Saiken sareta Urakami tenshudō" (The Reconstructed Urakami Cathedral), *Mainichi Shinbun*, June 10, 1959.

16. Kazuhiko Yokote and Brian Burke-Gaffney, *Nagasaki kyū Urakami tenshudō, 1945–58: Ushinawareta hibaku isan* (Nagasaki's Former Urakami Cathedral, 1945–58: An Atomic-Bombing Relic Lost) (Tokyo: Iwanami shoten, 2010), 70.

17. Agency of Cultural Affairs, Government of Japan, "Shiseki meishō ten'nen kinen butsu: Nagasaki genbaku iseki" (National Historic, Scenic, or Natural Monument: Nagasaki Atomic Bombing Ruins), Nationally Designated Cultural Property Database, https://kunishitei.bunka.go.jp/heritage/detail/401/00003956.

18. Takase, *Nagasaki*, 108.

19. Agency of Cultural Affairs, "Nagasaki genbaku iseki."

20. Takase, *Nagasaki*, 108.

21. Translations into English of the Japanese text on the signage at the sites discussed have been made by the author, based on a visit to Nagasaki in January 2020.

22. Takase, *Nagasaki*, 152.

23. Ibid., 10–11.

24. Nagasaki Atomic Bomb Museum, "Nagasaki Atomic Bomb Museum," museum guide map (in English), https://nabmuseum.jp/wp-content/uploads/english.pdf.

25. McClelland, *Dangerous Memory in Nagasaki*, 57.

26. Tomoe Otsuki, "The Politics of Reconstruction and Reconciliation in U.S.-Japan Relations: Dismantling the Atomic Bomb Ruins of Nagasaki's Urakami Cathedral," *The Asia-Pacific Journal: Japan Focus* 13, no. 32 (August 2015): 21, https://apjjf.org/2015/13/32/Tomoe-Otsuki/4356.html.

27. Diehl, *Resurrecting Nagasaki*, 145; Diehl, "Resurrecting Nagasaki," 190.

28. Interestingly, the guide's theory for its disappearance was one of censorship by the American occupation forces, which did not want a remaining symbol of the atomic bombing, particularly upon a large contingency of

Christians, which presented an "inconvenient" (*tsugō ga warui*) circumstance for the United States despite the occupation's having ended in 1952.

29. Takase, *Nagasaki*, 17–18.

30. Ibid., 141.

31. Yokote and Burke-Gaffney, *Nagasaki kyū Urakami tenshudō*.

32. Ibid., vii.

33. Ibid., vi.

34. Diehl, "Resurrecting Nagasaki," 7–9, 95, 233.

35. For example, see Pascale Marcotte and Laurent Bourdeau, "Tourists' Knowledge of the UNESCO Designation of World Heritage Sites: The Case of Visitors to Quebec City," *International Journal of Arts Management* 8, no. 2 (Winter 2006): 4–13. While many studies have also shown that World Heritage status tends to lead to an increased likelihood that visitors come away disappointed after experiencing the site, an assumed correlation between touristic revenue and designation status continues to pervade much of heritage literature; indeed, World Heritage status may still entice visitors, regardless of their reactions *following* the visit. Maria Gravari-Barbas, Laurent Bourdeau, and Mike Robinson, "World Heritage and Tourism: From Opposition to Co-production," in *World Heritage, Tourism and Identity: Inscription and Co-production*, ed. Laurent Bourdeau, Maria Gravari-Barbas, and Mike Robinson (New York: Routledge, 2016), 4, 9–10.

36. Owen Beazley, "A Paradox of Peace: The Hiroshima Peace Memorial (Genbaku Dome) as World Heritage," in *A Fearsome Heritage: Diverse Legacies of the Cold War*, ed. John Schofield and Wayne Cocroft (London: Routledge, 2016), 41.

37. Diehl, *Resurrecting Nagasaki*, 155.

38. K. E. Foote and M. Azaryahu, "Toward a Geography of Memory: Geographical Dimensions of Memory and Commemoration," *Journal of Political and Military Sociology* 35, no. 1 (2007): 128.

39. The inclusion of the hypocenter in this designation creates some ambiguity about the status of the Urakami Cathedral wall fragment that is now located there. Because the wall fragment lacks signage indicating its status as a nationally designated historic monument and the full designation statement of significance does not explicitly refer to the wall fragment (the only atomic monument at the hypocenter mentioned specifically is the display of the archaeological stratum from the time of the bombing), I will consider it undesignated.

40. Law for the Protection of Cultural Properties of 1950 (Japan), law No. 214 (May 30, 1950), https://elaws.e-gov.go.jp/document?lawid=325AC1000000214 #Mp-At_31-Pr_3. See chapter 7 of the law.

41. Agency of Cultural Affairs, Government of Japan, "Cultural Properties: Measures," https://www.bunka.go.jp/english/policy/cultural_properties/overview/index.html.

42. Agency of Cultural Affairs, "Nagasaki genbaku iseki."

43. Kaori Yoshida, Huong T. Bui, and Timothy J. Lee, "Does Tourism Illuminate the Darkness of Hiroshima and Nagasaki?" *Journal of Destination Marketing & Management* 5 (2016): 338.

44. Foote and Azaryahu, "Toward a Geography of Memory," 128.

45. Jing Xu, "The Old/New Unit 731 Museum: A Place of Memory and Oblivion," in *Affective Architectures: More-than-Representational Geographies of Heritage*, ed. Jacque Micieli-Voutsinas and Angela M. Person (New York: Routledge, 2021), 47.

46. For example, Article 15 of the International Charter for the Conservation and Restoration of Monuments and Sites (the "Venice Charter")—considered one of the earliest attempts to codify international preservation standards, which still remains influential in cultural heritage management practice today—insists that "reconstruction work" of any kind should "be ruled out '*a priori*.'" International Council on Monuments and Sites, "International Charter for the Conservation and Restoration of Monuments and Sites (The Venice Charter 1964)," https://www.icomos.org/charters/venice_e.pdf. In 2018 the various advisory bodies and representatives of the World Heritage Convention States Parties reaffirmed this sentiment in the Warsaw Recommendation on Recovery and Reconstruction of Cultural Heritage, which deemed that reconstruction could "be undertaken only in exceptional circumstances" that satisfy "the test of authenticity and conditions of integrity." UNESCO World Heritage Centre, "Warsaw Recommendation on Recovery and Reconstruction of Cultural Heritage," May 2018.

47. Cornelius Holtorf, "Embracing Change: How Cultural Resilience Is Increased through Cultural Heritage," *World Archaeology* 50, no. 4 (2018): 645–648.

48. Francesca Piazzoni, "What's Wrong with Fakes? Heritage Reconstructions, Authenticity, and Democracy in Post-Disaster Recoveries," *International Journal of Cultural Property* 27, no. 2 (May 2020): 246–252.

49. Margaret Wetherell, Laurajane Smith, and Gary Campbell, "Introduction: Affective Heritage Practices," in *Emotion, Affective Practices, and the Past in the Present*, ed. Laurajane Smith, Margaret Wetherell, and Gary Campbell (London: Routledge, 2018), 1, 3.

50. Hamzah Muzaini, "Personal Reflections on Formal Second World War Memories/Memorials in Everyday Spaces in Singapore," in *Memory, Place and Identity: Commemoration and Remembrance of War and Conflict*, ed. Danielle Drozdzewski, Sarah De Nardi, and Emma Waterton (New York: Routledge, 2016), 40.

51. For reasons of data privacy and research ethics, I will report information based only on reviews posted on TripAdvisor in aggregate, anonymous format, without any identifying information about individual users.

52. Laurajane Smith, "'We are . . . we are everything': The Politics of Recognition and Misrecognition at Immigration Museums," *Museum & Society* 15, no. 1 (2017): 76.

53. Ibid., 73.

54. As of August 2021, under "Things to Do" for Nagasaki, TripAdvisor has distinct pages for "Urakami Cathedral," "The Former Urakami Cathedral Belfry," "Urakami Cathedral Wall," and "Nagasaki Atomic Bomb Museum." In addition to these pages, specific reviews were isolated and included for study if they made reference to the cathedral wall or Urakami Cathedral on the "Hypocenter of Atomic Bombing" and "Nagasaki Peace Park" pages. The photographs uploaded to each of these pages were also analyzed. The only site of the ones described in this essay that does not have a separate page on TripAdvisor is the marker for the stone wall surrounding the Urakami Cathedral grounds. Indeed, its relative obscurity is confirmed by the fact that, despite the prevalence of a page for a particular Urakami Cathedral-related site containing images of and review text about other sites, the plaque for the stone wall was mentioned in only one review and shown in one photograph uploaded to TripAdvisor, out of the more than four thousand reviews and four thousand photographs uploaded since 2010 analyzed for this study.

55. Yoneyama, *Hiroshima Traces*, 127.

56. There were twenty-eight reviews for the Urakami Cathedral that articulated the visitor's opinion of the effectiveness of the site to impact visitors, particularly in terms of an experience that brought insight or affective response about the atomic bombing of Nagasaki. Of these, nineteen (roughly 68 percent) were negative. Meanwhile, on the whole, the belfry was the most favorably reviewed site of those listed, with only one comment that reflected disappointment out of twenty-one reviews that explicitly addressed the quality of the visitor's encounter with the site.

One Fine Day
The Allied Occupation of Nagasaki and "Madame Butterfly House"

By Brian Burke-Gaffney

The Allied occupation of Nagasaki began on September 23, 1945, three weeks after Japanese representatives signed the Instrument of Surrender aboard USS *Missouri* in Tokyo Bay. The atomic bombs dropped by American forces the previous month had devastated Hiroshima and Nagasaki and precipitated Japan's defeat in the Pacific War. By the time the occupation forces arrived in Nagasaki, where two-thirds of the city's population had been killed or injured, most of the corpses lying in the charred rubble or festering on riverbanks had been collected and cremated, but the stench of death and conflagration hung in the air as though permanently imprinted there.

The former Nagasaki Foreign Settlement, once the site of a thriving multinational community, had also suffered damage from the blast but remained largely intact owing to its distance from the hypocenter and the protection of hillsides and canals. The occupation forces immediately requisitioned a large number of buildings for use as living quarters and offices, including the former Glover House, a deserted nineteenth-century Western-style residence on the Minamiyamate hillside overlooking Nagasaki Harbor. The American inhabitants soon began to use the whimsical nickname "Madame Butterfly House" when referring to the house, enchanted by its eclectic style and scenic location evoking scenes from the famous opera. It was only a matter of time before the nickname caught the attention of Japanese officials searching for ways to rebuild Nagasaki and revive the regional economy.

Arrival of Occupation Forces

A task force including several American warships and the hospital ship USS *Haven* arrived in Nagasaki Harbor on September 11, 1945, the first American vessels to call at the port since the outbreak of World War II. The warships dropped anchor in the middle of the harbor while USS *Haven* pulled up to Dejima Wharf, the landing stage used formerly by the sister ships *Nagasaki-maru* and *Shanghai-maru* on the regular Nippon Yusen Kaisha service from Kobe to Shanghai via Nagasaki.

The view from the wharf was bleak: many buildings had been destroyed by fire and their carcasses left to the mercy of the wind and rain; those still standing were invariably ramshackle and grime-laden. At night, the entire city was shrouded in darkness because the electrical grid had still not been restored. Other essential facilities, such as water and gas supply lines, hospitals, schools, banks, and government offices, languished in a similar state of paralysis.

Nagasaki Prefecture Governor Nagano Wakamatsu met the American officers and agreed to cooperate in the release of prisoners-of-war and to make all necessary preparations for the arrival of occupation forces, expected before the end of the month. The governor issued orders to the heads of cities, towns, and villages for citizens to stay away from the areas demarcated for use by occupation forces and to desist from picking up any of the foodstuffs and other supplies dropped by American airplanes into former prisoner-of-war camps.[1] The task force immediately took over the Dejima Wharf office and constructed a row of showers, as well as makeshift facilities for the reception and examination of former prisoners-of-war. Electricity and steam were supplied from the hospital ship. Over the following days, several thousand emaciated and bedraggled men arrived from various parts of Kyushu, stepping off the train only to shed tears of joy at the sounds of "Hail, Hail, The Gang's All Here," "Beer Barrel Polka," and other welcoming numbers played by the band from USS *Wichita*. After a warm shower, the men were given fresh clothing and, depending on their physical condition, either transferred to one of the warships for repatriation or admitted to a ward in the hospital ship. Further information and photographs related to the task force are available online.[2] Although their sole mission was the rescue and treatment of prisoners-of-war, the American medical staff did not ignore the atomic bomb victims. A few of the USS *Haven* physicians traveled to the hypocenter and also paid a visit to a provisional hospital (probably the relief station established in Shinkōzen Primary School), where they witnessed the carnage caused by the bomb.[3]

The formal occupation of Nagasaki began on Sunday, September 23, 1945 with the arrival of dozens of warships and transports carrying the Second Marine Division of the Sixth Army, previously stationed in Saipan. Mission accomplished, USS *Haven* steamed out of Nagasaki Harbor two days later and headed to Okinawa. The *Nagasaki City Sixty-Five-Year History* describes the landing of troops and the reaction of Nagasaki citizens:

> The expression on the faces of the Occupation troops was surprisingly cheerful if somewhat nervous, and the citizens of Nagasaki showed no dismay, peacefully greeting the inevitable under the clear autumn sky. . . . The city was calm, and there was no sign of agitation among the citizens as the troops passed by. It was unpleasant, however, to see some [Japanese] people rummaging through the shops that had opened overnight to sell souvenirs to the soldiers. Armed American military police made the rounds, but most citizens paid no attention to them and faithfully carried on with their duties. There was a feeling that the rushed setup of Occupation facilities would rob the city of vitality, but the day passed peacefully without any unfortunate incidents.[4]

The occupation forces lost no time in confiscating weapons and military equipment, arresting suspected war criminals, and beginning the process of creating a democratic system of government under American control. They requisitioned school dormitories to billet the hundreds of soldiers coming ashore and converted the former Nagasaki Customs Building in Semba-machi for use as occupation headquarters. The Western-style buildings remaining in the former Nagasaki Foreign Settlement and now in Japanese hands were also earmarked on the day of landing, including the former Holme, Ringer & Co. office on the Ōura waterfront. The two-story wood and stucco building provided ideal space for an officers' club. One of the houses acquired for officer quarters was the former residence of British merchant Thomas B. Glover and his family at No. 3 Minamiyamate, an elegant colonial-style bungalow perched on a hillside overlooking Nagasaki Harbor.

The Iconic Hillside House

From the time of its construction in 1863, the residence of Scottish merchant-adventurer Thomas B. Glover (1838–1911) was one of the most conspicuous buildings in the Nagasaki Foreign Settlement, a wooden bungalow with a fanshaped roof, stone-paved veranda and front garden commanding a panoramic view over Nagasaki Harbor. Glover made a fortune selling ships, guns and other merchandise to the domains of southwestern Japan during the 1860s. He also helped young samurai steal out of Japan to study abroad and provided the machinery and expertise needed to launch the first modern sugar refinery, coal mine, and ship-repair dock. Built beside a lone pine tree visible from afar, his house nestled on the Minamiyamate hillside like a new-generation castle, symbolizing the importance of commercial wealth and international exchange as Japan transformed from an isolated backwater into a world power.

In a 1918 article contributed to the magazine *The New East*, William B. Mason, coauthor of *Murray's Handbook to the Japanese Empire*, describes the Scotsman's house as follows: "His picturesque residence 'Ipponmatsu' or 'Single Pine Tree' derives its name from an old tree around which the house was built, its trunk rising straight up through the roof. The building has, accordingly, a unique arrangement of rooms, and the situation, overlooking the beautiful harbour with its island-studded approach, is one that long haunts the memory."[5]

Glover declared bankruptcy in 1870 but continued to contribute to Japanese business and industry as a consultant to the Mitsubishi Company. The same year as the bankruptcy, he fathered a son out of wedlock with a Japanese woman and later brought the boy up with the help of his common-law wife, Awajiya Tsuru. The boy attended a mission school in Nagasaki and Gakushūin (Peers School) in Tokyo before traveling to the United States to study at Ohio Wesleyan University and the University of Pennsylvania. He returned to Nagasaki in 1892 and took up a position with the British firm Holme, Ringer & Co., later acquiring Japanese citizenship and assuming the legal name Kuraba Tomisaburō (the surname Kuraba fashioned to simulate the sound of Glover).[6]

Kuraba married a British-Japanese woman named Nakano Waka in 1899 and moved with her into the family house in 1909. The couple served over the following decades as a bridge between the Japanese and foreign communities, but the construction of the mammoth battleship *Musashi* at the Mitsubishi Nagasaki Shipyard, which was clearly visible from Minamiyamate, brought an unexpected upheaval. Kuraba sold the house to Mitsubishi in April 1939 and moved with his wife to another location lower on the hillside.[7] Although the circumstances remain unclear, the transaction terminated the Glover family connection with the Minamiyamate house. During World War II, Mitsubishi apparently provided the building for military uses, but no definitive record exists.

Kuraba Waka died of tuberculosis in 1943 and left her husband alone to experience the atomic bombing and Japan's surrender. On the morning of August 26, 1945, Kuraba strangled his dogs and hanged himself, apparently dying not only of despair over the destruction of his beloved hometown but also of fear that his Japanese citizenship would be construed as an act of treason by the British and American victors soon to land. The occupation forces found the former Glover House empty and requisitioned it for use as officer housing, summarily applying the code name JPNR 1163.[8]

The Nagasaki Military Government Team

The Second Marine Division of the Sixth Army was deactivated in June, 1946, and replaced by a division of the Eighth Army. Before leaving Nagasaki, the former held a football game, complete with a band to play pep songs and marches, in an area of the atomic wasteland cleared to make an airstrip. They called the game the Atomic Bowl, showing scant consideration toward the atomic bomb survivors and the spirits of the countless dead.[9]

On September 23, 1946, exactly one year after the arrival of the first wave of Occupation forces, Colonel Victor E. Delnore assumed the position of first commander of the Nagasaki Military Government Team (NMGT), a body formed in conjunction with a nationwide change of emphasis in occupation policy from military to civilian administration. Under Delnore's supervision, the NMGT moved its headquarters to a threestory building in Shindaiku-machi, later to become the office of the Atomic Bomb Casualty Commission (ABCC) and a center for research into the late effects of atomic-bomb radiation. The NMGT also established a camp in the neighborhood of Katafuchi-machi and named it Camp Patton, after the famous armor strategist General George S. Patton. With its insular structure and Western-style buildings, the camp resembled the former foreign settlements of Nagasaki and Yokohama and presaged the American naval bases of today.[10]

By early 1947, many of the American officers were bringing their families to Nagasaki and taking up lodgings in requisitioned houses. The Delnore family lived in a large Japanese house in Atago-machi. Many other staff members found accommodations in the former Nagasaki Foreign Settlement, including Captain Joseph C. Goldsby, an engineer stationed in Nagasaki since September 1945. Goldsby's wife Barbara arrived from the United States in 1947 and moved with her husband into the former Alt House at No. 14 Minamiyamate. Goldsby was granted an honorable discharge in August the same year but stayed in Nagasaki to assume new duties as a civilian employee. It was at this juncture that Joseph and Barbara Goldsby moved into the former Glover House at No. 3 Minamiyamate, becoming the last people to inhabit the historic building. Around the time of the move, Goldsby posed for a photograph with two other uniformed officers in front of the house (figure 1). The jeeps parked in the background show that the Americans widened the old hillside path to provide access for motor vehicles. On the back of the photograph, Goldsby wrote the words "Mme. Butterfly House,

Figure 1. Joseph Goldsby and colleagues in front of the former Glover House and the inscription on the back of the photograph. Personal collection.

1947," evidence that the American occupation personnel in Nagasaki were already using the nickname to refer to the former Glover House.[11]

Madame Butterfly in Japan

Madame Butterfly is the tale of a young Japanese woman (Cho-cho-san, i.e. Miss Butterfly) who falls in love with an American naval lieutenant named Pinkerton and, after his departure from Nagasaki, gives birth to a son and waits in a hillside house, convinced that she is legally married, waiting for "One Fine Day" when her husband will return. When the lieutenant returns to Nagasaki three years later, however, he is accompanied by his American wife, and Cho-cho-san commits suicide out of grief and despair. Based to a large extent on Pierre Loti's 1887 travelogue *Madame Chrysanthème*, the story started as a novelette by American writer John Luther Long, developed into a stage play by Broadway virtuoso David Belasco, and finally surprised the world in 1905 as an opera by the famed Italian composer Giacomo Puccini.

From the beginning, *Madame Butterfly* was made by and for Westerners and attracted little if any attention in Japan. The opera may in fact have elicited feelings quite the opposite of interest or appreciation. The Japanese reaction to a Western opera set in Japan is indicated by the widely reported protests against British performances of the Gilbert and Sullivan farce *The Mikado* in 1907. In an interview in London that year, Kikuchi Dairoku, former Tokyo University president and Japanese minister of education, expressed the Japanese position:

> Of course, the play is an old one, and was written, I suppose, before our China war, when the general impression seemed to be that Japan was not a country to be treated seriously. A Japanese who had never been out of his country before would probably be more hurt at seeing a matter which is almost a religious one treated in so light a manner. The Mikado is a subject of which our conception is almost sacred, and to see him represented as a figure for buffoonery is obviously one which would not be pleasing.[12]

The opera *Madame Butterfly* did not directly insult the emperor, but the glorification of a prostitute's illicit relationship with a foreigner, the archaic images paraded across the stage, the confusion of Chinese and Japanese artifacts in costumes and sets, and the degrading portrayal of male characters—not to mention Puccini's use of the Japanese national anthem "Kimigayo" to embellish a scene in which the cunning pimp Goro appears on stage—were bound to offend Japanese audiences.

Only weeks after the arrival of the occupation forces in Nagasaki in 1945, an enterprising young woman named Kogano Tomiko opened the Takarazuka Dance Hall in the downtown neighborhood of Hamanomachi and hired legions of young women to serve as companions for the American servicemen free on leave, flush with back pay, and eager for a respite from boredom and loneliness.[13] Almost as quickly and in even larger numbers, women came out of the cracks to work as prostitutes, tapping into a lucrative new source of income and, in many cases, saving their families from starvation. The mingling of foreign servicemen and Japanese women became so prevalent that, as early as March 1946, GHQ-SCAP (General Headquarters of the Supreme Commander for the Allied Powers) issued a ban on kissing and other public displays of affection because it was inappropriate for members of the occupation forces to associate so intimately with the former enemy.[14] An alarmed GHQ-SCAP also stepped up efforts to control sexually transmitted diseases and ordered nocturnal roundups of women in public places, thereby weeding out infected prostitutes but subjecting many innocent women to the humiliation of medical examinations.

Until now an invisible presence behind the guns and barricades, Japanese women surprised and charmed the battle-weary soldiers, providing, as they saw it, both a sexual refuge and a bridge into the heart of an otherwise inimical culture. As John W. Dower points out, "The defeated country itself was feminized in the minds of the Americans who poured in. The enemy was transformed with startling suddenness from a bestial people fit to be annihilated into receptive exotics to be handled and enjoyed ... Japan—only yesterday a menacing, masculine threat—had been transformed, almost in the blink of an eye, into a compliant, feminine body on which the white victors could impose their will."[15]

Opera as Occupation Strategy

Since foreign civilians were still barred from visiting Japan, the authorities naturally turned to Japanese musicians and singers to provide entertainment, particularly those who at home in classical music, jazz, and other Western genres. The latter came forward willingly to please their new overseers, if only because of the huge financial rewards. One of the performances noisily demanded by the Americans was Giacomo Puccini's opera *Madame Butterfly*.

Nagato Miho, a soprano who had spent several years in Germany as a child and undergone voice training, won first place in the singing division of the 1934 Japan National Music Competition. Soon after the war's end, she established the Nagato Miho Opera Company to cater to occupation forces stationed in Tokyo. The company presented Japan's first full-fledged performance of *Madame Butterfly* at the Tokyo Gekijō Theater in November 1946, with Nagato playing the lead. According to the soprano, it set a world record because she played the grueling role of Cho-Cho-san nine times in three days.[16]

Japanese-British tenor Fujiwara Yoshie also remembers how his opera company responded to requests from the occupation forces for musical performances, and he cites *Madame Butterfly* as the favored selection: "In the early postwar period, musicians were enlisted to perform at the American Navy Headquarters in Yokosuka. My opera company was also invited many times to present *Madame Butterfly*. Upon departure, we received a supply of coffee, cigarettes, chocolate and other souvenirs, and we stuffed these into our valises and violin cases before heading off to the train station."[17]

The occupation forces seem to have had something more on the agenda than mere recreation when they insisted on *Madame Butterfly* and other Western operas set in Japan. This conjecture is supported by the fact that, in June 1947, the Nagato Miho Opera Company presented Japan's first performance of *The Mikado* directly under orders from GHQ-SCAP.[18] If the mission of the occupation was to erase all traces of militarism and emperor worship from Japan's psychological landscape, then *The Mikado* served the purpose ideally because, couched in the form of entertainment, it negated the warrior-aggressor image of prewar Japan, emphasized the triumph of Western values, and brought the emperor down to a level where he could be viewed and, if necessary, ridiculed in a democratic manner. The presentation by Japanese singers of *The Mikado, Madame Butterfly,* and other Western operas and plays that had been rejected as ludicrous if not insulting prior to World War II—and yet were being performed now as though they had a bona-fide place in the files of Japanese art—poignantly symbolized Japan's subjugation to the whims of the victors.

In the case of *Madame Butterfly,* there was in fact an uncanny similarity between the scenes unfolding on stage and the Allied occupation taking Japan by storm in the early postwar years. The irresponsible Lieutenant Pinkerton enjoying a sexual romp in the exotic Far East corresponded to the Occupation forces; the guileless geisha Cho-Cho-san devoted to her fickle patron represented the legions of Japanese women catering to American sexual needs in the aftermath of World War II; the pimp Goro and the military officer Yamadori who fails in his bid to win Cho-Cho-san's heart mimicked the male component of the Japanese population, incapacitated and demasculinized by defeat.

The son of the fictional Cho-Cho-san and Pinkerton, born after his father's departure and named "Trouble," also found a real-life counterpart in the so-called GI babies born to Japanese women and foreign men during the occupation period. Most of the babies were ignored by their fathers. Some disappeared into Japanese society, but many others were abandoned by their destitute mothers and ended up on the street. Fearing an anti-American backlash, GHQ-SCAP censored all discussion of the children in the Japanese press. It was not until after the departure of the occupation forces and the restoration of Japan's sovereign rights that the subject came to light. One of the journalists to report on the plight of the GI babies was Peter Kalischer, a United Press reporter who had been covering the Allied Occupation since 1945. Kalischer contributed a long article to a popular American magazine complete with color photographs of Euro- and Afro-Asian tots stranded in a Yokohama orphanage. Not surprisingly, the article is entitled "Madame Butterfly's Children."[19]

The First "Culture Festival"

Aside from the fact that Thomas Glover's wife was Japanese and lived on a hillside overlooking Nagasaki Harbor, there is nothing in prewar sources, including the letters, photograph albums, and Glover family documents, to indicate any connection between the former Glover House and the story, play, or opera *Madame Butterfly*. The nickname "Mme. Butterfly House" scribbled on the back of Joseph Goldsby's 1947 photograph was obviously a figment of the imagination of occupation personnel aware that Nagasaki was the setting of the famous opera but ignorant of the history of the house and its former owners. Victor E. Delnore, NMGT commander from 1946 to 1949, reiterated this opinion in a 1996 letter: "As to your query about Madame Butterfly's house, I attribute the remark to Joe Goldsby. The embellishment of his remark came from his wife, Barbara. I never heard anyone else say anything regarding this subject. When it was brought up in the presence of the Japanese, they would smile condescendingly and pass it along."[20]

A twenty-six-page English-language booklet entitled *Nagasaki Souvenir* published for NMGT personnel includes a photograph taken from the garden of the former Glover House and the caption "Nagasaki City seen from Madam Butterfly's Home," indicating that the nickname was common knowledge among the American community in Nagasaki. Nowhere else in the booklet, however, is there a single reference to the house. One of the articles in the booklet discusses the opera *Madame Butterfly* and its relationship to Nagasaki, introducing a Nagasaki Museum employee named Shimauchi Hachirō who had been "chasing the Madame Butterfly legend for more than 20 years." As the article discussed Shimauchi:

> One promising trail led him to Omura where it was stated that Cho Cho-san began life as the daughter of a down and out samurai. Investigations in this city banged up against a dead end, and since that day he has been following leads of all kinds, but he confessed that he was nowhere from where he started. 'It's a kind of a wil o' the wisp story which you cannot pin down,' he said.[21]

It is noteworthy that Shimauchi's twenty-year-long search had not led him to Thomas Glover or the Glover family residence on the Minamiyamate hillside. By May 1948, however, the Nagasaki Museum employee had turned his attention to the house. In a conversation with a *Mainichi Shinbun* reporter, Shimauchi revealed a plan to erect a monument to Madame Butterfly at the former Glover House, parroting Joseph and Barbara Goldsby and either failing to mention or deliberately ignoring Kuraba Tomisaburō, who had committed suicide less than three years earlier:

> Nagasaki means Madame Butterfly, and Madame Butterfly means Nagasaki. Nagasaki is famous worldwide for the atomic bomb and Madame Butterfly, but there is nothing here to remind visitors of Madame Butterfly. Because of this, a group of interested persons including myself is working on a project

to establish a Madame Butterfly monument. And so what about the place to put it? Of course, the house in Minamiyamate is the best choice. It fits perfectly with the image of Madame Butterfly.²²

Alerted to the use of the nickname by American residents, Shimauchi and his colleagues decided to exploit the Madame Butterfly theme as a way to attract foreign tourists and rescue Nagasaki from the economic doldrums dogging the city since the atomic bombing. Soon after the interview, a Mainichi reporter and photographer visited the former Glover House and asked Barbara Goldsby to pose for a photograph in the front garden. An article entitled "House of 'Madam Butterfly' Discovered" appeared in *The Mainichi*, the English-language edition of the newspaper, along with the photograph of Goldsby posing with a parasol held coquettishly over her shoulder, apparently in imitation of Cho-Cho-san. Remarkably enough, the article appeared on August 6, 1948, the third anniversary of the Hiroshima atomic bombing, months after the reporter visited the former Glover House. The full text of the article reads:

NAGASAKI, Aug. 5—The house in which "Chocho-san," heroine of the famous opera "Madam Butterfly" [sic] by Puccini lived and ended her life tragically has been discovered on the eve of the cultural festival commemorating the third anniversary of the atom bombing of this city. The house, a pseudo-western style building, is situated at 12 Minami Yamate-cho [sic], and all data and information indicated it to be the most probable house in which "Madam Butterfly" lived. The credit for this historical discovery goes to Hachiro Shimauchi and other native historians, who have conducted the search with undying enthusiasm on the theory that the girl whose tragic life was adapted into the famous opera actually existed. A plan is underway to construct a memorial tower within the "house," to be completed before the 400th anniversary of the arrival of St. Francis Xavier in April, next year. The house and its beautiful garden will be used in minute details as the scene of the opera Madam Butterfly to be presented by the Nagato Miho Opera Company at the Tokyo Theater beginning August 28, this year. (The photo shows the 'Madam Butterfly residence' and its beautiful garden. Strolling in the garden is Mrs. Goldsby, who now occupies this house.)²³

None of the so-called data and information proving the building to be "the most probable house in which Madam Butterfly lived" is provided. Moreover, the name Glover is nowhere to be found, evidence that the prewar history of the building had nothing to do with the "discovery." The mistaken identification of the address as No. 12 Minamiyamate (instead of No. 3 Minamiyamate) further reflects the lack of scrutiny regarding the former Glover House and its true history.

Four days later, on August 10, 1948, a verbatim translation of the article, with the same photograph of Barbara Goldsby, appeared in the Japanese-language *Mainichi Shinbun* beside an article describing the "culture festival" held the previous day to commemorate the third anniversary of the Nagasaki atomic bombing (figure 2). Entitled *Atomu Nagasaki: Heiwa e no inori* (Atom Nagasaki: Prayers for Peace), the latter reports that more than a thousand citizens gathered for the *bunkasai shikiten* (culture festival ceremony) in Matsuyama-machi on August 9. After an address by Nagasaki Mayor Ōhashi Hiroshi, messages from General Douglas MacArthur (Supreme Commander for the Allied Powers), Colonel Victor E. Delnore (NMGT commander) and Ashida Hitoshi (prime minister of Japan) were read to the audience, in that order. These were followed by addresses from local politicians and finally with the delivery of Nagasaki's first "Peace Declaration" by a city council member named Mizogami Tarō, representing the citizens of Nagasaki. The newspaper report ends with the full wording of the Peace Declaration and the message from Victor E. Delnore. The former reads:

> Nagasaki is the place where the atomic bomb brought an end to the war and turned unprecedented devastation into a bright hope for peace. In that sense, Nagasaki is the most remarkable place on Earth. I believe without a doubt that we will establish permanent peace for mankind by shouting that atom [i.e., atomic-bombed] Nagasaki must never be repeated. On the occasion of this cultural festival ceremony, we declare "No More Nagasakis" and hope that this motto will be proclaimed widely to the world.[24]

The message from Victor E. Delnore, translated from an English version provided beforehand by the NMGT, reads as follows (retranslated into English):

> We are gathered here today in Urakami to commemorate the anniversary of the atomic bombing, which astonished the people of the world and made them realize that war ultimately leads to human destruction. [The atomic bombing] proves that war is not simply futile in solving the problems of mankind, but rather increases misery and hardship, and destroys culture. [Our gathering today] is important to warn an unstable world and to remember the deaths of the victims. The people of the world pray that such an event

will not happen again, and the American people will spare no effort to cooperate with [the citizens of Nagasaki].[25]

Why did the *Mainichi Shinbun* wait until the third anniversaries of the Hiroshima and Nagasaki atomic bombings to report, in its English- and Japanese-language editions respectively, the purported discovery of the Madame Butterfly House? In the Japanese article, a photograph of a bereaved family praying at the Nagasaki hypocenter is printed directly beside that of Barbara Goldsby holding her parasol. The jarring juxtaposition of the two photographs not only illustrates the disparate realities of Occupation personnel and *hibakusha* but may even represent an attempt on the part of American authorities to subvert painful memories of the atomic bombings and prevent a surge in anti-American feelings among the Japanese populace.

Indeed, from the beginning of the occupation period, GHQ-SCAP banned newspaper articles and other reportage on the atomic bombings. The NMGT

Figure 2. From the August 10, 1948 issue of the *Mainichi shinbun* newspaper. The Glover House article with the Barbara Goldsby photograph is on the left side of the image.

called on Nagasaki citizens to turn over all atomic bomb–related materials and artifacts, citing the need to protect military secrets. As a result, the majority of Japanese people were left in the dark about the atomic bombings, including the late effects of radiation exposure. Only after the San Francisco Peace Treaty of 1952 did Japanese newspapers begin to publish in-depth articles and photographs dealing with the calamities of Hiroshima and Nagasaki.[26]

The fact that the commemoration of the Nagasaki atomic bombing was called a "culture festival" under the supervision of GHQ-SCAP also reveals an effort to pull a cloak over the raw truth. The first Nagasaki Peace Declaration was blue-penciled by GHQ-SCAP censors to ensure that no expression of resentment or call for revenge crept into the rhetoric, a fact indicated by the opening assertion that the Nagasaki atomic bombing "brought an end to the war and turned unprecedented devastation into a bright hope for peace." The expression "No More Nagasakis," which today is invariably rendered by Japanese speakers and writers as "No More Nagasaki," also exposes the American intervention in the composition of the first Peace Declaration.

The use of the words *culture* and *peace* to camouflage the atomic bombing continued even after the departure of occupation forces. Nagasaki authorities eventually discarded the "culture festival" euphemism, but the commemoration of the Nagasaki atomic bomb anniversary, referred to as a Peace Memorial Ceremony, has been held in Peace Park near the Peace Statue every subsequent year. In 1949, the Japanese government passed the Nagasaki International Culture City Construction Law and the Hiroshima Peace Memorial City Construction Law to promote the restoration of the atomic-bombed cities, In Nagasaki, the first atomic bomb museum was opened in a building called the Nagasaki International Culture Hall. To this day, schoolchildren in Hiroshima and Nagasaki engage in "Peace Studies," which in fact dwell exclusively on the horror of the atomic bombings and the sufferings of the *hibakusha*.

Truth or Tourist Appeal

Japan's tourism industry, stagnant since the late 1930s, received an injection of new energy in the summer of 1947 when GHQ-SCAP authorized visits by a small number of business representatives entering Japan to begin the process of establishing commercial links. On December 28, a group of eighty wealthy American tourists arrived in the port of Yokohama on the USS *President Monroe* and embarked on a tour of Kamakura, Nikko, and other sightseeing spots in the Tokyo area.[27] More and more groups followed, both by ship and by the airplanes that started service in October 1948. The network of destinations gradually extended from Tokyo to Kyoto and Nara and, by the end of the decade, to Nagasaki and other parts of southwestern Japan. The money spent by the affluent visitors on hotels, meals, and souvenirs constituted a vital source of revenue in the wake of the war and brought enormous benefits to the municipalities with attractions popular among foreigners. Already famous for the atomic bombing, Nagasaki gained further renown when news about the Madame Butterfly House spread among occupation personnel and foreign tourists.

While perusing the Glover family photograph albums in the hope of solidifying the connection between the house and famous opera, Shimauchi Hachirō and his Nagasaki Museum colleague Miyazaki Kiyoshige noticed that Thomas Glover's wife Tsuru often wore a kimono with a butterfly mark on the sleeve. Digging deeper, they realized that Tsuru's gravestone at Taiheiji Temple was embellished with an *agehachō* (butterfly with raised wings) crest. This in itself meant little, because the butterfly crest was used widely by foreigners' consorts who, because they did not engage in conventional marriages, were barred access to traditional family crests. The butterfly design was often used deliberately by geisha and other women in the entertainment industry because the metamorphosis from humble caterpillar to beautiful butterfly expressed the geisha's dream to find a wealthy patron and to be reborn as a lady of high standing.[28] Although Shimauchi and Miyazaki insinuated that the *agehachō* crest was unique to Tsuru, it can be seen on the gravestones of several Japanese women who married foreigners and who are buried today in Nagasaki's international cemeteries.[29]

Tsuru's use of the crest simply indicated that she was a former geisha married to a foreigner, but it was just what Shimauchi and Miyazaki needed to exploit the former Glover House as a tourist attraction. On July 2, 1949, the newspaper *Nagasaki Nichinichi Shinbun* reported the discovery of Tsuru's photographs and the opinion of Shimauchi and Miyazaki that she had served as a model for the tragic heroine in the opera. Tellingly, however, the article refers to the Minamiyamate house as "the home of Mr. Goldsby" and completely ignores both Thomas Glover and Kuraba Tomisaburō.[30] Several expert observers, including Watanabe Kurasuke, a university professor who had studied the history of the opera prior to World War II, rejected the idea that Tsuru had served as a model for Cho-Cho-san. Refusing to back down but hoping to dodge criticism, the organizers tried to conciliate the two conflicting opinions by doing away with the name "Madame Butterfly House" and using the ambiguous moniker *Chō chō fujin yukari no chi* (Place Connected with Madame Butterfly) (figure 3).

The duplicitous attitude of Nagasaki officials is evident in an article, entitled, "Madame Butterfly and the Glover House," by Yoshimatsu Yuichi, councilor of the Nagasaki International Culture Association, carried in the September 25, 1951 issue of a local newspaper:

> There are some who claim that Thomas Glover's wife Tsuru was the model for Madame Butterfly or that the property behind the Glover house was called the "land of Madame Butterfly" in old days. But even if these claims are untrue, there is probably no other place in Nagasaki aside from the garden of the Glover House that evokes the famous scene in which Madame Butterfly sings the aria *One Fine Day*.... In Fukushima Prefecture, near Kurozuka Station, there is a statue called Kurozuka Kannon. This is represented in scrolls and other historic documents as the place where the Adachi-ga-Hara Devil Woman lived. Even Matsuo Basho, in his book *Narrow Road to the Deep North*, mentions stopping there. But a closer look reveals this to be merely a legendary site fabricated on the basis of a poem. Most so-called famous sites and legendary spots come into existence this way, and after many years they can develop into immovable objects of local worship. In this light, I do not think that it is inappropriate to make the Glover House "the famous site connected with Madame Butterfly."[31]

Figure 3. Postwar picture postcard of the former Glover House without any mention of the Glover family. Personal collection.

It is clear that the Nagasaki officials trying to transform the former Glover House into a tourist mecca were fully aware that they had no historic foot to stand on. They simply pushed ahead with the project because they considered the need to promote economic growth more important than responsibility to convey the truth.

The falsehood of the Madame Butterfly House campaign continued to raise questions. Even Shimauchi Hachirō suffered pangs of conscience about his role in creating the sham. On November 5, 1953, when the opera *Madame Butterfly* was presented in Nagasaki for the first time by the Nagato Miho Opera Company, a message from Shimauchi, entitled "Joy at Welcoming the Opera," appeared in the opera program. In his message, the retired Nagasaki Museum employee, now referred to as a poet, expresses more repentance than joy:

> Local historians argued vehemently about whether or not *Butterfly* is fiction. They argued even more vehemently about whether the Glover House was the real setting. It was Ishida Hisashi, chief judge of the Nagasaki Court and myself who, in the midst of these arguments, suggested that the Glover House be designated as the setting. Our reason was that the house is aesthetically appropriate. As a result, we now have the "Garden Connected with Madame Butterfly," but I have been severely castigated over it, and so I think that the naming should be changed to the "Garden Reminiscent of Madame Butterfly."[32]

Another person vexed by the falsification was Harold S. Williams, an Australian resident of Kobe since the 1920s and the foremost authority on the history of the former foreign settlements of Japan. As Williams wrote in an essay entitled "Miss Butterfly and Miss Chrysanthemum,"

> At first when the Nagasaki City authorities decided to whip up the tourist trade by putting on the "Madame Butterfly House" hoax, they described it rather obliquely, or shall we say with calculated ambiguity. But now the gloves are off. The Butterfly romance, we are now being told, really happened in the Glover mansion, and both the lady and the house are now given a prominent place in the tourist attractions along with the memorial to the twentysix Christian martyrs, and the other truly historic monuments of Nagasaki's past. We say this in sorrow more than in anger, because we always receive the most kind treatment from all the officials there whose assistance we seek in our researches. It is sad to know that most of the tourists, both Japanese and foreigners, who visit the delightful villa overlooking the harbour, leave

believing they have seen the actual house wherein the Madame Butterfly romance and tragedy occurred, and they will remember it as such, rather than as the home built in the early days by the highly respected British merchant, Thomas B. Glover, who lived there with his wife and children.[33]

Despite the disavowal by Shimauchi and the appeals of experts like Harold S. Williams, Nagasaki authorities made no effort to change the designation of the house or to dissuade tourists from assuming that Tsuru was the model for Cho-Cho-san. On the contrary, the tendency to choose atmosphere over history only grew stronger in subsequent years. The Madame Butterfly theme was used extensively in advertisements, signs, and pamphlets and in various other efforts to bolster Nagasaki's tourism industry. Even bus guides showing people around the house were required to learn the aria "Un Bel Di" (One Fine Day) and sing it for the entertainment of customers. But for people like Harold S. Williams who remembered Nagasaki in its prewar heyday as an international port, it was painfully clear that the Madame Butterfly craze came in the same parcel with hot dogs, bobby socks, striptease, and all the other Americana flooding Japan in the wake of defeat.

In 1957, the Mitsubishi Nagasaki Shipyard donated the former Glover House to Nagasaki City as part of its centennial celebrations. Four years later, the Japanese government designated the house an Important Cultural Property, second only to National Treasure. The honor was based solely on the architectural value of the house as the oldest European building in Japan: as long as alterations to the physical structure were carefully avoided, Nagasaki City was free to decide on the style of presentation and the content of displays. In 1963, the city installed a statue of Japanese prima donna Miura Tamaki (who had gained worldwide fame prior to World War II playing the leading role in the opera *Madame Butterfly*) directly beside the house, trying to draw another provocative if fallacious connection between the opera and the house.

As research on the life and work of Thomas B. Glover and his son Kuraba Tomisaburō deepened, however, municipal authorities decided to move the statue of Miura Tamaki to a spot higher up the hillside, where it remains to this day. The "Place Connected with Madame Butterfly" moniker also eventually fell out of favor and now rarely appears in discussions related to the former Glover House. From 2019 to 2021, the building underwent a thoroughgoing restoration for the first time in more than fifty years. The interior displays were also completely revamped on the basis of scholarly research, not whimsy as in the past. One small panel shows the 1947 newspaper article entitled "House of 'Madam Butterfly' Discovered" and the photograph of Barbara Goldsby holding a parasol over her shoulder. But the article and photograph are offered, not as historical evidence *per se*, but as an example of how the former Glover House was misrepresented during the Allied occupation period, a time when the people of Nagasaki were struggling to pick up the pieces of their city and reestablish their lives in the aftermath of the atomic bombing.

Notes

1. Nagasaki City, ed., *Nagasaki shisei rokujūgo nen shi* (Nagasaki City Sixty-Five-Year History) (Nagasaki: Nagasaki-shi sōmubu chōsa tōkeika, 1959).

2. "Remembering the Days of Liberation: Finding Our POWs, Allied POWs Under the Japanese," http://www.mansell.com/pow_resources/evacuation/finding_our_pows.html.

3. A report by one of the physicians, Dr. Tom Harris, is also available online here: Lt. Cmdr. (MC) U.S.N. Tom Harris, "Hospital Ship 'Haven' in Nagasaki," May 29, 2009, http://www.storagemojo.com/wp-content/uploads/2009/05/hospital-ship-haven-in-nagasakitxt.pdf.

4. *Nagasaki shisei rokujūgo nen shi*, 966. All translations from Japanese herein are by the author.

5. "Thomas Glover: Pioneer of Anglo-Japanese Commerce." Reproduced in *The Nagasaki Press*, February 21, 1918.

6. See, e.g., Brian Burke-Gaffney, *The Former Glover House: An Illustrated History* (Nagasaki: Flying Crane Press, 2015), 25–35.

7. *Senkan Musashi kenzō kiroku: Yamatogata senkan no zenbō* (The Construction of the *Musashi*: A Portrait of the Yamato-class Battleships), eds. Makino Shigeru and Koga Shigeichi (Tokyo: Atene shobō, 1994), 77.

8. Burke-Gaffney, *The Former Glover House*, 25–35.

9. Second Marine Division Special Services Section, ed., *Pictorial Arrowhead: Occupation of Japan by Second Marine Division* (1946). The handmade booklet was produced as a souvenir for the Marines leaving Nagasaki.

10. For a detailed discussion of Delnore's activities in Nagasaki, see Lane R. Earns, "Victor's Justice: Colonel Victor Delnore and the U.S. Occupation of Nagasaki," in *Crossroads: A Journal of Nagasaki History and Culture* 3 (1995): 75–97, http://www.uwosh.edu/faculty_staff/earns/home.html.

11. Burke-Gaffney, *The Former Glover House*, 36–42.

12. Quoted in *The Nagasaki Press*, June 23, 1907.

13. Earns, "Victor's Justice," 88.

14. *Nippon Times*, March 24, 1946. Any soldier caught kissing or walking hand in hand with a Japanese woman was to be charged with disorderly conduct.

15. John W. Dower, *Embracing Defeat: Japan in the Wake of World War II* (New York: New Press, 1999), 138.

16. Nagato Miho, "Watakushi no rirekisho" (My Curriculum Vitae) in *Watakushi no rirekisho bunkajin 14* (My Curriculum Vitae, Person of Culture 14) (Tokyo: Nihon keizai shinbun, 1984), 533–534.

17. Fujiwara Yoshie, *Ryūten nanajūgo nen: Opera to koi no hansei* (Meandering for 75 Years: A Life of Opera and Love) (Tokyo: Nihon Tosho Center, 1998), 266. Fujiwara Yoshie (1898–1976) probably felt an affinity to the *Madame Butterfly* story because he himself was the illegitimate son of a British father and Japanese mother abandoned at a young age. He went on to gain fame as the "Japanese Rudolph Valentino." During a visit to the United States, he took in a performance of *Madame Butterfly* by the New York City Opera, and he reports that it was "painful to watch" because Japanese culture was portrayed so inaccurately.

18. Nagato, "Watakushi no rirekisho," 535.

19. Peter Kalischer, "Madame Butterfly's Children," *Collier's Magazine*, September 20, 1952, 15–18.

20. Victor and Catherine Delnore to Lane R. Earns, April 3, 1996.

21. Written by a certain M. Okamoto, the booklet contains a series of short articles on Nagasaki history and culture as well as advertisements for local shops. The printer, Fujiki Hakueisha Co. of Nagasaki, is still in business but has no record of the publication. Although undated, the booklet was probably published between late 1946 and early 1948. (Copy in possession of the author.)

22. Yanagimoto Kenichi, ed., *Gekidō nijūnen* (Turbulent Twenty Years) (Tokyo: Mainichi Shinbun sha, 1965), 172. Meaning "A Turbulent Twenty Years," this is a collection of reminiscences by a Mainichi reporter about events in postwar Nagasaki.

23. *The Mainichi* (English edition of the Japanese newspaper *Mainichi Shinbun*), August 6, 1948.

24. *Mainichi shinbun*, August 10, 1948.

25. Ibid.

26. Yokote Kazuhiko, *Nagasaki Urakami Cathedral. 1945–1958: An Atomic Bomb Relic Lost*, trans. Brian Burke-Gaffney (Tokyo: Iwanami shoten, 2010), 79.

27. *Nippon Times*, December 28, 1947.

28. Kondō Masaki, *Onna mon: Ketsuen no fōkuroa* (Women's Crests: The Folklore of Blood Relations) (Tokyo: Kawade shobō, 1995), 199.

29. For more on these cemeteries, see Brian Burke-Gaffney, "Secret Tales of the Nagasaki International Cemeteries," *Crossroads* 2 (1994), http://www.uwosh.edu/faculty_staff/earns/tales.html.

30. *Nagasaki Nichinichi Shinbun*, July 2, 1949.

31. *Nagasaki minyū*, September 25, 1951.

32. Program of the Grand Opera Madam Butterfly presented at the Mitsubishi Kaikan, Nagasaki on November 5 and 6, 1953, by the Nagato Miho Opera Company and hosted by the Nagasaki City Board of Education, the

Nagasaki Music Promotion Association, and the Nagasaki Amateur Music Association. Nagato visited the Glover House during her stay in Nagasaki and sang an aria from the opera in the garden overlooking Nagasaki Harbor.

33. Harold S. Williams, *Foreigners in Mikadoland* (Rutland, VT: Charles E. Tuttle, 1963), 230–231.

The Titan and the Arch
Regulating Public Memory through the Peace Statue

By Nanase Shirokawa

Pain, especially bodily pain, resists representation by lacking an object in the external world. We can often identify the source of pain, but we do not experience pain "for" or "of" anything in the way that other human sensations relate themselves to a referent—one touches *x*, possesses desire for *y*, and fears *z*.[1] In order to express or allude to the pain of others, we must reach even further into the depths of our imagination and attempt—often in vain—to construct an entity that can serve as a prism through which we can communicate such sentiments and fill the void of objectlessness. When memorializing the suffering inflicted by the atomic bombs, the task at hand is further complicated by the lack of visual precedent and the ontological challenges posed by a form of violence whose physical and environmental effects have never been fully understood.

The aesthetic language around nuclear energy often errs on the side of ambiguity, inscrutability, and invisibility. This uncertainty itself reflects a key feature of the civic language of remembering employed in both Hiroshima and Nagasaki, though each city has in turn pursued distinct avenues of action amidst this sweeping fog of vagueness. The imbalance of public attention and scholarship on the narratives of memory in the two cities has made itself starkly evident, as disparities began to unfurl even from the early days after the bombings. Like many other elements of the collective memory practices surrounding the two events, the Hiroshima Peace Memorial Park has enjoyed proportionally greater attendance and scholarly analysis than its Nagasaki counterpart. While both spaces are guided by the overarching language of peace (*heiwa*) that dominates postatomic bomb discourse in Japan, the constructions and appearances of the two parks are markedly different.

One of the most visible contrasts in the two cities' approaches to remembering is found in the memorial centerpieces of each peace park. If Tange

Kenzō's concrete-laden Hiroshima Peace Park and memorial cenotaph (1955) exhibit a modernist sensibility that pays hefty homage to Le Corbusier (figure 1), the statue that sits in the center of Nagasaki's Peace Park derives from an entirely different visual genealogy (figure 2). Completed in the same year, the boxy, thirty-two-foot (9.7 m)-high Peace Memorial Statue (*Heiwa kinen zō*) by Nagasaki-born sculptor Kitamura Seibō—commonly referred to by the mononym Seibō—feels far less cosmopolitan by comparison, and the awkwardly neoclassical, figurative approximation of a titan is rarely treated as an artistic object worthy of visual analysis. Rendered in bronze and treated with a turquoise patina, the nude towers over its beholders, taking on the appearance of an icon of worship through its authoritative presence.

This essay discusses the Peace Statue through a comparative study with its Hiroshima pendant and inquires into the politics of its production in order to examine the state-sanctioned memory paradigms embedded into the object, and the means by which the bodily form of the statue invokes questions around social order and surfaces alternate paths of collective remembrance. Particular attention will be devoted to the symbolism of

Figure 1. Tange Kenzō, Cenotaph for the Atomic Bomb Victims (Hiroshima), 1955. Photograph by author.

Figure 2. Kitamura Seibō, Peace Memorial Statue (Nagasaki), 1955. Photograph by author.

their respective forms, material qualities, and the means by which they command space and orient visitors. While the Hiroshima memorial complex dives headlong into the vision of an egalitarian landscape of a future city driven by the positive and productive capacities of the atom, the Nagasaki monument is less lucid in terms of its relationship to nuclear violence and civic responsibility. The deity gestures but does not direct; it neither looks to the past nor imagines a future, instead invoking spiritual and masculine order as assurances of peace. The two sites are ripe sources for examining the different dimensions of how Japan relates and responds to its past and confronting the perennial question of what exactly "peace" signifies, and for whom.

The Body in the Public Sphere

Public opinion on the Nagasaki Peace Statue ranges from apathy to disdain, and at times even heightening to vitriol. *Hibakusha* often invoke its existence as a symbolic dumping ground for their frustrations, and many critics view it as a manifestation of the inadequate and misguided efforts of disengaged authorities. In August 1955, two days after the statue was unveiled to the public on the occasion of the tenth anniversary of the bombing, Nagasaki *hibakusha* and antinuclear activist Fukuda Sumako wrote the following poem, pointing out how the statue in fact did nothing to aid in the real-life struggles of the survivors:

> Everything became intolerable
> The huge statue of peace that stands tall in the atomic field is fine
> That's fine
> But couldn't they have done something with the money?
> "The stone statue is inedible; it does not feed the hungry"
> Do not say that we are selfish.
> These words come at the survival on brink of ten years of the bombing
> With the unflinching heart of a *hibakusha*[2]

According to records from the Nagasaki National Peace Memorial Hall, the ¥50 million (increased from the initial budget of ¥30 million) statue was funded almost entirely through public donations, save for the stone pedestal and other minor details, which were financed by the city government.[3] A civilian organization dubbed the Peace Statue Construction Cooperative was tasked with soliciting donations from both the local citizenry and from overseas groups. These contributions comprised more than half of the final expenditures.[4] Seibō claimed to have invested his own savings into the production when unexpected costs arose, though the exact amount he provided remains unclear.[5]

Tange's design, too, received similar criticism for its use of a trendy, Euro-inflected modernist language. The assertively flat spaces and structures were perceived by some as an attempt to sanitize imperial travesties and the physical and psychological traumas of war, and many raised concerns that the construction fees could have been redirected to support *hibakusha* instead.[6] Yet the Hiroshima cenotaph has not been subjected to nearly the same degree of criticism and disdain that the Peace Statue has faced during its entire existence. At the 1974 Peace Memorial ceremony, *hibakusha* Taniguchi Sumiteru made mention of the statue in a speech advocating for nuclear disarmament, resurfacing the collective displeasure with both the cost and appearance of the sculpture. Standing in front of the source of his resentment, he respectfully and curtly directed his words at the artist: "Apologies to Kitamura-san, but I too have absolutely no emotions for this statue."[7] The statue is not embraced as a unifying agent for the community, nor does its purported role as a "guardian" appear to have resonated much with residents since its creation. The late Father Kawazoe Takeshi, head priest of Urakami Cathedral and a survivor of the bombing, claimed he was never able to approach let alone pray in front of that "giant work of art ... no matter how many times it bears the word 'peace' in its name."[8] Nagasaki historian Brian Burke-Gaffney has described in frank terms the inadequacies of the memorial function of the statue and its aesthetic shortcomings: "the figure is touted as an East-West hybrid, but you don't need a degree in art history to recognize it for what it is: a clumsy approximation of a Greco-Roman deity."[9]

What might happen, however, if we slow down to "read" this statue as an art object? At first glance, the use of "art" implies a sort of ascribed aesthetic value, coupled with a connoisseurly overture. The formalist reading enacted here is not in service of a Greenbergian mode of assumed objectivity and does not seek to reduce analysis to the level of the self-referential and self-enclosed medium. Nor, in embarking on a visual analysis of the object itself, do I seek to refocus attention away from the *hibakusha* and citizen responses to the controversial piece. Yet much of the scholarly discourse around the statue has focused on the reactions induced by its presence, and less so on the visual nuances of the object, the circumstances that enabled its existence, and its location amid systems of power and exchange.[10] While the label of "public art" itself could be considered somewhat of an anachronism (or to some, a misnomer—how could it be considered "art" to begin with?), the term enables us to examine the sculpture as part of a rich network of exchanges and engagements. Public art is produced with the conditions of the "public" in mind—a public that is in turn imagined by the desires and beliefs of the artist and the commissioning body. Environmental and civic concerns also take part in the shaping of its program. Though it certainly develops alongside urban policy and cultural movements, it is a slippery category that lacks no definitive historical genesis or discernible common aesthetic. These peace monuments are premised upon certain imagined visions of an ideal public sphere that are in turn made visible through the materialization of the artwork.

To situate the object as an artwork also encourages a sensitivity toward its affective textures and emphasizes the moment of encounter with the beholder, as mediated by physical, textual, sociocultural, and environmental conditions. How, in its failure to be embraced as a representative for civic identity and collective remembering, does it in turn reveal attitudes, desires, and frustrations circumscribing the act of memorializing what resists being remembered? Ugliness and representational inadequacy should not be considered obstructions to understanding, but rather as impetuses for contemplating how narratives of remembering are produced by individuals and groups, and what they reveal about priorities, desires, and fears of those who construct and engage with them.

Sociologist Rafael Narvaez writes, "embodied collective memory involves a *structure of possibilities*, which helps individuals apprehend not only the past and the present—but also the possible" (emphasis in original).[11] Memorials to nuclear violence are sites of activities that not only present pathways for remembering and forgetting but also open up regenerative potentialities. Such a framework enables us to attempt to comprehend nuclear trauma on a more expansive model that goes beyond the common discursive framing of the bombings—specifically, the Hiroshima bombing—as the genesis of a new "nuclear" age. Rather than situating the events as a turning point, and the erection of physical memorials as part of a mere routine of modern bureaucracy, I propose a discussion of the Peace Statue that parses through the social conditions that enabled its existence and examines the extant traditions and ideas that encouraged it to shape collective memory through the medium of the body.

Traces of Empire and War

On August 6, 1945, the Little Boy uranium bomb pierced the nexus of Hiroshima, detonating midair around 1,970 feet (600 m) above the Shima Hospital. The deployment took place just 1,300 feet (400 m) southeast of the intended target of Aioi Bridge and walking distance from the famed late-sixteenth century Hiroshima Castle, at the time operating as the headquarters for the Second General Army and Fifth Division of the Imperial forces. The decision to bomb Nagasaki three days later was the product of a last-minute change of plans after low visibility conditions over the initial target of Kokura, in Fukuoka Prefecture, prompted the B-29 carrying the Fat Man plutonium bomb to change course. Ground zero in Nagasaki is located around 1.25 miles (2 km) north of the city center in the Urakami district, an area historically associated with the city's Catholic community. The geographic siting of violence, coupled with the extant tensions between the minority group and the rest of the city, set spatial obstacles to centralizing urban memory from the onset.[12] In order to better construct—or reconstruct, to a certain extent—the phenomenological encounter with the statue and situate it as a node within a greater memoryscape rather than view it as an isolated entity, it will be useful to examine the institutional underpinnings of the park.

The concept of the "Peace Park" first requires a bit of unpacking. Discussions of reconstruction arose immediately after the surrender, and both Hiroshima and Nagasaki rallied to receive special funding that set them apart from dozens of other cities that suffered under air raids, owing to the extraordinary circumstances of their destruction.[13] In early 1949, Hiroshima mayor Hamai Shinzō proceeded to singularly seek claim to the identity of the atomic-bombed city by presenting the Hiroshima Peace Commemoration City Construction Law to the National Diet, much to the dismay of Nagasaki officials who sought a more collaborative approach to representing and codifying nuclear memory.[14] Though mentions of "peace" (*heiwa*) eventually came to figure prominently in the narratives of remembering designed in both cities, Hiroshima's swift claim to the title of "peace city" in legislation in turn prompted Nagasaki to settle for the designation of "international city," a generalized term that sought to play up the city's history of cross-cultural encounter and trade. The municipal prioritization of internationalism was taken by some survivors as an affront to their localized experiences, and to the rest of Japan it made the city appear apathetic to the bombings, especially in comparison to Hiroshima's self-fashioning as the nexus of atomic memory and peace production.[15] Seibō himself declared his desire for the Peace Statue to become a representative tourist destination for Nagasaki and eventually rise to the level of a world heritage monument.[16] Thus, marketing potential with a global audience in mind is explicitly built into the rhetoric of the sculpture itself. In aspiring to be a timeless, internationally recognized artwork, the statue was endowed with the responsibility of spurring the cultural and economic growth of the city.

From the onset, the name recognition of the designers involved in the Hiroshima site clearly outweighed that of their Nagasaki counterpart. Tange Kenzō (1913–2005), an up-and-coming architect, had established himself by securing a number of design competition wins, including most notably the Greater East Asia Co-Prosperity Sphere Commemorative Building Competition in 1942. The proposal, which was never realized, toed a strategic line by borrowing from the international style chastised by nationalists for being unpatriotic or even anti-Japanese while simultaneously infusing it with Japanese traditional references in order to express a distinctly and singularly "Japanese" ethos of modernism.[17] In a questionnaire accompanying his submission, Tange boldly proclaimed his allegiance to the imperial mission: "We must ignore both Anglo-American culture and the preexisting cultures of the Southeast Asian races. . . . We should start out with an unshakable conviction in the tradition and the future of the Japanese races. Architects were given the task of creating a new Japanese architectural style in order to contribute to the supreme and inevitable project of the foundation of the Greater East Asia Co-Prosperity Sphere."[18] In 1987, he would go on to receive the Pritzker Prize, jump-starting a lineage of Japanese architects who would be endowed with the preeminent international award.

Tange had invited Japanese-American artist Isamu Noguchi to design a cenotaph and bridge railings for Hiroshima's Peace Park. The two railings, *Yuku* (To Depart) and *Tsukuru* (To Build), remain in place today. The sculptor's proposal for a polished, heavy-set black granite arch whose legs extended into an underground sanctum accessed through a set of stairs was rejected by the park's adjudicating committee during the final stages of the planning process. Titled *Memorial to the Dead, Hiroshima*, the proposal centered the process of remembrance on the contemplation of the victims' pain and the connective fibers between the living and the dead. Natural light would stream into the chamber through a trapezoidal aperture between the legs of the arch, creating a calming aura that sought to both offer the living an opportunity to quietly reflect and provide the deceased with a place to rest, safe from the dangers of the world above. The phrase "peace" rarely makes an appearance in the artist's descriptions of the work.

Tange hurriedly drafted a substitute inspired by Noguchi's design in the days following, an airy barrel arch that blends in seamlessly with his concrete ensemble. The piece, which remains today, was ultimately titled *Cenotaph for the Atomic Bomb Victims* (Genbaku shibotsusha ireihi), though it is also referred to more generally as the Hiroshima Peace City Monument. Cenotaphs became more commonly seen in Japan after the war, and the use of the typology demonstrates a reckoning with mass death in the absence of physical remains.

Budgeting concerns played a role in determining the final form of both monuments. The failure of Noguchi's proposal was attributed to financing and aesthetic concerns, both of which the artist questioned, remarking that such qualms had never been raised during the initial stages of the process. The artist perceived the primary, unsaid reason behind the rejection to be his hybrid identity, lamenting the failure of officials to see his Americanness as anything but a political roadblock.[19] The complications behind the construction of the Hiroshima monument help illuminate the aesthetic debates at play in the challenge of remembering and visualizing nuclear violence, and in turn shed light on how Nagasaki's path to establishing a language of civic memory deviated from the approach taken by Hiroshima. In weaving through the following comparative discussion of the peace monuments, I seek not to uphold the dichotomous trope of "Hiroshima rages, Nagasaki prays" but rather to illustrate the fraught and multivalent processes of civic memory-making in these two cities, which converge and diverge from one another at various points.

Born in Minami-Arima-chō (now Minami-Shimabara), Nagasaki Prefecture, in 1884 to a wealthy agriculturalist father who was an ardent follower of the Buddhist New Pure Land Sect (Jōdo Shinshū), Seibō was formally trained in sculpture at art universities in Kyoto and Tokyo.[20] During his years at the School of Fine Arts in Tokyo ("Geidai"), he found himself leaning more toward *chōso*, or modeling with clay and plaster to produce molds for metal sculptures, rather than *mokuchō*, or woodworking, a method he perceived to be more traditionally Japanese.[21] The stylistic tension between East and West finds parallels in Tange's pursuit of an ethnically Japanese modernist language, gesturing to an ongoing aesthetic struggle taking place in the designs of wartime and postwar built testaments to national memory.

In the summer of 1955, when the statue was unveiled to the public, Seibō was seventy years old, firmly established in his career as both a practitioner and as an educator at Geidai, where he was hired as a full professor in 1921.[22] Seibō worked continuously until his death in 1987 at the age of 102, producing a rich body of sculptural work that can be found across the archipelago. Nevertheless, the Nagasaki statue is arguably the best-known of his pieces. According to the sculptor, the idea to create something that would "represent the bombing, take a step forward, and pray for peace" came to him immediately following the aftermath of the war.[23] He was insistent that the work be titled "Peace Memorial Statue" rather than "Atomic Bomb Memorial," further underscoring the thematic centrality of peace while expanding the memorial referent beyond the scope of the bombing.[24]

Seibō himself wrote about the process and the artwork in remarkably charged and impassioned terms. In a June 1954 essay, titled "My Thoughts on the Peace Statue" (Heiwa kinen zō to watashi no kimochi) and published a little over a year before its completion, the artist groused over the unexpected obstacles he encountered during the production of the work. Issues raised included the technical challenges of the metalsmithing process, the need for increased personnel, the difficulty of communicating through bureaucratic channels, and the many letters he received from postmarked Nagasaki addresses chastising his design and calling for the project to be aborted.[25] His tone reveals the weathered expertise and grievances of an artist working in the public sphere, navigating and balancing the divergent interests of civic leadership, citizens, and his own artistic license and personal beliefs. Seibō was by no means oblivious to the criticisms of his work both during and after its production, and he utilized them as a rhetorical device to emphasize the trials and tribulations he endured in order to bring this piece to fruition.

Like Tange, he too undertook commissions for the imperial regime and was renowned among civic officials for his equestrian statues and depictions of military heroes throughout the 1920s and 1930s.[26] His enthusiastic support for these commissions made him a respectable and, importantly, safe choice for Nagasaki municipal leaders. In October 1950, members of the Nagasaki city council met with a group of Nagasaki-born artists and architects in Tokyo. Seibō's audacious proposal to build a statue that would echo the scale of the forty-nine-foot (15 m)-tall Nara Daibutsu and appeal to the people of Japan, and more broadly the citizens of the world, was eventually selected.[27] The artist's brazen conviction in the potential of the piece may also have to do with the fates that befell many of his earlier sculptures. During the Allied occupation of Japan (1945–1952), the General Headquarters of the Allied Powers (GHQ) and the Civil Information and Education Section (CIE) ordered the removal of militaristic statues from public view and banned the production of any new works that fell under this category, Seibō's previously celebrated sculptures began to lose their sheen of prestige.[28] As Tomoe Otsuki suggests, the Nagasaki project provided the sculptor with the opportunity to rehabilitate his career, secure his place in the Japanese art historical canon, and create a seemingly impenetrable work at a monumental scale that would demonstrate his adaptability to the new priorities of the nation while maintaining his signature style and aesthetic values.

While Tange's postwar efforts sought to diffuse or downplay his wartime design practice in service of the Empire, Seibō's work, even after the war, demonstrates a much less obfuscated image of artistic continuity and consistency in subject matter. In 1950, he completed a statue of a kamikaze pilot that he donated to an association of air force veteran's families in 1976.[29] The triumphal figure eventually made its way into the collection of the Yūshūkan Museum of Yasukuni Shrine, and an enlarged version, recast in 1999 by a former student of Seibō, stands today at the entrance of the museum. The dual contexts of the so-called institutions of "peace" and "war" appear at first glance contradictory, but such ambiguity and fluidity of meaning is not unusual in Japanese history. In practice, these dichotomies dissipate in state-sanctioned narratives of nuclear and imperial memory, which operate by enabling the protraction and abstraction of history in order to selectively "forget" aspects of history that threaten to undermine the coherence of postwar national identity.

The Peace Park as System

In the central area of the Hiroshima Peace Memorial Park, there are no immediate human referents in sight. Planarity and the light gray hues of concrete define the landscape, and broad, open paths create clean lines of movement and visibility for parkgoers across the main plaza. Tange's cenotaph, park plan, and Peace Center remain intact and well-preserved to this day, escaping the fate of most Japanese modernist buildings constructed in the 1950s that have been subjected to demolition or retrofitting.[30] The arch rests on a concrete platform in the reflecting pool, rising from a bed of white gravel. Located at the center of the rectangular plaza, the cenotaph can be viewed from all sides. While the Hiroshima park complex is unified under the vision of the single "genius" who wielded the common medium of concrete, the Nagasaki Peace Park lacks the same degree of visual and conceptual orchestration across its built components.

The forty-four-acre (18 ha) Nagasaki Peace Park, located atop one of Nagasaki's many steep hills, is divided into five "zones": the Wishing Zone—where the statue and Peace Fountain are located—the Prayer Zone, the Learning Zone, the Gathering Zone, and the Sports Zone. The latter two consists of athletic facilities including a baseball stadium, track, a soccer field and public pool, while the Prayer Zone and Learning Zone are home to the hypocenter and memorial museums. The JR train line along Route 206 bisects the park, separating the recreational areas from the institutions and memorials to the east of the tracks.[31] These subdivided areas were developed not during the original construction of the park in the immediate postwar years, but rather emerged as a result of the Peace Construction Plan formulated in 1993, in preparation for the fiftieth anniversary of the bombing.[32]

After the passing of the Nagasaki International Cultural City Construction Law in the National Diet, the Peace Statue was officially commissioned in the spring of 1951, approved through an overwhelming majority in the Nagasaki City Council.[33] The project arose alongside the construction of the Nagasaki International Cultural Center, a multipurpose space that would serve as a museum, archive, and community space. Located on a hill overlooking the hypocenter, the six-story building was designed to echo the United Nations Headquarters in New York City that had been completed in 1952, revealing parallel desires to Hiroshima's vision of a modernist city while declaring a symbolic connection to the postwar international political organ of peacemaking. The structure was built using reinforced concrete and locally sourced stones from the Gotō Islands. Its front facade was made up of a grid of balconied windows that looked out onto a rectangular reflecting pool.[34] The final outcome, however, might be considered a loose interpretation of the International Style at best and a paltry misnomer at its worst.

By the 1990s, the cultural hall had fallen into disrepair, and the city initiated a ¥5.6 billion project to replace the hall with the Nagasaki Atomic Bomb Museum, which houses and displays the majority of the artifacts and archival matter preserved from the bombing.³⁵ The lack of preservationist attention is not only a byproduct of the sweeping downfall of modernist buildings across Japan in the late twentieth century, but also a symptom of administrative neglect that befalls many institutions dedicated to atomic memory, particularly in Nagasaki. The museum's first and currently sole curator, Okuno Shotarō, was hired by the city shortly after graduating from Kumamoto University in 2008 and has spoken openly of the need for expanding conservation efforts and preserving material and immaterial narratives in the face of a diminishing *hibakusha* population. According to city officials, the position of the curator had never been established because it had not been stipulated by the original Nagasaki International Cultural City Construction Law (the Hiroshima Peace Memorial Museum currently has eight curators).³⁶ Adjacent to the museum is the Nagasaki National Peace Memorial Hall for the Atomic Bomb Victims, a ¥4.4 billion, glass-bound, and largely subterranean memorial space designed by Kuryū Akira and completed in 2003.³⁷ The memorial hall possesses a decidedly more individualizing bent, oriented specifically toward the remembrance of individual victims.

Proceeding north through the Learning Zone, one enters the Prayer Zone, which contains the hypocenter memorial. A simple, slender rectangular obelisk emerges from the center of a series of concentric paved circles. The spaces between each circle are filled with trimmed grass and inlaid bricks, enhancing the illusion of a radiation impact diagram while creating an interplay between built and organic elements. The austerity of the space, coupled with the circumambulatory environment create a markedly different correlate to the dynamism of the Peace Fountain and the linear path towards the towering statue. From the hypocenter, the visitor may cross the street and make their way up two flights of stairs to the Wishing Zone. The body of the statue gradually reveals itself as one ascends the steep hill, beginning with the raised right arm and culminating in the dramatic splendor of its full form. The scale is impressive in its own right, and its incremental unveiling heightens the drama of the encounter. The park as an object cannot be consumed through singular vantage points, as in Hiroshima, but rather exists as a collection of discrete visual and spatial encounters that are in part mediated by the natural contours of the landscape. Though initially planned to be located at the hypocenter, the statue was eventually erected on higher ground, at the site of the former Urakami branch of the Nagasaki Prison.³⁸

The organization of the circulation paths and the placement of the statue at the northern periphery of the zone indicates its function as a final destination—an altar at the end of a nave, so to speak.

Designed by Nagasaki-born architect Moto'ō Take and completed in 1969, the Fountain of Peace greets visitors as they enter the Wishing Zone and ambulate down the axis of the park toward the statue. Two slender, arced columns of water curve inward to frame the titan, merging to align with the two lines of Victorian-style lampposts that flank the stone path to the statue. The rise and fall of the fountains and the concave orientation of two rows of spouts is also described as echoing the movement of the wings of a dove of peace, and as a reference to the city itself, which has been colloquially dubbed "Port of Cranes." When viewed from above, the coastline of the peninsula is said to resemble the shape of the bird with its wings outstretched.[39]

A small inset juts into the circular pool, where a rectangular plaque is installed along the same axis as the Peace Statue.[40] The inscription features a diary entry of a *hibakusha* who recounts being unbearably dehydrated, and eventually succumbing to drinking the only water she could find, which was coated with an oily film. The credit line is phrased with a poetic ambiguity characteristic of the language used across civic narratives of the nuclear bombs: "Written by a Girl on That Day." The text, selected by Moto'ō, was excerpted from the reflections of a girl who was nine at the time of the attack.[41] Moto'ō's fountain, along with his designs for the Nagasaki Aquarium (1959) and Nagasaki Civic Auditorium (1962), grew out of the 1955 Nagasaki International Cultural Center Building Commission, an addendum to the initial 1949 law.[42]

The girl's blended use of kanji and hiragana, rendered in shaky, slightly uneven strokes, evokes a poignant humanness and youthfulness. Sandwiched between two walls, the plaque hovers above the surface of the pool, creating a niche to draw water from during prayer services.[43] Thirst and the lack of clean water are mentioned frequently in recollections of suffering by *hibakusha*, and imagery of the black rain from nuclear fallout appears time and time again across mass media and artistic responses. As one looks head on through the pulsating threads of water and encounters the haptic immediacy of the inscription, for a brief moment, the statue is dwarfed and humbled amid the expanse of the sky. By crafting an open, legible spatial relationship between the two memorials, the fountain operates as a transparent, plastic foil to the inert and unflinching statue.

In Hiroshima, the barrel arch also serves as a strategic framing device within the space of the park. At annual commemorative ceremonies and visits by significant figures, cameras are positioned to capture faces and figures through the legs of the arch, sometimes including the Genbaku Dome (known also as the Atomic Dome or Peace Dome) as a blurry specter in the distance. In an image of Prime Minister Abe Shinzō and President Obama shaking hands at the latter's 2016 visit to the city, the arch visually crafts a political narrative of unity that obscures the complexities surrounding the first visit to the memorial by a sitting U.S. president. As a result, it provides a legible reading of spatiotemporal continuity and symbolic closure by allowing the trauma and remnants of the past to be understood through the lens of the future, demarcating a shift toward the new, even at the expense of forgetting.

Commemorative media images taken in Nagasaki fail to have the same degree of recognizability held by their Hiroshima equivalents. This can be gleaned from a simple image search comparison of the two ceremonies. For the Nagasaki annual ceremony, a white stage is typically set up in front of the statue, spanning across the width of the reflecting pool and rising just high enough to hide the thirteen-foot (4 m)-tall stone base. Folding chairs are arranged in horizontal rows facing the statue, further reinforcing the frontal nature of the encounter. The camera is often situated amid or behind the crowd of mourners in order to capture the breadth of the crowd, inevitably affirming the dominance of the statue as he towers over the faceless masses. While the lens in the Hiroshima "money shot" is typically placed relatively close to level with the human subject, in Nagasaki there is no effective way to capture individuals in detail while including the body of the titan in full. Thus, speakers at the podium are often captured with the generic green backdrop of the artificial grass that covers a trapezoidal swatch of the constructed wall, echoing the form of the pedestal. The wall is emblazoned with the abstracted forms of an origami crane, a nod to the bird's symbolic associations with peace and good health and an ode to the Port of Cranes epithet.

The Body of Peace

The Peace Statue is seated upon a rectangular plinth of irregularly shaped rocks, whose mottled gray hues bring a tonal along with structural contrast to the light blue-green of the patina and the angular contours of the figure. The entire structure is surrounded by a still reflecting pool, while the statue's backside is flanked by a thicket of trees. The base was initially planned to be constructed with stones collected from around the world and intended to serve double duty as an ossuary for an unnamed Buddha, to be emblazoned with a copper plate engraved with the names of the dead. Both features were eventually cast aside due to budgetary and sizing concerns, as the statue became larger than initially planned.[44]

This landscaping and structural placement enacts a spatial mediation that informs the beholder's relationship to the statue. One must approach frontally, maintain a distance, and view from below. The artist's privileging of the head-on encounter is articulated not only by the positioning and stiffness of the figure itself, but also by the lack of attention given to the profile of the statue.[45] Viewed from the side, the nose and features reveal themselves to be remarkably flat. The shallowness between the chin and the trunklike neck gives the statue a stunted quality that undermines his rigidly defined musculature and facial expression seen from the front.

The titan is sheathed in a gauzy fabric that drapes across his left shoulder and lap, slinking around and tucking under his right leg, which bends and rests upon the seat. The cloth does not indicate status or identity in the manner that a toga would, nor is it distinctive enough to provide any hints toward determining a historical or mythic reference work. While the textural treatment of the folds harkens to the thin, rippling garments typical of Buddhist statuary, the minimal coverage of the loose cloth bears little resemblance to the layered robes that sheathe the forms of Buddhas and bodhisattvas.

The statue's expression is stoic and impenetrable. His left leg is planted firmly on the ground, perpendicular to the left arm, which is stretched taut, palm open and facing the ground. The softer bend of the right calf echoes the subtle curvature of the right arm, which gestures upward, a slight bend hinting at his relaxed muscles. The right hand, too, lacks tension, fingers unclenched as the index signals towards the heavens. In an inscription on the reverse of the plinth, reproduced in the artist's own handwriting, Seibō walks the spectator through a series of symbolic cues. The figure's eyes are said to be closed in prayer for the victims of the attack. The right hand points skyward in reference to the dropping of the bomb, while the left extends laterally to point toward "peace" (*heiwa*). Whether "peace" refers to a concrete and whole object, or a distant and abstracted aim that the statue orders the visitors to pursue, remains open and undefined. The left hand, which points southeast, was planned to be oriented toward the hypocenter (southwest) in an earlier iteration, which would have likely supported a more integrated reading between the elements of the park.[46] Owing to the final location of the statue, the meaning of the left arm was tweaked to simply refer to peace itself.

The vague instrumentalization of *heiwa* is not at all unusual, and in turn demonstrates the operations at play in its use as a diplomatic tool. Through the upward gesture, the bomb itself is spiritualized, loosely referred to as an entity that derived from an indeterminate heavenly source rather than human innovation and deliberation. Even Hiroshima, without the inflection of a Catholic background, made use of this language of fate and responsibility in dealing with the rubble of the aftermath. Itō Yutaka, chairman of Hiroshima's reconstruction committee, wrote in a letter soliciting donations for the project: "We consider it a duty given to us by Providence to reconstruct Hiroshima."[47] In order to absolve Emperor Hirohito, and by extension, his political adherents, of his wartime executive actions, the government released an imperial rescript on August 15, 1945, effectively presenting the end of the war not as a defeat but as a conscious decision on the part of the emperor and implying that without his intervention, weapons like the atomic bombs would threaten to extinguish both the Japanese people and human civilization. The emperor merely sought peace, as the narrative came to be understood, while the militarists were to blame for the atrocities. The discourse surrounding his "divine decision" to intervene and end the war set the tone for Japan's postwar trajectory of strategic compliance and selective forgetting. Needless to say, there is no mention in the monuments in Nagasaki and Hiroshima of who was responsible for dropping the atomic bombs. The Peace Parks in both cities thus function as operatives of a sanctified notion of peace, creating environments of "reflection" that instruct beholders to understand the civic meaning of peace through a tightly controlled political vision.

Seibō sought to not only create an image that avoided clear visual allegiance to any singular category, but that would also be accepted and embraced by all peoples, regardless of race, nationality, and faith. Laudatory writings of the piece specifically emphasize the statue's "abundant musculature" and "quietly meditative face," focusing on the bodily features as the harbingers of prayer and peace.[48] The artist describes the statue as a "human who transcends differences of race," and yet would also be accepted by all peoples, regardless of faith, race, and nationality.[49] By both upholding a hyperidealized image of the human form and endowing it with an iconology of peace that claims relevance to all people, the work thus equates the physical body with a body of knowledge that leaves no room for accommodating difference. Peace is created in the image of the statue and is proposed as an "affair of will," as Michael Lucken puts it—an entity that can be enacted through the choices made by the artist at the scale of his work, or the government at the scale of society.[50] Peace is conceived through a corporeal referent that directs human action from the vantage point of a deity with an undefined body of faith while modeling behaviorally and physically the shape that it takes in an individual body.

The style of the Peace Statue could be classified as neoclassical in its subject matter, but aesthetically it fails to fit neatly to any established category in the way that Tange's cenotaph clearly declares its ties to European modernist architecture. The blunt angularity and scale calls to mind contemporaneous Soviet statues, while the nudity and brazen assertion of muscularity finds parallels in the physical forms found in monuments to Italian fascism.

The seated posture, however, sets it apart from the heroic standing poses or equestrian staging assumed by many of these war monuments, and it instead echoes the forms of *daibutsu* and *dai-kannon* figures found across East Asia. The bodhisattva Kannon is often evoked in memorials to the war as an embodiment of peace. Seibō himself designed a twenty-six-foot-(8 m)-tall, standing *bosatsu* figure as a memorial to the bombings in 1975 that stands in Hiroshima today.[51] Though its position loosely echoes the visual language of Buddhism, the angularity of the Nagasaki titan's features appears oppositional to the fluid, organic contours that articulate sculptural representations of Buddhas and bodhisattvas. The monumentality was intended to allude to the evergreen spiritual heft of the Nara Daibutsu, whose unyielding presence and colossal scale functioned as a means of affirming unity among disparate feudal states and asserting the fortitude of a common Buddhist identity among the Japanese.[52]

According to Seibō, the figure was also intended to oscillate between references, presenting itself as "sometimes Buddha, sometimes God" (*Toki ni hotoke, toki ni kami*).[53] The crossed right leg indicates meditation, while the grounded left symbolizes salvation, further enhancing the dual nature of the deity.[54] The stylistic in-betweenness coupled with the symbolic vacillation enables the statue to elude any hard referent while maintaining claim to a unifying, seemingly apolitical common power. It becomes evident that the statue is ontologically tasked with upholding, reifying, and yet simultaneously surpassing and thus rendering inconsequential different sociocultural paradigms that are at once contained within a single body.

This muddily defined project of the body serves as an enactment of the "dual process of expression and repression of the past in postwar cultural discourse" in Japan, as described by Yoshikuni Igarashi.[55] In the wake of a dismembered body politic, a new body of national identity had to be reassembled and brought back to health through maintaining continuities while selectively effacing facets of trauma that could undermine state-sanctioned discourse of reticence and silence. The efforts to conceal scars and dismiss bodies that failed to support an official narrative of war were laborious by necessity, in order to counteract what Peter Sloterdijk terms the "awareness of a radically new dimension of latency" invoked by the atomic bombs. For Sloterdijk, the power of the bombs lay in their capacity to surface "the long concealed, the unknown, the unconscious, the never-known, the never-noticed and the imperceptible."[56] Yet while Sloterdijk's argument privileges the atmospheric conditions of violence now brought into the realm of consciousness, the body should not be relegated to the periphery as a mere matter of scale. The expression-repression interplay does not emerge merely from the acts of imperial collapse and nuclear disaster, but rather in their capacity to elucidate the existing fissures, desires, and threats inherent in the stability of the nation that could be dealt with only through silencing. The two monuments grapple with this hunger for ontological stability and impenetrability through prisms of time, space, and gender.

Both Noguchi's proposition and Tange's extant concrete adaptation of the arch contain symbolic nods to Japanese antiquity. Noguchi's thick, dense arch recalled the wide-set handles of *dōtaku,* the distinctive, hulking ceremonial bells from the Yayoi period whose functions to this day remain shrouded in mystery. The artist also found inspiration in the forms of *haniwa* sculptures from the Kofun period, reanimating their curvatures in the swelled form of the arch.[57] In Tange's saddlelike arch, the apexes of the catenary ends stretch upward and out, alluding to the distinctive roofs of *haniwa* houses. These allusions to the premodern era tap into desires to both express a uniquely "Japanese" spirit and revisit an era supposedly unencumbered with the technological ills of the present. In the two cenotaphs, a sense of movement outward from the occupied volume of the object—skyward (Tange) or subterranean (Noguchi)—is expressed in its physicality.

The Peace Statue, on the other hand, actively aspires to be something more encompassing, universalizing, and free from the grip of time and history. This desire for a cosmic order that surpasses not only the differences between men but also the very nature of humanness itself is in turn coupled with the oppositional force of organizing society around the rationality of man—what Lucken refers to as "the foundation of the contemporary Japanese nation."[58] It aspires to a stabilizing, immobile force that resists being subordinated to the status of a referent instead of a subject.[59]

Tange's quotation of Le Corbusier's *pilotis* in the Peace Museum, and the fluid curves of the concrete arch, which neatly and airily frames the ruins of the Genbaku Dome, craft a starkly different relationship between ground and air than does the Nagasaki Peace Statue in its negotiations with its surrounding space. The statue obstinately entrenches itself in its seat, its rectilinear contours negating any possibility of the effusion of form into air. The transparency and rhythmic order evoked by the main plaza of the

Hiroshima park is transformed in Nagasaki to a pathway of ruptures and discoveries, pockmarked moments of declaration and reflection.

The arch in the Hiroshima park—the fraught and harried circumstances of the final design notwithstanding—is not intended to serve as a centerpiece so much as an organizing principle that balances the constituent elements in the main plaza. In Nagasaki, the statue instead takes on the role of a compound monument, wherein the desires to reconstitute and eternalize nuclear histories consolidated within a single main object of focus.[60] Thus, in its aggressively frontal and singular nature, the statue spatially dominates the discursive arena of the memorial environment, making it difficult for alternate narratives to make themselves visible.

While both Pope John Paul II in 1981 and Pope Francis in 2019 paid visits to Hiroshima and Nagasaki to honor victims and advocate for nuclear deterrence and disarmament (each to varying degrees), neither included the Peace Statue as part of their itinerary. Motoshima Hitoshi, mayor of Nagasaki at the time of John Paul II's arrival and a practicing Catholic, claimed that the pope's avoidance of the statue was due to the prohibition of idolatry in Catholic practice.[61] Yet the Vatican has never provided a clear reason for why one of the most significant, albeit vexed, landmarks of Nagasaki civic memory was conspicuously omitted from these tours. Perhaps because the statue leans so heavily into the language of prayer and agglomerates the prototypical indicators of divinity (the scale of a *daibutsu*, the musculature of a Greek deity, topped off with wavy Christlike tresses) to accord the state ideology of peacemaking with the air of an organized faith, it presents itself to the Church as a slippery object that errs dangerously close to ecclesiastical sacrilege.

Using a single human body as the primary representative for the memory—a masculine, and seemingly Western one at that—is a striking move to pursue when navigating the possibilities of collective memory. Despite repeated assertions that the statue claims to exceed differences of race, nationality, and faith, the category of gender is never mentioned in both accompanying texts and writings by the artist himself. The externalized, impenetrable nature of the statue, and the verticality and emergent movement of the Hiroshima arch both distinguish themselves from the entrenched quality of the "maternal thighs" of Noguchi's arch that would have extended underground into the "womb-like" chamber.[62]

The aggressively coherent, virile form of the statue also presents itself in direct opposition to the scarred and erased bodies that characterize the experiences of both the dead and the survivors of the bomb. The brazen masculinity exuded by the statue finds an intriguing counterpart in a scarred statue of Mary, salvaged from the ruins of the Urakami Cathedral. At a ceremonial mass held at the Urakami baseball stadium, Pope Francis shared the stage with the wooden bust, whose hollowed-out eyes and charred surfaces imbue the icon with a haunting aura of grief and evoke the corporeal traces of the bomb's violence.[63] That the Mary icon endures only as a disembodied head and neck is all the more salient when seen in relation to the structurally sound, singular body of the titan. During times of persecution in the Edo period, Nagasaki Christians adopted the gender-ambivalent bodhisattva Kannon as a stand-in for the Virgin to conceal their faith.[64] As W. J. T. Mitchell writes, "The fictional ideal of the classic public sphere is that it includes everyone; the fact is that it can be constituted only by the rigorous exclusion of certain groups—slaves, children, foreigners, those without property, and (most conspicuously) women."[65] The Peace Statue expresses no desire to engage in dialogue with other symbolic figures specific to the site or to any legacies of spatial concealment and social repression. In aspiring to an all-encompassing monument unencumbered by the iconographic references of the past, the statue derives its power to create a masculine, dominant narrative by pushing forth a narrative of absolute coherence, aggressive superficiality and frontal visibility that works against feminized legacies of occlusion, subversion, and nonvisual modes of sensory experience.

Further, the power of the male body operates as a strategic application of a postwar rhetoric pushed forth by both Japanese and American authorities. The aforementioned inscription by the artist also reads: "A wise and holy visage like a mountain/that evokes the fortitude and bravery of a healthy man" (*Yama no gotoki seitsu/Sorewa takumashii dansei no kenkōbi*).[66] The notion of virile beauty, or *kenkōbi*, had figured prominently throughout Seibō's oeuvre, and work produced during the war aided in the promotion of imperial efforts to promote fit and healthy national bodies under the auspices of the Healthy Citizen Movement (Kenmin Undō). In 1942, a male nude by Seibō was featured in a traveling exhibition commissioned by the Imperial Rule Assistance Association. Staged at eight auditoriums and department stores across Tokyo, the Healthy Citizenry Sculpture Exhibition (Kenmin Chōso Tenjikai) sought to model ideal forms of being through artistic exhibitions sited across the metropole.[67]

The continued assertion of the unequivocally muscular, unfazed man in the aftermath of war perhaps also served as a means of reinvigorating and rehabilitating national identity in the wake of American occupation. After enduring the social and medical pathologization of Japanese bodies under U.S. practices, which include the dehumanizing lab research conducted on *hibakusha* by the Atomic Bomb Casualty Commission (ABCC) and the extensive spraying of DDT at the level of both individual bodies and landscapes to mitigate the spread of infectious diseases, the brazen physicality of the statue may have operated as a fervent attempt to restore patriotic dignity through the medium of the body.[68]

The image of the hygienic body and omniscient psyche of the statue, and its proposed intent to unify all beings, is premised upon the vigorous omission of anything that threatened to undermine this presentation. To view this notion as a collective representation seems preposterous in the wake of a disaster characterized by the scarring, splintering, and eradication of human forms, both physically and psychologically. Thousands still suffered from the long-term effects of radiation poisoning and endured stigmatization from both political leaders and fellow citizens. The urban disfiguration enacted by the bomb was only further accentuated by the heedless bulldozing undertaken by American troops upon their arrival in Nagasaki and the controversial decision to demolish and rebuild the cathedral, a symbolic move that stands in diametric opposition to Hiroshima's preservation of the blown-out remains of the Genbaku Dome.[69]

Behind depictions of human or humanoid bodies is typically the service of a figure model. For Seibō, his corporeal reference came in the form of Yoshida Hiroichi, a former captain in the 55th Division of the Imperial Japanese Army who fought in the New Guinea and Burma campaigns.[70] Yoshida became a professional weightlifter following the war, weighing in at 187 pounds (85 kg) and standing six feet (184 cm) tall. A photograph taken in the 1950s reveals the clear parallels between Yoshida and the resulting sculpture (figure 3). The camera captures him fully frontal and from a low angle, imbuing him with a herculean, unyielding aura. Arms akimbo, Yoshida squints into the sunlight, which vividly bounces off the contours of his chiseled, triangular torso.[71] A six-time middleweight weightlifting national champion, Yoshida bore the flag of the Japanese team at the second Asian Games in 1954 in Manila. His broad shoulders and tightly cinched waist, neatly accentuated by a wide black belt, are visibly echoed in the bronze statue. The crosslike division between Yoshida's pectorals, too, is noticeable in the final work. That Seibō would draw inspiration from a highly articulated male form, one that emerged physically intact from the losses of war and embodied the fortitude of the nation, as his model is telling.

Amid the culturally fragmented postwar landscape of the nation, bodies such as Yoshida's served as the ultimate vision of an idealized unity that Japanese authorities desperately sought during a period of hybrid, fluctuating autonomy under the auspices of American jurisdiction. Yoshida's status as

Figure 3. Yoshida Hiroichi. Photograph used with permission of the *Yomiuri Shimbun*.

both a decorated veteran and an impeccably fit male worked to counteract the feminized role of the conciliatory, forgetful servant assumed by the state during the reconstruction years in order to play victim to American forces while absolving themselves of imperial wrongdoings. The statue may describe itself as a guardian of peace. What it successfully buttresses, however, is the puncturing of state-sanctioned memory by lived narratives that undermine the continuity of the coherent body politic under the imperial regime through the postwar period. On the level of the state, the Peace Statue carved out an avenue for expressing national coherence and fortitude as a means of not only reassuring its citizenry but also asserting to the world that Japan was not in the same state of disorder and disrepair that its former colonial outposts still suffered under, a decade after the end of the Pacific War.

In the closing sentences of Seibō's 1954 text, he finishes off the passage with the bravado of a late-career artist, essentially declaring the work to be his magnum opus. He claims no interest in the financial or professional gains to be received from the work while expressing hopes for the sculpture to rise to the level of a national treasure, impressing upon the country a legacy that he hoped would endure for millennia.[72] Yet in 1980, when asked in an interview about how he thought the goal of perpetual peace would be achieved, he laughed and replied, "That will never happen. Human nature is, after all, avaricious."[73] As callous as these words may sound coming from the maker of a monument so reviled for its perceived vacuousness, there is a degree of truth to them. Monuments primarily exist to alleviate the guilt of the living rather than appease the souls of the dead. We may even say that the erection of monuments in the public sphere enables us to displace the burdens and labors of memory onto the monuments themselves.[74] The materialization of memory always makes evident what is lacking. Moreover, memorials are perhaps contingent on this very lack in order to articulate their representational form.

The Peace Statue is a site of latency and obfuscation, where the pushes and pulls, affirmations and denials, reclamations and relinquishments of memory-making take place. It is also by no means the only site of controversy and flux in the Peace Park. After decades of lobbying, the first government-sponsored memorial to the thousands of Korean victims of the bomb was unveiled in November of 2021.[75] In 1996, the hypocenter pillar came close to being replaced by a statue of a mother holding her infant child by one of Seibō's Nagasaki-born protegees, Tominaga Naoki through a nearly unilateral decision put forth by the mayor. After protests from antinuclear groups, which offered the defense that the extant monument had, through years of prayer, taken on "the character of a cenotaph" (without necessarily being labeled as one), the statue was eventually sited in a different location within the Prayer Zone, although still within site of the hypocenter pillar.[76] Each node of encounter that emerges within the park is evidence of the active, ongoing production and negotiation of memory. The overwhelmingly apathetic or hostile responses to the statue also aid in the construction of new responsive paradigms to encompass scarred, nonconforming bodies and absent or lost narratives. By revisiting these organs of memory-making and the system failures of their prescribed programs, we can not only examine the select features of past they seek to reify but also recognize the body as a malleable canvas of memory-making that is uniquely sensitive to its surrounding conditions, enabling us to imagine possible futures that emerge beyond the scope of these built testaments.

Notes

1. Elaine Scarry, *The Body in Pain: The Making and Unmaking of the World* (New York: Oxford University Press, 1985), 161.

2. Hisashi Tomokuni, "'Samoshii to itte kudasaimasu na' Fukuda Sumako-san no omoi genbaku o seotte" ("Don't Call Me Selfish"—Sumako Fukuda, Carrying the Weight of the Atomic Bombing), *Nishi Nippon Shinbun*, August 6, 2020, https://www.nishinippon.co.jp/item/n/624208/.

3. Nagasaki Atomic Bomb Damage Records, Part 3: Rescue and Medical Relief, Chapter 2: International Culture City: available at Nagasaki National Peace Memorial Hall for the Atomic Bomb Victims, https://www.peace-nagasaki.go.jp/abombrecords/b030402.html. The Nagasaki International Cultural Hall, which was planned and built concurrently with the statue, was fully funded by the national, prefectural, and municipal governments. The allocation of financial responsibility for a public art piece to civilians, a common practice in memorial-making, perhaps provides the illusion of a communal, "cultural" undertaking while absolving authorities of a degree of direct complicity in the making of the project.

4. Nagasaki Atomic Bomb Damage Records; Tomoe Otsuki, "Reinventing Nagasaki: The Christianization of Nagasaki and the Revival of an Imperial Legacy in Postwar Japan," *Inter-Asia Cultural Studies* 17, no. 3 (2016): 411.

5. Kitamura Seibō, "Heiwa kinen zō to watashi no kimochi" (My Thoughts on the Peace Statue) in *Heiwa kinen zō no dekiagarumade* (The Making of the Peace Statue), ed. Nagasaki Teachers' Union and the Peace Statue Construction Cooperative (Nagasaki: Nagasaki Teachers' Union and the Peace Statue Construction Cooperative, 1955), 20.

6. Ran Zwigenberg, *Hiroshima: The Origins of Global Memory Culture* (Cambridge: Cambridge University Press, 2014), 58.

7. Taniguchi Sumiteru, "'Heiwa e no chikai' ni buchimaketa ikari: Genbaku o seotte" (Raging against the "Vow of Peace," Carrying the Weight of the Atomic Bombing), *Nishi Nippon Shinbun*, August 23, 2020, https://www.nishinippon.co.jp/item/n/631219/.

8. Yamasaki Takeshi, "Inori to ishitsu na kyodai geijutsu: Heiwa kinen zō: Hōō wa konkai mo tachiyorazu" (Prayers and Strange Massive Sculpture: Pope Again Avoids Peace Statue Visit), *Nishi Nippon Shinbun*, October 27, 2021, https://www.nishinippon.co.jp/item/n/554327/.

9. Brian Burke-Gaffney, "Thoughts on the Peace Statue," *Nagasaki Perspectives*, July 26, 2011, https://railwayrider-nagasakiperspectives.blogspot.com/2011/07/thoughts-on-peace-statue.html.

10. W. J. T. Mitchell, "Utopia and Critique," in *Art and the Public Sphere*, ed. W. J. T. Mitchell (Chicago: University of Chicago Press, 1992), 2–3.

11. Rafael Narvaez, "Embodiment, Collective Memory, and Time," *Body and Society* 12, no. 3 (2006): 66.

12. Chad R. Diehl, *Resurrecting Nagasaki: Reconstruction and the Formation of Atomic Narratives* (Ithaca, NY: Cornell University Press, 2018), 71.

13. Ibid., 14.

14. Ibid., 31–32.

15. Chad R. Diehl, "Envisioning Nagasaki: From 'Atomic Wasteland' to 'International Cultural City,' 1945–1950," *Urban History* 41, no. 3 (August 2014): 516. While Hiroshima was the only city to receive the "peace city" designation, the title of "international city" was shared by other municipalities including Kyoto, Nara, and Beppu (510–511).

16. Kitamura, "Heiwa kinen zō to watashi no kimochi."

17. Hyunjung Cho, "Hiroshima Peace Memorial Park and the Making of Japanese Postwar Architecture," *Journal of Architectural Education* 66, no. 1 (2012): 72–74. The similarities between this proposal and the Hiroshima park plan have invited greater critical attention in recent years, with scholars such as Inoue Shōichi viewing the "recycling" of the design as both a nostalgic restoration of wartime values, while also a reconstitution of the ruins of destruction into an utterly modern, future-oriented paradigm, turning the "negative" into an entirely "positive" site of urban identity production. See Inoue Shōichi, *Senjika Nihon no kenchikuka* (Architects in Wartime Japan) (Tokyo: Asahi Shinbun sha, 1995), and Michael Lucken, *The Japanese and the War: Expectation, Perception, and the Shaping of Memory*, trans. Karen Grimwade (New York: Columbia University Press, 2017), esp. ch. 11, "From Monument to Museum: The Difficult Path to Healing."

18. Tange Kenzō, "Dai tōwa kenchiku ni okeru kaiin no yōbō" (Requests of the Greater East Asia Architecture), *Kenchiku zasshi* 56, no. 690 (September 1942): 744, trans. Hyunjung Cho, "Hiroshima Peace Memorial Park and the Making of Japanese Postwar Architecture," *Journal of Architectural Education* 66, no. 1 (2012): 74. For more on the design competition, organized by the Architectural Institute of Japan (AIJ), see Funo Shūji, "Dai tōa kenchiku yōshiki" (The Greater East Asian Architectural Style), *hiroba* (April 2001): 16–19.

19. Isamu Noguchi, "Project: Hiroshima Memorial to the Dead," *Arts and Architecture* 70, no. 4 (April 1953): 16.

20. Michael Lucken, "The Peace Statue at Nagasaki," in *Japan's Postwar*, ed. Michael Lucken, Anne Bayard-Sakai, and Emmanuel Lozerand, trans. J. A. A. Stockwin (London: Routledge, 2011), 181–182.

21. Ibid, 182.

22. Ibid.

23. Kitamura Seibō, "Heiwa kinen zō no kansei ni atatte" (On the Completion of the Peace Statue), in *Heiwa kinen zō no seishin: Genbaku jushūnen kinen shikiten kiroku* (The Spirit of the Peace Statue: Records of the 10th Anniversary Commemorative Ceremony) (Nagasaki: Nagasaki City and the Peace Statue Construction Cooperative, 1955), 14.

24. Otsuki, "Reinventing Nagasaki," 410.

25. Kitamura, "Heiwa kinen zō to watashi no kimochi."

26. Michael Lucken, *The Japanese and the War: Expectation, Perception, and the Shaping of Memory*, trans. Karen Grimwade (New York: Columbia University Press, 2014), 244.

27. Kimishima Ayako, "Heiwa mo'nyumento to kannon-zō: Nagasaki-shi Heiwa Kōen nai no chōzō ni okeru shinkō to kenshō" (Peace Monuments and Kannon Statues: Faith and Shapes Seen in the Statues of Nagasaki Peace Park), *Shūkyō to shakai* (Religion and Society) 24 (June 2018): 100.

28. Otsuki, "Reinventing Nagasaki," 409.

29. Lucken, *The Japanese and the War*, 244.

30. Igor Fracalossi, "AD Classics: Hiroshima Peace Center and Memorial Park / Kenzo Tange," *ArchDaily*, August 29, 2011, https://www.archdaily.com/160170/ad-classics-hiroshima-peace-center-and-memorial-park-kenzo-tange.

31. Nagasaki City, "Heiwakōen" (Peace Park), last modified April 13, 2018, https://www.city.nagasaki.lg.jp.e.jc.hp.transer.com/sumai/630000/632000/p005153.html.

32. Nagasaki Atomic Bomb Damage Records.

33. Ibid.

34. Ibid.

35. Daniel Seltz, "Remembering the War and the Atomic Bombs: New Museums, New Approaches," *Radical History Review* 75 (1999): 103.

36. Mizuki Enomoto, "Nagasaki Curator Strives Alone to Preserve A-Bomb Artifacts," *Asahi Shinbun*, August 23, 2021, https://www.asahi.com/ajw/articles/14416184.

37. "Heisei no Nagasaki: Kokuritsu Nagasaki genbaku shibotsusha tsuitō heiwa kinenkan ga kaikan: Heisei 15 (2003)" (Heisei-Era Nagasaki: Nagasaki National Peace Memorial Hall for the Atomic Bomb Victims Opens [2003]), *Nagasaki Shinbun*, November 29, 2018, https://nordot.app/439022632128529505. The memorial hall and its counterpart in Hiroshima were both established as a result of commissions issued by the Ministry of Health, Labor, and Welfare, hence the inclusion of "National" in the building name. The Hiroshima Memorial Hall was also designed by Tange, further underscoring the authorial and aesthetic unity of the park. Kuryū's design possesses some qualities that resonate with Noguchi's proposal; namely, in its construction of a subterranean space dedicated to quiet reflection, and the use of ceiling apertures to filter in light from above.

38. Ohira Teruhisa, "Nagasaki genbaku rakka chūshin-hi ni miru mo'nyumento no kōchiku" (Social Construction of Nagasaki Atomic Bomb Hypocenter Monument), *Kyūshū chiku kokuritsu daigaku kyōiku kei, bunkei kenkyū ronbun-shū* (Joint Journal of the National Universities in Kyusyu: Education and Humanities) 5, no. 1 (2017): 2. Fragments of the prison's foundations have been preserved within the park, functioning as one of the few indexical traces of ruination present in the area. Of the eighty-one prisoners

killed by the blast, thirty-two were Chinese and thirteen were Korean. The remains of the stone walls of the building lie low to the ground along the path leading to the main gathering plaza, making them easy to miss and impossible to identify without the aid of the accompanying plaque.

39. Ministry of Internal Affairs and Communications, "Heiwa no izumi" (The Peace Fountain), https://www.soumu.go.jp/main_sosiki/daijinkanbou/sensai/virt plaque ual/memorialsite/nagasaki_nagasaki_003/index.html.

40. Ibid.

41. Shimada Yoshiko, "Shōwa-ki ni katsudō shita kenchikuka Motoō Take (1910–2005)" (Motoō Take, an Architect Active during the Shōwa Period [1910–2005]), *Nagasaki Shinbun*, April 20, 2015, https://www.nagasakicitylegacy.info/topics/2375/.

42. Ibid.

43. "Kawaki to kanashimi o urusu heiwa: Nagasaki asu genbaku no hi" (Peace to Quench Thirst and Sorrow: Nagasaki to Hold Atomic-Bombing Memorial Service Tomorrow), *Chūnichi Shinbun*, August 8, 2020, https://www.chunichi.co.jp/article/101909.

44. Kimishima, "Heiwa mo'nyumento to kannon-zō," 101.

45. Lucken, "The Peace Statue at Nagasaki," 193.

46. Otsuki, "Reinventing Nagasaki," 410. The project site was an intense topic of debate. Municipal leaders, *hibakusha*, other consultants and constituents debated on various possible locations even after Seibō was well into the process. Records from the *Nagasaki Minyū Shinbun* in 1952 illustrate the back and forth between proponents for placing the statue at Kazagashira Park, where it could be seen from afar by Nagasaki city residents (but not from Urakami) and visitors arriving at the port, and those who supported erecting it in the Urakami area, where the bulk of the physical destruction had taken place. See Araki Takeshi, "The Reconstruction Effort and Construction of the Peace Statue in Nagasaki," *Genbaku bungaku kenkyū: Tokushū "sengo 70 nen" renzoku wākushoppu* (Atomic Bombing Literature Research: Special Issue "70 Years After the War" Workshop Series) (2015): 181–204, for a discussion of this topic.

47. Ran Zwigenberg, "The Most Modern City in the World: Isamu Noguchi's Cenotaph Controversy and Hiroshima's City of Peace," *Critical Military Studies* 1, no. 2 (2015): 105.

48. Kino Fumio, "Heiwa no mamori zō" (The Protective Statue of Peace), in *Heiwa kinen zō no seishin: Genbaku jushūnen kinen shikiten kiroku* (The Spirit of the Peace Statue: Records of the 10th Anniversary Commemorative Ceremony) (Nagasaki: Nagasaki City and the Peace Statue Construction Cooperative, 1955), 21.

49. Kitamura, "Heiwa kinen zō sakusha no kotoba."

50. Lucken, "The Peace Statue at Nagasaki," 193.

51. Lucken, *The Japanese and the War*, 221.

52. "Heiwa kinen zō wa dōshite tsukurareta no ka" (Why the Peace Statue Was Built), in *Heiwa kinen zō no dekiagaru made* (The Making of the Peace

Statue), ed. Nagasaki Teachers Union and the Peace Statue Construction Cooperative (Nagasaki: Nagasaki Teachers Union and the Peace Statue Construction Cooperative, 1955), 8–9.

53. Ibid., 9.

54. Ibid., 8.

55. Yoshikuni Igarashi, *Bodies of Memory: Narratives of War in Postwar Japanese Culture, 1945–1970* (Princeton, NJ: Princeton University Press, 2000), 14.

56. Peter Sloterdijk, *Terror from the Air* (Los Angeles: Semiotext(e), 2009), 58.

57. Bert Winther-Tamaki, *Art in the Encounter of Nations: Japanese and American Artists in the Early Postwar Years* (Honolulu: University of Hawaii Press, 2001), 124–126. *Dōtaku* also teeter delicately along the interlacing beams in a model for Noguchi's unrealized project, *Bell Tower for Hiroshima*.

58. Lucken, *The Japanese and the War*, 247.

59. I note the statue's obstinate quality not merely to set up a visual counterpoint to the Hiroshima arches but also to set it even further apart from memorials that engage with transience, translocation, and malleability as part of their artistic program. The "counter-monument" movement in late twentieth-century Germany, encompassing works such as Jochen Gerz and Esther Salev-Gerz's *Harburg Monument against Fascism* (1986) self-effacing pillar, is one of many useful reference points for comparing design programs of civic monuments. See James E. Young, "The Counter-Monument: Memory against Itself in Germany Today," *Critical Inquiry* 18, no. 2 (Winter 1992): 273.

60. Ibid., 245.

61. Yamasaki, "Inori to ishitsu na kyodai geijutsu."

62. Winther-Tamaki, *Art in the Encounter of Nations*, 124–126.

63. Gwyn McClelland, "Urakami Memory and the Two Popes: The Disrupting of an Abstracted Nuclear Discourse," *Religions* 12, no. 11 (2021): 950.

64. Ibid.

65. W. J. T. Mitchell, "The Violence of Public Art: *Do the Right Thing*," in Mitchell, *Art and the Public Sphere*, 35. The blanketing municipal and state discourses of "national peace" have also effectively repressed or excluded the experiences and suffering of minority ethnic groups including Chinese and Korean victims (many of whom were indentured laborers), along with the *burakumin* population.

66. Yamasaki, "Inori to ishitsu na kyodai geijutsu."

67. Hirase Reita, *Chōkoku to sensō no kindai* (Sculpture and War in Modernity) (Tokyo: Yoshikawa Kōbunkan, 2013), 83.

68. For more on DDT during the occupation, see Igarashi, *Bodies of Memory*, 65–67.

69. Diehl, *Resurrecting Nagasaki*, 59–60.

70. "Sensen o ikinuita tsuyo-sa to yasashi-sa: Kishu hansen no arubamu" (The Strength and Kindness That Survived the War: A Flag-Bearer's Antiwar Album), *Yomiuri Shinbun*, August 9, 2020, https://www.yomiuri.co.jp/s/ims/yoshidaalbum/.

71. "Owaranu natsu <9> Nagasaki heiwa inoru 'kenkō-bi'... heiwa kinenzō moderu to sa reru Yoshida Hiroichi rikugun taii no jijo Inoue Jun-san (68)" (A Never-Ending Summer, no. 9) Nagasaki: Praying for Peace "Healthy and Beautiful," Inoue Jun (68 [Years Old]), the Second Daughter of Army Captain Yoshida Hiroichi, Said to Be the Model of the Peace Statue), *Yomiuri Shinbun*, August 9, 2020, https://www.yomiuri.co.jp/pluralphoto/20200809-OYT1I50012/.

72. Kitamura, "Heiwa kinen zō to watashi no kimochi."

73. As quoted in Otsuki, "Reinventing Nagasaki," 410.

74. Young, "The Counter-Monument," 273.

75. Ryo Sasaki, "Monument for Korean Atomic Bomb Victims Set up in Nagasaki," *Asahi Shinbun*, November 7, 2021, https://www.asahi.com/ajw/articles/14476801.

76. Ohira, "Nagasaki genbaku rakka chūshin-hi ni miru mo'nyumento no kōchiku," 6.

Part IV
Reflections

How I Came to Criticize Nagai Takashi's Urakami Holocaust Theory
By Shinji Takahashi
Translated by Chad R. Diehl

In the autumn of 1985, I gave a presentation, titled, "Criticizing the Nagai Takashi 'Urakami Holocaust Theory'" (Nagai Takashi "Urakami hansai setsu" hihan), at an interdisciplinary academic meeting of the Society for the History of Social Thought (Shakai shisōshi gakkai), at Kumamoto Shōka University (now Kumamoto Gakuen University). Looking back, that moment became a turning point in Nagasaki's postatomic discourse because it forced a long overdue reconsideration of the dominance of Nagai as representative voice of the atomic experience. In many ways, his interpretation of the bombing, which was loaded with religious ideas and terminology, made reckoning with the trauma of the bombing difficult for *hibakusha* (atomic-bombing survivors).[1] What follows is a recounting of how I came to publicly criticize what I have termed the "Urakami holocaust theory" of Nagai Takashi.

I would like to begin with a short explanation of how and why I have used the word "holocaust." The word originally meant "burnt offering" in Judaism, originating from the ritual offering unto God of burning a whole calf, lamb, or goat for atonement, and the word is used in some translations of the Old Testament of the Bible to mean such a burnt offering. The word I use in Japanese is *hansai*, also meaning, literally, a burnt offering. The term "holocaust" in English, in addition to coming to represent the Holocaust of the Second World War, has been used by some scholars to describe mass atrocities in general, including the atomic bombings.[2] However, I use the word as Nagai Takashi himself intended: to describe what he saw as the martyrdom of his Catholic community in the form of a burnt offering on God's altar that ended the Second World War.

When I commented on Nagai Takashi's ideas and called it his Urakami holocaust theory, I was criticized for rehashing old criticisms of his works and was accused of not knowing the kindness of Nagai-sensei. But of course that was not the case. I did not imitate others to criticize Nagai, nor did I criticize him because I was unaware of his kindness as a human being. It was a natural extension of the research I was engaged in at the time, and so even more than its having been natural, I was intellectually bound (*hitsuzenteki ni*) to undertaking a critical commentary of Nagai and his works. Ever since my "Criticizing the Nagai Takashi 'Urakami Holocaust Theory,'" was made public, including into the present, many people have used it as a reference point for discussing his place in Nagasaki's postwar history and the atomic-bombing literature. However, no one has yet mentioned how I developed a criticism of Nagai's interpretation of the atomic bombing of Nagasaki. Therefore, I wanted to take the opportunity of being invited to contribute to the first-ever edited volume in English about postatomic Nagasaki to relate the intellectual origins of my criticism of Nagai Takashi and his Urakami holocaust theory.

The NGO International Symposium on the Damage and Aftereffects of the Atomic Bombings of Hiroshima and Nagasaki

It was half a century ago, in 1973, when I was just thirty-one years old, that I completed my graduate work in Tokyo and relocated to Nagasaki for work. I was fortunate because in 1977, an unprecedented weeks-long event took place that forever changed discourse on the atomic bombings in Japan. Sponsored by nongovernmental organizations associated with the United Nations, the first International Symposium on the Damage and Aftereffects of the Atomic Bombing of Hiroshima and Nagasaki (NGO Hibaku mondai kokusai shinpojiumu) was held in Tokyo, Hiroshima, and Nagasaki from July 21 through August 9, 1977.[3]

In the background of the 1977 symposium, as I will refer to it, appeared the harsh reality of the Cold War, when the nuclear superpowers of the United States and the Soviet Union faced off with nuclear weapons. Fearing that it would erupt into a hot war, world leaders decided to hold the first-ever Special Session on Disarmament at the United Nations (SSOD-I) in 1978. As part of the preparations for the special assembly, the 1977 symposium in Japan was organized to discuss the "damage and aftereffects of the atomic bombings of Hiroshima and Nagasaki." The International Peace Bureau (IPB) made the core aim of the symposium the idea that the mobilization of public opinion was the key to the abolition of nuclear weapons and to disarmament more generally. To prepare for the symposium and invigorate dialogue, the Japan Preparatory Committee (Nihon junbi i'inkai) was established, as were preparatory committees all throughout the prefectures of Japan, including the Nagasaki Preparatory Committee.

How I Came to Criticize Nagai Takashi's Urakami Holocaust Theory | 297

I had gradually settled in at my position, lecturing on philosophy and other subjects at Nagasaki College of Naval Architecture (called the Nagasaki Institute of Applied Science since 1978), when I began to collaborate with my university colleagues on the Nagasaki Preparatory Committee for the 1977 symposium. My colleagues Kamata Sadao, Katayose Toshihide, and Ōkubo Tokuyuki and I exchanged views with medical scientists working at Nagasaki University's School of Medicine, such as Dr. Nishimori Kazumasa, Dr. Takei Hiroshi, Dr. Ichimaru Michito, and others to produce various reports about the human damage and social ruptures created by the atomic bombing.[4] I also came to know members of the Peace Education Subcommittee, such as Sakaguchi Tayori, Tsuiki Shōhei, and Imada Ayao, who were experienced teachers engaged in peace education in Nagasaki.

However, the most important acquaintances I made at the time were the *hibakusha*, such as Dr. Akizuki Tatsuichirō, chief physician at Nagasaki Saint Francis Hospital, and Yamaguchi Senji, president of the Nagasaki Atomic-Bombing Survivors Council (Hisaikyō, for short), as well as the many other activist-survivors, including Taniguchi Sumiteru and Shimohira Sakue. Once, in 1977, a colleague named Hibino Masami and I brought two members of an international research team, Mary Kaufman (an American specialist in international law and prosecutor at the Nuremburg war-crimes trials) and Uvais Ahamed (at the time head of educational administration in Sri Lanka), to visit a *hibakusha* named Watanabe Chieko at her home in Otonashimachi town in the northern part of Nagasaki City. Chieko had been working at the Mitsubishi Electric Works at the time of the atomic bombing, and the factory's steel-framed roof fell on her, trapping her beneath it. As a result of her injuries, she was paralyzed from the waist down. For me, that meeting and resulting exchange between Chieko and two members of an international research team remains an unforgettable and beautiful memory. Chieko began to use a wheelchair for mobility at the encouragement of Hibino Masami. This empowered her to speak about her atomic-bombing experience abroad, traveling the following year to Geneva, Switzerland, to participate in the 1978 International NGO Disarmament Conference. There she gave a speech in which she appealed for the realization of a nuclear-free world as soon as possible, which was met with thunderous applause and excitement from the audience.

As a result of the work leading up to the 1977 symposium, and of course the symposium itself, something else happened that was important for my intellectual journey. With Dr. Akizuki Tatsuichirō as the core activist, the Nagasaki Council for the Dissemination of Research on "Atomic-Bombing

Issues" (Nagasaki "genbaku mondai" kenkyū fukyū kyōgikai, hereafter Genfukyō) was established in Nagasaki the following year, in 1978, to carry out the work and develop the remaining issues inherited from the symposium. As a member of the Genfukyō's research subcommittee, I worked with researchers and research institutes at Nagasaki University and the Nagasaki Institute of Applied Science on the compilation and analysis of the "general survey" portion of the *hibakusha* survey that was conducted on the occasion of the 1977 Symposium. Our work produced several publications. Kamata Sadao, Dr. Takei Hiroshi, and others edited and published books, such as *Report from Nagasaki* (in English, 1978, revised 1980, third edition 1985).

For my part, I edited volumes such as *Hibakusha no genzai* (Present Conditions of the *Hibakusha*, 1984), *Nagasaki kara no uttae* (Appeals from Nagasaki, 1985), and *Appeals from Nagasaki* (the English version of *Nagasaki kara no uttae*, 1991). I also read the 804 survey responses of the *hibakusha* that were the subject of the 1977 symposium's "general survey" and created four charts based on the data. Figure 1 has appeared in several of my publications, including *Nagasaki ni atte tetsugaku suru* (Philosophizing in Nagasaki, 1994).[5]

On the "general survey" was a free-response question, asking about any "disadvantages to daily life brought on by having experienced the atomic bombing." Researchers at Nagasaki University with whom I was working input the data into a computer and subdivided the results into forty-six items. After having carefully read the responses, I found that I could divide the results into five areas that each represented an inextricable aspect of human life: life and death (*inochi*), body (*karada*), employment (*hataraki*), family life (*kurashi*), and mind (*kokoro*).[6] The center of figure 1[7] illustrates, in condensed form, the nexus among these areas of a survivor's daily life.[8] The chart reveals how the atomic bombing confined the *hibakusha* within a "vicious cycle of illness and poverty" through their "incapacity to work" because of the effect of the bomb's inherent lethality—the heat rays, blast, and radiation—on their bodies. Moreover, the nexus of suffering shown here reveals that the atomic bombing has forced the *hibakusha* who survived into an existence in which they alternate between "death" and "anxiety and anguish" (*fuan to kunō*).[9]

For decades, the *hibakusha* had been seeking the enactment of a relief law (Hibakusha engo hō) in order to end the mutually amplifying and "vicious cycle of illness and poverty." Furthermore, it was not a request for a support law for social security or welfare for the *hibakusha*, but rather for a relief law that based national compensation on the state's war responsibility. As outlined in figure 2, the demands of the support law as envisioned

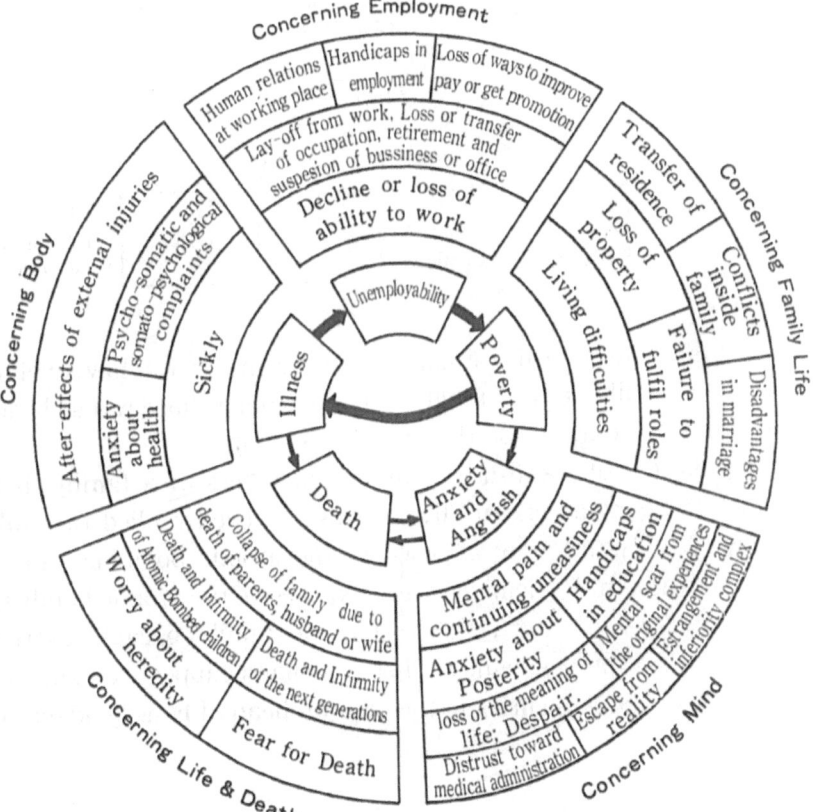

Figure 1. Chart related to the various causes of atomic-bombing damage (Genbaku higai no sho yōin kanren zu). Source: Shinji Takahashi, ed., *Appeals from Nagasaki* (Nagasaki Association for Research and Dissemination of Atomic Bomb Survivors' Problems, 1991), 36.

by the *hibakusha* corresponded to the sustained totality of atomic-bombing related suffering—life and death, body, employment, family life, and mind.[10] Even so, the goals of the *hibakusha* to bring about the enactment of a relief law were not limited to achieving changes in domestic affairs. Their vision, as they saw it, had to include goals of an international peace movement, such as the abolition of nuclear weapons and the desire for world peace, which are illustrated in figures 1 and 2. As the hibakusha saw it, there could be no true release for them from their existence between "death" and "anxiety and anguish" without the disposal of nuclear weapons and the actualization of world peace.[11]

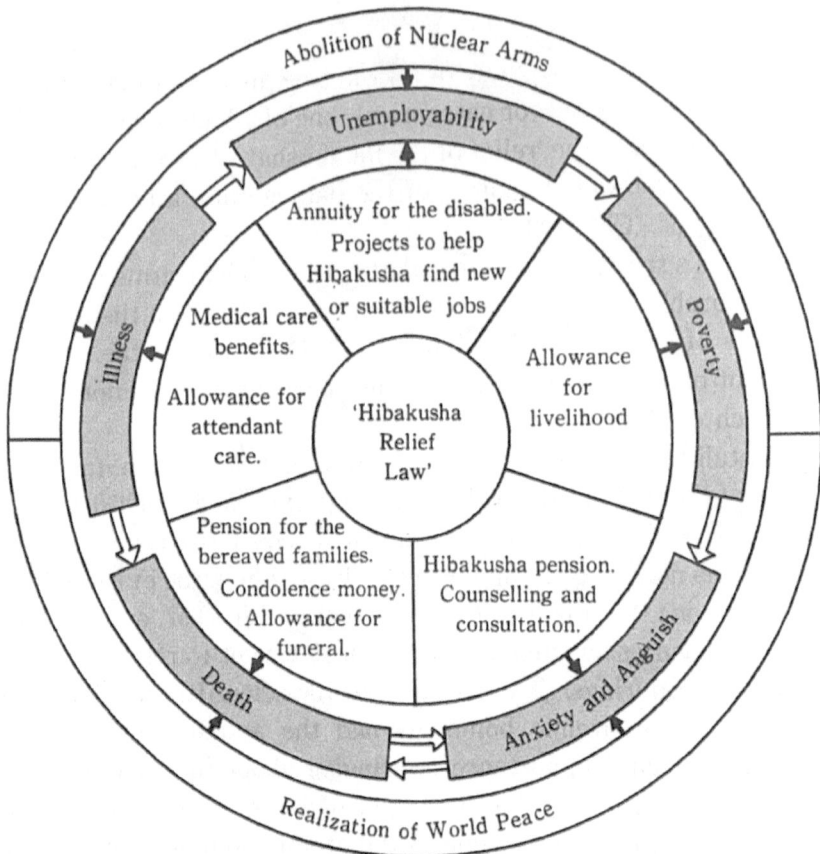

Figure 2. Atomic-bombing damage and the appeals of the *Hibakusha* (Genbaku higai to hibakusha no uttae). Source: Shinji Takahashi, ed., *Appeals from Nagasaki* (Nagasaki Association for Research and Dissemination of Atomic Bomb Survivors' Problems, 1991), 44.

From Nagasaki to Tokyo and on to New York

I sought to share the knowledge gained from the years of collaborative research, publications, and activism beyond Nagasaki. In 1981, I presented at a large symposium sponsored by the Science Council of Japan (Nihon gakujutsu kaigi) that took place at the council's auditorium in Roppongi, Tokyo, on November 26–28, called "The Crisis of Nuclear War and Conditions for the Survival of Humanity: Exploring the Contemporary Significance of the Russell-Einstein Manifesto."[12] I then set off for New York City the following year, in June 1982. I was fortunate enough to be included as a member of the delegation from the Japan Confederation of Atomic-Bomb and Hydrogen-Bomb Sufferers Organizations (Nihon gensuibaku higaisha dantai kyōgikai, hereafter Nihon hidankyō), to participate in the United Nations Second Special Session on Disarmament (SSOD-II) and related events.[13]

On June 4, Dr. Akizuki Tatsuichirō, who had also traveled to New York, presented an important report, titled, "Medicine is Powerless at 'That Time,'" at the "International Symposium on the Morality and Legality of Nuclear Weapons." On the same day, I headed over to the City University of New York (CUNY) for a meeting called Social Scientists and Nuclear War. There I presented a talk titled "Damage from the Atomic Bombing and the Appeal of the Hibakusha" (Genbaku higai to hibakusha no uttae), using twenty-one slides over the course of thirty-two minutes. Reflective of how scholarly interest in the atomic bombings transcended national boundaries at the time, the venue was full at four hundred audience members, and everyone remained quiet and listened to my talk. Afterward, the moderator, psychologist Howard E. Gruber of Columbia University, commented that my talk was "moving and revealing."

When I returned to my seat on the panel, Robert J. Lifton, who was also well known in Japan at the time, and who had written the monumental psychoanalytic study on the atomic-bombing experience, *Death in Life: Survivors of Hiroshima* (Random House, 1967), encouraged me by telling me that my research was "an important study." I do not consider the words of Gruber and Lifton as simply diplomatic language. This was an academic setting, of course, but I also had come to know from other experiences presenting at similar gatherings that Western scholars could be quite frank in their feedback. When I think about it now, within the deep, solemn tranquility of the venue, perhaps a feeling of guilt (*tsumi ishiki*) was at work among the American citizens whose country had dropped the atomic bombs on Hiroshima and Nagasaki. I was fortunate to have been able to travel as a member of the Nihon hidankyō, which allowed me to present the findings of the *hibakusha* survey from the 1977 symposium in this way in front of the social scientists, teachers, and citizens gathered from all around the United States.[14]

On June 12, I participated in the world's largest, at a million people, antinuclear peace rally, where Dr. Akizuki and I walked for three hours from the United Nations up to Central Park, with people along the road supporting the marchers with applause and cheers.[15] On the way back, together with Sekiya Ayako, director of the YWCA, we interacted with American citizens at a gathering organized by the University of Hawai'i, and I presented on the "present-day conditions of the *hibakusha*" of Nagasaki, showing them the two charts discussed earlier (figures 1 and 2).

On June 24, Yamaguchi Senji gave a fiery speech at the plenary session of SSOD-II at the United Nations as the first-ever representative for Nagasaki atomic-bombing victims (*higaisha*), titled "Never Allow the Hell of Another Nuclear War!" For his closing remarks, Yamaguchi proclaimed: "May there be no more Hiroshimas! No more Nagasakis! No more wars! No more *hibakusha*!"[16]

Criticizing the Nagai Takashi Urakami Holocaust Theory

My years of work with the hibakusha peace activists in the 1970s and 1980s had led me, ultimately, to reevaluate and criticize the work and legacy of Nagai Takashi. The religious interpretation put forth by Nagai did not reflect the lived experience of the survivors, namely their trauma and continued suffering. Participating in the 1977 symposium, forming the new group Genfukyō in Nagasaki, and compiling a series of short books analyzing the results of the general survey of the lived experience of the *hibakusha* gradually led me to present and publish analyses of my own from the mid-1980s through the mid-1990s.

In 1978, an interdisciplinary academic group was formed, called the Society for the History of Social Thought (Shakai shisō shi gakkai, hereafter Shashikai), for which Mizuta Hiroshi served as its representative secretary. In 1985, as one of the secretaries of the Shashikai myself, I wondered if there was not something I could do to make a suitable contribution related to the fortieth anniversary of the atomic bombing to an academic meeting that was to take place in the neighboring prefecture of Kumamoto. What came to my mind was to present on how the lived experience of the *hibakusha* (*hibakusha no genzai*), which I had been researching since 1977, defied the ideas put forth by Nagai Takashi, who had become so famous—and continued to be so even decades after he had died in 1951—that he appeared to be the representative voice of all *hibakusha*. I therefore assigned myself the task of taking what I had concluded from reviewing and conceptualizing the *hibakusha* surveys of 1977 (as well as my work with *hibakusha* peace activists) and scrutinizing the ideas of Nagai Takashi regarding the significance of the bombing.

To prepare for the talk at the Kumamoto meeting, I reread the works of Nagai Takashi carefully, especially his "Eulogy for the Joint Funeral for Those Who Died in the Atomic Bombing," which was delivered on November 23, 1945, three months after the bombing, and his "Eulogy for the Urakami Joint Memorial Service," presented on August 9, 1946, the first anniversary of the bombing.[17] I termed Nagai's peculiar way of framing the significance of the atomic bombing the "Urakami holocaust theory" and summarized it in the following way. As I later wrote it in *Nagasaki ni atte tetsugaku suru* (1994), "When we think about the atomic bombing of Nagasaki, we ask, (1) How do we view the bombing in the first place? (2) How do we view those who died in the bombing? And, finally, (3) What should the surviving hibakusha do? When Nagai Takashi answered these questions through his interpretation of the bombing with (1) providence, (2) holocaust, and (3) trial (*shiren*), he established what I call the 'Urakami holocaust theory.'"[18]

I also came to the conclusion that the historical significance of Nagai's interpretation of the bombing lies in the way it contains a "double exemption of responsibility" (*nijū menseki*). As I once phrased it, "If the atomic bombing of Nagasaki is the providence of God, then the responsibility of the leaders of Japan, headed by the Emperor, who started, carried out, and delayed the end of a reckless fifteen-year war, would be exempted. Similarly, the responsibility of the leaders of the United States of America who used the atomic bomb would be exempted."[19]

Last, the significance of the Urakami holocaust theory is not limited to the way it doubly exempts war responsibility and the dropping of the atomic bomb. In his eulogy of November 1945, a version of which was later reproduced in one of his bestselling books, Nagai stated: "Precisely because Urakami became a sacrifice the war was brought to an end. I believe that because of this sacrifice, billions [*jūsūoku*] of people [*jinrui*] were saved from the calamity of war." I concluded that Nagai's approval of the Nagasaki bombing in this way opens the way to an affirmative view of atomic bombs in general.[20] In the discussion that followed my presentation of the preceding analysis and conclusions at the Kumamoto Conference, one member of the audience, Itō Naruhiko, commented that I "at last pointed out a special characteristic of the Nagasaki atomic bombing."

One year after my presentation in Kumamoto, I published it in the Shishikai's annual report, *Shakai shisō shi gakkai nenpō* 10 (1986), and sent an offprint of the essay to Nagasaki poet and *hibakusha* Yamada Kan (at the time on staff at the Nagasaki Prefectural Library).[21] Shortly after I had moved to Nagasaki for work, I began working with Yamada's poetry magazine, *Hōbō*, and contributed original poems and essays.[22] I was inspired to join him in Nagasaki's literary activism because of how the sharpness and depth of his poetry and essays unequivocally denounced the atomic bombing.[23] When I sent him a copy of my essay criticizing Nagai's interpretation, he replied to me with a postcard (*hagaki*) that included the following message:

Greetings. Winter has arrived since last we spoke. I have read the offprint from *Shakai shisō shi kenkyū* that you recently sent me. Your discussion is based on precise logical composition, and so I have bound a copy of it and stored it as a document in the Historical Materials Division [of the Nagasaki Prefectural Library]. It will be of value. Thank you very much. If the Bible's doctrine to love thy neighbor as thyself [*onore no gotoku hito o ai su beki*] was transferred to real life in the middle of Mr. Nagai's postwar [experience], it would have immediately changed into an antilaborer [*hanrōdōsha*] and anticommunist philosophy. I continue even now to find it difficult to comprehend the thinking [*naimen*] of the saint [Nagai], who was an extremely political person [harboring] so much intense contempt [for his fellow human]. Thank you for your hard work. Sincerely yours.

My academic criticism of Nagai's interpretation of the bombing was not paid much attention at the time of the Kumamoto symposium or the article's publication. However, after the publication of my 1994 book, *Nagasaki ni atte tetsugaku suru* (Philosophizing in Nagasaki), which included the essay, things changed completely. On the occasion of the fiftieth anniversary of the atomic bombing and the end of the war, the president of Nagasaki Immaculate Heart University, Sister Kataoka Chizuko (Congregation of the Sisters of the Immaculate Heart of Mary), the daughter of the famous Nagasaki scholar Kataoka Yakichi, who himself was an authority on the history of Japanese Christians, resolutely and severely criticized my essay in a public lecture aimed at city residents.[24] Sister Kataoka then published her response to my criticism in a book in 1996 titled *Hibakuchi Nagasaki no saiken* (Reconstruction of Atomic-Bombed Nagasaki).[25] Her main argument, in brief, was that I did not understand the "true meaning of Nagai Takashi's words."

After Kataoka's response to me in her book, as if a dam had broken, literary scholars and historical researchers from all around Kyushu, including local Nagasaki intellectuals, began sharing their scholarly opinions to participate in the controversy and debate. Moreover, the scholarly criticism and conversation surrounding Nagai traveled beyond regional discussions in Nagasaki in the early 2000s, with Nishimura Akira's article in the field of religious studies, titled "Inori no Nagasaki: Nagai Takashi to genbaku shisha" (Nagasaki of Prayer: Nagai Takashi and the Atomic-Bombing Dead).[26] Recently, there have also been new perspectives and fresh research conducted overseas on Nagai and postatomic Nagasaki in general, such as Chad R. Diehl's *Resurrecting Nagasaki*.[27] There have also been scholarly articles in Korea, such as Park Sukyung, "The Transformation of Thought in Atomic-Bombed City 'Praying' Nagasaki."[28] Other recent research has focused on the

Urakami Catholics in particular, such as Shijō Chie's *Urakami no genbaku no katari* (Atomic-Bombing Narratives of Urakami) and Gwyn McClelland's *Dangerous Memory in Nagasaki*.[29]

The Pope's 1981 Visit and Catholic Discourse on the Bombings

In February 1981 Pope John Paul II traveled to Japan, visiting Tokyo, Hiroshima, and Nagasaki. In Hiroshima, on February 25, the pope gave a speech, "Appeal for Peace," in front of the atomic-bombing memorial cenotaph in the city's famous Peace Park. In the speech, the pope declared: "War is the work of humankind. War snatches away human life. War is death. To reflect on the past is to take responsibility for the future. To remember Hiroshima is to reject nuclear war. To remember Hiroshima is to take responsibility for peace."[30] The pope then visited Nagasaki on February 26, and amid heavy snowfall held a large, outdoor mass at the Matsuyama track and field stadium near the hypocenter. I also participated in the outdoor mass.[31] He also visited places related to the history of the persecution of Christians in Nagasaki, including the site of the twenty-six martyrs of 1597. The Pope's visit was, in a way, the realization of an ultimate hope—a visit by the Holy Father to Japan—historically held by the hidden Christians who had suffered so terribly in the past.[32]

Some scholars have pointed to the visit of Pope John Paul II to Japan in February 1981 as a turning point in the discourse on the significance of Nagasaki's bombing, and especially for the Urakami Catholics.[33] In his speech in Hiroshima, the pope, although not mentioning Nagai Takashi directly, delivered an interpretation of the bombing as a Catholic leader who contradicted Nagai. The pope stated that war—and by extension the atomic bombings—was the work of humankind, not God. For the first time, Catholics in Nagasaki were given permission, so to speak, to break with Nagai and his interpretation and speak of the trauma and suffering that the bombing caused for their community. For some Catholic *hibakusha*, the pope's words lifted a burden and gave meaning to their life for the first time since the bombing in a way that reflected their lived experience.[34]

In *Nagasaki no kane* and other works published shortly after the Pacific War—or, as Ienaga Saburō has correctly termed it, the Asia-Pacific War— Nagai Takashi related his interpretation of the atomic bombing of Nagasaki in the form of the Urakami holocaust theory. I have strongly criticized this theory as doubly exempting the responsibilities of the leaders of Japan for colonialism and waging an imperialist war, as well as the political and military leaders of the United States who dared to drop two types of atomic bombs, uranium and plutonium, on Hiroshima and Nagasaki in the final stages of the Second World War. I believe there is still much to learn, even for me, from further scholarly arguments and controversies related to Nagai, especially by looking to other fields of study, such as historical philosophy.[35]

In this short chapter, I have simply tried to convey the importance of a specific ten-year span to the development of my criticism of Nagai's theory—from 1985, when I first wrote an analysis of the experience of the *hibakusha* based on the data collected from the 1977 symposium's related survey through 1994, when I published my first book exclusively about postatomic Nagasaki. Considering the image of the *hibakusha* that emerged from that survey—one of "death, anxiety, and anguish" stemming from a "vicious cycle of illness and poverty" (figure 1)—it is no wonder they felt compelled to give meaning to their trauma through activism, both in demanding the enactment of a national system of compensation for medical costs related to having experienced the bombing, which became known as the Hibakusha Relief Law, and in being active members in the antinuclear peace movement (figure 2).

In contrast to these *hibakusha* activists, from the early years after the war when the American military occupied Japan from September 23, 1945, a relentless Nagai recited his Urakami holocaust theory based on a particular understanding of the ideas of "providence, holocaust, and trial." Were they not once-in-a-lifetime "theatrical"[36] comments made by a Nagai who was fully aware they would be transmitted from the Nagasaki occupation forces to general headquarters in Tokyo and then to Washington, DC? In other words, was not his framing of the bombing in peculiar religious terms aimed at maximizing theatrical effect?

For the hibakusha who had experienced the Nagasaki bombing and survived, Nagai's Urakami holocaust theory was a useless idea because it was too detached from their postwar reality. To speak about that reality, Nagasaki *hibakusha* and other activists working with them have been publishing a journal since 1969 called *Nagasaki no shōgen* (Nagasaki Testimony), which includes survivor essays and poetry. The first volume, published on August 9, 1969, included as its lead essay a piece by Dr. Akizuki titled "Genbaku no jittai o kataru koto koso watashitachi no gimu" (To Speak about the Reality of the Atomic Bombing Is Precisely Our Duty). For the cover of the next volume in summer 1970, the publishing team, including Kamata Sadao and Dr. Akizuki, chose to use the shocking image of the bright-red back of Taniguchi Sumiteru, which had been burned to the bone in the bombing. The image was from less than a year later, when Taniguchi

How I Came to Criticize Nagai Takashi's Urakami Holocaust Theory | 307

was still recovering from the burns when he was still a boy.[37] The journal continues to publish to this day.

Notes

1. The word *hibakusha* has long been used to refer to atomic-bombing survivors in international discourse on nuclear weapons since the late 1970s. Its origins in Japanese discourse related to the atomic bombings dates back to the first medical relief law passed in 1957. However, at a meeting of scholars in Nagasaki on August 8, 1977, which was part of a larger weeks-long international symposium that took place in Tokyo, Hiroshima, and Nagasaki—and which is explained in more detail here—Barbara Reynolds, an American author and peace activist who was living in Hiroshima at the time, suggested that *hibakusha* be used untranslated in non-Japanese discussions of the survivors.

2. For example, the American psychiatrist Robert J. Lifton includes as case studies of "holocausts" in the modern era the Nanjing Massacre, the mass extermination of the Jewish people by the Nazis, the killing of humans in the atomic bombings of Hiroshima and Nagasaki, and atrocities against civilians during the Vietnam War. See, e.g., Robert J. Lifton, *Death in Life: Survivors of Hiroshima* (New York: Random House, 1967), where he refers to the atomic bombing of Hiroshima as the "atomic holocaust" and "holocaust" throughout the book, as well as to other mass disasters as "other holocausts" (e.g., on page 46).

3. I have used the English translation of the name of the symposium as it appears in Committee for the Compilation of Materials on Damage Caused by the Atomic Bombs in Hiroshima and Nagasaki, *Hiroshima and Nagasaki: The Physical, Medical, and Social Effects of the Atomic Bombings*, trans. Eisei Ishikawa and David L. Swain (New York: Basic Books, 1981), 341, 635. —Trans.

4. Through his research from the early 1950s, Ichimaru Michito brought to light the fact that blood cancers and leukemia frequently occurred in *hibakusha*. In 1981, he attended the first-ever meeting of the International Physicians for the Prevention of Nuclear War (IPPNW) in Airlie, Virginia, and shared his personal experience of surviving the atomic bombing. He also discussed the destruction of Nagasaki from the perspective of an "atomic-bombing medical student" (*hibaku igakusei*). For his account, see *Last Aid: The Medical Dimensions of Nuclear War*, eds. Eric Chivian, Susanna Chivian, Robert Jay Lifton, and John E. Mack (W. H. Freeman & Company, 1982), 43–47; in Japanese: Ichimaru Michito, "1945 nen hachi gatsu kokonoka: Hibaku igakusei no nikki" (August Ninth 1945: The Diary of a Hibaku Medical Student), in *Last Aid: Kaku sensō to igaku* (Last Aid: Nuclear War and Medicine), ed. Kaku sensō bōshi kokusai ishikai (Tokyo: Nikkei saiensu sha, 1983), 30–32.

5. My book was the first in what would become a three-volume series: *Nagasaki ni atte tetsugaku suru: Kakujidai no shi to sei* (Philosophizing in Nagasaki: Death and Life in the Nuclear Age) (Tokyo: Hokuju shuppan, 1994);

Nagasaki ni atte tetsugaku suru, II: Genbakushi kara heiwa sekinin e (Philosophizing in Nagasaki: From Atomic-Bombing Death to Peace Responsibility) (Tokyo: Hokuju shuppan, 2004); and *Nagasaki ni atte tetsugaku suru III: 3.11 go no heiwa sekinin* (Philosophizing in Nagasaki: Peace Responsibility after 3.11) (Tokyo: Hokuju shuppan, 2015).

6. I have used the English translations of these five terms as found in Takahashi Shinji, ed., *Appeals from Nagasaki* (Nagasaki: Nagasaki Association for Research and Dissemination of Atomic Bomb Survivors' Problems, 1991), 36. —Trans.

7. I have translated the title of figure 1 here from the text that the author contributed for the present volume. The 1991 book from which the chart comes gives the title in English as "Interrelated Chart of Handicaps Due to Atomic Bombing." —Trans.

8. Itō Takeshi, one of three representatives of the Japan Confederation of Atomic-Bomb and Hydrogen-Bomb Sufferers Organizations (Nihon gensuibaku higaisha dantai kyōgikai, or Hidankyō for short) had created a chart in 1977 called "Genbaku higai no zentai zō" (Complete Picture of Atomic-Bombing Damage), which categorized *hibakusha* postwar life into just three fields: life and death (*inochi*), family life (*kurashi*), and mind (*kokoro*). In response to this, I added the two additional fields of body (*karada*) and employment (*hataraki*) in a chart that I developed to more fully articulate the daily struggles of the *hibakusha* (figure 1). The charts that I have made and included in my various books and essays have been featured by scholars such as Hamatani Masaharu as part of the work of "the second generation who have accessed (*sannyū*) the hibakusha surveys." See Ishikawa Atsushi, Hashimoto Kazutaka, and Hamatani Masaharu, eds., *Shakai chōsa: Rekishi to shiten* (Social Research: History and Perspective) (Minerva shobō, 1994), 300.

9. The term *hibakusha* can include the people who died in the bombing, or later as a result of its effects on their body. Also, I have translated *kunō* as "anguish" instead of "suffering," following the English translation as it appears in Takahashi's charts. —Trans.

10. I have translated the title of figure 2 here from the text that Takahashi contributed for the present volume. His 1991 edited book from which the chart comes gives a different title in English, "Appeals and Demands of *Hibakusha* in Relation to their Handicaps." —Trans.

11. For a detailed discussion in English of how Nagasaki *hibakusha* fought for a national system of medical relief and worked as activists in the antinuclear peace movement during the first two decades after the war, see, Chad R. Diehl, *Resurrecting Nagasaki: Reconstruction and the Formation of Atomic Narratives* (Ithaca, NY: Cornell University Press, 2018), ch. 5; for a discussion of both Hiroshima and Nagasaki activism, see also James J. Orr, *The Victim as Hero: Ideologies of Peace and National Identity in Postwar Japan* (Honolulu: University of Hawai'i Press, 2001), ch. 6. —Trans.

12. See Eguchi Bokurō, Fukushima Yōichi, Okakura Koshirō, and Iijima Sōichi, eds., *Nihon gakujutsu kaigi shinpojiumu: Kaku sensō no kiki to jinrui no seizon* (Symposium of the Science Council of Japan: The Crisis of Nuclear War and the Survival of Humanity) (Tokyo: Sanseidō, 1985), 62–67.

13. See United Nations, Office for Disarmament Affairs, https://www.un.org/disarmament/topics/ssod/. —Trans.

14. A summary of my lecture in New York was reproduced as Shinji Takahashi, "Relief for the Hibakusha," *Bulletin of Atomic Scientists* 40, no. 8 (October 1984): 25–26.

15. Dr. Akizuki Tatsuichirō said of participating in the march that it was "pleasant memory to take to the afterlife" (*meido no miyage ni*) and that "it was worth it to come to New York."

16. For the English version of Yamaguchi's speech, see *Appeals from Nagasaki*, ed. Shinji Takahashi (Nagasaki: Nagasaki Association for Research and Dissemination of Atomic Bomb Survivors' Problems, 1991), 12–16. —Trans.

17. The former was included in Nagai's 1949 book, *Nagasaki no kane* (known as *The Bells of Nagasaki*), and the latter in his 1948 book, *Rozario no kusari* (Rosary Chain).

18. Takahashi, *Nagasaki ni atte tetsugaku suru*, 198–199.

19. Ibid., 201.

20. Ibid., 202.

21. Even today, the Local History Division of the Nagasaki Prefectural Library contains the copy of my essay that Yamada self-bound and stored there.

22. The *kanji* (Chinese characters) of the title of Yamada's poetry magazine, *Hōbō* (炮氓), mean "people who were engulfed in flames, burned, and killed" (*hi ni tsutsumarete, yakarete, horobosareta min*).

23. Yamada Kan was the most vocal critic of Nagai Takashi for decades, beginning in the early 1970s. —Trans.

24. Kataoka Yakichi was friends with Nagai Takashi. He also wrote a biography of Nagai, called *Nagai Takashi no shōgai* (The Life of Nagai Takashi) (Tokyo: Chūō shuppan sha, 1952). —Trans.

25. Kataoka Chizuko and Kataoka Rumiko, *Hibakuchi Nagasaki no saiken* (The Reconstruction of the Atomic-Bombed Land of Nagasaki) (Nagasaki: Nagasaki Junshin Daigaku hakubutsukan, 1996).

26. Nishimura Akira, "Inori no Nagasaki: Nagai Takashi to genbaku shisha" (Nagasaki of Prayer: Nagai Takashi and the Atomic-Bombing Dead), *Tōkyō daigaku shūkyō gakunen hō* (Tokyo University Annual Review of Religious Studies) 19 (2000): 47–61.

27. Diehl, *Resurrecting Nagasaki*. I wrote a review of Diehl's book for the *Nagasaki Shinbun* newspaper titled "Yomigaeru 'Nagasaki': Toshi saiken no taseiongaku" (Resurrecting "Nagasaki": The Polyphony of City Reconstruction), December 30, 2018.

28. Park Sukyung, "Genbaku toshi 'inori no' Nagasaki no shisōteki tenkan: Nagai Takashi kara Oka Masaharu e" (The Transformation of Thought in Atomic-Bombed City 'Praying' Nagasaki: From Nagai Takashi to Oka Masaharu), *Nihongo kyōiku* (Journal of Japanese Language Teaching) 73 (2015): 169–193.

29. Shijō Chie, *Urakami no genbaku no katari: Nagai Takashi kara Rōma kyōkō e* (Atomic-Bombing Narratives of Urakami: From Nagai Takashi to the Pope) (Tokyo: Miraisha, 2015); Gwyn McClelland, *Dangerous Memory in Nagasaki: Prayers, Protests and Catholic Survivor Narratives* (New York: Routledge, 2020).

30. Here I have rendered Takahashi's Japanese text of the pope's speech into English rather than rely on English translations of the pope's speech found elsewhere. The excerpt here was inscribed in a plaque that now sits in Hiroshima's Peace Memorial Museum: see "Pope John Paul II's Appeal for Peace," Hiroshima Peace Tourism, https://peace-tourism.com/en/spot/entry-79.html. —TRANS.

31. Amid the heavy snowfall on the day of the pope's mass in Matsuyama Stadium, there were moments of occasional sunshine, but because of the persistent freezing temperature there were more than a few people who fell sick and required medical attention, and I distinctly remember the constant sound of ambulance sirens that day. In retrospect, I find it significant that it was Dr. Akizuki Tatsuichirō who was in charge of the medical team that day.

32. For more on the history of the oppression of the hidden Christians, see Kataoka Yakichi, *Nihon Kirishitan junkyō shi* (History of the Martyrdom of Japanese Christians) (Tokyo: Jiji Tsūshinsha, 1979).

33. See, for example, Shijō, *Urakami no genbaku no katari*, and McClelland, *Dangerous Memory in Nagasaki*.

34. See, for example, the story of Kataoka Tsuyo, as recorded in Jack Wintz, O.F.M., "Nagasaki: A Peace Church Rises from the Nuclear Ashes," *American Catholic*, July 9, 2015, https://web.archive.org/web/20150709210645/http://www.americancatholic.org/Features/WWII/feature0283.asp. —TRANS.

35. I am thinking here, for example, of the work of Pierre Nora, especially *Les lieux de mémoire* (1984; published in Japanese translation in 2002). Also, since the days of writing my MA thesis so many years ago, I have relied on the work of R. G. Collingwood, especially his approaches to metaphysics, philosophy of history, art philosophy, and political science. See, e.g., R. G. Collingwood, *The Idea of History* (Oxford: Oxford University Press, 1946).

36. Akizuki Tatsuichirō knew Nagai Takashi very well. Akizuki graduated from Kyoto Imperial University's School of Medicine in March 1940, returned to Nagasaki, and began studying radiology under Nagai in June. According to Akizuki, among the doctors who studied radiology under Nagai, many called him "theatrical" (they would use the German word *theatralisch*) because he made statements and undertook activities they viewed as somewhat cringeworthy, such as seeking to build a section in the university library called the "Nagai Takashi Bookshelf" (*bunko*) (this was not completed); his planting of "Nagai senbon

zakura" (One Thousand Sakura Trees of Nagai); and the creation of "Our Bookshelf," a children's library.

37. Taniguchi also later used this image of his back on his peace-activist business card. The American military film footage from which the image came can be viewed online at my personal YouTube page: https://www.youtube.com/watch?v=d0mf7xer4yk (see from around the nineteen-minute mark for footage of Taniguchi's wound being cared for by doctors; the scene at around 20:57 became the image which appeared on his card and on the cover of the 1970 volume of *Nagasaki no shōgen*).—TRANS.

On Rereleasing *The Bells of Nagasaki* to the World

By Tokusaburō Nagai

Translated by Chad R. Diehl

The year 2021 marked seventy years since my grandfather, Nagai Takashi, left this world and twenty years since I began my tenure as the appointed director of the Nagasaki City Nagai Takashi Memorial Museum. To commemorate the occasion, I planned a reprint of the English translation of Takashi's popular book *Nagasaki no kane* (The Bells of Nagasaki) and published it in February 2022.[1] Working on the new English version has added an additional unforgettable memory for 2021, because *The Bells of Nagasaki* became the one book I have reread more than any other in my life. Takashi himself declared the book his "masterpiece" (*daihyōsaku*). The book traces the atomic-bombing experiences of the Nagasaki Medical College staff, including his own, and was first published in the early postwar years, becoming widely known in Japan and elsewhere as a realistic account of the Nagasaki bombing. The 1984 English translation was also popular, but it has been out of print for a long time.

Among other things, the following revisions have been made to the English translation in order to increase its value as a document (*shiryō*).

1. Corrected errors in place names and personal names.[2]
2. Investigated the names and occupations of people who appear in the book and added annotations for reference.
3. Included also, in parallel, the original text in Japanese for language and translation study.

As I look now at this bilingual edition of *The Bells of Nagasaki*, I know that it is not perfect, but I am satisfied with how it has turned out. I would like to make the book available to anyone who would like a copy, so please feel free to contact me at seitan@nagai100.jp with your name and mailing address, and I will try to get a book to you as soon as possible. This book once again takes on the role of conveying both the reality of the atomic bombing and Takashi's thoughts on peace (*heiwa shisō*), and so I hope that it will be read widely by people across the world.

Having read through Takashi's *The Bells of Nagasaki* so many times in preparation for the new edition, I have recognized once again the fact that his books are an interesting subject for study because they have so many "mysteries" (*nazo*). Takashi decided to write the book when the *Nagasaki Shinbun* newspaper asked him in the spring of 1946 to write about the atomic bombing as part of a book series it planned to publish called New Cultural Books (Shin bunka shoseki). The newspaper approached Takashi for the series because he had been the main author of a widely read report that had recorded his medical team's relief activities immediately following the bombing. He had been suffering from leukemia since before exposure to the atomic bomb and was not expected to live much longer. Even so, Takashi took on the writing project because, he thought, "There are so few survivors who were near the hypocenter of the bombing, and even fewer among them who could write of their experience. Moreover, no one else is studying nuclear medicine [*genshi igaku*]. I am the appropriate person to write this record, and it is also my duty."[3]

Takashi continued his work as a doctor while working on the book, always thinking that "recording the truth [about the atomic bombing experience] will prevent another war."[4] He completed the first draft of the book in summer of the same year. The original title that Takashi gave the manuscript was *Genshi jidai no kaimaku* (The Opening of the Atomic Age), which left the impression it was a formal research essay.[5] The final title, *Nagasaki no kane* (The Bells of Nagasaki), was not Takashi's idea, but rather that of Dr. Shikiba Ryūzaburō, a psychiatrist who supported Takashi in all aspects of the publication of the book. Shikiba was a cultural person (*bunkajin*) active in fields beyond his own profession, such as establishing newspapers and publishing companies and introducing to the world Yamashita Kiyoshi, who was a wandering painter. There is no mistake that Takashi's career as a writer would also have been different had he not met Shikiba.

I had many doubts about the manuscript that Takashi had written. More than a firsthand account of the experience, the book has the style of a "nonfiction novel," complete with a continuous narrative structure, beginning with the atmosphere (*fūkei*) before the atomic bombing and taking the reader through the bombing, injuries (*fushō*), relief activities, the end of the war, and reconstruction activities (*seikatsu*). Takashi himself also appears in the book, and drama develops among many of the characters. The book ends with the sound of the Urakami Cathedral's Angelus bell ringing on

Christmas Eve, which presents a true symbol of peace and hope and impresses the reader deeply.

However! Did the newspaper request of Takashi, who himself recognized that he was an amateur who knew nothing of the world of publishing, that "we want you to write in the style of a novel"? Did he have the writing ability to then respond to their request and produce a work of writing that would have satisfied them? I do not think so. But this is not to say that he lacked writing ability. He composed tanka and wrote screenplays for the stage, so he certainly had the talent of a writer. However, I do not think that the content of the manuscript that Takashi titled *The Opening of the Atomic Age* made it a particularly novelistic or dramatic work. Rather, when it comes to his writing on the atomic bombing, his 1948 *Seimei no kawa* (River of Life), which Shikiba also helped bring to publication, is more suited for that topic and better fits the title of *The Opening of the Atomic Age*. However, a publisher would never request that an author "write us a book that can't sell." It is feasible that Nagai wrote the book [which would become *The Bells of Nagasaki*] in response to a request that he write it in an informal manner, and as something that could be easily understood, so that it would sell well. In fact, *River of Life* did not sell well. Also, considering the Press Code [censorship] during the Allied occupation at the time, one probably had to choose words carefully. While he was writing the book, he had thought of quitting many times. Whenever that happened, the publisher would encourage him, and in the end he was able to complete the book. We can presume, then, that he had several occasions to discuss the content with people in his orbit.

Now back to the story. In the end, despite Takashi's efforts, the plan to publish the book as part of the New Cultural Books series disappeared because the publisher dissolved, and so it seemed that his work lost an opportunity to be released to the world. However, out of this a new drama was born. The newspaper reporter who had initially asked Nagai to write something for the series had visited Takashi on a regular basis and encouraged him along the way. He felt compelled by something in Takashi's manuscript to continue working to get the book published even after the collapse of the series, and so he visited several publishers in Tokyo and negotiated with them on Takashi's behalf. No publisher was interested in books about the atomic bombing written by an unknown doctor from the countryside until meeting Dr. Shikiba Ryūzaburō. He, too, felt compelled by something in Takashi's manuscript, and so he took on the publication of the books and spared no effort in spreading the name of this unknown writer to the world. Shikiba let Takashi contribute writings to the newspapers and magazines that he or his relatives operated, and he also gathered and published the writings as books, such as *Rozario no kusari* (Rosary Chain, 1948) and *Kono ko o nokoshite* (Leaving These Children Behind, 1948).[6] These books became bestsellers, and Takashi joined the ranks of popular writers at the time who became celebrities (*yūmeijin*). Even so, prolonged negotiations with the Supreme Commander for the Allied Powers (SCAP) made publishing *Nagasaki no kane* difficult, which leaves me with the following doubts (*ginen*).

SCAP allowed the publication of *Nagasaki no kane* with the condition that the book include a record of the Japanese invasion of Manila in the Philippines, called, "Manira no higeki" (The Tragedy of Manila). But was that the only condition? What comes to mind here is the text of the "eulogy" (*chōji*) included in the book, which is still the subject of criticism of Nagai Takashi. I wonder if it was not also a condition for publication to include this eulogy?

The story and subject of *Nagasaki no kane* throughout most of the book are the conditions immediately before and after the atomic bombing, as well as the relief activities afterward. Then, in the final two chapters, "Gōsha no kyaku" (Visitors to My Hut) and "Genshino no kane" (The Bells of the Atomic Waste), the tone of the book suddenly takes on a religious hue.[7] "Visitors to My Hut" includes the eulogy that Takashi gave on the occasion of the joint funeral in Urakami on November 23, 1945. In the book's final chapter, "The Bells of the Atomic Waste," there is a scene where Takashi is talking with his children, Makoto and Kayano, about the atom, and their conversation spells out the book's original title, "The Opening of the Atomic Age." Then, when the sound of the Angelus bell rings, the father and his children pray, a scene which closes the book. Was the inclusion of these final two chapters presented as conditions for publication? I think that more firmly now. And I certainly do not mean it only in a negative way. With the chapter "Visitors to My Hut" Takashi asks the question, "What was the atomic bombing?" And in the chapter "The Bells of the Atomic Waste," he provides an answer with a discussion of the future potential of the atom, as well as its dangers, from his perspective as a specialist. However, it does not seem strange to me the fact that Takashi's eulogy as it appears in *Nagasaki no kane* "does not completely match the important points" of the original manuscript he delivered at the funeral in November 1945. Even if it is the case that Takashi "was telling us the rough content of the eulogy," the text, which was "read aloud at the funeral," should not have changed when it was included in the book. It seems unnatural considering both the original title, "The Origins of the Atomic Age," and the overall flow of the book to end with a Catholic prayer.

How satisfied must Takashi have felt to clearly state what he had truly wanted to through writing books like *The Bells of Nagasaki* and *River of Life* in the final years of his life. The only thing that could answer my questions (*ginen*) would be to read Takashi's original manuscript of that which he named "The Opening of the Atomic Age." Most likely, the content of that manuscript and the book that the world knows as *The Bells of Nagasaki* is different, but, unfortunately, I have not had the opportunity to do so to this day, and I probably never will. Why? Because I think the manuscript probably disappeared—no, was erased—due to "special circumstances."

As I reread the book over and over, I found one more "answer" to my doubts and impressions. That is, even if it had been changed from its original form, the book would still have attracted a lot of excitement and sympathy from being known widely in the world, endured occasional criticism, and still exist and be read today, and that, I think is "providence" (*setsuri*). At the same time, the fact that *The Bells of Nagasaki* is still in demand is proof that true peace has yet to arrive in the world. The capabilities of nuclear weapons today are not comparable to the atomic bomb, because one can now attack and destroy enemy countries while remaining within one's own country. The so-called remote work that has become popular with the current coronavirus pandemic began a long time ago. If another great war were to begin now, there would be no winners or losers, and the resulting wasteland (*kōya*) would far surpass that of "Hiroshima" and "Nagasaki." It has been seventy years since Takashi died. In order to let him rest in peace, we must always reinforce the spirit of peace and neighborly love (*rinjin'ai*).

"Love your neighbors as you love yourself."

Notes

1. *Nagasaki no kane* was first published in 1949 by Hibiya shuppan, and the first English translation appeared in 1984 as *The Bells of Nagasaki*, trans. William Johnston, published by Kodansha International. The original Japanese title refers to a single bell (*kane*) that was excavated in late winter 1945 from among the ruins, the story of which is recounted in the last part of the book. The bell was lifted and preserved as a symbol of peace for more than a decade. The conventional English translation of *Nagasaki no kane*, immortalized by Johnston's published translation, has pluralized it as *The Bells of Nagasaki*, which refers to the sounds of ringing *bells*, and so I have retained it here. Johnston had also made other changes to the original text in his translation, most of which Tokusaburō has corrected for the 2022 version. —Trans.

2. There is one correction made for the new version of the English translation that should be singled out here because it relates to the subject of the present volume. Johnston's 1984 translation had replaced Nagai's word "Urakami" with

"Nagasaki" in the eulogy in which Nagai proclaimed the bombing an act of God's Providence and love for the Catholics. The replacement of "Urakami" with "Nagasaki" eliminated the particular historical and contemporaneous contexts surrounding Nagai's interpretation of the bombing, making it seem that he considered the entire city of Nagasaki as a "worthy sacrifice" to end the war. He did not. The Urakami region of the city had a centuries-long history of Catholic martyrdom and survival, and it was hardest hit by the initial blast of the atomic bombing. Tokusaburō's reinstatement of his grandfather's original words brings to English readers the original intent, context, and significance of the eulogy and Nagai's interpretation of the bombing more generally. —TRANS.

3. Nagai Takashi, *Hana saku oka* (Hill of Blossoming Flowers) (Tokyo: San Paolo, 1976), 277.

4. Ibid.

5. I have elsewhere translated this title as *Raising the Curtain on the Atomic Age*, but in this case I have chosen "The Opening" for *kaimaku*. —TRANS.

6. Shikiba Shunzō, the younger brother of Ryūzaburō, was one of the founders of the Tokyo-based publisher Hibiya shuppan, which released *Nagasaki no kane* in 1949. —TRANS.

7. The word *genshino* can also be read *genshiya*, but Nagai was careful to use *genshino* when referring to the devastated landscape of Urakami, sometimes writing the reading out in his texts (*furigana*) and using it in interviews: see, e.g., an interview that aired on the radio on August 9, 1950, https://www.nhk.or.jp/archives/shogenarchives/no-more-hibakusha/library/bangumi/ja/1/. Also, the word *genshino*—which originally was a Japanese translation of the English "Atomic Field" label for the area (which included an airfield) that American personnel used in Nagasaki—is sometimes translated back into English from the Japanese as "atomic wasteland," but I have kept the version used in the English translation of the book, "atomic waste." —TRANS.

Acknowledgments

There are always so many people involved in bringing a book to life, and in so many ways. First and foremost, I would like to thank Fred Nachbar at Fordham University Press for believing in the book and for giving it a home. He always showed genuine patience and enthusiasm when it mattered most. To the many other people involved in the book's production with Fordham University Press, including Eric Newman, Kem Crimmins, and Gregory McNamee, I extend to you all a genuine thanks.

The book would also not have come to life if not for the dedication of each of the contributing authors included in the pages that follow, most of whom have been with the project from its start two years ago. I am grateful to each for their brilliant insights, and for joining me in working to establish a field of Nagasaki studies in English-language scholarship. Our scholarship, however, would never be possible without the decades of work by the *hibakusha* (survivors) and other memory activists, not to mention the scholars in Japan, who have dedicated their lives to illuminating the atomic experience of Nagasaki.

I am forever in debt to Takahashi Shinji for taking me under his wing when I was on a Fulbright fellowship for one year at Nagasaki University in 2003–2004. Takahashi introduced me to the city's history and memoryscapes, as well as to several *hibakusha* memory activists whose work was influential during my formative years as a scholar of Nagasaki, including Akizuki Tatsuichirō, Ikeda Sanae, Taniguchi Sumiteru, Sister Kataoka Chizuko, and former mayor Motoshima Hitoshi. During that year, also thanks to Takahashi, I was fortunate enough to meet and speak with Nagai Kayano (Nagai Takashi's daughter) and Nagai Tokusaburō (Nagai's grandson, son of Makoto). Tokusaburō in particular has been supportive of my work ever since, granting me access to archives and continuously showing me genuine kindness whenever we meet up in the city for dinner or by chance at a *sentō*. To these residents of Nagasaki and so many more I am neglecting to name here, thank you for shaping my career and life trajectory.

I would not have found my way to editing a volume about postatomic Nagasaki without the influence of mentors and colleagues at the various institutions I have found myself at over the years. Carol Gluck has always shown genuine care and provided professional guidance well after I completed my graduate work at Columbia University. Also at Columbia, Marianne Hirsch introduced me to the vibrant field of memory studies, and Kim Brandt first showed me the complexities of the American occupation of Japan. Before that, at Montana State University, Brett L. Walker introduced me to Japanese history and has been a steadfast source of professional support ever since. Yuka Hara, Mary Murphy, and Timothy LeCain, also at MSU, helped shape the scholar I have become in important ways.

At Emmanuel College in Boston I am grateful to Jeff Fortin, Bill Leonard, Javier Marion, Clare Mehta, Melanie Murphy, Adam Silver, Petros Vamvakas, and Todd Williams. At Loyola University Maryland, deep and warm thanks to Sara Scalenghe, Betsy Schmidt, and Keith Schoppa, as well as to my many other colleagues and friends there, including Fr. Charles Borges, Jack Breihan, Katherine Brennan, David Carey, Kelley DeVries, Bill Donovan, Jane Edwards, Steve Hughes, Angela Leonard, Matt Mulcahy, Toja Okoh, Brandon Parlopiano, Austin Parks, Tom Pegram, Andrew Ross, and Willeke Sandler. At the University of Virginia, I have had the pleasure of working with and benefiting from conversations with Claudrena N. Harold, Erik Linstrum, and Joseph Seeley of the History Department, and my colleagues in the office of Learning Design & Technology, including Jason Bennett, Yitna Firdyiwek, Hope Fitzgerald, Judy Giering, Gail Hunger, Keith Samuels, and Jessica Weaver-Kenney.

I am also grateful to the two publishers who have granted permission for me to reproduce earlier works of mine for this volume. Chapter 1 is from my 2018 book *Resurrecting Nagasaki* and is included here by permission of Cornell University Press. Chapter 6 previously appeared in the journal *Japanese Studies* in 2017 and is reprinted by permission of Taylor & Francis Ltd. on behalf of the Japanese Studies Association of Australia.

I have been fortunate to enjoy the company of friends old and new during the production of this volume. Huge and loving thanks to Kate Johnston, Peiting Li, Duong Phan, and Tim Yang. In early 2022, I was excited to meet and collaborate with Gabriele Di Comite, who shares a passion for postatomic Nagasaki and especially the history of Catholicism there. Thanks to him, I have begun to view Nagasaki in new ways, especially relating to Nagai Takashi.

To my family in Montana, I send unwavering love: my parents Gay and Joe, brother Matt, sisters Erin and Korie, sister-in-law Makiko, nephews

Keegan and Austin, niece Maya, and late brother-in-law Pete Krebs. My mom, Gay Kathleen Diehl, passed away suddenly on June 19, 2023. I am overwhelmed by the weight of the loss, and I miss her dearly. Her warmth and brilliance, which has always burned with the intensity of a thousand suns, has comforted and guided me on life's many journeys, and continues to propel me upward and out of the darkness of grief. I look forward now to seeing her in the faces of my own children, and striving to be the superhero for them that she was to me.

To the love of my life, Anri, and my two wonderful little girls, Yuzu and Beni: you three are truly my world and nothing would ever be possible without being surrounded by your love, laughter, and good spirits. I love you all more than anything.

Contributors

Brian Burke-Gaffney was born in Winnipeg, Canada, in 1950 and came to Japan in 1972, going on to train for nine years as an ordained monk of the Rinzai Zen Sect. He moved to Nagasaki in 1982. He is currently professor of cultural history at the Nagasaki Institute of Applied Science and honorary director of Glover Garden. He received the Nagasaki Prefecture Citizens Award in 1992 and the Nagasaki Shinbun Culture Award in 2016. He has published several books in Japanese and English, including *Starcrossed: A Biography of Madame Butterfly* (EastBridge, 2004) and *Nagasaki: The British Experience 1854–1945* (Global Oriental UK, 2009).

Chad R. Diehl received his PhD from the Department of East Asian Languages and Cultures at Columbia University in 2011, specializing in modern Japanese history. He has researched the atomic bombing of Nagasaki and its aftermath since 2003 and published his first monograph, *Resurrecting Nagasaki: Reconstruction and the Formation of Atomic Narratives*, with Cornell University Press in 2018.

Anna Gasha is a doctoral candidate in historic preservation at Columbia University's Graduate School of Architecture, Planning, and Preservation. Her research interests include the relationships between disasters and preservation and the history and politics of science and technology within preservation practice. She graduated with a BA in history of art and architecture and an ScB in materials engineering from Brown University, and she holds an MS in structural engineering, mechanics, and materials from University of California, Berkeley. She is of Japanese and Okinawan descent.

Anthony Richard Haynes received his PhD in Christian ethics and practical theology from the University of Edinburgh in 2018. He wrote his doctoral thesis on the connection between art and mysticism in the life and thought of the French Catholic philosopher Jacques Maritain. He has since worked as an adjunct professor and visiting lecturer in philosophy and religious studies for several universities, including Lakeland University (Japan Campus) and, most recently, the University of Santo Tomas (Philippines). His academic research centers on the practical expression of religious belief and experience, particularly in fiction, visual art, and ascetic ways of life.

Michele M. Mason is associate professor of Japanese cultural studies at the University of Maryland, College Park. Her interests include colonial and postcolonial studies, gender and feminist theory, masculinity studies, environmental humanities, and contents tourism. Mason is also dedicated to the study of Hiroshima and Nagasaki in literature and history, nuclear abolition, global *hibakusha* movements, and nuclear power. She is the author of *Dominant Narratives of Colonial Hokkaido and Imperial Japan: Envisioning the Periphery and Nation-State* (Palgrave Macmillan, 2012) and coproduced, with Kathy Sloane, the award-winning documentary film *Witness to Hiroshima* (witnesstohiroshima.com).

Gwyn McClelland is an oral historian who studies the impact of trauma in religious narratives. He is currently lecturer in Japanese studies at the University of New England, Anaiwan Country, Australia, and is the author of *Dangerous Memory in Nagasaki: Prayers, Protests and Catholic Survivor Narratives* (Routledge, 2020). His work has also recently been published in *History Workshop Journal* and *Journal of Cultural Economy*, and he is a recent Japan Foundation Fellow researching the experiences of Hidden Christians and Catholics in the Goto Archipelago.

Tokusaburō Nagai is the grandson of Takashi Nagai and the director of the Nagasaki City Nagai Takashi Memorial Museum.

Maika Nakao is an associate professor at Hiroshima University. She received her PhD in the history of science from the University of Tokyo and is an expert in the nuclear history of Japan. She also worked at Nagasaki University from 2018 to 2021. She coedited the book *The Seventy-Five Years after the Atomic Bombing: Tracing the Memories and Records of Nagasaki* (Shoshi tsukumo, 2021) and has published two monographs: *Scientists and the Sorcerer's Apprentice: The Border between Science and Non-Science* (Seidosha, 2019) and *Allure of Nuclear: Science Culture in Prewar Japan and the Emergence of "Atomic Utopia"* (Keisō shobō, 2015).

Haeseong Park is currently an instructor in the Community Faculty at Metropolitan State University. She has published several journal articles, including many on Christianity in Korea, such as "Christian Feminist Helen Kim and Her Compromise for the Service to Syngman Rhee" in *Korea Journal* (2020).

Franklin Rausch received his PhD from the University of British Columbia and is an associate professor in the History and Philosophy Department at Lander University in Greenwood, South Carolina. His research focuses on Korean religious history, particularly Catholicism. He has published several articles, including "The Late Chosŏn Korean Catholic Archives: Documenting this World and the Next" in *Journal of Korean Studies* (October 2019). He has also contributed two articles on Korean Catholicism to *The Palgrave Handbook of the Catholic Church in East Asia*. His recent translation with Jieun Han, *An Chunggŭn: His Life and Thought in His Own Words*, was published by Brill in 2020.

Nanase Shirokawa is a graduate student at the Massachusetts Institute of Technology studying art and architectural history. Her research focuses on memory and visual culture in postwar Japan.

Shinji Takahashi is one of the foremost scholars of the atomic bombing of Nagasaki and was formerly a professor at Nagasaki University. He has written and coedited numerous books on Nagasaki and has been active in the antinuclear peace movement since the 1970s.

Anri Yasuda is an assistant professor of modern Japanese literature at the University of Virginia. Her monograph *Beauty Matters: Modern Japanese Literature and the Question of Aesthetics, 1890-1930* is forthcoming from Columbia University Press.

Index

ABCC. *See* Atomic Bomb Casualty Commission
Abŏji ŭi moksori (Father's Voice) (Pak), 76
abolition activism, 211n11
"abyss of darkness," 166
An Account of the Nagasaki Atomic Bombing (*Nagasaki genbaku ki*) (Akizuki), 179–80
Agamben, Giorgio, 160
Agawa Hiroyuki, 59
air-defense facilities, 37
Akizuki Mineral Therapy, 184
Akizuki Tatsuichirō, 297, 301, 309n15, 310n31; background of, 181; bomb detonation and, 182; bombing experience of, 179–84; bombing silence noted by, 163; Catholic baptism of, 184; *hibakusha*'s traumatic memory and, 18; on hypocenter, 186–88; on lack of bombing criticism, 163; Maika writing about, 22; marriage of, 183; on Nagai as theatrical, 310n36; on religion's power, 188; Sugako wife of, 183
Akutagawa Award, 14, 131
Akutagawa Ryūnosuke, 21, 131–32; arts multiculturalism and, 137; Christian characters in stories by, 133; cultural fusion by, 144; identity crisis of, 143; Japan's cultural identity from, 138–39; Kirishitan works of, 133–35, 139; mysterious creatures by, 146; on Nagasaki as calm and beautiful, 144; "Nagasaki Diary" published by, 144–45; Nagasaki vision of, 148; sense of displacement by, 147–48; *Shaba o nogareru kappa* by, 146, 148; *Suiko*

banki no zu by, 145, 145–46; Tokyo depictions by, 141–42
Allied occupation: bulldozing done by, 284; censorship bureau of, 45, 47, 58–59, 61, 239n28; disorderly conduct during, 261n14; forces arrival for, 243–45; Glover House misrepresented during, 260–61; of Japan, 273; *Madame Butterfly* demanded by, 250–51; of Nagasaki, 23; newspaper articles banned by, 255–56
Amakusa Shirō, 133
Ambrose, Mary, 51–52
Amino Isao, 66n68
anamnesis, 113–20
Angelus bell, 314–15
Anri Yasuda, 21
antinuclear peace movement, 8, 152, 171, 175n1, 187
antiwar message, 57–58
The Apostle of Peace (*Heiwa no shito*) (Nagai), 94
"Apostle of True Love, Dr. Nagai Tak'asi" (*Ch'am sarang ŭi sado, Nagai Tak'asi paksannim kke*) (Yi Howŏn), 86
"Appeal for Peace" (John Paul II), 305
Appeals from Nagasaki (*Nagasaki kara no uttae*), 298
Araragi school, 95
art, 287n3; Akutagawa and multiculturalism in, 137; emotions preserved through, 110; Nagai importance of, 94–96; Namban-style artworks as, 138
artistic life, 93
Asahi Shinbun (newspaper), 14, 154–55
Ashida Hitoshi, 254

Asia-Pacific War, 305–6
Assmann, Aleida, 4–5
"As Yourself Association" (Yŏgi Aein), 72, 81–88, 89n4
"As Yourself Cottage" (Nyokodō), 72
Atarashiki asa (New Morning), 95
Atomic Battlefield Psychology ("*Genshiun Senjo Shinri*") (Nagai), 50
Atomic Bomb Casualty Commission (ABCC), 187, 247, 284
Atomic Bomb Dome (*Genbaku dōmu*, also Atomic Dome, Peace Dome), 26n19, 197–98, 216, 224, 226–28, 232, 277, 281, 284
atomic bombing: Akizuki experience of, 179–84; Akizuki noting lack of criticism about, 163; anniversary ceremony of, 206, 208; belfry's destruction by, 222; Catholic community understanding of, 96; children in attack of, 200; damage from, 299; destructive power of, 51; divine love transfiguring suffering from, 101–2; as divine punishment, 209–10; Fat Man bomb in, 169, 269; *Genbaku* as, 8, 15–16, 24n1; *Ground Zero, Nagasaki* approach on, 192–93; *hibakusha* and human destruction of, 168; *hibakusha* appeals from, 300; *hibakusha* as survivors of, 4, 25n13, 307n1; *hibakusha* trauma from, 174–75; Hiroshima as symbol of, 10; Hiroshima's experience of, 1–4, 11, 16; human experience of, 17; Inferior Atomic-Bombed City and, 9–11; *kataribe* interpretation of, 125; literature on, 57, 59–60, 151–52; Little Boy bomb in, 168, 269; Midori death in, 95, 107, 159; miseries of war in, 232; Nagai and God's Providence in, 12, 14, 38, 40, 42, 46–47, 51–52, 96–98, 106, 155, 197; Nagasaki's divine punishment by, 34; Nagai's experience of, 11–15; Nagai's memoryscape of, 11–12; Nagai's religious interpretation of, 11, 40–42, 71; Nagai's Urakami sacrifice by, 35, 40–44, 51–52, 99–100; Nagasaki as inferior city and, 6–8; Nagasaki decision for, 269; *Nagasaki no kane* and experience of, 312–16; Nagasaki ruins after, 237–38; Nagasaki's experience of, 1–4, 125, 217–18; Nagasaki's perceived muted protest of, 8, 114–16; no-life-in-the-atomic wilderness theory and, 106; Ōura Cathedral surviving, 63n23; over Urakami district, 6, 39, 96–100; Ozaki during, 121–23, *122*; Ozaki victimization by, 127n16; pain and suffering from, 63n29; pastoral approach to, 99; Hiroshima as peace commemoration city after, 154; personal trauma from, 162, 168–73; poetic tradition ruptured by, 172; preserving sites of, 219–20; return of life after, 106; scientific record of, 186; Seirai literature on, 22; suffering from, 299; survivors poetry after, 158–59; time stopped by, 225; traumatic memories of, 184–85; Urakami Cathedral ruins from, *2–3, 7, 217, 221*; Urakami Catholics horrors of, 177n38; Urakami Valley tragedy of, 43, 93, 96–100; by U.S., 168–69; Yamada on poetry about, 165–66. *See also* nuclear weapons
"Atomic Bombing" and the Thirty Years Since (*"Genbaku" to sanjūnen*) (Akizuki), 180
Atomic-Bombing Hypocenter (*Genbaku bakushinchi*), 187
"The Atomic Bomb Inside Me" (*Watashi no naka no genbaku*), 156
"The Atomic Bomb Survivors' Medical Support Law" (*Genshi bakudan hibakusha no iryō nado ni kan suru hōritsu*), 25n13, 196, 211n10, 306, 307n1
atomic energy, 102–3
atomic experience, 16, 60–61
Atomic Field, 317n7
Atomic Jesus (painting) (Nagai), 103, 162
atomic science, 44–45, 102
atomic wasteland (*genshino*), 177n34, 317n7
atonement (*tsugunai*), 210

Index | 329

"At the very bottom is the great earth" (*Donzoko ni daichi ari*), 106
Auschwitz, 112, 124–25
Auschwitz (painting), 10
authenticity: historical, 233–34; Hypocenter Park structures lacking, 232–33; rebuilt sites for, 234; in reconstruction, 241n46; Urakami Cathedral lacking, 237; Urakami Cathedral pieces for, 23
Awajiya Tsuru, 246
Azaryahu, Maoz, 229, 233

Bara za (Rose theater group), 65n51
Barefoot Gen (cartoon), 127n16
Bastian no kamiyama (The sacred mountain of Bastian), 123
Battleship Yamato (*Senkan Yamato*) (film), 65n51
Belasco, David, 248
belfry, Urakami Cathedral's original, 221–23, 230–32, 242n56
The Bells of Nagasaki. *See Nagasaki no kane*
The Bells of Peace That Also Reverberate Today (*Kyō mo narihibiku heiwa no kane*), 19
Beloved Children (*Itoshigo yo*), 76
"Between Belief and Doubt" (*Shin to gi no aida*) (Seirai), 209
Between Sadness and Nothingness (*Kanashimi to mu no aida*) (Seirai), 192–94
Bible, 62n16, 98, 134
Blossoms of Holland (*Oranda no Hana*) (Akutagawa), 135, 137
Bodhisattva Avalokiteśvara, 103
books: from Catholic community, 19; censorship bureau suppressing, 58–59, 61; *hibakusha* facing challenges publishing, 56–60; Nagai donating royalties from, 52–54; Nagai publishing, 45, 84; opinion poll on, 48–49; Yi Sŏngwu translation of, 73–74
Bravo hydrogen bomb test, 196
Breaking Down the Walls of Silence (*Chinmoku no kabe o yabutte*), 18
bricks, from Urakami Cathedral, 223

Buddhist goddess (Kannon), *136*
"*Bungei-teki na, amari ni bungei teki-na*" (Literary, All Too Literary) (Akutagawa), 141
Burke-Gaffney, Brian, 23, 227, 268
burnt offering (*hansai*), 12, 63n31, 98–99, 210, 295. *See also hansai*
Burnt Offering Theory, 210. *See also Urakami hansai setsu*
The Burnt Rosary Beads (*Yaketa rozario*), 116, *117*
butchering, of animals, 127n30

Café Ground Zero, 195
calligraphic works, 106, 118
Campbell, Gary, 234
cancer, 115; leukemia and, 307n4; pancreatic, 118; radioactivity and, 167; Yamaguchi Tsutomu's death from, 169
capital transfer taxes, 68n90
Caruth, Cathy, 153, 159
catharsis, 151
cathedral bell, 65n53
Catholic catechism (*Kōkyō yōri*), 36
Catholic community: Akizuki baptized into, 184; atomic bombing horrors of Urakami, 177n38; bombing understanding in, 96; books from, 19; martyrdom of, 10–11, 13; memoryscapes of, 4–6; new cathedral built by, 9; pope's visit important for, 128n39; relics after bombing of, 2; survivor guilt of, 115. *See also* Urakami Catholics
Catholicism: "As Yourself Association" and, 81–88; *chōgata* and, 62n7; in Christianity, 134; faith in God in, 75; Nagai's conversion to, 36, 78; prejudices about, 74–75; Roman Catholics in, 50; Yi Sŏngwu translation and, 73–76
Catholicism Bulletin (*Katorikkukyō hō*), 36–37, 62n13, 162
Cenotaph for Atomic Bomb Victims (*Genbaku shibotsusha ireihi*), 265, 271
censorship bureau, 45, 47, 58–61, 153, 239n28

Chaeil, Kim, 80
Ch'am sarang ŭi sado, Nagai Tak'asi paksannim kke ("Apostle of True Love, Dr. Nagai Tak'asi") (Yi Howŏn), 86
cherry blossoms, *105*, 107
cherry trees, 54
Chiaki Minoru, 48, 65n51
children, 106, 115, 200
Children of Urakami (*Urakami no kodomo*), 103
China, 37–38, 62n18, 138
Chinmoku no kabe o yabutte (Breaking Down the Walls of Silence), 18
Chō chō fujin yukari no chi (Place Connected with Madame Butterfly), 257, 260–61
chōgata, 62n7
Chŏng Sŏngho, 76
Chŏng Sunghŏn, 85–86
Chŏn Ŭnok, 73
Cho Yangwuk, 77–79, 90n25
Christian image of ground zero, 6–9, 16, 35, 152, 179
Christianity, 72; Akutagawa stories with, 133; banning of, *136*, 196–97, 216; Catholicism in, 134; in Japan, 37–39; martyrs in, 123–24; Nagai finding God and, 49–50; Nagai's sentiment of, 46–47; in Nagasaki, 21, 283; values of, 140–41; for world peace, 81
Christian martyrdom, 198
Christian socialism, 81
Chūgoku Shinbun (newspaper), 193
Civil Information and Education Section (CIE), 273
climate change, 233
Cold War, 296
collective memories, 5
commemorative ceremonies, 276–77
Committee for the Preservation of Atomic Bombing Materials (*Genbaku shiryō hozon i'in kai*), 218
Common Knowledge of the Criticism of Communism (*Kyōsan shugi hihan no jōshiki*), 65n54
Communism, 55, 75

Communist Party, 35, 55–56, 163
Concentric Circles of Death (*Shi no dō shin'en*) (Akizuki), 179–80
Le Corbusier, 265
corpses, rivers of, 170
cosmic order, 281
counter-monument movement, 291n59
crematorium, 182
"The Crisis of Nuclear War and Conditions for the Survival of Humanity" (symposium), 300–301
"Criticizing the Nagai Takashi 'Urakami Holocaust Theory'" (*Nagai Takashi "Urakami hansai setsu" hihan*) (Takahashi), 295–96
"The Cross of Jeronimo" (*Jeronimo no jūjika*) (Seirai), 192, 198
crucifixes, 2, *2–3*
culture: festival for, 251–56; fusion of, 144; heritage management of, 241n46; hybrid, 133; international, 5, 21, 227; production of, 229

daibutsu figures, 280
dai-kannon figures, 280
"Damage from the Atomic Bombing and the Appeal of the Hibakusha" (*Genbaku higai to hibakusha no uttae*), 301
Dangerous Memory in Nagasaki (McClelland), 28n31
dark era *(kurai jiki)*, 5–6
Dawson, Graham, 119
Dazai Osamu, 48
"The Dead Raven" (*Shinda karasu*) (Yamada), 165–66
death: as greatest gift, 83; in Hiroshima, 171; of Kuraba Waka, 246–47; by leukemia, 60; of Midori, 95, 107, 159; Nagai's views on, 38, 46; not meaningless, 99; Ozaki facing own, 116; ravens of, 165–68; Urakami Catholics with meaningful, 109–10; Yamaguchi Tsutomu's cancer causing, 169
Death in Life (Lifton), 301
Deleuze, Gilles, 131–32, 134

Delnore, Victor E., 58, 247, 252, 254
delusional schizophrenia, 201
Diehl, C., 20, 28n31, 179, 304; *hibakusha* as memory activists from, 198; Nagai's reconstruction focus and, 71; symbols of tragedy and, 226
discrimination, 195–96
Discussing the Thoughts of Dr. Nagai Takashi (*Nagai Takashi hakase no shisō, o kataru*) (Yamauchi), 19, 27n22
disorderly conduct, 261n14
divine love, 101–2
divine providence, 209
divine punishment, 34, 209–10
"Dr. Nagai's Eulogy" ("*Nagai hakase no chōji*") (Seirai), 14, 209
Dr. Nagai Takashi's Love, Peace, and Faith (*Nagai Tak'asi paksa ŭi sarang kwa p'yŏnghwa, kŭrigo sinang*) (Sŏ), 84
documentary film, 178n67
Doing Peace Studies from Nagasaki (*Nagasaki kara heiwa gaku suru!*) (Takahashi and Funakoe), 19
donations, by Nagai, 52–54
Donzoko ni daichi ari ("At the very bottom is the great earth"), 106
double *hibakusha* (*nijū hibakusha*), 168–69
Doubly Atomic-Bombed 2 (*Nijū hibaku II*), 178n67
Dower, John W, 250

earth, natural world of, 104–7
Earthiness, 105, 109
Edo-period (1603–1868), 135
emotions, 110, 193, 202–3
empowerment, 151, 158
Endō Shūsaku, 115, 126n12, 138, 192
Enomoto (*Asahi* biographer), 115–16, 124
Essays from As Yourself Cottage (*Nyokodō zuihitsu*) (Nagai), 74
ethnic groups, minority, 291n65
ethos of modernism, 270
eulogy, Nagai presenting, 40, 43, 96, 209, 302–3, 315–16

"Even the tail has a role" (*shippo mo hitoyaku*), 107

faith, 201–2, 206–8
Falk, Ray, 66n68
family, paintings of, 107–10
The Fate of Man at Nagasaki (Nagai), 51
Father's Voice (*Abŏji ŭi moksori*) (Pak), 76
Fat Man bomb, 169, 269
The Field Affair (magazine), 64n35
fifteen-year war, 41, 303
final lecture, of Ozaki, 118–20
financial crisis, 80
Fire (mural), 1
Fire of Life (*Inochi no hi*), 164
First World War, 172
flesh-eating birds, 167
Foote, Ken, 229, 233
forbidden fruit, 206–7
fountain, 276
"Fragmented Memory" (Gasha), 23
fragment signage issues, 229–31, 240n39
Francis (Pope), 282–83
Franciscan monk, 112
free verse poetry, 159–60, 162
From isolation we are saved by love (*Kodoku o suku'u no wa ai*), 121
From the Flames (*Hono'o no naka kara*) (Tagawa Seikō), 185
Fujiki hakuei sha (publisher), 59
Fujiwara Yoshie, 250, 262n17
Fukuda Masako, 48
Fukuda Sumako, 22, 154–55, 267
funeral, mass, 40
Furusato wa isshun ni kieta (My Hometown Disappeared in an Instant), 18

Gajowniczek, Franciszek, 124
Garden of Eden, 205, 206–8
Gasha, Anna, 23
Genbaku (the atomic bombings), 8, 15–16, 24n1, 216, 226
Genbaku bakushinchi (Atomic-Bombing Hypocenter), 187
Genbaku Dome (*Genbaku dōmu*). *See* Atomic Bomb Dome

332 | Index

Genbakugo no 75 nen (The Seventy-Five Years after the Atomic Bombing), 19
Genbaku higai to hibakusha no uttae ("Damage from the Atomic Bombing and the Appeal of the Hibakusha"), 301
Genbaku no zu (The Hiroshima Panels), 1–4, 2–3, 8–10, 24n1, 25n5, 26n18
Genbaku shibotsusha ireihi (Cenotaph for Atomic Bomb Victims), 265, 271
Genbaku shiryō hozon i'in kai (Committee for the Preservation of Atomic Bombing Materials), 218
"*Genbaku*" to sanjūnen ("Atomic Bombing" and the Thirty Years Since) (Akizuki), 180
General Headquarters of the Supreme Commander for the Allied Powers (GHQ-SCAP), 249–51, 255–56, 273
Genshi jidai no kaimaku (Raising the Curtain on the Atomic Age) (Nagai), 45
Genshi jidai no kaimaku (The Opening of the Atomic Age) (Nagai), 313–16, 317n5. See also *Nagasaki no kane*
genshino (atomic wasteland), 177n34, 317n7
"*Genshiun Senjo Shinri*" (Atomic Battlefield Psychology) (Nagai), 50
Gerson, Joseph, 195
Gerz, Jochen, 291n59
Ghosts (mural), 1
GHQ-SCAP. See General Headquarters of the Supreme Commander for the Allied Powers
Giblin, Ruth, 43, 51
Glover, Thomas B., 23, 245–46, 260
Glover, Tsuru, 257
Glover House, 243, 245–47, 248, 251–53, 255; Allied occupation misrepresenting, 260–61; Nagato visiting, 262n32; postcard of, 258; as tourist attraction, 257, 259. See also Madame Butterfly House
Glynn, Paul, 72, 79
God: atomic energy as gift from, 102–3; Catholic's faith in, 75; difficulties dealt with through, 80; faith and, 206–8; Nagai finding, 49–50; Nagasaki bombing willed by, 97; Ozaki imagining words of, 121; people rejected by, 204–5; Providence of, 12, 14, 38, 40, 42, 46–47, 51–52, 96–98, 106, 155, 197; trustful surrender to, 100; Urakami Catholics as instruments of, 161; Urakami Catholics faith challenged in, 40, 100–104; Urakami Catholics love from, 163
Goldsby, Joseph and Barbara, 247, 248, 252–54, 255
González, Antonio, 104, 105, 110
Gotō Minako, 151, 153, 174
Grand Opera Madam Butterfly, 262n32
Grant Me Something Eternal (*Horobinu mono o*) (Nagai), 73–75
ground zero: Christian image of, 6–9, 16, 35, 152, 179; history of, 195–96; hypocenter and, 186–88; in Japan, 195–96; literature on, 22, 27n26, 196; Seirai and literature on, 191; in U.S., 195–96
Ground Zero, Nagasaki (Seirai): atomic bombing approach in, 192–93; Honey chapter of, 205–11; insects chapter in, 202–5; nails chapter of, 199–202; as post-atomic-bomb literature, 198–99
Ground Zero: The Sky of Nagasaki (film), 192
Gruber, Howard E., 301
guardian angel, 203
guardian lion-dog (*komainu*), 104
Guattari, Felix, 131–32, 134

"Haguruma" (Spinning Gears), 142
haiku poetry, 160
Hamai Shinzō, 270
hansai (burnt offering), 12, 63n31, 98–99, 160, 210, 212n19, 295. See also holocaust
Han Su'gan, 79
Hara Tamiki, 59
Harburg Monument against Fascism (Gerz and Salev-Gerz), 291n59
Hashida Tōsei, 169
Haven, USS, 243–44
Hayashi Kyōko, 192, 194

Haynes, Anthony Richard, 20
healing, process of, 114
Healthy Citizen Movement (*Kenmin Undō*), 283
heavenly ascension, 102, 109–10
Heiwa no shito (The Apostle of Peace) (Nagai), 94
Heiwa Suishin Kyōkai (Nagasaki Peace Wing Organization), 118
Heiwa wa Nagasaki yori ("Peace starts from Nagasaki"), 57
Heretic Religion ("*Jashūmon*"), 139
Hersey, John, 48, 51
Hibakuchi Nagasaki no saiken (The Reconstruction of the Atomic-Bombed Land of Nagasaki) (Kataoka, C. and Kataoka, R.), 13, 19
hibakusha: atomic bombing appeals from, *300*; as atomic-bombing survivors, 4, 25n13, 307n1; atomic trauma of, 174–75; bombing's human destruction and, 168; cancer and leukemia of, 307n4; defining, 175n1; double, 168–69; empowerment of, 158; Hiroshima subject of, 59–60; in illness and poverty cycle, 298–99; *kunō* and, 308n9; listening to voices of, 188; as memory activists, 198; Nagai not representative of, 12–13, 33; *Nagasaki no shōgen* by, 306–7; Nagasaki publications by, 17–18; oral histories of, 115, 119; Ozaki as, 112–13; poetry by, 21–22, 152–53, 158–59; poetry empowering, 174–75; publishing challenges faced by, 56–60; radiation anxieties of, 167–68; recovery process for, 151; Seirai fear of criticism from, 194; social discrimination faced by, 153–54; statue construction fees and, 267; struggles of, 308n8; suffering by, 24; Tanaka poetry as, 157; traumatic memories and, 18, 152; walls of silence faced by, 153–57; Yamada as poet of, 22, 303
"Hibakusha Continue to Die" (*Hibakusha zokuzokuto shibō*) (article), 6, 7
Hibakusha no genzai (Present Conditions of the Hibakusha), 298

The *Hibakusha* of "Nagasaki" ("*Nagasaki*" *no hibakusha*) (Nishimura), 18, 28
Hibakusha zokuzokuto shibō ("*Hibakusha* Continue to Die") (article), 6, 7
Hibino Masami, 297
Hibiya Shuppan, 316n1
hidden Christians (*kakure Kirishitan*), 104, 123, 127n30, 200, 204
Hirohito (Emperor), 49, 65n56–57, 66n59, 279
Hiroshima: antinuclear peace movement from, 8, 152; "Appeal for Peace" speech in, 305; Atomic Bomb Dome in, 216, 226; as atomic bombing symbol, 10; atomic experience of, 1–4, 11, 16; commemorative ceremonies of, 276–77; Genbaku Dome in, 232, 284; *hibakusha* writing about, 59–60; Little Boy bomb dropped on, 168; Nagasaki symbolically inferior to, 6–8; Peace Center and memorial cenotaph in, 23, *265*, 271; as peace commemoration city, 154, 227, 270; postatomic memory in, 215–16; Yamaguchi Tsutomu witnessed deaths in, 171
Hiroshima (Hersey), 48, 51
Hiroshima (painting), 8, 10
Hiroshima Memorial Hall, 289n37
The Hiroshima Panels (*Genbaku no zu*), 1–4, *2–3*, 8–10, 24n1, 25n5, 26n18
Hiroshima Peace City Monument, 271
Hiroshima Peace Commemoration City Construction Law, 270; also Hiroshima Peace Memorial City Construction Law, 256
Hiroshima Peace Memorial Park, 264–65, 273–74, 282, 288n17
Hiroshima Rages, Nagasaki Prays (*Ikari no Hiroshima, Inori no Nagasaki*), 8, 152, 179, 209
Hiroshima's Peace Park, 271
Hisako (Yamaguchi Tsutomu's wife), 169
historical authenticity, 233–34
historic landmark, 231, 240n39
Hōbō (poetry magazine), 303, 309n22

holocaust: burnt offering and, 41, 295; *hansai* as, 12, 63n31, 98–99, 160, 210, 212n19, 295; Lifton studies of, 307n2; Nagai's reference of, 41, 160; Nagai's poem, 160
Holtorf, Cornelius, 233
Holy Water (Seisui), 192
Honey chapter, of *Ground Zero, Nagasaki*, 205–11
Hongchung, Kim, 73
Hong Sŏngmin, 77
Hono'o no naka kara (From the Flames) (Tagawa Seikō), 185
Honorary Citizen, 54–55, 68n98
Hori Tatsuo, 131
Horobinu mono o (Grant Me Something Eternal) (Nagai), 73–75
human-kind, 105; atomic bombing experience of, 17; atomic bombing's destruction to, 168, 170; atomic power discovered by, 102; atonement for sins of, 13, 40–43, 98; avaricious nature of, 286; body burned black as coal, 170–71; insects relationship with, 205; love and peace for, 107; trauma experiences of, 159
human rafts (*ningen ikada*), 169–70
Huong T. Bui, 232
hybrid culture (*Namban shumi*), 133
Hyōgen sha (publisher), 59
Hypocenter Park, 223–24; authentic structures absent from, 232–33; historic monument and, 240n39; wall section at, 230, 236
hypocenter, restoring, 186–88

Ichimaru Michito, 297, 307n4
Ichiro Shirato, 50
identity crisis, of Akutagawa, 143
Ikari no Hiroshima, Inori no Nagasaki ("Hiroshima rages, Nagasaki prays"), 8, 152, 179, 209
"*Ikiru to wa kodoku to deai*" (to live is isolation and encounter), 118
Image of a Suiko Returning Home in the Evening (*Suiko banki no zu*), 145, 145–46
Immaculate Conception Cat, 197

imperialism, 72
Imperial Silver Cups, 56
"Inferior Atomic-Bombed City," 9–11
Inochi, translation of, 118
Inochi no hi (Fire of Life), 164
Inori no Nagasaki (Nagasaki of Prayer), 304
Inoue Hisashi, 27n22, 27n25, 47
Inoue Shōichi, 288n17
Insects chapter, in *Ground Zero, Nagasaki*, 202–5
international cultural city (*kokusai bunka toshi*), 10–11, 288n15
international culture, of Nagasaki, 5, 21, 227
international peace, 81–82, 299
International Peace Bureau (IPB), 296
international recognition, 43–44, 50
International Symposium on the Damage and Aftereffects of the Atomic Bombing of Hiroshima and Nagasaki (*NGO Hibaku mondai kokusai shinpojiumu*), 296
internet blog, 120
IPB. *See* International Peace Bureau
Ishida Hisashi, 259
Ishida Masako, 58–59
isolation, life in, 109, 120–23, 125
Itō Hisa'aki, 25
Itō Naruhiko, 303
Itoshigo yo (Beloved Children), 76
Itō Takeshi, 308n8
Itō Yutaka, 279
Iwaguchi Natsuo, 219, 226

Japan: Akutagawa and cultural identity of, 138–39; Allied occupation of, 273; antinuclear peace movement in, 175n1; China in battles with, 37–38, 62n18; Christianity banned in, 136, 196–97, 216; Christianity in, 37–39; ethos of modernism in, 270; fifteen-year war initiated by, 41, 303; ground zero in, 195–96; imperialism of, 72; Korea's cooperation with, 85; Korea's reconciliation with, 88; landmarks designation in, 231–32; *Madame Butterfly* in, 248–50; modernization process in, 149n12;

sin-consciousness in, 115–16; social problems in, 47–48; tourist industry in, 256–61
Japanese-Christian iconography, 137
Japan Preparatory Committee (*Nihon junbi i'inkai*), 296
"*Jashūmon*" (Heretic Religion), 139
"*Jashūmon hikyoku*" (Secret Songs of the Heretic Religion), 133
Jeronimo no jūjika ("The Cross of Jeronimo") (Seirai), 192, 198
Jesty, Justin, 25n5
Jesus Christ, 82–84, 100; atomic heart of, 103, 162; life of, 133–34; Nagai compared to, 86; nails in crucified, 202; sacred heart of, *101*, 101–2, 109–10; self-sacrifice of, 140–41
Jidō fukushi hō (Juvenile Social Welfare Law), 48
John Paul II (Pope), 124, 128n39, 199–200, 282, 305, 310n31
Johnston, William, 72, 316n1–2
Jū nana sai no natsu (The Seventeen-Year-Old's Summer) (Ozaki), 120–21
Juvenile Social Welfare Law (*Jidō fukushi hō*), 48

Kagawa Toyohiko, 81
kakure Kirishitan (hidden Christians), 104, 123, 127n30, 200, 204
Kalischer, Peter, 251
Kamata Sadao, 163, 184, 297, 298, 306
"*Kamigami no bishō*" (The Smiles of the Gods), 137–38
Kamohara Haruo, 144
Kanashimi to mu no aida (Between Sadness and Nothingness) (Seirai), 192–94
kanji characters, 138
Kannon (Buddhist goddess), *136*
Kaori Yoshida, 232
kappa, ink paintings of, 145–48
A Kappa Fleeing Worldly Suffering (*Shaba o nogareru kappa*), 146–48, *147*
Kataoka Chizuko, 13, 304
Kataoka Rumiko, 13
Kataoka Yakichi, 35, 53–54, 82–84, 164, 304

kataribe (public speaker about atomic experience), 118, 120, 125
Katayose Toshihide, 297
Katorikukyō hō. See Katorikkukyō hō
Katorikkukyō hō (Catholicism Bulletin), 36–37, 62n13, 162
Katsutoshi (Yamaguchi Tsutomu's son), 169
Kaufman, Mary, 297
Kawazoe Takeshi, 267
Kayano (Nagai's child), 49, 54, 60, 159, 315; Nagai's paintings of, *108*, 108–9; pictures drawn by, 94
Kazagashira Park, 290n46
Keiji Nakazawa, 127n16
Keller, Helen, 50
Kelley, Francis Clement, 67n77
Kenmin Undō (Healthy Citizen Movement), 283
Kettō Ganryūjima (film), 65n51
Kikuchi Dairoku, 249
Kino Fumio, 162
Kinoshita Mokutaro, 133
Kirishitan stories, 133–35, 139
Kitahara Hakushū, 133
Kitamura Seibō, 23, 265, *266*; criticism of, 272–73; Peace Statue by, 277–86; as sculptor, 270
Kitaoka Nobuo, 169
Kiyomi (pseudonym), 201–2
Knights of the Holy Mother (*Seibo no Kishi*), 123–24
kodoku (solitude), 121
Kodoku o suku'u no wa ai (From isolation we are saved by love), 121
Kōfukuji Temple, 144
Kogano Tomiko, 249
kokusai bunka toshi (international cultural city), 10–11, 288n15
Kōkyō yōri (Catholic catechism), 36
Kolbe, Maximillian, 78, 112–14, 124; anti-Semitic sentiment of, 128n35
komainu (guardian lion-dog), 104
Konno Setsuzo, 55
Kono ko o nokoshite (Leaving These Children Behind) (Nagai), 45–48, 50, 76, 94; family theme in, 107–8; lambs sacrificed in, 97–98; opinion poll on, 65n54

336 | Index

Korea, 75–76; Japan's cooperation with, 85; Nagai criticized by, 88; Nagai interest in, 72–73; Nagai's name romanization in, 89n13; *Nagasaki no kane* causing discomfort in, 80–81; North, 81, 123; victims from, 286; Yi Munhŭi seeking Nagai understanding in, 83
Koromogawa Maiko, 59
Koyubi ga moeru (Little Finger Burning) (Seirai), 192
Kozawa Setsuko, 25n5
Kume Masao, 141
kunō, 308n9
Kuraba Tomisaburō, 246, 252, 260
kurai jiki (dark era), 5–6
Kurihara Sadako, 153
Kurozuka Kannon statue, 258
Kuryū Akira, 275, 289n37
Kyō mo narihibiku heiwa no kane (The Bells of Peace That Also Reverberate Today) (Takami), 19
Kyōsan shugi hihan no jōshiki (Common Knowledge of the Criticism of Communism), 65n54
Kyūshū region, 133
Kyūshū Times Culture Award, 54

LaCapra, Dominick, 153
landmarks designation, 231–32
Leaving Beloved Children Behind (*Sarang hanŭn ai tŭl rŭl namgyŏ tugo*) (Nagai), 76–77
Leaving These Children Behind (Nagai). See *Kono ko o nokoshite*
Lee, Timothy J., 232
leukemia, 307n4, 313; Nagai with, 38, 42, 60, 71, 95
The Life of Nagai Takashi (*Nagai Takashi no shōgai*) (Kataoka Yakichi), 84, 164
Lifton, Robert J., 301, 307n2
Literary, All Too Literary ("*Bungei-teki na, amari ni bungei teki-na*") (Akutagawa), 141
literary voices, 164–65
Little Boy bomb, 168, 269
Little Finger Burning (*Koyubi ga moeru*) (Seirai), 192

Long, John Luther, 248
loss, of Urakami Cathedral, 225–29
Loti, Pierre, 248
Lucken, Michael, 279
Lyotard, Jean-Francois, 113

MacArthur, Douglas, 254
Madame Butterfly: Allied forces demanding, 250–51; Fujiwara and, 262n17; in Japan, 248–50; in Nagasaki, 252–53; at Tokyo Gekijō Theater, 250
"Madame Butterfly and the Glover House" (Yoshimatsu), 258
Madame Butterfly House, 243, 247–48, 252–53, 259–60; *Mainichi Shinbun* discovering, 254–55; nickname given to, 23; tourism to, 257
Maika Nakao, 19, 22
Mainichi Shinbun (newspaper), 254–55, 255
Makoto (Nagai's child), 60, 78, 84, 159, 315; father's military service talk of, 90n28; Hirohito encouraging, 49; infrastructure improvement for, 54; pictures drawn by, 94; writings by, 82–83
male body, 283
Malli muyŏng (Bright Moonlight with No Shadows) (Nagai), 74
Manchurian Incident, 41
The Man from the West ("*Saihō no hito*"), 133–34
Maria-Kannon statue, 135, *136*
"Mari-no-kyō" (the teachings of Mari), 139, 149n15
Marshall, Bruce, 52, 67n77
martyrdom, 10–11, 13, 123–24
Maruki, Toshi and Iri, 1, 2–3, 8–10
Masako taorezu (Masako Shall Not Perish) (Ishida), 58–61, 69n108
masculinity, 282–84
Mason, Michele M., 22, 27n26
Mason, William B., 246
Matsumoto Tsunehiko, 149n15
Matsuo Atsuyuki, 153
Matsuo Basho, 258
McClelland, Gwyn, 21, 28n31, 218
Medical Relief Law, 25n13

medical training, 38, 43, 70–71
"Medicine is Powerless at That Time" (report), 301
Meiji Enlightenment, 134–35
memorial cenotaph, in Hiroshima, 23, 265, 271
memorial landscape, 215–16
memorials, 237
Memorial to the Dead, Hiroshima, 271
memory-making, 286
memoryscapes, 3–6, 11–12; memories in, 114, 152; of Nagasaki, 16–17; post-atomic, 193–94, 215–16; trauma in, 17–18, 151–53, 172, 184–85; Urakami Cathedral and lost, 9
Metz, Johann Baptist, 114
Midori, Maria, 36; bombing death of, 95, 107, 159; heavenly ascension of, 102; Nagai's paintings of, 99, *100*
Mihoko (pseudonym), 206–8
minority ethnic groups, 291n65
missionary prophecy, 63n29, 161
Mitchell, W. J. T., 283
Mitsubishi kōjō ato (Remains of the Mitsubishi Steel Works), 8
Mitsubishi Nagasaki Shipyard, 246, 260
Mitsubishi Shipbuilding Corporation, 168
Mitsubishi Steel Works (painting), 26n18
Mitsuko (pseudonym), 202–5
Miura Tamaki statue, 260
Miyamoto Musashi (Yoshikawa), 48, 156
Miyazaki Kiyoshige, 257
Mizogami Tarō, 254
modernization process, in Japan, 149n12
Mokusu Nyojō, 144
monuments, 231, 237, 240n39, 271
morally indefensible, 207–8
moral sin, 207
Moriyama family, 36
mother, vanishing, 119–20, 125
Mother and Child (mural), 1
Moto'ō Take, 276
Motoshima Hitoshi, 282
Mukchu al (Rosary Beads) (Nagai), 74
multiculturalism, 137
murals (*Genbaku no zu* as), 1–4
Murray's Handbook to the Japanese Empire (Mason, W. B.), 246

Musashi (battleship), 246
Muzaini, Hamzah, 234
My Beloved Children (*Sarang hanŭn nae aidŭra*) (Nagai), 76
My Hometown Disappeared in an Instant (*Furusato wa isshun ni kieta*), 18
mysterious creatures, 146

"*Nagai hakase no chōji*" ("Dr. Nagai's Eulogy") (Seirai), 14, 209
Nagai Takashi: Amino's letter to, 66n68; antiwar message from, 57–58; art importance to, 94–96; "As Yourself Association" publishing books by, 84; "As Yourself Association" spreading words of, 85–86; atomic age remarks of, 102–3; atomic bombing's divine punishment from, 34; atomic experience of, 11–15; atomic narratives shaped by, 60–61; atomic science dedication of, 44–45; awards won by, 54–56; background of, 35–37, 94–95; bombing and Urakami sacrifice from, 35, 41–44, 51–52, 99–100; bombing as God's Providence by, 12, 14, 38, 40, 42, 46–47, 51–52, 96–98, 106, 155, 197; bombing's religious interpretation by, 11, 71; books published by, 45, 84; calligraphic works of, 106; Catholicism conversion of, 36, 78; chapters on, 20; Christian image of ground zero embodied by, 35; Christians and finding God by, 49–50; Christian sentiment from, 46–47; criticisms of, 27n22, 73; death views of, 38, 46; desire for peace by, 82; devotional paintings of, 103; dignitaries taking note of, 49; diversified translations of, 76–81; donations by, 52–54; eulogy presented by, 40, 43, 96, 209, 302–3, 315–16; family paintings by, 107–10; hibakusha not represented by, 12–13, 33; Hirohito's connection to, 66n59; historical context analysis of, 87–88; holocaust reference by, 160; as Honorary Citizen, 54–55, 68n98; ink paintings of,

338 | Index

Nagai Takashi *(continued)* 107; international recognition of, 43–44, 50; Jesus compared to, 86; Korean criticism of, 88; Korean romanization of, 89n13; Korea's interest in, 72–73; with leukemia, 38, 42, 60, 71, 95; life's true treasures by, 161; literary voices muffled by, 164–65; makeshift hut life of, 39, 52, 64n34; medical training of, 38, 43, 70–71; memoryscape cast by, 11–12; Midori paintings by, 99, *100*; as militaristic, 62n18; Nyokodō visitors welcomed by, 95; objective discussion about, 15; poetry by, 152–53, 159–63; postatomic memoryscapes of, 12; reconstruction support by, 33–34, 44, 53; royalties donated by, 52–54; as Saint of Urakami, 35, 55, 64n46, 156; "Shira bara" written by, 98; short stories published by, 67n76; simplicity and humanity of, 77–78; Takahashi criticizing, 12–13, 24, 27n25; *tanka* poetry by, 93, 108–9; tax rate paid by, 68n82, 68n90; as theatrical, 310n36; theological explorations of, 20–21, 109–10; as untouchable, 164; Urakami Catholics leadership by, 33–34, 36–37, 39; Urakami Holocaust Theory from, 295–96; "Urakami holocaust theory" of, 13–14; Urakami Valley return of, 39–40; U.S. criticism omitted by, 13–14, 61, 71–72; Virgin Mary paintings by, 103–4; wall of silence created by, 162–63; writings of, 13–14, 20, 45, 50–52, 73–77, 79, 180, 302–6, 315; Yamada critical of, 163–64; Yi Howŏn praising, 86–87; Yi Munhŭi seeking Korean understanding of, 83; Yi Sŏngwu translating books of, 73–74. *See also* Kayano; *Kono ko o nokoshite*; Makoto; *Nagasaki no kane*
Nagai Takashi hakase no shisō o kataru (Discussing the Thoughts of Dr. Nagai Takashi) (Yamauchi), 19, 27n22

Nagai Takashi Memorial Museum, 24, 85, 89n4, 94, 176n17, 312
Nagai Takashi no shōgai (The Life of Nagai Takashi) (Kataoka Yakichi), 84, 164
Nagai Takashi "Urakami hansai setsu" hihan ("Criticizing the Nagai Takashi 'Urakami Holocaust Theory'") (Takahashi), 295–96
Nagai Tak'asi paksa ŭi sarang kwa p'yŏnghwa, kŭrigo sinang (Dr. Nagai Takashi's Love, Peace, and Faith) (Sŏ), 84
Nagami Tokutarō, 135
Nagano Wakamatsu, 244
Nagaoka Some, 41
Nagasaki: Akutagawa's vision for, 148; Allied forces arrival at, 243–45; Allied occupation of, 23; atomic experience of, 1–4, 125, 217–18; atomic ruins of, 237–38; Auschwitz journey back to, 112; bombing decision, 269; bombing's muted protest from, 114–16; calm and beauty of, 144; as Christian city, 21, 283; Fat Man bomb dropped in, 169; God willed bombing of, 97; *hibakusha* publications on, 17–18; Hiroshima and symbolically inferior, 6–8; as inferior atomic-bombed city, 6–8; international culture of, 5, 21, 227; *Madame Butterfly* is, 252–53; memoryscapes of, 16–17; Nagai assisting with reconstruction of, 33–34, 44, 53; Nagai Takashi Memorial Museum in, 24; no air-defense facilities in, 37; Okamoto on history of, 262n21; Peace Declaration in, 254; Peace Statue in, 23; Pope John Paul II visiting, 199–200; postwar history of, 24; research on, 15–24; return of life to, 106; testimonies of, 184–86; Urakami Cathedral no longer in, 226–27, 237–38; wall of silence within, 155–57; as worthy sacrifice, 316n2
Nagasaki (mural), 1–2
"Nagasaki" (Akutagawa), 143–44
Nagasaki 2021 Peace Declaration, 113

Index | 339

Nagasaki Atomic Bomb Museum, 191, 216, 224–25, 231, 275
Nagasaki Atomic Bomb Record Society (*Nagasaki genbaku kiroku no kai*), 184
Nagasaki Christians, 283
Nagasaki City Sixty-Five-Year History, 245
"Nagasaki Diary" (Akutagawa), 144–45
Nagasaki Foreign Settlement, 245
Nagasaki: Fushoku suru rekijitsu no soko de (Nagasaki: In the Depths of Decaying Calendar Days) (Yamada), 185
Nagasaki genbaku ki (An Account of the Nagasaki Atomic Bombing) (Akizuki), 179–80
Nagasaki genbaku kiroku no kai (Nagasaki Atomic Bomb Record Society), 184
Nagasaki International Cultural Center, 274
Nagasaki International Cultural City Construction Fund, 53
Nagasaki International Cultural City Construction Law, 256, 274
Nagasaki International Cultural Hall, 287n3
Nagasaki kara heiwa gaku suru! (Doing Peace Studies from Nagasaki) (Takahashi and Funakoe), 19
Nagasaki kara no uttae (Appeals from Nagasaki), 298
Nagasaki: Kieta mō hitotsu no "genbaku dōmu" (Nagasaki: The Other "Atomic Dome" That Disappeared) (Takase), 224, 226
Nagasaki kyū-Urakami tenshudō (Nagasaki's Former Urakami Cathedral) (Yokote and Burke-Gaffney), 227
Nagasaki: Life after Nuclear War (Southard), 28
Nagasaki Life Writing Group (*Nagasaki seikatsu o tsuzuru kai*), 184
Nagasaki Military Government Team (NMGT), 247–48
Nagasaki National Peace Memorial Hall, 275

Nagasaki ni atte tetsugaku suru (Philosophizing in Nagasaki) (Takahashi), 13, 18, 209–10
"*Nagasaki" no hibakusha* (The Hibakusha of "Nagasaki") (Nishimura), 18, 28
Nagasaki no kane (film), 65n51
Nagasaki no kane (The Bells of Nagasaki) (Nagai), 14, 20, 24, 48–49, 65n53, 72; atomic bombing experience in, 312–16; atonement for sins in, 98; bell excavated in, 316n1; dignitaries given copy of, 65n56; divine providence in, 209; English translation of, 67n75; Korean's uncomfortable with, 80–81; Nagai eulogy in, 45, 72, 315, 316n2; return of life in, 106; Shikiba and publishing of, 317n6
Nagasaki no shōgen (Testimonies of Nagasaki), 156, 184–86, 306–7
Nagasaki of Prayer (*Inori no Nagasaki*), 304
Nagasaki Peace Declaration, 256
Nagasaki Peace Statue, 281
Nagasaki Peace Wing Organization (*Heiwa Suishin Kyōkai*), 118
"*Nagasaki saiken no kōsō*" (Planning the Reconstruction of Nagasaki), 25
Nagasaki seikatsu o tsuzuru kai (Nagasaki Life Writing Group), 184
Nagasaki's Former Urakami Cathedral (*Nagasaki kyū-Urakami tenshudō*) (Yokote and Burke-Gaffney), 227
Nagasaki Shinbun (newspaper), 6, 42, 47, 119
"*Nagasaki shōhin*" (A Short Nagasaki Story) (Akutagawa), 135, 137–41, 143–44
Nagasaki's Peace Park, 265; zones of, 274–76
Nagasaki: The Other "Atomic Dome" That Disappeared (*Nagasaki: Kieta mō hitotsu no "genbaku dōmu"*) (Takase), 224, 226
Nagasak'i ŭi chong ŭn miso chit nŭnda (The Smiling Bells of Nagasaki) (Makoto), 82–83

Nagasaki ūi norae. *See* Song of Nagasaki
Nagasaki University Medical School, 38
Nagato Miho, 262n32
Nagato Miho Opera Company, 250, 253, 259
Nails chapter, of *Ground Zero, Nagasaki*, 199–202
Nakajima Banri, 222
Nakamura Akitoshi. *See* Seirai Yūichi
Nakano Waka, 246–47
Nakashima-Brock, Rita, 114
Namban shumi (hybrid culture), 133
Namban-style artworks, 138
Nanase Shirokawa, 23
Nara Daibutsu, 280
Narrow Road to the Deep North (Matsuo), 258
Narvaez, Rafael, 269
National Diet, 35, 48, 55–56
national fortitude, 285–86
national historic monument (*shiseki kinenbutsu*), 231
national peace, 291n65
"*Natsu no hana*" (Summer Flowers) (Hara), 59
natural world, of earth, 104–7
Nazis, 124
"Negi" (Spring Onions), 141–42
New Cultural Books (*Shin bunka shoseki*), 313–14
New Morning (*Atarashiki asa*), 95
New Nutrition (Sakurazawa), 181
newspaper articles, 255–56
New Zealand, 208
NGO Hibaku mondai kokusai shinpojiumu (International Symposium on the Damage and Aftereffects of the Atomic Bombing of Hiroshima and Nagasaki), 296
Nihon junbi i'inkai (Japan Preparatory Committee), 296
Nijū hibaku II (Doubly Atomic-Bombed 2), 178n67
nijū hibakusha (double *hibakusha*), 168–69
9/11 terrorist attack, 195
ningen ikada (human rafts), 169–70

Ningen ikada (Yamaguchi Tsutomu), 169
Ningen shikkaku (No Longer Human) (Dazai), 48
Nishida Hideo, 41
Nishimori Kazumasa, 297
Nishimura Toyoyuki, 18
Niwa Kankichi, 218
NMGT. *See* Nagasaki Military Government Team
Noboru (Nagai's father), 35
Noguchi, Isamu, 271, 281–82, 289n37
no-life-in-the-atomic wilderness theory, 106
No Longer Human (*Ningen shikkaku*) (Dazai), 48
nomadic living, 132
"*Nō moa Hiroshimazu*" (No More Hiroshimas) (journal), 175n3
North Bell Tower, 232
North Korea, 81, 123
nuclear energy, 264
nuclear violence, 271
nuclear weapons, 80–81; abolishment of, 113, 180; destructive power of, 217–18; as morally indefensible, 207–8; peace goal and, 235–36; world conference against, 154. *See also* antinuclear peace movement
Nyokodō (Nagai's wooden hut), 39, 42, 52–53, 72, 95
Nyokodō zuihitsu (Essays from As Yourself Cottage) (Nagai), 74

Oana Ryūichi, 146
Obama, Barack, 277
obituary, 116, 118
Ogin story, 139–41
Ogura Toyofumi, 59
Ōhashi Hiroshi, 254
Okamoto, M., 262n21
Ōkubo Tokuyuki, 297
Old Testament, 98
"One Fine Day," 23
Ōniwa Hideo, 65n51
Ono Tomoaki, 44
The Opening of the Atomic Age (*Genshi jidai no kaimaku*), 313–16. *See also Nagasaki no kane*

oral histories, *of hibakusha*, 115, 119
Oranda no Hana (Blossoms of Holland) (Akutagawa), 135, 137
Order of the Rising Sun, 38
Organtino, Padre, 137–38
orphanages, 48
Oshino story, 139–41
Ōta Yōko, 57, 59
Otsuki, Tomoe, 225, 273
Ōura Cathedral, 63n23
outcaste community, 127n30
Ozaki Tōmei, 21, 112–13; anamnesis of, 114, 118; background of, 123–25; during bombing, 121–23, *122*; bombing victimization of, 127n16; childhood sicknesses of, 115; death faced by, 116; Endō assisted by, 126n12; final lecture of, 118–20; God's words imagined by, 121; *Jū nana sai no natsu* by, 120–21; Kolbe story told by, 124; life as isolation from, 120–23, 125; mother attachment of, 120; mother vanished of, 119–20; obituary words of, 116, 118; renderings of life from, 118; rosary beads claimed by, 117, *117*; superiority complex feelings of, 119

paintings, 8–10, 26n18; Children of Urakami series, 103; of family, 107–10; of fruits, 107; *kappa* as ink, 146–48; of Kayano, *108*, 108–9; memoryscapes in, 3–4; of Midori, 99, *100*; Nagai love of, 94; Nagai's devotional, 103; Nagai's ink, 107; *Suiko banki no zu* as, *145*; of Virgin Mary, 103–4. *See also* art
Pak Ilhwa, 76
Pakpahan, Binsar, 114
Pak Sugyŏng, 73
pancreatic cancer, 118
Park Chunghee, 76, 87
Park Haeseong, 20
Park Sukyung, 304
past, unrecoverable, 113
pastoral approach, 99
patriotism, of Urakami Catholics, 37–39
Patton, George S., 247

peace, 154, 268; Nagai's desire for, 82; nuclear weapons and goal of, 235–36; studies, 19–20
Peace Center, in Hiroshima, 23
Peace Clause, 84
Peace Declaration, in Nagasaki, 254
Peace Memorial Statue, 265–69, *266*, 272
Peace Park, 154, 269–70
"Peace starts from Nagasaki" (*Heiwa wa Nagasaki yori*), 57
Peace Statue, 23, 277–86, 290n46
Pearce, Charles A., 50–51
Peron, Eva, 50
personal trauma, 151–53, 157–59, 168–73
Philosophizing in Nagasaki (*Nagasaki ni atte tetsugaku suru*) (Takahashi), 13, 18, 209–10
Piazzoni, Francesca, 234
Pinkerton, Lieutenant, 251
Pius XII (Pope), 44, 50, 60, 78
Place Connected with Madame Butterfly (*Chō chō fujin yukari no chi*), 257, 260–61
Planning the Reconstruction of Nagasaki ("*Nagasaki saiken no kōsō*"), 25
Pletzing, Christian, 128n35
poetic resemblance (*sanagara*), 98
poetic tradition, 172
poetry: *Atarashiki asa* collection of, 95; catharsis and empowered through, 151; censors rejecting, 153; "The Dead Raven" as, 165–66; free verse, 159–60, 162; by Fukuda Sumako, 22, 154–55, 267; *haiku*, 160; by *hibakusha*, 21–22, 152–53, 158–59; *hibakusha* empowered through, 174–75; holocaust, 162; "*Jashūmon hikyoku*" as, 133; by Nagai, 152–53, 159–63; Nagai's *tanka*, 93, 108–9; *Nagasaki: Fushoku suru rekijitsu no soko de* of, 185; personal trauma in, 157–59; by Seeger, 172–73; Shinshisha, 133; "Shira bara" as, 98; of survivors of atomic bombing, 158–59; by Tanaka, 157; *tanka*, 93, 95, 108–9, 158–59, 160; by Yamada, 163–68; Yamada on atomic bombing,

342 | Index

poetry *(continued)*
165–66; by Yamaguchi Tsutomu, 168–75
Port of Cranes, 276
postatomic-bomb literature, 198–99
postatomic memory, 215–16
postcard, of Glover House, 258
postwar memories, 193–94
postwar public diplomacy, 238n8
poverty, 52
Prayer of the Rosary (*Rosario ŭi kido*) (Nagai), 77, 79
Prayer Zone, 275
Present Conditions of the *Hibakusha* (*Hibakusha no genzai*), 298
preservation campaign, 219–20, 231–32
President Monroe, USS, 256
Primavesi, Anne, 93, 105
Prime Minister Award, 56
prison, fragments of, 289n38
Proudhon, Monfette, 67n77
Pruden House, 183
psychosexual musings, 203
public art, 287n3
public speaker, about atomic experience, 118, 120, 125
public testimony, 211n11
Puccini, Giacomo, 248–49

radioactivity, 106, 167–68, 173–74
radiology, 70
Raguet, Emil, 62n17
Raising the Curtain on the Atomic Age (*Genshi jidai no kaimaku*) (Nagai), 45. See also *Nagasaki no kane*
The Rape of Nanking (painting), 10
Rashōmon (film), 48
Rausch, Franklin, 20
ravens, of death, 165–68
rebuilt sites, 234
RECNA. *See* Research Center for Nuclear Weapons Abolition
reconstruction, 6–7; authenticity in, 241n46; Nagai's support for, 33–34, 44, 53; policies for, 154; of Urakami Cathedral, 220–21, 238, 239n15
The Reconstruction of the Atomic-Bombed Land of Nagasaki (*Hibakuchi Nagasaki no saiken*) (Kataoka, C., and Kataoka, R.), 13, 19
recovery process, 151
reflecting pool, 277
reflective obituary, 115
religion, power of, 188
"Remains of the Cathedral," 8
The Remains of the Cathedral (painting), 26n18
"Remains of the Mitsubishi Steel Works" (*Mitsubishi kōjō ato*), 8
renderings of life, 118
Research Center for Nuclear Weapons Abolition (RECNA), 191–92
research ethics, 241n51
"Responding to Criticism of Nagai" (Takahashi), 27n25
Resurrecting Nagasaki (Diehl), 20, 28n31, 304
Reynolds, Barbara, 307n1
Rilke, Rainer Maria, 41
River of Life (*Seimei no kawa*) (Takashi), 314
Rogers, Irvin W., 58
Roman Catholics, 50
Romans 8:36, 62n16
Rosario ŭi kido (Prayer of the Rosary) (Nagai), 77, 79
rosary beads, 116–17, *117*, 120
Rosary Beads (*Mukchu al*) (Nagai), 74
Rosary Chain (*Rozario no kusari*) (Nagai), 74, 77, 315
Rosary series, 103
Rozario no kusari (Rosary Chain) (Nagai), 74, 77, 315
ruin mementos, 218
Rutherford, Mary, 51

sacred heart, of Jesus, *101*, 101–2, 109–10
The sacred mountain of Bastian (*Bastian no kamiyama*), 123
sacrificial lambs, 11, 34, 38, 41, 43, 51, 96–98, 155–56, 160, 165, 168, 174, 295
"*Saihō no hito*" (The Man from the West), 133–34
Saint of Auschwitz., Kolbe as, 113
Saint of Urakami, Nagai as, 35, 55, 64n46, 156

Saint Paul's publishing, 78, 90n25
St. Francis Clinic, 183
Sakurazawa Nyoichi, 181
Salev-Gerz, Esther, 291n59
sanagara (poetic resemblance), 98
San Francisco Peace Treaty (1952), 256
Santo Montani, 144
Sarang hanŭn ai tŭl rŭl namgyŏ tugo (Leaving Beloved Children Behind) (Nagai), 76–77
Sarang hanŭn nae aidŭra (My Beloved Children) (Nagai), 76
Sarang ŭro purŭnŭn p'yŏnghwa ŭi norae (A Song of Peace Sung with Love) (Makoto), 82
Sasaki (pseudonym), 202–4
Sasaki Katsuhiko, 65n51
Sasaki Takamaru, 65n51
scientific records, 186
sculpture gardens, 221, 225
Secret Songs of the Heretic Religion ("*Jashūmon hikyoku*"), 133
Seeger, Alan, 172–73
Seibo no Kishi (Knights of the Holy Mother), 123–24
Seiji Kaya, 186
Seiji Lippit, 141, 149n12
Seimei no kawa (River of Life) (Takashi), 314
Seirai Yūichi: Akutagawa Prize won by, 14; atomic-bombing literature by, 22; Christian martyrdom and, 198; ground zero literature and, 191; *hibakusha* criticism fears of, 194; mothers, powerlessness of, 194; postwar memories of, 193–94; writings by, 14, 192–94, 198, 209
Sekiya Ayako, 301
self-sacrifice, 140–41
self-surrender, 106
sen (monetary unit), 68n85
Senkan Yamato (Battleship Yamato) (film), 65n51
Setoguchi Chie, 170
The Setting Sun (*Shayō*) (Dazai), 48
Seven Samurai (film), 48
The Seventeen-Year-Old's Summer (*Jū nana sai no natsu*) (Ozaki), 120–21

The Seventy-Five Years after the Atomic Bombing (*Genbakugo no 75 nen*), 19
seventy-year sterility theory, 39
sexual desire, 207
sexual vitality, 205
Shaba o nogareru kappa (A Kappa Fleeing Worldly Suffering), 146–48, *147*
shadows, 4–5, 11–12
Shadows of Trauma (Assmann), 4–5
Shakai shisō shi gakkai, hereafter Shashikai (Society for the History of Social Thought), 302
Shayō (The Setting Sun) (Dazai), 48
Shiba Kōkan, 135–37
Shiga Naoya, 141
Shikiba Ryūzaburō, 49, 65n56, 313
Shikiba Shunzō, 317n6
Shimabara Rebellion (1637), 133
Shimauchi Hachirō, 252–53, 257, 259–60
Shimohira Sakue, 297
Shimokawa Ōten, 56
Shin bunka shoseki (New Cultural Books), 313–14
Shinda karasu ("The Dead Raven") (Yamada), 165–66
Shi no dō shin'en (Concentric Circles of Death) (Akizuki), 179–80
Shinshi-sha poets, 133
Shin to gi no aida ("Between Belief and Doubt") (Seirai), 209
Shinto shrine (Suwa Jinja), 34
Shinzō, Abe, 277
Shioura Shintarō, 116, *117*
shippo mo hitoyaku ("Even the tail has a role"), 107
"*Shira bara*" (White Roses) (poem), 98
Shirachi no karasu ("White Blood Raven") (Yamada), 166–67
shiren (tests), 100
shiseki kinenbutsu (national historic monument), 231
A Short Nagasaki Story ("*Nagasaki shōhin*") (Akutagawa), 135, 137–41, 143–44
short stories, Nagai publishing, 67n76
shrine worship, 39

Shūkan asahi (journal), 175n3
Silverman, Herbert B. L., 50
Simek, Nicole, 114
sin-consciousness, 115–16
Sloterdijk, Peter, 280
The Smiles of the Gods ("*Kamigami no bishō*"), 137–38
The Smiling Bells of Nagasaki (*Nagasak'i ŭi chong ŭn miso chit nŭnda*) (Makoto), 82–83
Smith, Laurajane, 234–35
smooth spaces, 131–32, 139–40
Sŏ Chunhong, 72, 84
social activism, 22
social discrimination, 153–54
social problems, 47–48
Society for the History of Social Thought (*Shakai shisō shi gakkai*, hereafter Shashikai), 302
solitude (*kodoku*), 121
Solovskoy, George P., 58
Song of Nagasaki (Glynn), 72, 79
A Song of Peace Sung with Love (*Sarang ŭro purŭnŭn p'yŏnghwa ŭi norae*) (Makoto), 82
Song Sŏhyŏn, 86
Southard, Susan, 28
South Korea, 75–76
Sŏ Yun'gyo, Peter, 84
Special Session on Disarmament at the United Nations (SSOD-I), 296
Spinning Gears ("*Haguruma*"), 142
spiritual betterment, 100–102
Spring Onions ("*Negi*"), 141–42
SSOD-I. *See* Special Session on Disarmament at the United Nations
stable path, 132
statues, 221; construction fees for, 267; Kurozuka Kannon, 258; Maria-Kannon, 135, *136*; Miura Tamaki, 260; Peace Memorial, 265–69, *266*, 272. *See also* Peace Statue
stone wall, of Urakami Cathedral, 223–24, 236, 242n54
striated spaces, 131–32, 139–40
suffering, 299
Sugako (Akizuki's wife), 183
Sugimoto Waka (Terugiku), 144
Suhwan, Kim, 87

Suiko banki no zu (Image of a Suiko Returning Home in the Evening), *145*, 145–46
Summerfield, Penny, 119
Summer Flowers ("*Natsu no hana*") (Hara), 59
Sunghoe, Kim, 79
superiority complex, 119
survivor guilt, 115
Suwa Jinja (Shinto shrine), 34
symbols, of tragedy, 226

Tadokoro Tarō, 27n22, 27n25
Tagawa Seikō, 185, 226, 238n8
Tagawa Tsutomu, 60, 218–19
Tagawa Wasa, Clara, 119–20, 123
Taishō-period (1912–1926), 131
Takahara Itaru, 227
Takahashi Shinji, 6, 10–11; Nagai criticized by, 12–13, 24, 27n25; on pope's speech, 310n31; *Testimonies of Nagasaki* movement and, 180; writings by, 18, 19, 209–10, 295–96
Takase Tsuyoshi, 222, 224
Takashi, Paulo, 36. *See* Nagai Takashi
Takatani Shigeharu, 187
Takei Hiroshi, 297–98
Takeyama Hiroshi, 177n38
Tamai Reiko, 59
Tanaka Kishirō, 157
Tange Kenzō, 264–65, 270–71, 281; Cenotaph for Atomic Bomb Victims by, *265*; Hiroshima Memorial Hall designed by, 289n37; Peace Center designed by, 23
Taniguchi Sumiteru, 18, 267, 297, 306, 311n37
tanka poetry, 93, 95, 108–9, 158–60
Taue Tomihisa, 113
taxes, 53–54, 68n82, 68n90
the teachings of Mari ("*Mari-no-kyō*"), 139
Terugiku (Sugimoto Waka), 144–45
Testimonies of Nagasaki (*Nagasaki no shōgen*), 156, 184–86, 306–7
Testimonies of Nagasaki movement, 180
tests (*shiren*), 100
The Mikado (play), 249–51

theological explorations, 20–21, 109–10
theological understanding, 83
A Thousand Plateaus (Deleuze and Guattari), 131
"The Titan and the Arch" (Nanase), 23
Tokusaburō Nagai, 24, 316n2
Tokyo depictions, 141–42
Tokyo Gekijō Theater, 250
to live is isolation and encounter (*"Ikiru to wa kodoku to deai"*), 118
Tominaga Naoki, 286
Tosŏ Ch'ulp'an Apsan mit puk k'ap'e (publisher), 85
tourism, in Japan, 256–61
transcendental truth, 74
traumatic memories, 17–18, 151–53, 172, 184–85
Treat, John, 57, 59, 157–58
Trinity test, 195
TripAdvisor, 235–36, 241n51, 242n54
tsugunai (atonement), 210
Tsukasa Uchida, 187
Tsunoo Susumu, 182
tuberculosis, 115, 123, 181–82
tunnel factory, 121–23
"Twenty-Three Years since That Day" (report), 184–85

UNESCO World Heritage Convention, 227
United States (U.S.): atomic bombs dropped by, 168–69; ground zeros in, 195–96; Nagai omitting criticism of, 13–14, 61, 71–72; postwar public diplomacy of, 238n8
Urakami Cathedral: Angelus bell ringing in, 314–15; atomic bombing ruins of, 2, 2–3, 7, 217, 221; authenticity lacking at, 237; authentic pieces of, 23; belfry plaque at, 222–23; categorizing fragments of, 220–24, 221; demolish approval of, 218–19; destruction of, 6, 197–98; fragment signage issues at, 229–31, 240n39; historical authenticity and, 233–34; historical value of, 219; Hypocenter Park relocation of, 223–24; memorial landscape of, 215–16; memoryscapes lost in, 9; Nagasaki no longer has, 226–27, 237–38; narrative of loss about, 225–29; new cathedral replacing, 9; original belfry of, 221–23, 230–32, 242n56; partial replica of, 225; preservation campaign for, 216–20; preservation policy issues for, 231–32; reconstruction of, 220–21, 238, 239n15; ruin mementos of, 218; ruin sites dispersion of, 234–37; stone wall and bricks of, 223–24, 236, 242n54; visitor reviews of, 235–37, 242n56; World Heritage status of, 227
Urakami Catholics: atomic bombing and sacrifice by, 35, 41–44, 51–52, 99–100; bombing horrors of, 177n38; faith in God challenge of, 40, 100–104; God's love for, 163; *hansai* symbolic resemblance and, 98–99; as instruments of God, 161; Nagai leadership for, 33–34, 36–37, 39; patriotic duty of, 37–39; relatives' deaths meaningful for, 109–10; as sacrificial lambs, 155–56, 160; shrine worship refusal by, 39; sins of human-kind atonement by, 13, 40–43, 98; spiritual betterment of, 100–102; way of expiation for, 99–100
Urakami First Hospital, 181–82
Urakami hansai setsu (Urakami Holocaust Theory) (Takahashi on Nagai), 13–14, 97–98, 180, 302–6
Urakami no kodomo (Children of Urakami), 103
Urakami Valley: atomic bomb exploding over, 6, 39, 96–100; bombing tragedy in, 43, 93, 96–100; cherry trees planted in, 54; destruction of, 8–9; devastated landscape of, 317n7; Nagai's return to, 39–40; Ōura Cathedral in, 63n23
U.S. *See* United States
Uvais Ahamed, 297

Virgin Mary, 98, 103–4, 109–10
visitor reviews, 235–37, 240n35, 242n56

walls of silence, 152, 154; Christian image of ground zero and, 179; *hibakusha* facing, 153, 155–56; Nagai creating, 162–63; within Nagasaki, 153–57
war, miseries of, 232
warm-blooded woman, 202–3
war responsibility, 14
Watanabe Chieko, 297
Watanabe Kurasuke, 144, 257
Watashi no naka no genbaku ("The Atomic Bomb Inside Me"), 156
Watashitachi wa Nagasaki ni ita (Bright Moonlight with No Shadows) (Nagai), 74–76
way of expiation, 99–100
Weber, Max, 63n29, 160
We of Nagasaki (Nagai), 20, 50–52, 72
Wetherell, Margaret, 234
What Is Eternal (*Yŏngwŏn han kŏt ŭl*) (Nagai), 73
What Is Eternal, Rosary Beads (Kataoka Yakichi), 82
"White Blood Raven" (*Shirachi no karasu*) (Yamada), 166–67
White Roses ("*Shira bara*") (poem), 98
Wichita, USS, 244
Williams, Harold S., 259–60
The World, the Flesh, and Father Smith (Marshall), 52
World Heritage Convention States Parties, 241n46
World Heritage site, 227–28, 235, 240n35
world peace, 81
World Trade Center, 195
worship, temporary place for, 217–18

X-rays, 38, 95

Yaketa rozario (The Burnt Rosary Beads), 116, *117*
Yamada Kan, 12, 152, 174, 309n23; "abyss of darkness" in, 166; on atomic bombing poetry, 165–66; as *hibakusha* poet, 22, 303; literary theory of, 165; Nagai criticism from, 163–64; poetry of, 163–68; traumatic memories from, 17–18; writings by, 165–67, 185
Yamaguchi Aijirō, 59, 218–19
Yamaguchi Senji, 11, 297, 302
Yamaguchi Tsutomu, 22, 152–53, 159; cancer death of, 169; documentary film with, 178n67; as double *hibakusha*, 168; Hiroshima deaths witnessed by, 171; Hisako wife of, 169; Katsutoshi son of, 169; *Ningen ikada* poem collection by, 169; personal trauma of, 170; poetry of, 168–75; radioactivity worrying, 173–74; rivers of corpses described by, 170; traumatic memory ruptured and, 172
Yamauchi Kiyomi, 13–14, 19, 27
Yasuda Mitsuru, 164
Yi Howŏn, 86–87
Yi Munhŭi, 72, 82–83
Yi Sŏngwu, 73–76, 78
Yi T'aesŏk, 87
Yŏgi Aein (As Yourself Association), 72, 81–88, 89n4
Yokote Kazuhiko, 227
Yokoyama Michiko, 116
Yoneyama, Lisa, 215, 235
Yŏngwŏn han kŏt ŭl (What Is Eternal) (Nagai), 73
Yoshida Hiroichi, 284, *285*
Yoshida Shigeru, 60
Yoshikawa Eiji, 48–49, 156
Yoshikuni Igarashi, 280
Yoshimatsu Yuichi, 258

World War II: The Global, Human, and Ethical Dimension
G. Kurt Piehler, *series editor*

Lawrence Cane, David E. Cane, Judy Barrett Litoff, and David C. Smith, eds., *Fighting Fascism in Europe: The World War II Letters of an American Veteran of the Spanish Civil War*

Angelo M. Spinelli and Lewis H. Carlson, *Life behind Barbed Wire: The Secret World War II Photographs of Prisoner of War Angelo M. Spinelli*

Don Whitehead and John B. Romeiser, *"Beachhead Don": Reporting the War from the European Theater, 1942–1945*

Scott H. Bennett, ed., *Army GI, Pacifist CO: The World War II Letters of Frank and Albert Dietrich*

Alexander Jefferson with Lewis H. Carlson, *Red Tail Captured, Red Tail Free: Memoirs of a Tuskegee Airman and POW*

Jonathan G. Utley, *Going to War with Japan, 1937–1941*

Grant K. Goodman, *America's Japan: The First Year, 1945–1946*

Patricia Kollander with John O'Sullivan, *"I Must Be a Part of This War": One Man's Fight against Hitler and Nazism*

Judy Barrett Litoff, *An American Heroine in the French Resistance: The Diary and Memoir of Virginia d'Albert-Lake*

Thomas R. Christofferson and Michael S. Christofferson, *France during World War II: From Defeat to Liberation*

Don Whitehead, *Combat Reporter: Don Whitehead's World War II Diary and Memoirs*, edited by John B. Romeiser

James M. Gavin, *The General and His Daughter: The Wartime Letters of General James M. Gavin to His Daughter Barbara*, edited by Barbara Gavin Fauntleroy et al.

Carol Adele Kelly, ed., *Voices of My Comrades: America's Reserve Officers Remember World War II*, foreword by Senators Ted Stevens and Daniel K. Inouye

John J. Toffey IV, *Jack Toffey's War: A Son's Memoir*

Lt. General James V. Edmundson, *Letters to Lee: From Pearl Harbor to the War's Final Mission*, edited by Dr. Celia Edmundson

John K. Stutterheim, *The Diary of Prisoner 17326: A Boy's Life in a Japanese Labor Camp*, foreword by Mark Parillo

G. Kurt Piehler and Sidney Pash, eds., *The United States and the Second World War: New Perspectives on Diplomacy, War, and the Home Front*

Susan E. Wiant, *Between the Bylines: A Father's Legacy*, Foreword by Walter Cronkite

Deborah S. Cornelius, *Hungary in World War II: Caught in the Cauldron*

Gilya Gerda Schmidt, *Süssen Is Now Free of Jews: World War II, The Holocaust, and Rural Judaism*

Emanuel Rota, *A Pact with Vichy: Angelo Tasca from Italian Socialism to French Collaboration*

Panteleymon Anastasakis, *The Church of Greece under Axis Occupation*

Louise DeSalvo, *Chasing Ghosts: A Memoir of a Father, Gone to War*

Alexander Jefferson with Lewis H. Carlson, *Red Tail Captured, Red Tail Free: Memoirs of a Tuskegee Airman and POW, Revised Edition*

Kent Puckett, *War Pictures: Cinema, Violence, and Style in Britain, 1939–1945*

Marisa Escolar, *Allied Encounters: The Gendered Redemption of World War II Italy*

Courtney A. Short, *The Most Vital Question: Race and Identity in the U.S. Occupation of Okinawa, 1945–1946*

James Cassidy, *NBC Goes to War: The Diary of Radio Correspondent James Cassidy from London to the Bulge*, edited by Michael S. Sweeney

Rebecca Schwartz Greene, *Breaking Point: The Ironic Evolution of Psychiatry in World War II*

Franco Baldasso, *Against Redemption: Democracy, Memory, and Literature in Post-Fascist Italy*

G. Kurt Piehler and Ingo Trauschweizer, eds., *Reporting World War II*

Kevin T Hall, *Forgotten Casualties: Downed American Airmen and Axis Violence in World War II*

Chad R. Diehl, ed., *Shadows of Nagasaki: Trauma, Religion, and Memory after the Atomic Bombing*

www.ingramcontent.com/pod-product-compliance
Lightning Source LLC
Chambersburg PA
CBHW020351080526
44584CB00014B/973